P9-DWS-914

Principles
For Navigating

BIG
DEBT
CRISES

RAY DALIO

PART 2: DETAILED CASE STUDIES

GERMAN DEBT CRISIS AND HYPERINFLATION (1918–1924)
US DEBT CRISIS AND ADJUSTMENT (1928–1937)
US DEBT CRISIS AND ADJUSTMENT (2007–2011)

CALGARY PUBLIC LIBRARY

JAN   2019

BRIDGEWATER

1 Glendinning Pl
Westport, CT 06880

Copyright © 2018 by Ray Dalio

All rights reserved.

Bridgewater is a registered trademark of Bridgewater Associates, LLP.

First edition published September 2018.

Distributed by Greenleaf Book Group. For ordering information or
special discounts for bulk purchases, please contact Greenleaf Book
Group at PO Box 91869, Austin, TX 78709, 512.891.6100.

Printed in the United States of America on acid-free paper.

Cover design by Andrew Greif.
Book design by Creative Kong.

ISBN 978-1-7326898-0-0
ISBN 978-1-7326898-4-8 (ebook)

Table of Contents

German Debt Crisis and Hyperinflation (1918–1924)

German Debt Crisis and Hyperinflation (1918–1924)

This section provides a detailed account of the most iconic inflationary depression cycle in history—the German debt crisis and hyperinflation that followed the end of World War I and carried into the mid-1920s, which set the stage for the economic and political changes of the 1930s. Much like my accounts of the 2008 US Financial Crisis and the 1930s Great Depression, this study goes through the particulars of the case in some detail with reference to the template laid out earlier in the "Archetypal Inflationary Depression." Although the German hyperinflation took place almost a century ago, and amid exceptional political circumstances (Germany's defeat in the First World War and the imposition of a huge reparation burden on it by the Allies), the basic dynamic of debt cycles, economic activity, and markets described in the template drove what happened. Noting the differences between this inflationary depression case (and other inflationary depression cases) and the deflationary depression cases highlights what makes some inflationary and others deflationary. To provide a vivid sense of what was happening in real time, a newsfeed runs along the sides of my description of what happened.

July 1914–November 1918: World War I

World War I (July 1914–November 1918) set the stage for this big, dramatic cycle. During the war years Germany left the gold standard, accumulated a large stock of domestic and foreign debts, began the practice of money printing to finance its ever-growing fiscal deficits, and experienced its first bout of currency depreciation and inflation. Based on their experience of the Franco-Prussian War of 1870, the Germans had expected the war to be short, and they assumed it would ultimately be paid for by large indemnities levied on the defeated Allied powers. Instead it turned out to be an extremely long and expensive affair that was financed primarily through domestic debt, and Germany ended up having to pay a huge war reparation bill rather than collecting on one.

This was a classic case of war debts being built up by a country that then loses the war (though more extreme than most) and is also a classic case of a country with large foreign currency denominated debt that is held by foreign creditors. Knowing the dynamic described in the "Archetypal Inflationary Depression" section of Part 1, you should have a pretty good idea of how this story will play out.

Background

Like most countries at the time, Germany had been on the gold standard at the beginning of the war. All paper currency, including all government debt, was convertible to gold at a fixed rate. However, by 1914, the central bank did not have enough gold to back the stock of money in circulation at the fixed price,[1] as one might expect. As soon as the war broke out, smart German citizens rushed to exchange their paper money for bullion, which caused a run on the banking system. Within a matter of weeks, the central bank (the Reichsbank) and the Treasury had paid out 195 million marks' worth of gold to the public (i.e., about 10 percent of total gold reserves).[2] In order to prevent further losses, ensure liquidity in the banking system, and avoid a major contraction in the money

The News

July 29, 1914
Berlin Very Nervous: Big Banks Will Support Stocks—Keeping Gold in Vaults
"Although bankers insist that it is not justifiable to speak of a 'financial crisis' in Germany as a consequence of the danger of a general European war, conditions have undeniably grown graver in the last twenty-four hours. Runs on savings banks have increased in intensity, and the banks are paying out gold with the utmost reluctance."

July 30, 1914
Berlin Bourse on Cash Basis
"Gold has become scarce to the point of invisibility. The runs on Berlin savings banks are still going on."

August 2, 1914
German Bank Rate Up

August 3, 1914
Reichsbank Hoards Gold: Patriotic Appeal in Germany Not to Demand Coin
"Germany's financial and economic life are naturally greatly affected. The Reichsbank has raised the bank rate to 5 per cent and the Lombard rate to 6 per cent. The demand for gold continues, but up to the present time the Reichsbank has paid out comparatively little of it."

August 12, 1914
German Banks Helped; Financing of the Mobilization Has Been Successful

March 4, 1915
German Loan In Chicago: Bankers Ask for Subscriptions—First Offering by Belligerents

March 10, 1915
No Gold in German Banks; Patriots Urged to Exchange Hoarded Gold for War Loan Stock

April 10, 1915
Germany Faces Huge Debt; Means $500,000,000 a Year and Doubling of Taxes
"The Socialist newspaper Vorwaerts, discussing the new war budget, calculates that interest on war loans, deficit for war years, and the making good after the war will mean doubling all existing taxation. The annual increase of expenditure is figured at $625,000,000 to $730,000,000."

All news excerpts from *The New York Times*.

The News

September 22, 1915
Berliners Buy War Bonds; Rush for Subscriptions to Third German Loan Reported

March 12, 1916
German Food Crisis Seems Impending
"Newspapers just received from Germany contain many semi-official and seemingly inspired articles emphasizing the economic difficulties due to the Allies' blockade and the failure of the 1915 crop."

March 19, 1916
$10,400,000 for German War Loan

October 9, 1916
Fifth German Loan 10,590,000,000 Marks
"Berlin, announcing total, says subscriptions have exceeded the amount expected."

February 24, 1917
German Reichstag Votes 15,000,000,000 Marks
"A new war credit of 15,000,000,000 marks was introduced in the Reichstag today...This credit of 15,000,000,000 marks brings the total credit in Germany up to 67,000,000,000 marks, or, on the basis of values before the war, $16,750,000,000."

May 21, 1917
Germany to Borrow Bonds
"*The Exchange Telegraph*'s Amsterdam correspondent quotes the *Berliner Tageblatt* as saying that Germany's Finance Ministry, as a preliminary step to new methods of raising money, intends to call in all Swedish, Danish, and Swiss bonds and shares owned by Germans."

July 9, 1917
German Finance
"Saturday's cablegrams brought the result of the sixth German loan and the announcement of the ninth German credit. The latest loan produced 13,120,000,000 marks."

September 12, 1917
Germany Keeps Coal From Holland to Force Loan
"Germany is employing this method with a view to exerting pressure in order to induce Holland to fall in with the German desire to raise a loan here. It will be recalled that Germany put similar pressure on Switzerland a short time ago."

November 18, 1917
Latest German Loan Was Uphill Fight
"Every power of persuasion and pressure at the disposition of the German Government was brought into play to make a success of the seventh war loan of 15,000,000,000 marks, ($3,570,000,000 at normal exchange), according to reports found in German newspapers recently reaching London."

supply, policy makers suspended the conversion of money to gold on July 31, 1914.[3] The government also authorized the Reichsbank to buy short-term Treasury bills and use them, along with commercial bills, as collateral for the money it was printing.[4] The pace of printing that followed was rapid: By the end of August, the quantity of Reichsbank notes in circulation (i.e., paper marks) had increased by approximately 30 percent.

This is classic. Currency is both a medium of exchange and a store hold of wealth. When investors hold a lot of promises to deliver currency (i.e., a lot of debt denominated in a currency) and the supply of that currency is tied to something that backs it, the ability of the central bank to produce currency is limited. When investors want to convert their bonds to currency/money and spend it, that puts the central bank in the difficult position of having to choose between having a lot of debt defaults or floating a lot of currency, which can debase its value. **So, whenever (a) the amount of money in circulation is much greater than the amount of gold held in reserves to back the money at the designated price of conversion, and (b) investors are rushing to convert money into gold because they are worried about the value of their money, the central bank is in the untenable position of either reducing the supply of money in circulation (i.e., tighten credit) or ending convertibility and printing more money.** Central banks almost always choose suspending convertibility and printing more money versus allowing a credit contraction to take place, because it's less painful.

Printing a lot of money and depreciating the value of a currency causes just about anything denominated in that depreciated money to go up in price, and people like it when the things they own go up in value and they have more money to spend. This is also true in times of war. Policy makers attempting to marshal the economic resources of the country toward the war effort print money to give themselves more to spend. This printing helps prevent a liquidity crisis in the banking system or an economic contraction from taking place—either of which would be very disruptive to the war effort. It is for this reason that most of the countries fighting in WWI ended up suspending the gold standard at one point or another.

Fighting the war required the German government to significantly increase expenditures (government spending as a share of GDP would increase 2.5x between 1914 and 1917). Financing this spending would mean either raising new revenues (i.e., taxation) or increasing government borrowing. **As there was huge resistance to increasing taxation at home, and as Germany was mostly**

locked out of international lending markets, the war had to be financed by issuing domestic debt.[5] In 1914, German government debt was insignificant. By 1918, Germany had amassed a total local currency debt stock of 100 billion marks, about 130 percent of German GDP.

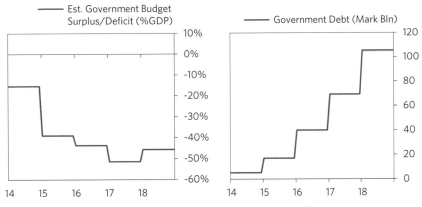

Source: Global Financial Data

Although this stock of debt was huge, prior to the German surrender and the imposition of war reparations, most of it was denominated in local currency.[6] Policy makers recognized that this was a good thing. According to the Reichsbank, "the greatest weakness in the war financing of the enemies is their growing indebtedness abroad [particularly to the US],"[7] as it forces them to scramble for dollars when needing to make debt-service payments. In contrast, most German debt taken on to finance the war (prior to reparations) was in local currency and financed by Germans.[8]

Up until the second half of 1916, the German public was both willing and able to finance the entire fiscal deficit by purchasing government debt.[9] In fact, war bond issuances were regularly oversubscribed. However, as the war dragged on and inflation accelerated, the Treasury found that the public was no longer prepared to hold all the debt it was issuing. This was partly due to the size of the deficit, increasing substantially as the war progressed, but also because wartime inflation had caused real interest rates to become very negative (government war bonds paid out a fixed interest rate of 5 percent throughout the war, whereas inflation had climbed above 30% by early 1915), which resulted in lenders not being adequately compensated for holding government debt.[10] The inflation was being driven by wartime disruptions and shortages, capacity constraints in key war industries, and currency weakness (the mark would fall about 25 percent against the dollar by 1916).[11] While some naive lenders clung to the hope that the government would return to the gold standard at the old exchange rate once the war was over, or compensate them for any losses due to inflation, others feared they would most likely be paid in money that had lost most of its purchasing power, so they ran out of debt denominated in that currency.[12]

The News

January 16, 1918
Berlin Food Scarcer: Population Forced to Keep to the Ration Quantity
"The population is compelled to exist almost entirely on the rationed quantities of bread, meat and potatoes."

February 18, 1918
New Taxes in Germany to Meet Big Deficit
"Dispatches received from Berlin say that the ordinary receipts and expenditures of the German budget for 1918 balance at 7,332,000,000 marks, as compared with approximately 5,000,000,000 marks last year. The increase is said to be due mainly to the higher amount required for interest on the national debt."

March 13, 1918
Germany Seeks New Loan
"A new German war loan of 15,000,000,000 marks will be issued soon, an *Exchange Telegraph* dispatch from Copenhagen says. The German war debt now amounts to 109,000,000,000 marks."

April 21, 1918
German Loan Passes 3-Billion Mark

May 21, 1918
German Exchange Falling
"Germany, judging by foreign exchange rates, has no prospect of smashing the opposition on the west front."

June 13, 1918
German Loan 15,001,425,000 Marks
"Subscriptions from the army to the eighth German war loan brought the total of the loan up to 15,001,425,000 marks, according to Berlin dispatches today."

October 27, 1918
Debts Now Exceed Assets: Germany's Financial Status as Shown in Recent Figures

October 27, 1918
Financiers Foresee Crash: Long Known Here That Germany Was Approaching Economic Abyss

November 7, 1918
Germany's Finances Near Breaking Point
"Debt Exceeding $35,000,000,000. Has Mortgaged Two-Fifths of Her National Wealth"

November 11, 1918
Armistice Signed, End of the War! Berlin Seized by Revolutionists: New Chancellor Begs for Order; Ousted Kaiser Flees to Holland

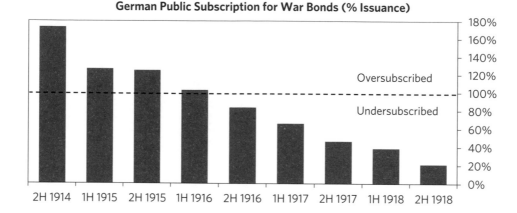

German Public Subscription for War Bonds (% Issuance)

The currency remained an effective medium of exchange while losing its effectiveness as a store hold of wealth. So, the government borrowed money to pay for its war expenditures, and the Reichsbank was forced to monetize the debt as investors came up short in supplying the money. This had the effect of increasing the money supply by an amount equal to the fiscal deficit not financed by the public. **As debt monetization is inflationary (there is more money in the economy chasing the same quantity of goods and services), a self-reinforcing spiral ensued—i.e., debt monetization increased inflation, which reduced real interest rates, which discouraged lending to the government, which encouraged additional debt monetization.** As the deficit was huge (averaging about 40 percent of GDP between 1914 and 1918), this led to the money supply increasing by almost 300 percent over the course of the war.[13]

The pace of money creation accelerated after 1917 as German citizens became increasingly unwilling to purchase government debt, and the central bank was forced to monetize a growing share of the deficit.[14] Although the number of marks in circulation almost doubled between mid-1917 and mid-1918, it did not cause a material decline in the currency. In fact, the mark rallied over this period as Russia's withdrawal increased expectations of a German victory. The mark only began falling in the second half of 1918, as a German defeat began looking increasingly likely.[15]

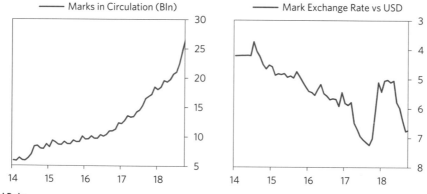

Source: Global Financial Data

In the last two years of the war, the German government began borrowing in foreign currencies because lenders were unwilling to take promises to pay in marks.[16] When a country has to borrow in a foreign currency, it's a bad sign. By 1918, the Reichsbank and private firms each owed about 2.5 billion gold marks in FX to external lenders.[17] A gold mark was an artificial unit used to measure the value of a paper mark to gold. In 1914, one gold mark equaled one paper mark.[18] A debt of 5 billion gold marks was therefore a debt denominated in gold, with the bill equal to the amount of gold that could be purchased by 5 billion marks in 1914.

Unlike local currency debt, hard currency (foreign currency and gold denominated) debt cannot be printed away. Debtors would have to get their hands on either gold or foreign exchange to meet these liabilities. While the hard currency debt was less than 10 percent of the total debt stock, it was still larger than the entire public gold reserves of the Reich.[19] The hope was that once Germany won the war, the mark would appreciate, making those debt burdens more manageable. And, of course, the losing countries would be forced to pay for most of Germany's foreign and domestic debts.[20]

Policy makers recognized that if Germany lost the war, or failed to extract large reparations, it would be extremely difficult to pay back these debts with hard money. According to the president of the Reichsbank, Rudolf Havenstein, covering those debts "will be extraordinarily difficult if we do not get a large war indemnity."[21] According to the German economist Edgar Jaffé, unless England paid between a third and a half of Germany's war costs, the result would be the "monstrous catastrophe" of "currency collapse" once German citizens learned that domestic debts would likely be paid in depreciated money, and government agencies and private firms scrambled to get their hands on foreign exchange to pay off external liabilities.[22]

Breaking the peg to gold and monetizing an ever-growing fiscal deficit, combined with wartime economic disruptions and shortages, led to a declining exchange rate and a pickup in inflation. By the beginning of 1918, the mark had lost about 25 percent of its value versus the dollar and prices had tripled.

However, in the context of WWI, this was pretty typical—i.e., it's what most countries did to fund their wars. German inflation, while high, was not significantly higher than that of other war participants, as you can see in the chart below.[23] But only a few of the war's many participants ended up with hyperinflation, for reasons I will soon explain.

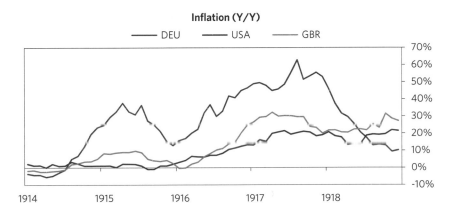

Inflation (Y/Y)

I bring up this point to underline the fact that WWI (and the accompanying monetization of debt) did not directly cause Germany's postwar inflationary depression. As mentioned in the archetype template, **while inflationary depressions are possible in all countries/currencies, they are most common in countries that:**

- **Don't have a reserve currency:** So there is not a global bias to hold their currency/debt as a store hold of wealth
- **Have low foreign exchange reserves:** So there is not much of a cushion to protect against capital outflows
- **Have a large stock of foreign debt:** So there is a vulnerability to the cost of debt rising via increases in either interest rates or the value of the currency the debtor has to deliver, or a shortage of available credit denominated in that currency
- **Have a large and increasing budget and/or current account deficit:** So there is a need to borrow or print money to fund the deficits
- **Have negative real interest rates:** So lenders are not adequately compensated for holding the currency/debt
- **Have a history of high inflation and negative total returns in the currency:** So there is a lack of trust in the value of the currency/debt

By the end of the war, the German economy met all of these conditions. Losing the war meant that the mark was not going to be the reserve currency of the postwar era. A large stock of external debts had been acquired,

The News

November 12, 1918
Revolt Still Spreads Throughout Germany

November 23, 1918
Ebert and Haase Deny Banks Will Be Seized: Uphold the War Loans
"For weeks, even before the revolution, there had been a steady run on German banks all over the country, not only causing an extremely painful dearth of currency, but the banks in many cities, among them Berlin, being compelled to print so-called Notgeld."

November 27, 1918
Firm for Forcing Germans to Repay; Allies May Occupy the Former Empire if Attempt is Made to Escape Reparation

November 30, 1918
High Mortality in Berlin: 15,397 More Deaths Than Births among Civilians Last Year

May 1, 1919
Germans Confident of Swaying Allies

May 1, 1919
Germany to Lose 70% of Iron and One-third of Her Coal

June 2, 1919
What Comes Next? Worries Germans: Allied Hostility to the Counter-proposals Causes Much Pessimism
"'What is going to happen now?' That is the question everyone is asking here, and now that the almost unanimously hostile attitude of the Entente press toward the German counterproposals is known, the answer is a very pessimistic one."

June 6, 1919
Germans Smuggle Wealth Abroad
"Some merely wish to escape the inevitably heavy taxation which must be shortly expected…the Government will not allow cash to be sent out of the country so the merchants smuggle their marks abroad and sell them at a large reduction, thereby still further reducing the value of the mark."

June 8, 1919
If Germany Doesn't Sign—Starvation
"Allies Are Ready to Enforce a Blockade More Rigorous Than Ever Before, Should Enemy Balk at Peace Terms."

June 15, 1919
Sees Germans Taxed $75 Each a Year
"Minister Wissell Doubts Wisdom of Importing Food to Be Paid for in Blood."

June 28, 1919
Germans Reach Versailles, Treaty to Be Signed Today

and it was very likely that the Allies would force Germany to pay them an additional sum in war reparations. Foreign exchange reserves were not sufficient to meet the existing stock of external debts, let alone any additional reparation payments. Real interest rates were very negative, and offered little compensation to creditors holding German currency/debt. The budget and the trade balance were also in very large deficits, meaning that Germany would remain dependent on borrowing/monetization to finance expenditures and consumption. Finally, the experience of high inflation, money printing, and negative total returns in holding the mark had begun to reduce trust in the German currency/debt as a store hold of value.

November 1918–March 1920: The Treaty of Versailles and the First Inflation

News of the German surrender in November 1918 was met with a wave of capital flight out of Germany. German citizens and firms rushed to convert their wealth into the currencies and assets of the victorious powers, not knowing what the terms of the peace would be or exactly how the German government would pay for its massive stock of liabilities now that it had lost the war. Over the next few months, the mark declined about 30 percent against the dollar, the German stock market lost almost half its real value, and government debt in local currency rose by about 30 percent, almost all of which had to be monetized by the central bank. As a result, the money supply grew by about 50 percent and the inflation rate climbed to 30 percent.

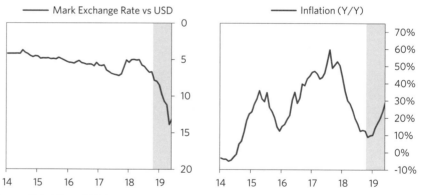

Source: Global Financial Data

This capital flight occurred despite initial optimism that the final terms of the peace would not be particularly harsh. Many members of the German negotiation team hoped that reparations would be limited to damage done in territories occupied by German forces, and would be paid primarily in goods instead of currency.[24] US President Woodrow Wilson's emphasis on self-determination also led many Germans to believe that there would be no annexations of German territory without at least a referendum. Many Germans therefore expected that their country would come out of the war with its territory and economic capacity intact, and that the reparation burden would not be too vindictive.[25]

When the final terms of the Treaty of Versailles were revealed, they came as a huge shock. Germany was to lose 12 percent of its territory through annexations, 10 percent of its population, 43 percent of its pig-iron capacity, and 38 percent of its steel capacity.[26] Germany was also required to compensate Allied citizens for all wealth seized during the war (within Germany and in occupied territories), but it would receive no compensation for its own assets (both real and financial) that had been confiscated abroad. The German government would also have to honor all prewar debts to Allied creditors, even if they were the debts of private citizens. As for reparations, a commission was to be established in 1921 that would determine the final bill after evaluating Germany's capacity to pay and giving its government another chance to be heard on the subject. In the interim, Germany would pay an equivalent of 20 billion marks in gold, commodities, ships, securities, and other real assets to compensate the Allies for the costs of occupation.[27]

Germany had no option but to agree to these terms or face total occupation. It signed the treaty on June 28, 1919. This triggered another sharp plunge in the exchange rate,[28] with the mark falling 90 percent against the dollar between July, 1919 and January, 1920. Inflation surged, hitting 140 percent by the end of the year. Once again, the mark's drop was driven primarily by **German citizens rushing to get their capital out of the country because they justifiably feared that these promises to deliver currency (i.e., these debt obligations) would make it very difficult, if not impossible, for the German government to meet its liabilities with hard money. To do that, the Reich would have to levy extortionately high taxes and confiscate private wealth. As the real wealth of private citizens was at risk, getting out of the currency and the country made sense.**

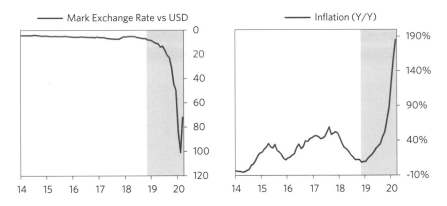

As the mark fell, German debtors with external liabilities saw the real expenses of their debts soar. They rushed to pay off as many of their foreign debts as they could, flooding the foreign exchange market. This further weakened the mark, triggering additional rounds of capital flight. This dynamic is also very common in countries with large foreign currency denominated debt during a debt/balance of payments crisis. As a prominent Hamburg industrialist noted at the time, "We are driving ourselves to destruction if everyone now… secretly sells mark notes in order to be able to meet his obligations. If things keep on this way, the mark notes will become unusable."[29]

To be clear: at this point money printing was not the source of the currency weakness so much as currency weakness was the cause of money printing. In other words, capital flight from the currency and the country was driving the currency down, which in turn helped drive higher inflation. That's classically how inflationary depressions happen.

The News

August 3, 1919
German Resources Are in Allies' Grip

August 9, 1919
Germans Approve Centralized Plan of Finance Minister
"This decision, which approves the Erzberger plan of unified imperial taxes, removes the rights of states to impose taxes and was bitterly contested."

August 10, 1919
Mark Goes Still Lower
"German marks, the value of which has been steadily falling recently in neutral countries surrounding Germany, reached their lowest point in history in Switzerland yesterday, being quoted at 35 centimes instead of the peace price of 125 centimes."

August 11, 1919
Billions in Paper in Deutsche Bank: But Report Admits Big Figures Don't Mean Real Gain in German Business
"The management remarks: 'It is true that the uncanny rise in the cost of operation is due to the depreciation of our money standard…but it is also materially due to the demand of the personal in connection with decreased labor output and shorter working day'"

September 7, 1919
Rigor in German Tax Hunt: Agents Empowered to Search Houses and Force Strong Boxes

September 13, 1919
German Industry Rapidly Reviving
"British observer says progress is greater than in any other country."

September 18, 1919
Mark Touches Lowest Point in the History of Germany
"Mathias Erzberger, Minister of Finance, today convened a conference of bankers and other financiers in order to discuss the decreased value of the mark and other financial problems."

September 26, 1919
Germans in Discord Over Heavy Taxes; Erzberger Hints at Resignation of the Government If Opposition Is Pressed

October 20, 1919
German Steel Output Up: Figures for July Show Big Gain during the Last Few Months

November 15, 1919
Won't Take German Money; Hanover Tradesmen Refuse Cash Bought at Low Exchange Rates
"A large number of Hanover tradesmen have decided to sell nothing to foreigners who wish to pay in German money which they bought with foreign money at the present low rates of exchange. Foreign money will, however, be accepted at the ordinary peacetime rates."

The News

November 29, 1919
Good Market Here for German Bonds
"Imperial war loans and securities of cities attractive to American speculators."

December 1, 1919
Germany Checks Exports Lest Country Be Stripped
"The Government's alarm over the manner in which the process of 'selling out Germany' continues has finally forced it to enact temporary measures which are calculated to put a radical check on exports."

December 5, 1919
Erzberger Offers Great Tax Budget; 60 Percent Levy on Biggest Incomes in Germany's Post-War Financing
"Discussing Germany's post-war economic obligations, Herr Erzberger said that the problems confronting the nation demanded the same universal solidarity among all citizens as did the responsibilities during the war. He hoped that the prospective tax reports would accelerate progress toward democracy, and contribute to the raising of a new Germany on the ruins of war."

December 17, 1919
Germany's Loan Falls Far Short; Only 3,800,000,000 Marks Subscribed, Instead of 5,000,000,000 Which Were Expected
"The Government is greatly disappointed by the failure of the Premium bond loan, for the preliminary figures show that it can hardly be represented as anything like the success which Erzberger and his colleagues expected."

January 2, 1920
Berlin Bourse Becomes Lively on Expectations of Treaty
"This was due chiefly to the understanding Germany had reached with the Entente with regard to the signing of the Peace Treaty and the expectation of better conditions for exports and imports."

January 23, 1920
Erzberger Serene Facing Many Foes

January 26, 1920
Germans Begin Evacuating Lands Lost by Treaty
"German preparations for the evacuation of Danzig, which is to become a free city under the terms of the Treaty of Versailles, had as one feature a final parade of the German troops this morning."

Naturally, as money leaves a currency/debt market, that puts the central bank in the position of having to choose between a) allowing the liquidity and debt markets to tighten up a lot and b) printing money to fill in the void. Central banks typically print money to fill the void, which causes currencies to decline. **While currency declines hurt importers and those with debts in foreign currencies, devaluations are stimulative for the economy and its asset markets, which is helpful during a period of economic weakness.** Currency declines provide a boost to exports and profit margins, as they make a country's goods cheaper on international markets. Simultaneously, they make imports more expensive, supporting domestic industries. Devaluations also cause assets to rise in value when measured in local currency, and they attract capital from abroad as a country's financial assets become cheaper in global currency terms.

From July 1919 through March 1920, the decline in the mark and negative real rates provided a boost to the German economy and its equity and commodity markets.

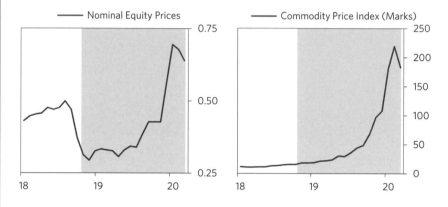

The export industry also thrived, unemployment declined, and as real wages remained low, business profitability improved. You can see the decline in unemployment and the pickup in exports in the charts below. (Note that all unemployment statistics from the time only show unemployment among trade union members, so they likely understate the true amount of unemployment and hardship in German society. However, they do show that employment conditions were improving.)

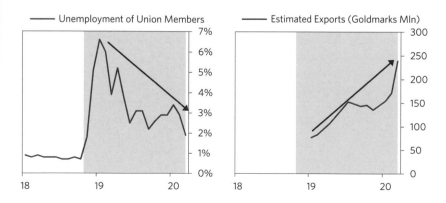

There was also the hope that by encouraging exports and discouraging imports, the mark's decline would be a one-off and would help bring the German balance of payments into equilibrium. According to one prominent German official:

"I regard our gravely ailing currency as an admirable means of dispelling the hatred felt abroad towards Germany, and of overcoming the reluctance to trade with us by our enemies. The American who no longer gets for his dollar 4.21 marks worth of goods from us, but 6.20 marks worth, will rediscover his fondness for Germany."[30]

German policy makers also began considering ways to deal with the domestic debt burden and the fiscal deficit. As one official described policy since the end of the war, "All we have done is keep printing."[31] To reduce the deficit, and raise revenues to meet debt liabilities, a comprehensive tax-reform package was proposed by finance minister Matthias Erzberger. Known as the "Erzberger Financial Reform," the package would transfer from the "haves" to the "have-nots" by levying highly progressive taxes on income and wealth (with top rates for income approaching 60 percent, and those for wealth at 65 percent).[32]

Passed in December 1919, the Erzberger Reforms would go on to increase the share of the Reich's income coming from direct taxes to 75 percent (the 1914 figure had been about 15 percent) and raise enough revenue to pay for all government expenditures except reparations by 1922.[33] Prior to these reforms, the majority of the government revenue came from public enterprises (primarily railroads), as well as specific duties on exports, imports, and coal.

The beneficial results of currency weakness led many German policy makers to advocate relying on currency weakness and inflation (from rising import prices and central bank printing) as an effective alternative to "confiscatory taxation."[34] One such official was Dr. Friedrich Bendixen, who argued that "every effort to collect the monstrous sum through taxes will weaken our productivity and thus reduce receipts and drive the Reich to economic collapse…only the transformation of the war loans into money can bring salvation."[35] Inflation would "cleanse" Germany of its local currency war debts and allow it to "begin a new life on the basis of new money." Although this program was explicitly rejected by the central bank, it recognized that things might "develop along these lines anyway." They did: inflation climbed to almost 200 percent, and by the end of 1919 it had reduced the domestic war-debt burden to about 25 percent of its original 1918 value. As you might imagine, those with wealth scrambled to buy foreign currencies or real assets to prevent their wealth from being either inflated or taken away.[36]

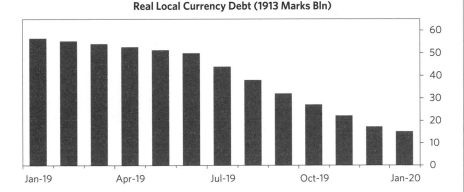

Real Local Currency Debt (1913 Marks Bln)

Jan-19   Apr-19   Jul-19   Oct-19   Jan-20

The central bank's alternative to allowing inflation to "naturally" reduce the real debt burden was to tighten monetary policy and engineer a

The News

January 31, 1920
Gold and Silver Bring High Prices in Berlin; Germans Pay 500 Paper Marks for 20-Mark Gold Pieces to Provide Against Collapse
"An unprecedented decrease in the German rate of exchange has caused a serious panic among business men and the public generally and has led to enormous prices being paid for gold and silver in coins, which many people seek to purchase now as a sort of an 'iron reserve' which will provide for them when the worst comes."

February 14, 1920
French Interested in Treaty Revision: but They Would Consider None That Lightened Germany's Burdens
"France sees in the possibility of changes opportunity of gains for herself, while the English advocates for alternations would ease the burden of Germany".

March 14, 1920
Troops Overthrow Ebert; Kapp, Prussian Pan-German, Declares Himself German Chancellor
"Germany today is in the throes of a counterrevolutionary movement which was successful this forenoon in turning the Ebert Government out of Berlin and setting up a new Administration in the capital."

March 28, 1920
German Rage Rises over Kapp Mutiny
"People angry over laxity in arresting and prosecuting the revolutionists. Threaten another strike; workmen demand that soldiers be withdrawn immediately from the Ruhr district."

April 12, 1920
German Prices Rise though Mark Gains; Food Conditions Grow Worse and Health of People Continues to Decline
"Financial circles in Berlin are recovering their spirits. The mark continues to improve."

May 16, 1920
War on Profiteers Fails in Germany
"Prices Continue to Soar Despite Berlin's Efforts and Rise in Marks. Up 650 per cent. Since 1914 increase in cost of necessities about 17 per cent. In First Two Months of 1920."

June 20, 1920
Germans Welcome Steel Price Drop
"With the announcement of an actual reduction in the producers' prices for steel and iron, effective from June 1, and the further statement that there would be no rise in the price of coal, the German press, in general, took occasion to rejoice over this concrete evidence of the fact that the Peak of high prices had been reached in these basic industries."

June 23, 1920
German Food Outlook
"Crops Not Up To Expectations And Farm Labor Threatens Strike—Food Riots Reported."

deflationary recession. This would allow the Reich to pay back its citizens something closer to the true value of their loaned wealth, but it would also crush domestic credit creation and demand, generating significant unemployment. **Germany faced the classic dilemma: whether to help those who are long the currency (i.e., creditors who hold debt denominated in it) or those who are short it (i.e., debtors who owe it). In economic crises, policies to redistribute wealth from "haves" to "have-nots" are more likely to occur. This is because the conditions of the "have-nots" become intolerable and also because there are more "have-nots" than "haves."**

At the time, relieving debt burdens and redistributing wealth were higher priorities than preserving the wealth of creditors. Unemployment was still high, food shortages were rampant, and a large mass of returning soldiers from the front needed jobs so they could be reintegrated into the economy. Clashes between capitalists and workers, as are typical in depressions, were also happening all across Europe. There had been a Communist revolution in Russia in 1917, and Communist ideas were spreading around the world. Commenting on the choice between inflation and deflation at the time, the legendary British economist John Maynard Keynes wrote: "The inflation is unjust and deflation is inexpedient. Of the two perhaps deflation is the worse, because it is worse in an impoverished world to provoke unemployment than to disappoint the rentier [i.e., the capitalist lender]."[37]

Although levels of activity remained very depressed, by late 1919/early 1920 Germany had inflated away most of its domestic debt, passed a comprehensive tax-reform package to generate new revenues, and was beginning to see a pickup in economic activity. There was also some good news on the reparations front. To relieve growing tensions between Germany and the Allies, the Allies invited Germany to submit its own proposal for how much the reparation bill should be. Critics of a harsh settlement, such as John Maynard Keynes, were finding increasing sympathy in official circles abroad. The exchange rate also began to stabilize.[38]

However, conflicts between the Left and Right remained intense in Germany. In March 1921, right-wing nationalist groups led by Wolfgang Kapp attempted to overthrow the Weimar government and institute an autocratic monarchist regime in its place. The coup collapsed within a matter of days after workers refused to cooperate with the new government and declared a general strike.[39] Although a complete failure, the "Kapp Putsch" was a reminder of how fragile the political environment remained, and was another example of how **the economic pain of deleveragings/depressions can give rise to populist and reactionary leaders on *both* the Left and the Right.** As one frustrated Berlin businessman put it:

"Just at the moment when we begin again to work more than before…when in London the recognition is mounting that through the imposition of the Versailles Treaty one has committed a fearful political stupidity, and that accordingly the exchange rate begins to improve, the military party…under the leadership of a man who is a notorious reactionary, again throws everything overboard and forces our workers into a general strike and demonstrations that are unnecessary because nothing will be achieved that way."[40]

March 1920 to May 1921: Relative Stabilization

The fourteen months between March 1920 and May 1921 were a period of "relative stabilization."[41] The mark halted its slide, prices remained stable, and the German economy outperformed the rest of the developed world. Germany wasn't collapsing from either economic or political chaos, as many had predicted, and those shorting the mark lost considerable sums (a notable case is John Maynard Keynes, who personally lost about £13,000 on the trade).[42]

The global backdrop at the time was one of severe contraction, driven by tightening monetary policy in the US and UK. For example, between 1920 and 1921, industrial production fell by 20 percent in the US and 18.6 percent in the UK, while unemployment climbed to 22 percent and 11.8 percent respectively.[43]

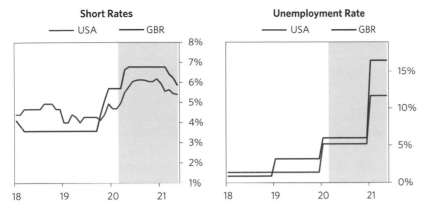

Source: Global Financial Data

In contrast to other central banks, the Reichsbank kept monetary policy very easy—the discount rate remained at 5 percent until 1922.[44] The Reichsbank also regularly intervened to inject additional liquidity when credit conditions tightened. For instance, in the spring of 1921, when business liquidity tightened moderately, the Reichsbank responded by accelerating its purchases of commercial bills (from 3.1 percent to 9 percent of bills outstanding).[45] Fiscal policy also remained accommodative, with real expenditures (ex-reparations) rising in 1920 and 1921.[46] Although the budget deficit narrowed, it remained huge—roughly 10 percent of GDP—and continued to be financed by the issuance of floating debt.

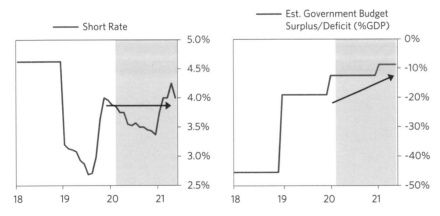

Source: Global Financial Data

The stimulative policies allowed Germany to escape the global contraction and enjoy relatively strong economic conditions. Between 1919 and 1921, industrial production increased by 75 percent! However, as you can see in the charts below, levels of economic activity remained extremely depressed (e.g., industrial production and real GDP were still well below 1913 levels), and there was considerable poverty and suffering in German society. This period should be understood as one of growth within a larger period of economic contraction.

The News

July 2, 1920
German Debt 265 Billion Marks

September 17, 1920
Exchange Decline Depresses Berlin; Proposed Tax On Capital, Financial Chaos And Despair Given As Reasons
"Germany is again suffering from a severe fit of depression. The mark has fallen heavily again today, being quoted at 210 to the pound sterling. That means a depreciation of 40 percent in the last six weeks."

October 3, 1920
Germany Abolishes Weak War Beer
"Berlin Is Now Enjoying Peacetime 8 Percent Brew—Tips Restored, Too."

October 7, 1920
Unexampled Boom in German Textiles; Huge Profits Announced by Many Woolen and Cotton Companies
"The German textile industry, which of late has begun even to invade England again, has had such an astoundingly successful year that its high records of peace times have been put completely in the shade. Several of the largest concerns are now issuing annual reports and declaring dividends."

November 2, 1920
German Industry Gets Big Orders
"Many Millions of Marks' Worth Placed and Payment Arranged. Coal Shortage Handicap. Serious Check on Trade Expansion Possible, a Conference at Dresden Is Told."

December 19, 1920
Germany's Foreign Trade; Remarkable Movement of Exports and Imports This Year

December 23, 1920
Reparation Issue Nearer Settlement
"Germans leave Brussels for conference recess taking allied suggestions for reforms. Full agreement expected."

January 7, 1921
Stocks in Germany Have Climbed Fast
"The way in which Germany's industries have gone ahead since the end of the war can be strikingly illustrated by reference to the Stock Exchange quotations of shares of the country's most important concerns."

January 27, 1921
French Hesitate About Indemnity
"Undecided Whether They Want Germany Ruined but Powerless or Able to Pay but Strong."

February 20, 1921
Germany's Growing Trade

February 26, 1921
Germans May Seek Reparation Delay; Are Now Said to Object to Immediate Fixing of Their Total Indemnity Obligation
"*The New York Times* correspondent has reliable information that the German proposals in London will be based on demands for delay in the fixing of the total of reparations, in order to afford Germany time for recuperation. This procedure, it is argued, would give the Entente an opportunity of judging just what Germany really could pay."

The News

April 2, 1921
Commodity Prices; Grains Sag to New Low Levels—General Weakness in the Provisions

April 3, 1921
Extent of World's Decline in Prices
"The fact that wheat declined last week to the lowest since 1915, that corn and oats fell to pre-war prices, that cotton is selling below many pre-war years and copper at the lowest since 1914, is adding interest to the scope of the general fall in prices in the different countries."

April 3, 1921
Inflation in Germany
"The Frankfurter Zeitung's index number of average commodity prices in Germany for March, taking the average of Jan. 1, 1920, as 100, places the present figure at 131, as compared with 136 in February, 148 in January and 156 on May 1920, which was the highest point ever reached."

April 9, 1921
German Note Asks All of Upper Silesia
"The German Ambassador delivered to the French Foreign Office last night a document of 500 pages asking that all of Upper Silesia be given to Germany."

April 16, 1921
Germans Hopeful on Loan

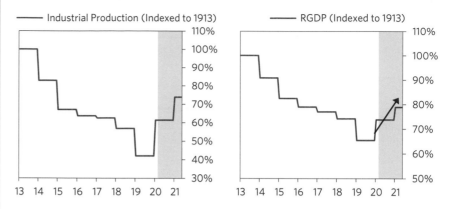

Rising economic activity and reflationary policies did not result in much inflation in Germany between March 1920 and May 1921, as domestic inflationary pressures were being offset by global deflationary forces. Import prices from the US and UK fell by about 50 percent, and rising capital flows into the outperforming German economy helped to stabilize the currency, which allowed for slower growth in the money supply. As you can see in the charts below, this was a significant turnaround. The mark rallied, inflation declined, and by early 1921 prices stopped rising for the first time since 1914.

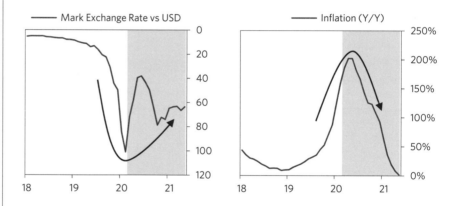

There was also considerable optimism about the German economy abroad—in fact, it became the new hot economy to invest in, as reflected by foreigners' willingness to pour money into it, which financed an ever-growing trade deficit. In fact, some commentators at the time began referring to Germany's surging capital inflows as a "tremendous" speculative bubble, with Keynes even calling it "the greatest ever known." **Many of those flooding the market with mark orders were new buyers, with no prior experience in the market they were trading—one of the classic signs of a bubble.** According to Keynes:

"[From those] in the streets of the capital…[to] barber's assistants in the remotest townships of Spain and South America…the argument has been the same…Germany is a great and strong country; someday she will recover; when that happens the mark will recover also, which will bring a very large profit."[47]

For some perspective on the size of these inflows, by 1921 almost a third of all deposits in the seven largest German banks were foreign-owned.[48] These speculative inflows supported a relative stabilization in the mark. **It also made the central bank's job much easier by reducing the inherent trade-offs** between growth and inflation. As explained in my description of the archetypal template, when capital is flowing into a country, it tends to lower the country's inflation rate and stimulate its growth rate (all other things being equal); when capital leaves, it tends to do the opposite, making the central bank's job much more difficult.

Strong capital inflows also meant that the German economy became increasingly dependent on "hot money" (i.e., speculative investments that could be pulled out at a moment's notice) continuing to come in, year after year, to finance fiscal and external deficits.[49] As is classic in the bubble phase of any balance of payments crisis, **increasing dependence on capital inflows to maintain levels of spending and economic activity made the economic recovery fragile, and sensitive to any minor event that could trigger a shift in sentiment** vis-à-vis the future prospects of the German economy.

The mark's sharp appreciation in early 1920 was an unwelcome development for policy makers because a falling mark was considered essential to maintaining German export competitiveness, supporting employment growth, and building a savings pool of hard currency earnings. It was considered the "one good fortune in the midst of misfortune," without which Germany would lose the possibility of exports.[50] The initial appreciation hit exports hard, with the chamber of commerce going as far as to say that industry had practically "ground to a halt."[51] Unemployment surged, with the number of trade union members reported as unemployed tripling. For these reasons, the economic ministry intervened between March and June 1920—aiming to deliberately depress the mark and stimulate employment. It worked. The mark fell, competitiveness returned, and unemployment once again began to decline.[52]

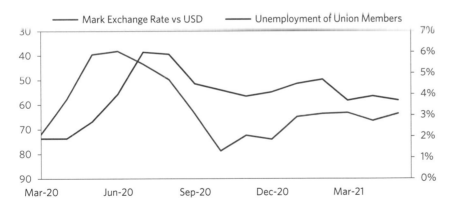

During this period, German policy makers were more concerned about deflationary forces spreading to Germany than the inflation that their stimulative policies could cause. Rising unemployment, and the potential social unrest it could cause, were considered much more menacing than the return of rising prices. As the reconstruction minister told a prominent industrialist:

"[I] am not afraid of the inflation…if the crisis which has already broken out to its full extent in England were not to come over to us, we should allow the printing press to do a bit more work and begin rebuilding the country. This activity would enable us to build a dam against the crisis."[53]

Of course, the stabilization of the mark, inflation, and economic conditions remained contingent on large speculative inflows into Germany and a stable balance of payments.

The News

April 23, 1921
Briand Vows France Will Get Her Dues; Drastic Action Will Convince Germany That She Can Pay, He Declares

April 30, 1921
Berlin Cabinet May Have to Quit Now: See No Way to Avert Further Penalties but Full Surrender to Paris Demands
"There is great talk tonight of a cabinet crisis caused by failure to induce America to act as mediator in the reparations dispute. In political circles the question is being discussed as to who shall succeed Chancellor Fehrenbach and Foreign Minister Simons if they should refuse to place their signatures to the Paris demands."

May 1, 1921
Could Move Troops May 7: French Military Plans Call For Occupation Of Ruhr In Two Days
"The territory to be occupied, subject, of course, to decisions reached at the meeting of the Supreme Council in London."

May 2, 1921
Allies to Give Germany an Ultimatum, While France Mobilizes Her Forces

May 3, 1921
French Start War Machine
"British opposition to the French plans has been strengthened by advices from Washington that the United States Government is opposed to military action against Germany."

May 6, 1921
M. Briand Faces Critics in Paris
"Premier Briand declared in an interview at the Quai d'Orsay tonight that if Germany accepted the allied conditions and subsequently did not fulfill them, military action would be taken without the formality of another allied conference."

May 8, 1921
German Note Circulation Increases

May 8, 1921
German Bonds' Prospects
"International bankers in New York who commented yesterday on the plans of the Reparation Commission for the issuance of a series of bonds by Germany, for cancellation of her debt to the Allies, expressed the opinion that the bonds could be sold in the New York market satisfactorily, only after they had received the endorsement of the allied governments, to whom the plan calls for their delivery."

May 15, 1921
Germany Shares Boom In Exchange
"Belief that she will pay her war bills sends marks up"

May 24, 1921
France Warns Germany That Invasion of Silesia Would be Regarded as War

May 27, 1921
Berlin to Pay Allies $200,000,000 Tomorrow
"Will Complete May 31 Reparation Payment by Treasury Bills in Dollars."

May 1921: The London Ultimatum

The arguments between Germany and the Allies over reparations came to a head with "The London Ultimatum" in May 1921, in which the Allies threatened to occupy the Ruhr Basin within six days if Germany did not accept the new reparation bill. Total reparations were set at 132 billion gold marks (about 330 percent of German GDP). Fifty billion was scheduled to be paid in quarterly installments, adding up to around 3 billion gold marks a year. This was a debt-service burden of around 10 percent of German GDP, or 80 percent of export earnings.[54] Payments for the remaining 70 billion would begin whenever the Allied powers, not Germany, determined its economy capable of doing so. Not only did Germany have to service a huge hard currency debt burden, it also had to live with the threat of its debt service payments tripling at a moment's notice.

The reparations demanded were enormous and dashed expectations that a far more conciliatory agreement would be reached. The structure of the payments was also deeply unnerving to potential investors and the German public, as it meant that debt service burdens would likely get bigger if economic conditions improved.[55] For context, the chart below shows the size of the hard currency debts imposed on Germany relative to other economies prior to entering major inflationary depressions. As you can see, Weimar Germany dwarfs every other case. The second chart shows Germany's debt as a percent of GDP between 1914 and 1922.

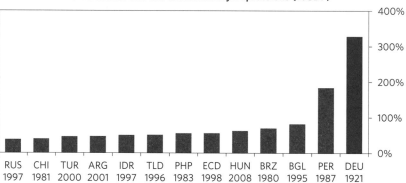

FX Debt Levels Prior to Inflationary Depressions (%GDP)

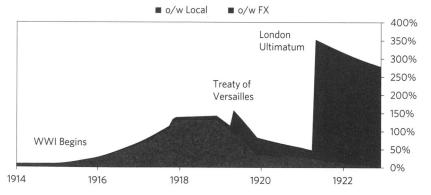

Estimated German Government Debt (%GDP)

As soon as the reparation burden was announced, the mark began selling off; it declined by 75 percent by the end of the year. Inflation also returned, with prices almost doubling over the same period. For one prominent German participant at Versailles, the ultimatum fulfilled his worst fears:

"The world must be made to understand that it is impossible to burden a country with debts and at the same time to deprive it of the means of paying them...the most complete collapse of the currency...cannot...be avoided if the peace treaty is maintained in its current form."[56]

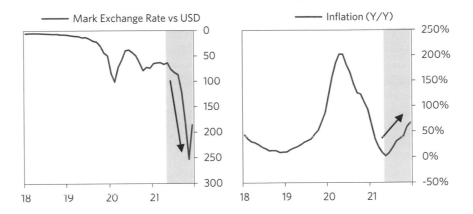

The reparation schedule created a balance of payments crisis. In many ways, a balance of payments crisis is just like any other serious problem faced by individuals, households, and corporations in making a payment. To come up with the money, a country must either 1) spend less, 2) earn more, 3) finance the payments through borrowing and/or tapping into savings, or 4) default on the debt (or convince creditors to give it relief). Unlike its domestic war loans, Germany could not print away the debt burden, as the debts were not denominated in paper marks. Policy makers would need to rely on some combination of the four levers outlined above.

Cutting Spending Would Be Extremely Painful and Politically Dangerous

Since about 50 percent of the German government's total revenues would have to be spent on reparations, cuts in nonreparation expenses would need to be drastic to make a difference.[57] Because most nonreparation spending was going towards essential social services—unemployment relief, subsidies for food and housing, and funding for leading public employers, such as the railways and shipyards—large spending cuts were considered "politically impossible." With the Bolshevik Revolution in Russia and its ongoing bloody civil war, as well as the growing Communist movement in Germany, policy makers feared a potential revolution from the left. Simultaneously, the increasingly humiliating demands of the Allied powers, and the economic pain that came from meeting them, were fueling far-right nationalism. Fears of political chaos intensified as strikes, riots, and acts of political violence became increasingly common. During the summer of 1920, a state of emergency had to be declared following widespread looting;[58] in March 1921, Communist groups seized control of several shipyards and factories and were only dispersed following firefights with police;[59] and in October 1921, finance minister Matthias Erzberger was assassinated by ultranationalists for his role in the 1918 surrender.[60] Given this context, it should not be surprising that the government refused to cut back on social spending and the Reichsbank refused to stop monetizing the deficit.

Tax Burdens Were Already Extremely High

While cutting spending was untenable, so was raising income by levying additional taxes. The problem was that the Erzberger Reforms of 1919 (discussed above) had already raised tax burdens considerably. Increasing this burden posed the same political/social risks as cutting back on spending—i.e., any additional tax increases would not only prove immensely difficult to pass (the Erzberger Reforms themselves had been watered-down significantly by opposition in the Reichstag), but would also be likely to accelerate capital flight. Commenting on the impossibility of meeting the reparation burden through taxation, Keynes wrote "the whips and scorpions of any government recorded in history [would not have been] potent enough to extract nearly half…[the required] income from a people so situated."[61]

Existing Savings Were Extremely Limited and Securing Lending in Sufficient Size Was Impossible

There were virtually no savings to draw on to service those debts. The Treaty of Versailles had essentially seized or frozen all of Germany's prewar foreign holdings and canceled all debts owed to Germans. Moreover, those with foreign currency savings (primarily exporters) were incentivized to keep their earnings in foreign bank accounts, precisely because they had reason to fear the reparations burden would encourage a government seizure of their wealth. As for the central bank's gold reserves, they were not enough to cover even the first interest payment.

Further, there was little appetite internationally to extend Germany credit on a scale that would allow it to spread out its reparation burden. This was for two reasons. First, most developed world economies were burdened by war debts of their own (primarily owed to the United States) and were also in the midst of severe recessions. Second, the German government (and most Germans) weren't creditworthy. For instance, when the head of the Reichsbank approached the Bank of England for a 500 million gold mark short-term loan to meet the second reparation installment, he was "politely refused."[62] According to the British Chancellor of the Exchequer at the time, "the difficulty was that there was a vicious circle. Germany said she could not stop the emission of paper money and repay her obligations unless she was able to raise a foreign loan, and she could not raise a foreign loan unless she could pay her obligations."[63]

Of course, defaulting on the debt unilaterally was impossible, because Germany had been threatened with an invasion. Though its leaders furiously and continuously tried to renegotiate the payments, bitter feelings from the war (which had ended just a couple of years earlier) made the victors, especially France, disinclined to make concessions.

Unlike a household facing a payment problem, a country can change the amount of existing currency, and by doing so affect its value. This gives it an additional lever to manage a balance of payments crisis. While the Reichsbank could try to defend the currency by raising rates and tightening credit, which would increase the returns on holding mark denominated assets/deposits for creditors, and thereby attract more capital from abroad while discouraging capital flight at home, it would also crush domestic demand, reduce imports, and help close the trade deficit. That would require an unimaginably severe contraction in consumption, which would have been intolerable for this already impoverished and conflict-ridden society to bear.

The only remaining alternative was to allow the currency to depreciate and print money to alleviate any potential tightening in liquidity that resulted from the flight of marks abroad.

As we noted in the template, **the most important characteristic of cases that spiral into hyperinflation is that policy makers don't close the imbalance between income and spending/debt service; instead, they fund and keep funding spending over sustained periods of time by printing lots of money.** Of course, some targeted money printing is typical in any balance of payments crisis—and, if not overused, is helpful, because it prevents the economic contraction from getting too severe. **But when there is too much reflationary printing of money/ monetization, and too severe a currency devaluation (which is reflationary) relative to the other levers for managing a deleveraging—especially the deflationary levers of austerity and debt restricting/default—the most severe inflationary depressions can and do occur.**

The reparation schedule—and the extreme difficulty of using austerity, dissaving, external borrowing, and debt defaults as levers—pushed German policy makers to rely exclusively on money printing to manage the crisis. While policy makers knew this would contribute to inflation, they wagered that it would be the least terrible of their terrible choices. In my opinion, they made a mistake in not trying to achieve a better balance between deflationary forces and inflationary ones.

June 1921–December 1921: The Emerging Inflationary Spiral

The second half of 1921 saw the **classic dynamics of an inflationary spiral emerge. Germany's impossible set of foreign debt obligations was contributing to currency declines, which caused inflation and a liquidity crisis. The central bank provided liquidity by printing money and buying debt, rather than allowing commerce to deeply contract. This, in turn, triggered further rounds of capital flight, inflation, tightening liquidity, and money printing, so the spiral accelerated.** In the midst of this, the central bank depleted a substantial portion of its gold reserves to cover the first reparation payments.

The spiral was still relatively contained compared to what was to come a year later, mainly as foreigners continued to support the German balance of payments by purchasing German assets. But reparation payments and local capital flight caused the mark to decline 75 percent over the period and inflation accelerated, approaching 100 percent per annum. The sharpest declines came in October 1921, following the League of Nation's decision to cede Upper Silesia (an important coal mining and industrial region) to Poland, despite a majority vote by its residents to remain in Germany.[64]

Rising inflation led to a surge in retail purchases. This pickup in demand was not a sign of increasing economic activity but rather a flight of income and savings into real goods before inflation could eat away at the purchasing power of money. The American Council of Hamburg spoke of a "vast amount of retail buying," while the *Hamburgische Correspondent* referred to a "monstrous lust for goods."[65] The situation soon came to be described as one of "general liquidation," because between foreigners buying a lot since the mark was cheap and Germans buying goods to escape inflation, the shelves in the shops were bare. A Berlin official reported shock at the "plundering of the retailers by foreigners with highly valued currencies," while a British observer lamented that "many shops declare themselves to be sold out; others close from 1 to 4 in the afternoon, and most of them refuse to sell more than one article of the same kind to each customer...Germans [are] laying in stores for fear of a further rise in prices or a total depletion of stocks."[66]

The same pressures led to a massive increase in consumer-durable and real-asset purchases. Auto sales climbed to all-time highs, the textile trade had bookings several months in advance, cotton firms refused to take new orders, and most industries found themselves operating at full capacity and having to introduce overtime to meet the growing demand for goods.[67] Once again, this burst of economic activity was not a sign of economic prosperity, but a classic flight into inflation-hedge assets. According to one Bavarian official:

"The fall of the mark...has brought a real anxiety among the propertied classes. Everyone seeks to do something with their money. Everything is bought that can be bought, not only for present need, not only for future use, but in order to get rid of the paper and have objects to exchange when the time comes that it is worth absolutely nothing."[68]

The News

June 1, 1921
Germany Preparing to Pay
"Now that the period of negotiation and hoping against hope has passed for Germany, she is grappling with the financial obligations involved in making her reparations payments."

June 20, 1921
Germany Seeking Additional Credits; Sounding Foreign Bankers on Establishment of Balances Secured by Reichsbank Silver
"Germany has used up a large proportion of her foreign credits in making the reparation payments which have already been concluded. How much in the way of credits still remains available in liquid form is a question which is causing much discussion."

June 23, 1921
Find German Industry Making Rapid Gains
"A commercial commission which has just returned from studying conditions in Germany reports that German factories and workshops of all kinds are working with all their might and that if nothing intervenes to impede her progress Germany will before very long become commercially superior to all other European countries."

June 23, 1921
To Tax Germans 20 Billions More; Wirth Tells National Economic Council's Reparations Committee What Is Impending
"Chancellor Wirth's 'reparation Government' is tackling the herculean task of raising funds for reparation with an intensive thoroughness and deadly earnestness commensurate with its intricate difficulties and unpopular thanklessness."

June 25, 1921
Change in Method of German Payment
"800,000,000 marks can be turned over in European currencies instead of dollars. Countries to take risk may involve depreciation of own money, but is expected to lower rate of dollar."

June 26, 1921
Germany Sets Pace for World's Trade
"A reflection of the powers of recuperation of Germany has been found in statistics of the imports and exports of the United States, as compiled by the Department of Commerce. They present an excellent picture of the manner in which the German Government, importers and exporters are thrusting themselves into the forefront of foreign trade."

June 30, 1921
Exchange Steady in German Payment
"The payment by Germany of her second instalment [sic] on her reparations bill, amounting to 44,000,000 gold marks, has been accomplished without disorganizing the foreign exchanges, as happened when the first payment was made."

The News

July 7, 1921
German Tax Bill 80 Billions a Year
"Wirth announces that figure in paper marks as necessary to cover obligations. The chancellor's dilemma is if he emphasizes direct tax he alienates the bourgeois; if indirect, the proletariat."

July 20, 1921
Mystery Cloaks Germany's Credits
"Local bankers believe that some of present heavy withdrawals are going abroad."

July 25, 1921
German Industries Entering on a Boom
"Artificially cheap labor and coal are basis of general revival in many branches."

August 6, 1921
German Debt Still Rises
"Up 8,339,040,000 marks in June, making total 135,031,060,000."

August 7, 1921
German Tax Plan Depends on Silesia
"The Wirth Government, wrestling continuously throughout the dog days with the tough problem of devising new tax schemes for saddling the additional billions on the German people needed to cover reparation charges and balance the deficit of the internal budget, has completed the first stadium of its thankless job."

August 28, 1921
Erzberger's Death Fires All Germany
"Responsibility for the murder attaches to the Nationalist skirts. Its effect on the radical masses is bound to assert itself."

As the central bank kept market interest rates anchored at 5 percent (by increasing purchases when liquidity tightened), and as inflation was generally 10x higher, **the real return on lending became very unattractive and the real cost of borrowing (i.e., real interest rates) plummeted.**[69] **This led to a surge in borrowing, which became extremely attractive.**[70] As a result, real investment reached prewar highs[71] and monthly bankruptcy rates declined by 75 percent.[72] However, there was very little in this investment that was productive. Firms would push borrowed money into capital less for its "use value" than for its "intrinsic value." Firms that did not do this, and kept most of their wealth in debt assets (such as bonds), suffered devastating losses. This time was called the "flight from the mark to the machine"; it resulted in many excessive investments that performed poorly once the inflation had passed.[73] Of course, all of this accelerated inflation and reinforced the spiral.

Growing demand for real goods led to increasing employment in the industries that produced those goods.[74] **So unemployment fell and workers' bargaining power increased as they pushed for wage increases and better working hours.** In the summer of 1921, numerous standoffs between employers and laborers led to large nominal wage gains. However, these gains were not enough to keep up with inflation and workers still saw their real incomes fall by about 30 percent.[75] This made tensions between the "haves" and the "have-nots" even worse.

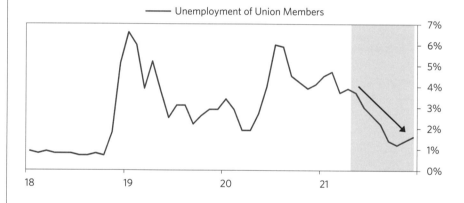

Unemployment of Union Members

The only sector of the economy that saw some clear benefit from the collapse of the mark was the export sector. Foreign sales increased as German goods became cheaper on the international market. However, the pickup in exports was less than it ordinarily would have been, given such a large decline in the currency, for two reasons: First, there was considerable hostility to German exports abroad, even as they became cheaper, which limited the potential gains from a depreciating currency. Second, labor costs were also declining in the rest of the developed world, as a result of deflation from the severe global recession, limiting the potential competitiveness gains from the depreciating mark.

The second half of 1921 also saw what one commentator called "an orgy of speculation" in the stock market.[76] Stocks nearly tripled in value over the period (in inflation-adjusted terms) and in August the Berlin stock exchange was so overloaded with orders that it was forced to shut down three times a week. By November, operating days were reduced to just one day a week and banks refused to take orders for shares after 10 a.m. According to one newspaper, "Today there is no one—from lift-boy, typist, and small landlord to the wealthy lady in high society—who does not speculate in industrial securities and who does not study the list of official quotations as if it were a most precious letter."[77]

Once again, **this bull market was not driven by improving economic fundamentals, or a more optimistic discounting of future economic conditions. It reflected a rush to get out of money or to get short money (i.e., borrow it) against a long "stuff" position.** According to one observer:

"Stock market speculation today is the organized flight from the mark...at a time when the return on an investment diminishes in the same ratio as the value of the paper mark and when therefore even the solid capitalist, if he does not want to impoverish himself from day to day, must acquire real values. This alone has led to an extraordinary increase in the stock market business."[78]

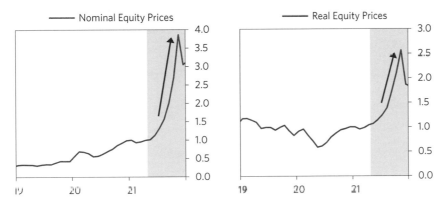

By the end of 1921, deteriorating economic conditions, the absence of faith in the mark, and rapidly rising prices began to threaten an economic and/or political collapse. At the time, the inflation rate was nearing 100 percent. The only thing preventing a total collapse was the foreigners' willingness to continue to buy marks and fund Germany's massive external deficit (about 10 percent of GDP). As the chart below illustrates, despite the loss of confidence in the mark at home, many foreigners kept purchasing German assets at cheap prices.

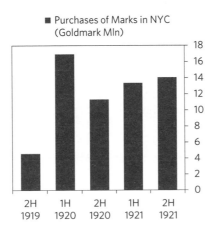

The News

September 4, 1921
Sees German Crash in False Success: Fall in Mark and Increase in Issue Is Inflating Prices, Says Moody
"'Germany's paper prosperity is leading to a crash,' says John Moody, President of Moody's Investors' Service."

September 5, 1921
German Reds Riot in Many Places

September 30, 1921
German Food Prices Rise
"Collapse of mark exchange affects every family in country."

October 21, 1921
Berlin and Warsaw Get Silesian Fiat: Allies Announce Adoption of League of Nations Partition of the Territory
"There will probably be a further outcry from the Germans, but with the French army on the edge of the Ruhr the Germans will accept the decision."

November 8, 1921
3 Marks for 1 Cent in Local Market: German Bank Statement of Vast New Inflation Sends Quotations Down
"The German mark touched the lowest figure in its history."

November 28, 1921
Germany Expects to Raise Foreign Credit

December 14, 1921
German Bank Statement: Further Increase of 1,846,000,000 Marks in First Week of December

December 17, 1921
Germany Asks for Time

December 21, 1921
Berlin Waits Result of London Conference: The Reichsbank Meanwhile Holds on to Its Reserve of Gold Marks

January 7, 1922
Rejects German Plea: Reparation Commission Refuses to Grant Delay on Next Payments

"In reply the Reparation Commission upholds its former standpoint and refuses to examine any possibility of delayed payment until Germany replies...regarding the length of postponement, what sums may be expected and what guarantees are given."

January 10, 1922
German Delegates Start For Cannes

"Berlin has been suddenly seized with unbridled optimism over the Cannes conference, and it was reflected on the Bourse today in its effect on the paper mark."

January 29, 1922
Germany Begs Off 1922 Cash Payment: Also Wants Allies to Reduce Money Demand and Increase Tribute in Kind

"Reply to reparations board tells of plans to re-establish financial stability: tax burden made heavier, in addition to forced levy, another internal loan is to help reduce floating debt."

February 6, 1922
New Perplexities In German Finance

"Government may be forced to resort to direct issue of paper money."

February 13, 1922
German Prices Up Again

"Public buying goods through fear of still further advance."

February 27, 1922
Renewed Rise of Prices In Germany; Markets Advancing On Withdrawal Of Government Subsidies And Fixed Values

"The tendency of German commodity markets last week, independently of the mark's movement on exchange, was toward rapidly rising prices, with renewed activity in production and trade, and with other symptoms which were shown during the great collapse of the mark in 1921."

February 28, 1922
Genoa Prospects Depress Germans

"Gloom Over Decision of Premiers to Exclude Reparations From Conference Discussion. Mark falls still lower."

March 2, 1922
Reparations Deal Opposed In Germany; Industrial Concerns Raise an Outcry Against Provisional Accord With Entente

"German industrials prophesy a death blow to German exports, also economic slavery and ultimate ruin, if the convention regarding material reparations, provisionally signed by representatives of the German Reconstruction Ministry...ever becomes operative."

March 10, 1922
Reply Shatters Germany's Hopes

"America's participation in future conference is still looked forward to."

March 22, 1922
Calls on Germany to Limit Paper Money: Allied Board Plans Partial Moratorium

January 1922–May 1922: Negotiating a Reparation Moratorium

Alarmed by the chaos in Germany, the Allied powers concluded that the German economy needed some relief from reparation payments.[79] This was encouraging because at this stage it was the reparation debt burden that was most crushing and most inescapable. Continuing with the status quo ran the risk of a total economic collapse, which would worsen the political chaos at the heart of Europe, while making it impossible to collect any reparation payments in the future. However, there remained considerable disagreement among the Allied powers as to the extent of such relief and what, if anything, Germany should be required to give in return.

Central to the matter was a tension between the desire for vengeance and the limitation of German power, and the recognition that economic realities dictated that some compromises be made. **This flavor of debtor/creditor standoff is classic during deleveragings. Naturally, the debtors (i.e., Germans) demanded as much relief as they could get and the creditors (i.e., the Allied powers) tried to get as much money back as they could without plunging the debtor economy into insolvency. The game of power brinksmanship was played by all.** Commenting on the dynamics at the time, J.P. Morgan, Jr. reportedly told a confidant:

"The Allies must make up their minds as to whether they wanted a weak Germany who could not pay, or a strong Germany who could pay. If they wanted a weak Germany they must keep her economically weak; but if they wanted her to be able to pay they must allow Germany to exist in a condition of cheerfulness, which would lead to successful business. This meant, however, that you would get a strong Germany, and a Germany that was strong economically would, in a sense, be strong from a military point of view also."[80]

The question of restructuring Germany's reparation payments was discussed at a conference in Cannes, France, in January 1922. A temporary compromise was reached under which the Reparations Commission reduced the debt service bill by 75 percent for the remainder of the year, provided Germany agreed to raise new taxes (including a forced loan of a billion gold marks on its wealthy citizens), reduced spending and money printing, and granted the Reichsbank formal independence from the government.[81] These concessions were mostly symbolic. The taxes agreed to were far too small to meaningfully close the budget deficit and the president of the Reichsbank, Rudolf Havenstein, said he welcomed more independence, as it would allow him to print as much money as was needed to ensure liquidity without constraints from fiscal policy makers.[82]

Renewed optimism about meaningful relief from reparations halted the mark's slide. By the end of January, it had risen 30 percent from its 1921 lows, and inflation, while remaining high (about 140 percent per annum), had stopped accelerating. The inflationary spiral was halted for now, providing much-needed relief to the German economy. As negotiations progressed, German policy makers pressed the Allies for additional concessions, arguing forcefully that it was the balance of payments, and not the central bank's money printing, that was ultimately responsible for the inflationary crisis. In a speech to the Reichstag on March 29, Foreign Minister Walter Rathenau told German lawmakers:

"Over and over again we encounter the notion that if the value of our money has been ruined this can only be because we have printed money. The recipe which we are given against this is: stop your printing press, bring your budget in order, and the misfortune is ended. A grave economic error!...[How is it possible] to make continuous gold payments without the help of foreign loans and at the same time keep the exchange rate intact? The attempt has never been made to give such a prescription and it cannot be given. For a country that does not produce gold cannot pay in gold unless it buys this gold with export surpluses [which Germany did not have] or unless it is borrowed [which Germany could not do]."[83]

As you can see, the mechanics of economics and markets were simple and basically the same then as they are now. While the central bank could easily extinguish its domestic currency denominated debt (in the ways previously described) it could not easily extinguish its external debts (for previously explained reasons).

From February until May, expectations surrounding the currency continued to be driven primarily by news of the reparation negotiations.[84] When news suggested there would be a comprehensive agreement, the mark rallied, and inflation expectations fell.[85] When new information suggested that an agreement was less likely, the mark fell and inflation expectations rose.[86] The mark experienced numerous 10 to 20 percent swings on such changes of sentiment, and by the end of May was down about 40 percent versus the dollar, as the prospects of a reparation agreement deteriorated.

The chart below gives a taste of how new pieces of information on the reparation negotiations led to major swings in the mark. As you can see from the below table, the markets chopped up and down in big moves every time there was essentially any update on reparation negotiations. Imagine having to trade through such volatility!

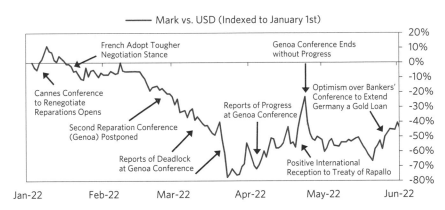

The News

March 25, 1922
Germany to Fight Reparation Terms
"Germany's quietest crisis in her post-revolutionary experience is likewise her most serious. There is no excitement in Berlin today. Neither the Teuton people nor the politicians betray signs of emotion. There is only the deadly calm of utter discouragement."

March 27, 1922
Mark's New Decline As Seen in Germany: Financial Circles Think Stipulations for German Home Finance Impracticable
"Prices are rising again. Fall in the Mark. After the first shock produced on financial markets by the conditions laid down last week by the Reparations Commission—a shock embodied in the sharp fall of the mark to a new low level—a somewhat calmer mood has followed."

March 30, 1922
French Are Deaf to German Pleas
"Will Not Believe Germans Cannot Pay for Restorations"

May 11, 1922
Germany Rejects Tax, Asks Loans
"Reparation reply offers to submit plan to cover expenditures and stop inflation."

May 12, 1922
Reparation Reply Displeases French
"They call it evasive and believe that Germany is playing for more time."

May 26, 1922
French Clear Way for German Loan; Poincare Working with Bankers Looking to Economic Settlement of Reparations
"The bankers conference is opening in conditions much more favorable than might be inferred from certain surface indications. The Poincare Government maintained a rigid stand against Lloyd George's strategy at Genoa, and the impression went abroad that if Germany failed in the engagements of May 31 there would be a resort to the penalties by France."

June 1, 1922
Allies Approve German Answer; Grant Moratorium
"After two days of consideration of the German reply to the demands of March 21 last, the Reparation Committee late this evening dispatched a note to the German Chancellor informing him that it was prepared to grant the partial moratorium on this year's reparations payments which had been scheduled."

The News

June 25, 1922
Berlin Assassins Slay Rathenau; Minister's Death Laid to Royalists; Germans Rally to Defend Republic
"Dr. Walter Rathenau, who was more closely identified than any other German with the efforts for the rehabilitation of his country since the war, was shot and killed."

July 3, 1922
Mark May Go Still Lower. German Government Buys Exchange From Exporters, Who Resell Marks
"Reichsbank officials declare that next two installments of reparations payments will undoubtedly be paid. The Reichsbank is still commandeering high currency bills from exporters, who, being reimbursed in paper marks, immediately re-convert such marks into foreign currencies. That policy will inevitably bring further depreciation of the mark."

July 26, 1922
Allied Representatives Decide Germany Must Continue to Pay 2,000,000 a Month

July 28, 1922
France Refuses Cut on Private Claims
"Germany Notified That She Will Have to Continue to Pay 2,000,000 a Month."

July 29, 1922
Urge German Loan and Cut in Budget; Experts on Guarantees Committee Submit Their Report to Reparation Commission.

July 31, 1922
Germans Near Panic as Mark Collapses; Crowds Storm Stores in Eagerness to Buy before Prices go Higher
"The prospects are all favorable to the continued and catastrophic decline of the mark."

August 2, 1922
The German Currency Crisis
"Practically all of Germany's accruing foreign obligations including purchases of food and material are being paid for with paper marks. The further the mark declines, the more of such paper is required to purchase abroad a bushel of wheat or a bale of cotton, or to meet a stimulated payment in gold on reparations account."

August 3, 1922
Hermes Asks Loan and Moratorium; Only Then Can Germany Balance Budget and Co-ordinate Her Currency
"Doctoring on symptoms is useless and senseless," was the opinion expressed today by Dr. Andreas Hermes, Minister of Finance, in discussing Germany's financial ills."

August 14, 1922
Rationing Project Urged in Germany

August 20, 1922
Another Increase in German Paper Issues
"Circulation Rises 6,811,000,000 in Second Week of August, 14,900,000,000 Since July."

June 1922–December 1922: Hyperinflation Begins

In June 1922, expectations of a reparation settlement collapsed, as did the mark. This was due to three interconnected events: First the French, who had always been the most reluctant among the Allied powers to reduce reparation burdens, declared they would no longer accept the conclusions of the Reparation Commission regarding Germany's capacity to pay.[87] Rather, France would make its own determinations on what German reparations should be, and would seize German assets, particularly some of its most productive assets (i.e., the coal mines in the Ruhr), if Germany defaulted.[88] Instead of a possible moratorium, Germany would now have to pay France whatever the French thought was appropriate, or risk a sustained occupation of some of its most valuable territory.

The French declaration also undermined an additional plan to support the German economy. An international committee had been established, headed by the American financier JP Morgan, Jr., to investigate the possibility of extending Germany a gold loan to rebuild its economy and ease the burden of external debt. However, this loan was contingent on progress on a reparation moratorium, for without it such a loan could almost certainly not be paid back. Following the French declaration, the loan committee was forced to conclude that extending credit to Germany was impossible.[89]

Finally, on June 24, Foreign Minister Walter Rathenau was assassinated by a right wing group. Rathenau, despite some of his belligerent speeches, was one of the few German politicians who was trusted by the Allied powers and enjoyed significant support at home.[90] If there was anyone who could mediate a settlement with the Reparations Commission and get it through the Reichstag, it was Rathenau. Of course, this also illustrates the threat of nationalism and extremist populism that was hanging over Germany.

Unlike earlier, foreigners now rushed to pull their capital from Germany. As noted previously, about a third of all deposits in German banks were foreign-owned, and foreign speculation had been a huge source of support for the German economy and balance of payments. Over the next few months, about two thirds of these deposits disappeared and capital inflows collapsed.[91] Simultaneously, capital flight of Germans wanting to get out accelerated; well-to-do citizens rushed to get their wealth out before the confiscatory taxes agreed to in the January compromise came into effect. The mark collapsed and hyperinflation began.

The result was an acute liquidity crisis in the German banking system that led to runs on the banks. The rate of central bank printing was no longer fast enough to keep up with the flight of marks abroad and rising prices. By July, banks were forced to go on three-day work weeks, and had to inform their depositors that they did not have enough cash on hand to either honor their deposits or make weekly wage payments for their large business clients.[92] Some even began printing their own marks, which was illegal. **The liquidity crisis was self-reinforcing. Depositors, seeing that the banks were struggling to honor their liabilities, began withdrawing their deposits in ever-growing numbers, which only made the liquidity crisis worse.**

By August 1922, the economy was on the brink of financial collapse. The central bank was forced to respond by rapidly accelerating the pace at which it was printing marks and monetizing a growing share of government debt.

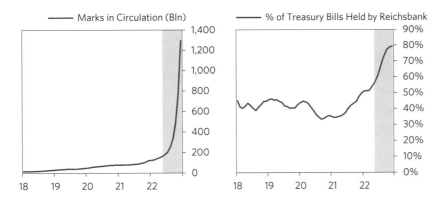

The central bank also began purchasing commercial bills en masse. As the liquidity crisis deepened in the fall, it additionally accelerated its provision of direct credits to the banking system. By the end of the year, the Reichsbank would end up holding about one third of all commercial bills in circulation and would have increased its credits to the banking system by 1,900 percent.[93] Such interventions helped prevent the financial system from collapsing, and led to a ten-fold increase in the money supply.

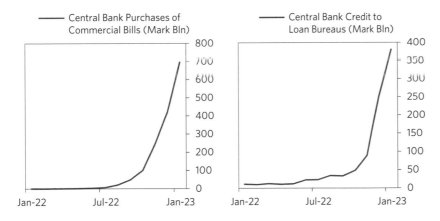

Unlike past bouts of currency depreciation and money printing, in which inflation would pick up substantially but never enter hyperinflation territory, this round of currency depreciation and money printing sent inflation skyrocketing. Part of this was due to the scale of the liquidity injection that was needed to offset the pullback in foreign capital, but part of it was also due to changing inflationary psychology. While most people had believed that inflation was being semi-managed, now most believed it was out of control.

The News

August 21, 1922
Germans Selling Marks for Dollars
"Frightened Stampede of the People to Put Money into Foreign Currencies."

August 21, 1922
Poincare Says All Germans Must Pay
"France must not listen to people who advise her to leave Germany unpunished for the wrongs of the war and forgive her the reparations she owes; France must and will find a way to make Germany pay."

August 30, 1922
Mark Note Famine Afflicts Berlin
"The scarcity of mark notes in circulation today has reached such an acute stage that the Reichsbank paid in cash only 40 percent of the amounts demanded."

September 2, 1922
Food Rioting Starts in Town Near Berlin; One Killed, 20 Hurt, as Police Fire on Mob
"The first blood has flowed in high cost of living riots...Other food riots have taken place in Berlin and in various other parts of Germany."

September 7, 1922
All Records Broken by German Paper Issue
"New Currency Put Out in Closing Week of August 22,978,000,000 Marks"

September 8, 1922
Germany Prepares for Unemployment

September 11, 1922
German Prices Double in Month of August
"Increasing use of gold values in transaction of ordinary business."

September 13, 1922
German Consumers Fight Dollar Basis; Protest to Government That Practice Undermines Confidence in the Mark.
"Dollar exchange was the subject of a concerted attack by German consumers today who protested against using the dollar as a basis for fixing domestic prices."

September 14, 1922
14 Billions Added to the German Currency
"Increase in first week of September second largest on record."

October 16, 1922
Will Use Foreign Money: German Business Men Mean to Continue Prices in Outside Currencies
"The basing of prices for home sales of goods upon foreign currencies is likely to continue notwithstanding the Government's new prohibition of the practice."

October 28, 1922
German Paper Issues Again Break Record
"New Currency Put Out in Third Week of October 35,466,969,000 Marks."

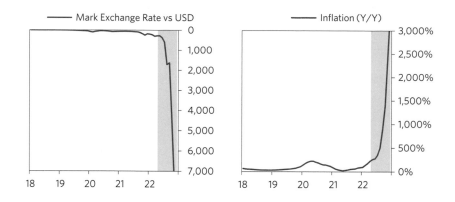

In inflationary depressions, it is classic that with each round of printing, more money leaves the currency instead of going into economic activity. As domestic currency holders see that investors that short cash (i.e., borrow in the weakening currency) and buy real/foreign assets are repeatedly better off than those who save and invest at home, they increasingly catch on and shift from investing printed money in productive assets to purchasing real assets (like gold) and foreign currency. Foreign investors no longer return because they have been repeatedly burned.

As early as August, with prices rising by over 50 percent a month and accelerating, policy makers recognized that they were approaching a hyperinflationary spiral, but they felt they had no alternative but to continue printing.[94] Why didn't they stop?

Once an inflationary depression reaches the hyperinflationary stage, it is extremely difficult to stop printing. This is because when extreme capital flight and extreme inflation feed off one another, money becomes harder to come by, even as it loses its worth. When Keynes visited Hamburg in the summer of 1922, still in the early phase of the hyperinflation, he vividly described the phenomenon:

"The prices in the shops change every hour. No one knows what this week's wages will buy at the end of the week. The mark is at the same time valueless and scarce. On the one hand, the shops do not want to receive marks, and some of them are unwilling to sell at any price at all. On the other hand...the banks were so short of ready cash that the Reichsbank advised them to cash no checks for more than 10,000 marks...and some of the biggest institutions were unable to cash their customers' checks for payment of weekly wages."[95]

To stop printing would result in an extreme shortage of cash and bring about a total collapse of the financial system and all commerce. As one economist noted at the time:

"[To stop the printing press] would mean that in a very short time the entire public, and above all the Reich, could no longer pay merchants, employees, or workers. In a few weeks, besides the printing of notes, factories, mines, railways and post office, national and local government, in short, all national and economic life would be stopped."[96]

People tend to think that hyperinflations are caused by central banks recklessly printing too much money, and all they need to do to stop it is to turn off the printing press. If it were that easy, hyperinflations would almost never occur! Instead, inflation spirals push policy makers into circumstances where printing is the least bad of several terrible options.

In the case of Weimar Germany, the cost of not printing was not only potential economic collapse, but political fragmentation. France's repeated threats to occupy German territory if reparations were not paid made halting the printing press an invitation to a foreign invasion. It also lowered hopes for productive reparations negotiations. As one prominent industrialist put it at the time:

"The Reichsbank can no more stop inflation than the Burgermeister of Hamburg can tell the patients in the hospital to stop being ill…as long as it is possible for the French to invade Germany, there can be no talk of a stabilization of our currency."[97]

By September, Germany was trapped in a classic hyperinflationary spiral. Extreme capital withdrawals and rapidly rising prices were forcing the central bank to choose between extreme illiquidity and printing money at an accelerating rate. As doing the former would result in a total collapse in business activity, there was really no choice. However, as the money supply grew, no one wanted to hold it in such a depreciating environment. The velocity of money accelerated, triggering even more capital flight, money printing, and inflation, and so on and so forth.

You can see this relationship most vividly in the chart below—which must be shown in logarithmic terms due to the exponential growth rates in inflation and the money supply. As you can see, currency weakness was leading inflation, which was leading money supply growth—not the other way around. **Reckless money printing was less the cause of the hyperinflation than what was required to prevent massive deflationary defaults by banks (and just about everyone else) and a deflationary economic collapse.**

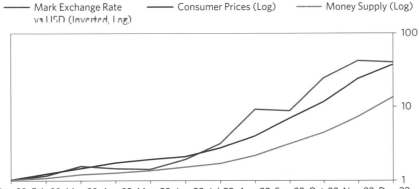

Remember that money and credit serve two purposes: As a medium of exchange and a store hold of wealth. As the spiral accelerated, the mark completely lost its status as a store hold of value. People rushed to exchange it for any available alternative—real goods, foreign exchange, and capital equipment. **Very soon, exponential rates of inflation made it impractical to trade in marks, so the currency also began to lose its status as a means of**

The News

October 30, 1922
Numerous Reasons for Fall in German Mark: Reserve Board Ascribes It to Deficit, Inflation, Reparations and Trade Balance.
"The Federal Reserve Board's bulletin for October ascribes the greatly accelerated fall in the German mark chiefly to the German budget, to reparations, to the balance of trade and to the flight of capital from Germany."

November 10, 1922
Berlin Once More Disappoints Allies.
"The Reparation Commission returns to Paris tomorrow empty-handed except for a brief final note from Chancellor Wirth predicating a complete moratorium and supporting action by an international financial consortium for temporary and final solution of the reparation problem and for permanent stabilization of the mark."

November 10, 1922
France Is Prepared to Coerce Germany
"Premier Poincare, speaking before the Senate today, declared that the only hope of getting any reparation payments from Germany lay in the Brussels conference, but that if this failed France was prepared to act alone again."

December 2, 1922
Poincare for Curb on Germany at Once
"Mark stabilization and reparations loan to follow control of German finance."

December 4, 1922
Money Very Dear on German Market
"Private Banks Still Get 20 Per Cent Through Fees and Commissions. Bank Rate May Go Up. Currency Inflation Now Being Increased By Rediscount Of Private Bankers At Reichsbank."

December 11, 1922
All Records Broken in German Inflation
"Paper Currency, Loans on Treasury Bills and Commercial Discounts Surpass Precedent."

December 17, 1922
German Debt Still Grows
"Increases 123,000,000,000 Marks In First Ten Days Of December."

December 23, 1922
German Deficit Nears One Trillion Marks
"Even ordinary expenditures are more than double the receipts from taxes."

December 25, 1922
Wild Increase in German Inflation
"Reichsbank discounts expand 172 billions in week, currency 123 Billions."

December 27, 1922
Germany Declared in Willful Default
"France gained an important victory in the Allied Reparation Commission today when the commission by a vote of 3 to 1 declared Germany in voluntary default in her wood deliveries for 1922."

exchange. Foreign currencies (especially the dollar) and even makeshift currencies became increasingly common in day-to-day transactions and price quotations. For instance, local branches of the Reichsbank found that they did not have enough actual paper notes for businesses to meet their payroll obligations.[98] So, the central bank and the finance ministry allowed some large depositors to print their own currencies. These were called Notgeld—which literally means "emergency money."[99] Soon, everyone began considering whether the mark would go extinct. According to the *Frankfurter Zeitung*, by October 1922:

"German economic life is…dominated by a struggle over the survival of the mark: is it to remain the German currency, or is it doomed to extinction? During the past few months foreign currencies have replaced it as units of account in domestic transactions to a wholly unforeseen extent. The habit of reckoning in dollars, especially, has established itself, not only in firms' internal accounting practice, but above all as the method of price quotation in trade, industry and agriculture."[100]

In a desperate attempt to calm the inflationary spiral, on October 12 1922, the government stepped in to stop the ever-growing flight into foreign currency. Restrictions were put on German citizens purchasing foreign FX.[101] **Such capital controls are a classic lever to control inflationary depressions; they are rarely successful. The reasons for this are that a) capital controls have limited effectiveness at best because they are usually pretty easy to get around and b) trying to trap people typically leads them to want to escape even more.** Not being able to get one's money out of the country triggers a psychology that is analogous to the inability to get one's money out of a bank: it produces fear that produces a run.

The stock market was one of the few remaining domestic escapes from the inflation. After declining 50 percent (in real terms) since June, stocks actually rallied in the second half of October—but like the fall of 1921, this rally had nothing to do with underlying economic conditions or the future prospects of the economy. In fact, in the fall of 1922, real profit margins were collapsing as the chaos of the hyperinflation hit productivity.[102] The rally was also extremely small in the context of the overall real stock market decline during the debt crisis.

See the charts below and imagine living through these conditions.

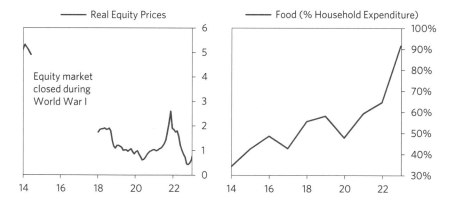

January 1923–August 1923: The Occupation of the Ruhr and the Final Days of Inflation

In January 1923, with the economy already in chaos and prompted by Germany missing a promised delivery of timber as a reparation payment, a French-Belgian force invaded Germany and occupied the Ruhr (Germany's primary industrial region). The French hoped that this action would pressure Germany to pay reparations more cooperatively and in the meantime allow France to extract payments in coal. The Germans responded by declaring "passive resistance."[103] Miners in the Ruhr would strike in an attempt to make the occupation as costly as possible for the French government. However, this resistance would need to be subsidized by the Reich, as both the miners and their employers would have to be paid. It also meant that about half of the country's coal supply would need to be imported, adding additional strain on the balance of payments.[104] As a result, government spending increased, the balance of payments deteriorated, liquidity shortages pushed the Reichsbank to print even more, and inflation, which was already at astronomical levels, accelerated even more.

France's aggression left an opening for Germany in the reparation negotiations, as the occupation of a country approaching economic ruin was widely denounced. To buy time, the Reichsbank began issuing dollar denominated debt (at a considerable discount to international prices due to its credit risk) in order to buy marks—with the central bank targeting a peg against the dollar. Between January and June of 1923, the Reichsbank sold about 400 million gold marks of borrowed foreign exchange and central bank reserves to defend the mark's peg against the dollar. The central bank also raised rates to 18 percent (but given that inflation was running at close to 10,000 percent this was mostly a symbolic move).[105] According to the president of the Reichsbank:

"The intervention did not…have as its purpose the permanent and final stabilization of the mark. Such an undertaking will only become possible when the reparations problem is seriously brought to a solution. What it had as its purpose was…to recover for the German economy…as long as possible…a time of somewhat calm…to free the market from wild and unscrupulous speculation and to protect the German people from a further rapid price increase which would have exhausted it."[106]

The FX intervention halted the mark's slide (it actually appreciated by 50 percent for the first three months of the intervention) and introduced a brief period of deflation that certainly hurt the shorts.[107] However, by May **it became clear that the Reichsbank did not have the reserves to pay out dollar denominated principal and interest payments and maintain the peg, so the fixed exchange rate policy was abandoned six months after it was put in place** and hyperinflation returned stronger than before (reaching 36,000,000,000 percent by November 1923).[108]

The News

January 9, 1923
Germans to Offer Passive Resistance
"The Cuno Government's immediate foreign policy will be based on the proposition that independent French occupation of the Ruhr tears up the Versailles Treaty and that consequently all reparations arrangements will be off."

January 11, 1923
French Enter Essen Unresisted at 4:45 A.M.; Germany Recalls Envoys in Paris and Brussels; Our Troops on the Rhine are Ordered Home
"The workers are apathetic regarding the presence of the French. They declare that they know they are being exploited by their own capitalists and now are working for their bread and therefore are indifferent as to what the French do, for their situation cannot be worse."

January 19, 1923
German Bank Rate Up From 10 Per Cent to 12; It Is Now the Highest in the World – Was 5 Percent in July

January 21, 1923
Time May Be Approaching When No One Will Buy German Paper
"It is the speculative buyer of marks, according to the year-end bulletin of the London County Westminster Parr's Bank of London, who has enabled Germany to 'carry on' as long as she has. German exports being, for the period since the war, almost invariably less than German imports, it is clear that she has not been able to pay for her needs in goods, as should be the case in normal times."

January 28, 1923
Fresh Slump in German Marks Carries Them to 28,500 to the Dollar

January 31, 1923
Paper Marks Increase 216 Billions in Week; All Records Broken by German Inflation in Third Week of January

February 12, 1923
Arrests and Riot Mark Day in Ruhr

February 12, 1923
Prices in Germany Up 248 ½ Per Cent in January; All Monthly Records of Increase Broken—7,159 Times Prewar Average

The News

February 15, 1923
Germany Protests Ruhr Export Barrier; Tells France She Is Reducing the Means of Paying the Other Allies

February 22, 1923
45,600,000,000 Marks Paid, Germany Says; Berlin Gives Official Compilation—Says Treaty Losses, Raise Total to 56,500,000,000.

March 1, 1923
French Lift Ban on Coal to Germany; Shipments Are Allowed Subject to 40 Per Cent Tax Imposed Prior to Occupation

April 9, 1923
Americans Ask $1,187,736,867 War Damages from Germany, Including Lusitania Losses
"The United States has tentatively fixed at $1,187,736,867 the amount which it will demand from the German Government in payment of the claims of the American Government and its citizens growing out of the World War. Notice to that effect has been served on the agent of Germany in the Mixed Claims Commission organized for the purpose of adjusting the claims of each country against the other."

April 16, 1923
Germany's Public Deficit: Expenditure in Fiscal Year 6 1/4 Trillion Marks above Revenue

April 30, 1923
Hopes Based on New German Bank Rate; Officials Claim 18% Charge Will Check Credit and Currency Inflation
"In German official circles great hopes are being based on last week's increase in the Reichsbank's discount rate from 12 per cent, to 18. It is expected to be supplemented this week by a Government decree further restricting dealings in foreign currencies and requiring registration of such holdings."

May 15, 1923
Suicides in Germany Now 80,000 Yearly; Toll Compares with 1,200 Before the War—Poverty Is Declared the Chief Cause

May 21, 1923
German Stock Exchange Now Keeps Open Only Three Days in Week

June 25, 1923
German Prices Rush Upward as Mark Falls; Rise of 41 Per Cent in Ten Days—Advance Increasingly Rapid Last Week

June 25, 1923
Effects of Germany's Disordered Currency; Old Investments Obliterated 100 Per Cent

August 1, 1923
Printers of German Paper Marks Walk Out; Berliners Call It Meanest Strike in History

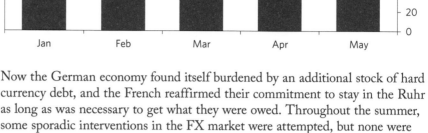

Now the German economy found itself burdened by an additional stock of hard currency debt, and the French reaffirmed their commitment to stay in the Ruhr as long as was necessary to get what they were owed. Throughout the summer, some sporadic interventions in the FX market were attempted, but none were able to curb inflation or prevent the downward spiral in the exchange rate.[109] Around this time, the president of the Reich asked his finance minister to find new measures "to avert the complete collapse of our mark." The finance minister replied "the complete collapse of the mark is already underway."[110]

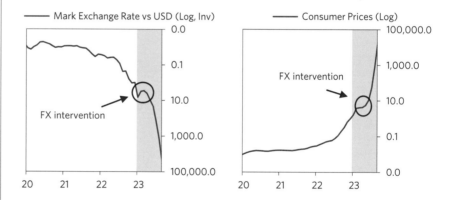

From July 1922 until November 1923 the mark depreciated by 99.99999997 percent versus the dollar (i.e., the cost of dollars increased 1,570 billion percent) and prices rose by 387 billion percent! For some perspective on what these numbers mean, in 1913 a total of six billion marks circulated as currency and coin in the whole German economy. By late October 1923, the entire stock of money in 1913 would just about get you a one kilo-loaf of rye bread.[111] Living through such chaos was immensely painful and traumatizing for German citizens—and experiences of the inflation would later serve to validate many of the criticisms made by Nazi politicians of the "disastrous" Weimar era.

Late 1923 to 1924: Ending the Hyperinflation

By late 1923, the hyperinflation had created intolerably painful conditions within Germany. Unemployment was rising rapidly, inflation was well above 1,000,000 percent, real tax revenues were diminishing at an alarming rate,[112] food was growing scarce, and transacting with marks had become almost impossible.[113] Without an effective means of exchange, the economic machine of the nation had ground to a halt. The resulting suffering stunned people of all walks of life. As one local mayor put it, "I have never encountered such hordes of people starving and wandering about."[114] And all recognized that the crisis would soon boil over into mass riots or revolution.[115] Rudolf Wissell, who would later serve as Germany's minister of labor, captured the prevailing sentiment of the period: "The inflation in which we find ourselves at this time is murdering the Republic. It will be the gravedigger of our Republic."[116]

The Allied powers concluded that without substantial reparation relief, German policy makers would remain helpless to avert a total collapse of the economy. So, in November 1923 they suspended reparations payments and reopened negotiations with the Germans on restructuring the debt.[117] This gave German policy makers the breathing room they needed.

German policy makers took five crucial steps to curb inflation, each following logically from the last:

1) To offload the reparations burden that started the crisis in the first place, policy makers renegotiated payments with the Allies, eventually reducing the debt service burdens to just 1 percent of GDP. With the crippling reparation burden made more manageable…

2) …A new currency was introduced, the rentenmark, which was backed by gold-denominated assets and land and pegged to the dollar. However, as the new currency could fail if investors believed that it would be used to monetize debt payments…

3) …Strict limits were placed on the amount of rentenmarks that could be printed and the amount of debt that could be monetized. However, a central bank can only credibly avoid monetizing debt if the government can pay its bills, so…

4) …The German government took action to raise its revenues and cut its expenditures, making deep, extremely painful cuts. Similarly, the central bank capped the amount they would loan to businesses and raised borrowing rates. To further build faith in the new currency…

5) …The central bank built up large reserves of foreign currency assets. They were able to do this by borrowing foreign exchange from the Allies and encouraging German citizens who had fled the currency during the hyperinflation to repatriate their savings.

Earlier one-off measures (e.g., the short-lived currency peg, capital controls) hadn't been enough—Germany needed a comprehensive and aggressive policy shift that abolished the currency, accepted hard backing, and placed extreme limits on monetization, credit creation, and government spending. It helped that years of economic crisis had made the public eager to find a currency that they could actually use. However, none of this would have been possible if the

The News

August 2, 1923
Plans Two Currencies Now For Germany: Cuno Cabinet Proposes Unlimited 'Near Gold' Loan, Scrip to Be Used as Money. Others Predict Failure. One Worthless Currency Is Bad Enough, Without Adding Another, They Assert
"With painful slowness and by devious ways the German Government is striving for all practical purposes to jettison the present paper mark and create a brand-new currency, which, it is hoped, will have a more confidence-inspiring character."

August 16, 1923
Germany's Changed Plans
"The new German Chancellor declares that his first energies must be wreaked upon domestic politics."

August 20, 1923
German Stocks Firm Since Recovery of the Mark

August 20, 1923
Last German Gold for New Currency; Finance Minister Hilferding Decides Not to Use It in Buying Paper Marks. Plans Fixed Values Basis. Berlin Raises Street-Car Fare to 100,000 Marks, and Demands Government Aid
"Finance Minister Hilferding denies that he plans another operation to save the life of the dying mark by buying worthless paper in foreign markets for what little gold is still at the disposal of the German Government. Contrarily, he means to make that gold the slender base of a new German currency."

August 29, 1923
Hunger-Driven Germans Die from Eating Toadstools

September 17, 1923
Basis of the Proposed New German Currency; Secured in Gold and Issued by New Bank Independent of State

September 23, 1923
Bodenmark New Unit of German Currency; Mortgages on Landed Property Throughout Country to Back Gold Bank
"Germany's new unit of currency is to be the 'bodenmark,' containing .358 of a gram of fine gold and equal to 100 'bodenpfennigs.' It became known today through publication of the measure providing for establishment of currency bank."

September 26, 1923
All German States Bow to Ruhr Peace
"It was officially announced this afternoon that the Premiers of the German Federated States at their conference with Chancellor Stresemann today unanimously agreed to abandonment of the passive resistance program, but at the same time expressed determination firmly to safeguard the unity of the country."

October 10, 1923
First Agreement in the Ruhr: Two Mine groups to Resume Work and Reparations in Kind
"The French Government today notified the Reparation Commission, the common agent for all the Allies, that General Degoutte concluded satisfactory arrangements yesterday with two Ruhr industrial groups for resumption of work and delivery of payments in kind on reparations account. He also notified that commission that other such accords would be negotiated."

October 13, 1923
Proposals for New German Currency; London Banking House Gives Outline of the Berlin Ministry's Proposals
"As outlined by international banking houses in London, the plan of the Stresemann Ministry for a new German currency makes the following provisions: Agriculture, industry, trade and banking shall provide means for the creation of a currency bank—'Waehrungsbank'—which will issue the new money in form of a 'ground-mark' or 'boden-mark.'"

October 15, 1923
German Stocks Rise with the Dollar; Impending Ruhr Settlement Also Stimulates Market—Bonds Also Advancing

October 16, 1923
Germany to Stop Worthless Marks
"The Cabinet tonight approved a bill granting a charter for a so-called gold annuity bank ... the Reichsbank will cease to discount the Government's Treasury bills, thus placing it in the position to accomplish an immediate curtailment of inflation."

October 29, 1923
German 'Rentenbank' Ready for Business: First Step in the Government's Efforts at Currency Reform

reparation burden was not substantially reduced. After all, why would any investor or saver want to hold German currency if they knew the government had huge external liabilities it could not pay?

Below, we walk through each of these measures in detail, moving roughly chronologically.

1) Restructuring the Reparations Debt

Although the process of negotiating with the Allies was slow, drawn out, and painful, some critical concessions were secured very early that provided the breathing room that was necessary to implement the policy changes that ended the hyperinflation.[118] Without reparation relief, the structural drivers of the inflation would have remained intact, and it would have been highly unlikely that any new currency could have commanded faith as a store hold of wealth.

Significant progress came as early as September 1923, when German industrialists in the Ruhr began to cooperate with the Weimar government in its negotiations with the French.[119] These industrial magnates had long resisted any concessions to France when it came to reparations payments, but as conditions continued to deteriorate and workers began to riot, they recognized the need for diplomacy, and eventually agreed to resume coal transfers.[120] By mid-October, the Weimar government was able to completely end its financial support of "passive resistance" to the Ruhr occupation, both opening the way for progress in talks with the French and eliminating one of its largest expenses.[121]

The Weimar government quickly built on the progress it had made in the Ruhr. By the end of November, British and French negotiators had created a new committee—the Dawes committee—to review and potentially reduce Germany's reparations obligations.[122] Critically, the committee agreed to suspend reparations payments until it came to its final conclusions—making it far easier for Germany to balance its budget during the stabilization period.[123] For the next 10 months, Germany did not have to make a single hard currency payment to the reparations commission. Moreover, when the Dawes Plan came into full force in August 1924, it significantly and permanently eased Germany's reparations burden.[124] Payments were rescheduled, and debt service costs reduced, to the point that reparations payments amounted to only one percent of German GNP in 1924 and 1925—a reduction of over 90 percent versus 1923.[125]

Although Germany would still have to pay the full 130 billion gold marks of reparations, payments were now so spread out that it was possible to meet them. The chart below gives some perspective on how significant this shift was by comparing what Germany could have been asked to pay at any moment between 1921 and 1923 (if the Allies had demanded Germany begin paying down the full reparation bill), what they actually had to pay between 1921 and 1923 (i.e., the London Schedule, under which some payments were suspended until the Allies thought Germany was capable of paying them), what debt service payments look like leading into the typical inflationary deleveraging, and what Germany had to pay after reparation payments were restricted in 1924 (i.e., the Dawes Plan). As you can see, the Dawes Plan dramatically reduced the FX debt service burden.

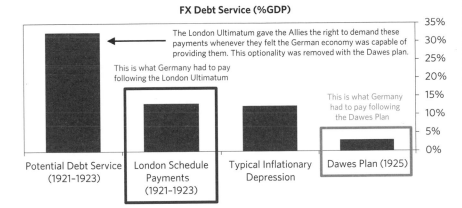

FX Debt Service (%GDP)

The London Ultimatum gave the Allies the right to demand these payments whenever they felt the German economy was capable of providing them. This optionality was removed with the Dawes plan.

This is what Germany had to pay following the London Ultimatum

This is what Germany had to pay following the Dawes Plan

Potential Debt Service (1921-1923) | London Schedule Payments (1921-1923) | Typical Inflationary Depression | Dawes Plan (1925)

With the reparations debt service substantially reduced and the domestic debt mostly inflated away, Germany's debt burden was largely relieved.

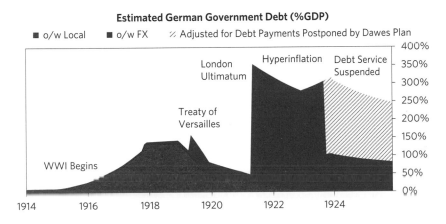

Estimated German Government Debt (%GDP)

■ o/w Local   ■ o/w FX   ⁒ Adjusted for Debt Payments Postponed by Dawes Plan

WWI Begins — Treaty of Versailles — London Ultimatum — Hyperinflation — Debt Service Suspended

2) Creating a New Currency

Creating a new currency with very hard backing is the most classic path that countries suffering from inflationary deleveragings follow in order to end them. In the Weimar case, this currency replacement process came in roughly three stages, beginning in August 1923 and ending in October 1924.[126]

The first steps toward replacing the mark were disorganized and reactive, driven by necessity rather than by any definite plan. By the summer of 1923, transacting in the mark had become so difficult that major institutions within Germany turned to alternatives, even though these had their own flaws.[127] Many resorted to using foreign exchange in place of domestic currency. From late 1922 onward, most major industries in Germany began to set prices in foreign currencies, and by 1923 much of the wholesale trade within Germany was conducted directly in dollars, francs, or florins.[128] Those who could not access foreign currency turned

The News

November 5, 1923
When Germany Issues Its New Currency
Berlin Believes Old Paper Marks Will
Disappear, New Marks Replacing Them

November 7, 1923
Must Aid Germans, Coolidge Believes;
President Learns Food Situation Is Serious,
Requiring Relief This Winter
"President Coolidge recognizes, as a result of official reports to the American Government brought to his attention by members of the Cabinet, that conditions in Germany are most serious, and the statement was authorized at the White House today that the President believes that the people of Germany will require relief from the outside world before the winter is over."

November 14, 1923
Reparation Board Invites Germany; Grants
Request for a Hearing on Reasons for Failure
to Make Payments

November 19, 1923
Germany Puts Out the New Currency;
Confusion in Financial Circles over Terms of
Issue and Conversion
"With the delivery of 142,000,000 new rentenmarks on Thursday by the new bank of issue to the Government, and with cessation of Reichsbank discounting of Treasury bills and of issue of paper marks against such discounts, the new German currency experiment has at least been initiated."

December 3, 1923
Germany's "Real Wages"; Workingmen's Pay
Estimated in Gold 44 to 60 7/8% of Pre-War
Rate

December 10, 1923
Further Decline of Prices in Germany; Social
Strain Relieved, but Financial Experts Are
Pessimistic of Future
"Social tension last week was considerably relieved by the heavy fall in prices, which for some goods reached 50 per cent."

December 14, 1923
Coolidge Tells Lenroot He Approves Private
Charity for German Relief

December 14, 1923
German Treasury Low; Barely Enough Money
to Keep the Government Going, It Is Said
"The desperate financial situation of Germany has compelled the Government to impose extraordinary taxes on the people, and even these will hardly suffice to keep the ship of State afloat. There is barely money enough in the treasury to pay the most pressing expenses for another ten days, though the salaries of most officials and Government employees have already been greatly reduced and thousands have been dismissed."

December 17, 1923
Many German Currencies; " Emergency
Issues" Now One-Fifth of Reichsbank
Circulation

December 23, 1923
Dawes and Owen Fitted to Aid German
Finance
"In selecting Charles Gates Dawes and Owen D. Young to aid in the solution of the knotty German financial problem, the Allies have chosen two Americans whose business lives exemplify success in its broadest meaning. Each is an outstanding figure in America's commercial life."

to "emergency money" as a last resort. These emergency bills were issued by local governments, trade associations, or companies, and were usually at least theoretically backed by real assets.[129] This emergency money, though often illegal, was easier to use than the paper mark, and by the fall of 1923, nearly 2,000 types of it were actively circulating in Germany.[130]

Recognizing the need for a currency with a stable value, the government attempted to give a stamp of authority to this informal system. Specifically, in August 1923 it began issuing very small-denomination debt, indexed to dollars, which it hoped would be used as a temporary currency until a better solution could be found.[131] These "Gold Loan" bills could either be circulated directly or used as a more secure backing for other emergency currencies.[132] And, though they were ultimately backed by nothing more than a stamp claiming they were "wertbestandig" (stable value) and a promise that the government could "raise supplements to the tax on capital" in order to honor them, they did retain their value.[133] In fact, the public was so desperate for a reliable store of wealth that the gold loan bills tended to be hoarded rather than used, and they disappeared almost entirely from circulation shortly after being issued.[134]

The second phase of the transition to a new currency began on October 15, 1923, when the government announced the creation of a new national bank—the Rentenbank—and a new stable-value currency, the rentenmark, which would enter circulation on November 15.[135] Unlike previous efforts to create a currency with "stable value," the more ambitious rentenmark scheme was an immediate, "miraculous" success.[136] Crucially, since rentenmarks could be exchanged for either a fixed quantity of paper marks or a fixed quantity of hard assets (and vice versa), the hard backing behind the rentenmark applied not only to newly issued bills (as had been the case with the gold loan bills), but to all of the paper marks already in circulation. Specifically, the rentenmark was pegged to the paper mark at a ratio of one to one trillion, and to the dollar at a ratio of 4.2 to one—a symbolically significant exchange rate, as it set the gold value of the rentenmark equal to that of the pre-war, peace-time mark.[137]

In the months that followed, both of these pegged rates held, and by December both the rentenmark and the newly-pegged paper mark were trading at par in foreign markets, while inflation had fallen to sustainable levels.[138]

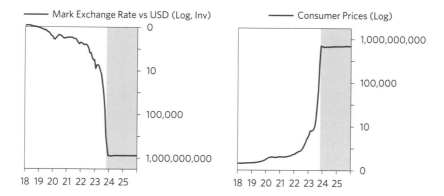

3) Imposing Limits on Money Printing

The key to the new currency's lasting success was that the Rentenbank issued relatively little of it and convincingly backed its issues with real assets. At the same time, there weren't large debts denominated in it—the total amount of credit the Rentenbank could extend was capped at 2.4 billion marks.[139] And, unlike the old gold loan bills, rentenmarks were directly secured by mortgages on 5 percent of all German agricultural and industrial property ("renten" refers to the annuities paid on these mortgages).[140] Even more important than this direct backing was the implicit security provided by the Reichsbank's gold reserves. By 1923 the real value of the money supply had been so reduced by the popular flight from paper marks that it could be backed entirely by the government's reserves.[141] This reduction in the value of circulating currency was reinforced as the Reichsbank began cracking down on illegal emergency money following the introduction of the rentenmark and withdrew its gold loan bills from circulation.[142]

As shown on the chart below, the monetary base in dollars had fallen to equal Germany's gold reserves by 1923.

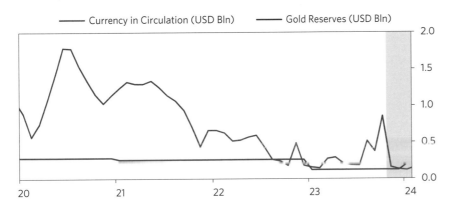

After a year of relative stability, German policy makers implemented the third phase of the currency transition. On October 11, 1924, they introduced another new hard currency (the reichsmark), which could be purchased with rentenmarks at a one to one ratio. Unlike the rentenmark, which had only been formally backed by mortgage bonds, the new reichsmark could be exchanged directly for bullion at the Reichsbank. Specifically, it could be converted into precisely the same quantity of gold as the pre-war mark.[143] All remaining paper marks were withdrawn from circulation by June 5, 1925, while the old currency (the rentenmark) was gradually phased out over the next decade.[144]

But as we will see, it took much more than a new currency to create a lasting stabilization. The rentenmark and reichsmark were crucial pieces of the reform process, but they weren't the only pieces. Currency depends on the credibility of the institutions issuing it. The fact that there were not a lot of promises to deliver currency (i.e., not a lot of debt denominated in the new currencies) meant that the central bank was not in the position of having to choose between inflationary monetization of debt and deflationary defaults on it. And the fact that the amount of the currency was limited to the amount of backing behind it meant it could be kept stable. The Rentenbank faced a difficult challenge as it attempted to gain credibility in the fall of 1923, but it succeeded because its fundamentals were solid.

The News

January 28, 1924
Berlin is Hopeful of New Gold Bank; Belief Expressed That It Will Restore International Faith in German Finance. Balanced Budget Assured; Hopes of New Plan to Check Inflation and Attract Foreign Capital
"Internal conditions in Germany are daily looking better. In the third taxation decree differences both in the Cabinet and between the republic and separate States has not appeared. It is believed the chief feature of this new legislation is the taxation away or expropriation of all gains made by paying off bonds and mortgages in paper marks."

January 29, 1924
Germany Awaits Arrival of Experts: Books and Other Data Ready for Dawes Committee Now on the Way
"The arrival of the Dawes committee tomorrow evening is hailed as an event of historic importance."

February 1, 1924
Germany Wipes Out Her Internal Debt; Other Drastic Steps.
"Private Bonds and Mortgages Restored to 10 Per Cent of Original Gold Value. Inflation Taxes Imposed. Independent Operation for Profit of State Railroad and Postal Services Decreed. Experts Hear Bank Plea. Schacht Urges Creation at Once of Gold Issue Institution."

February 2, 1924
Government Bonds of German Break; Debt Program Reacts Sharply in Market Here and Excited Trading Follows
"The market for bonds of the German Government and of German cities or corporations took on exceptional activity yesterday as the result of news dispatched telling of Germany's new program to cut down Government debts. In this program the German war loan and other issues have been scrapped and bonds of a corporate or private nature have been marked up to a value of 10 per cent of their early gold value."

February 4, 1924
Fixing Depreciation of German Mortgages; Allotment of 10 Per Cent Valuation—Savings Deposits Wiped Out

February 4, 1924
German Trade Recovery; Some Increase In Unemployment, but Much Less Short-Time Work

The News

February 18, 1924
Export Surplus for Germany in December; Measured in Gold Marks, Imports and Exports for 1923 Practically Balance

February 18, 1924
German Mortgages 'Valorized' at 15%; Had Expected Only 10%—Public Debt Repayments in Paper Marks Stopped
"The one difference in the formal decree is that mortgages are restored to 15 percent of their original value."

February 18, 1924
German Wartime Currency to Go; "Darlehnskassen" to Be Abolished at the Beginning of Next May
"One important announcement, in line with the return to normal conditions in the German currency, is that the Darlehnskassen, which were founded in August, 1914, for the purpose of granting easy-credit, are to stop functioning altogether at the beginning of May."

February 18, 1924
German Costs Down Again; Average Living Expenses Now 34 1/2 Per Cent Below Last November

February 20, 1924
German Revenues Increase; Surplus of Millions of Gold Marks Expected for First Time Since War

February 25, 1924
No Halt in German Trade Recovery; Continued Gradual Improvement of Industry, With 'Boom' in Textile Trade
"In German currency, finance and business the position continued to improve last week, the two first-mentioned gaining ground rapidly, the last more slowly, except in the textile and clothing branches. In those something of a boom is under way and manufacturers have already begun to refuse orders."

February 26, 1924
Britain Cuts Levy on German Imports; Impost of 26 Per Cent Drops to 5 Per Cent, With Berlin Pledging Payment

February 28, 1924
League May Audit German Finances; Dawes Committee Adopts Supervision as an Indispensable Part of Experts' Plan

March 10, 1924
Revival in German Industry Goes On; Unemployment in Labor Now Decreasing Rapidly From the Recent Figures. Steel Trade Recovering
"The trade situation throughout Germany continues to improve. One evidence is the fact that publicly supported unemployed workmen on Feb. 15 are stated to have been 1,301,270, as against 1,582,852 on Jan. 15. Even the partly unemployed decreased from 635,839 to 257,840."

4) Ending Monetization

In order to build confidence in a new currency, countries in inflationary deleveragings need to stop monetizing debt. As long as the government can force the central bank to print to cover its liabilities, there is a risk that the new currency will be debased and its supposedly hard backing abandoned. That is one of the reasons it is important that central banks be independent of the political system.

Reassurance that monetization would stop came in the form of two major announcements—one initially private and one quite public. First, on August 18, 1923, the Reichsbank informed the Weimar government that, beginning in 1924, it would not discount any additional government debt.[145] Though this memo was private, it quickly circulated among the industrial elite, and it spurred policy makers to seriously reconsider the need for fiscal reforms.[146] The second piece of reassuring news came on October 15, 1923, when central bank officials publicly stated that the new Rentenbank would cap total government credits (in this case at 1.2 billion rentenmarks). Additionally, its new policy would forbid the Reichsbank from monetizing any government debt after November 15.[147]

For a time, both the public and the government itself doubted that the central bank and the Rentenbank would honor these promises. After all, the Rentenbank lent the government the entirety of its 1.2 billion rentenmark allocation almost immediately.[148] And, by December 1923, the government had already requested an additional 400 million rentenmarks.[149] When officials at the Rentenbank stood firm, however, they successfully signaled the beginning of a new era of central bank independence—and the end of a long period of unchecked monetization.

5) Closing the Deficit

When the central bank stops monetizing debts during an inflationary deleveraging, the government can either find new creditors to finance its deficits, close those deficits, or take control over the central bank and continue monetizing debt. Since finding new creditors is usually impossible in an inflationary deleveraging, and monetizing debt only postpones the problem, the budget ultimately needs to be balanced.

By late 1923, the Weimar regime had come to the conclusion that it needed to close the deficits. There was no choice, and with the debts largely relieved, this was now possible. In the words of the German minister of finance, "If we do not succeed in cutting loose from the inflationary economy through ruthless choking off of Reich expenditures, then the only prospect we have is general chaos."[150]

The government had run budget deficits since the outbreak of the war in 1914.[151] However, in August 1923, the government took steps to address the problem by indexing certain taxes to inflation and passing additional emergency taxes.[152] By October, it had indexed all taxes to inflation.[153]

Additionally, the government took aggressive measures to reduce expenses, dismissing 25 percent of its employees and cutting the salaries of the remainder by 30 percent.[154] The Weimar regime ended its expensive subsidies to workers engaged in "passive resistance" in the Ruhr.[155] Such austerity was extremely painful, and would have been almost impossible to stomach a year or two before. But the hyperinflation had caused so much suffering and chaos by the end of 1923 that the German public was willing to do almost anything to bring prices back under control.

Most important, though, was the effect of more gradual inflation and a more stable exchange rate on the yield of existing taxes.[156] Temporary stabilization created a virtuous cycle of sorts: by reducing the rate of inflation, the stabilization increased real tax receipts, helping reduce budget strains and increasing the public's confidence in the government's ability to avoid future monetization. Following the introduction of the rentenmark in November, real tax receipts increased rapidly, rising from about 15 million gold marks in October 1923 to more than 300 million in December 1923.[157]

By January 1924, the government was running a surplus.[158]

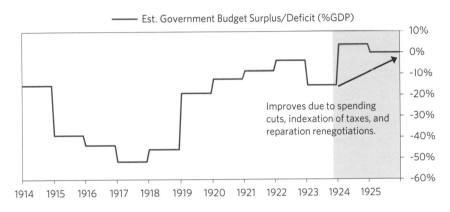

Improves due to spending cuts, indexation of taxes, and reparation renegotiations.

6) Tightening Credit

Officials decided to significantly tighten access to credit, so private credit wouldn't add to inflationary pressures. This tightening was implemented through two channels. First, the government announced in February 1924 that it would "revalue" some privately held debts (i.e., require debtors to give creditors more than face value).[159] These included mortgages, bank deposits, and industrial debentures whose values had fallen to almost nothing during the hyperinflation.[160] Although the policy was implemented to appease angry creditors, it also worked as a tightening.[161] Just as debt reductions have the effect of easing credit, weakening the currency, and increasing inflation, debt revaluations tighten credit, support currencies, and lower inflation.

Second—and more significantly—on April 7 1924, the Reichsbank decided to cap the total amount of credit it would extend to the private sector. It wouldn't call back any existing debt, but it would extend new credit only as prior debts were paid off.[162] This strict cap on new credit creation was painful for businesses in the short term, but it also meaningfully stabilized German inflation, which turned slightly negative in May 1924.[163]

The News

March 17, 1924
Further Improvement in Trade of Germany; Government Helped by Establishment of Nine-Hour Working Day

March 24, 1924
Continued Recovery in German Industry; Metal Prices Are Rising and Textile Industry Still Booming

April 3, 1924
German Gold Bank Ready; Will Start Business Next Week in the Reichsbank Building

April 10, 1924
Germans Criticize Terms; First Official View Is That Dawes Report Is Inacceptable as It Stands

April 10, 1924
German Resources Ample; Dawes Report Calls for Mortgage on Industry to Meet Payments. $200,000,000 Loan Proposed
"Germany's protestations during the last four years designed to make the world believe she could not pay reparations were refuted today when the Dawes Expert Committee reported to the Reparation Commission that Germany could pay. The committee fixes the minimum normal payments at 2,500,000,000 marks annually, subject to increases according to German prosperity."

April 15, 1924
Germany to Accept Dawes Board Plan as Basis of Parley; Reply Will Agree to Enter Negotiations for Settlement with Reparation Commission

April 16, 1924
France and Britain Approve in Full the Dawes Report; Germany's Acceptance of It as Basis of Discussion Is on Way to Paris

April 18, 1924
Reparation Board Adopts Dawes Plan; Sets Berlin to Work: Calls on Germans to Draft Laws and Name Officials to Put It into Effect

April 21, 1924
Credit Demand in Germany; Industrial Situation Improving and Loans Doubled in a Month

April 28, 1924
Germany Re-Entering Foreign Steel Trade; Large Orders Taken in Sweden—Said to Be Underbidding France and Belgium

April 28, 1924
German Surplus Revenue; Latest Period Shows 19,280,800 Marks Above Expenditure

April 29, 1924
Marx Talks of Dawes Plan; Defends Action of German Government in Accepting It.
"A speech on the Dawes report and the reasons which compelled Germany to accept it was delivered at an election meeting of the Centre Party here tonight by Dr. Marx, the German Chancellor."

The News

May 4, 1924
German Voters Go to Polls Today; Most Important Election Since the War Fails to Arouse Great Interest

"Thirty-five million men and women in Germany who have attained the age of 20 will have an opportunity tomorrow to give untrammeled expression to their political preferences, and upon their verdict will depend in a large measure the future of German politics and economics, as well as of the nation's foreign relations."

May 5, 1924
Bavarian Vote Divided: Hitler-Ludendorff Group Fails to Win Expected Victory

May 5, 1924
German Coalition for Dawes Plan Leads in Election: Despite Gains by Communists and Nationalists, Middle Parties Retain a Majority

"First returns from today's election indicate that, though as expected the German Nationalist Party standing at the extreme right registered substantial gains, the old Coalition from which the present government was formed—the German People's Party, the Centrum, and the Democratic Party—will form the next government, probably in conjunction with the Socialists."

May 6, 1924
German Coalition Holds 230 Seats to Opponents' 192; Present Cabinet Expects to Retain Office and Carry Out the Dawes Plan

"The result of German elections shows that a majority of Germans are for the 'policy of fulfillment' as against a definite break with the Entente, for qualified acceptance of the Dawes report as against summary rejection thereof, for continuance of the German Republic as against restoration of the German monarchy."

June 30, 1924
Germany Accepts Military Control; Asks Month's Delay and Limitation of Inquiry to Points Mentioned by Allies

July 31, 1924
French Ports again Open to Germans; Berlin Hears That from September Onward Ships from Fatherland Will Be Admitted

"French ports are to be thrown open to German shipping for the first time in ten years."

August 17, 1924
Allies and Germans Sign Agreement; French Will Quit Ruhr within a Year

7) Accumulating Foreign Exchange Reserves

Though all the programs, policies, and agreements described above put the German economy on progressively firmer footing, not everyone was convinced they would ensure a permanent stabilization. In fact, as Germany implemented its stabilization regime between November 1923 and October 1924, speculators continually bet against the mark.[164] As long as Germany lacked a meaningful foreign exchange reserve, these speculative attacks remained a threat to its continued stability.

Two major shifts helped restore Germany's depleted foreign exchange reserves. The first was the transfer of privately held foreign currencies to the Reichsbank. As institutions and individuals within Germany gained increasing confidence in the new rentenmark as a means of exchange, they began to convert the foreign currency they had hoarded during the hyperinflation into new bills.[165] Between November 1923 and January 1924 alone, foreign exchange holdings at the Reichsbank grew from about 20 million gold marks to nearly 300 million.[166] Though these foreign exchange flows paused as inflation rose in early 1924 (and individuals began accumulating foreign currencies again), they resumed once credit standards within Germany were tightened and inflation stabilized (as described above).[167]

The second major shift came through the Dawes Plan. In addition to reducing reparations burdens, the Dawes Committee also extended Germany a significant foreign exchange loan.[168] The loan, issued in October 1924, amounted to 800 million gold marks worth of foreign currency, divided mainly between dollars, pounds, and francs.[169] Though the amount was not extraordinarily large, it meaningfully improved the Reichsbank's credibility when it came to defending against speculative attacks.[170] It also sent a reassuring signal to foreign investors. In the four years following the implementation of the Dawes Plan, American investors poured money into German debt, attracted by its relatively high yields.[171]

By 1924, the crisis was largely over. Germany would enter a brief period of recovery before the Great Depression hit it hard a decade later. This second crisis was not only economically devastating but fueled the rise of right wing and left wing populists, Hitler's rise to power, and all that followed. But that's another story.

Works Cited:

Balderston, T. "War Finance and Inflation in Britain and Germany, 1914–1918." *The Economic History Review* 42, no. 2 (May 1989): 222-244. https://doi.org/10.2307/2596203.

Bresciani-Turroni, Constantino. *The Economics of Inflation: A Study of Currency Depreciation in Post-War Germany.* Translated by Millicent E. Sayers. London: Allen and Unwin, Ltd., 1937.

Eichengreen, Barry. *Hall of Mirrors: The Great Depression, the Great Recession, and the Uses—and Misuses—of History.* New York: Oxford University Press, 2016.

Feldman, Gerald D. *The Great Disorder: Politics, Economics, and Society in the German Inflation, 1914–1924.* New York: Oxford University Press, 1997.

Ferguson, Niall. *Paper and Iron: Hamburg Business and German Politics in the Era of Inflation, 1897–1927.* Cambridge: Cambridge University Press, 1995.

Graham, Frank D. *Exchange, Prices, and Production in Hyper-Inflation: Germany, 1920–1923.* Princeton, NJ: Princeton University Press, 1967.

Holtfrerich, Carl-Ludwig. *The German Inflation, 1914–1923.* Berlin: Walter de Gruyet, 1986.

Keynes, John Maynard. *The Collected Writings of John Maynard Keynes.* Vol. 17, *Activities 1920–1922: Treaty Revision and Reconstruction.* London: Macmillan, 1977.

Peukert, Detlev J.K. *The Weimar Republic: The Crisis of Classical Modernity.* New York: Hill and Wang, 1993.

Rupieper, H.J. *The Cuno Government and Reparations 1922–1923: Politics and Economics.* The Hague, The Netherlands: Martinus Nijhoff, 1979.

Taylor, Frederick. *The Downfall of Money: Germany's Hyperinflation and the Destruction of the Middle Class.* New York: Bloomsbury Press, 2013.

Webb, Steven B. *Hyperinflation and Stabilization in Weimar Germany.* New York: Oxford University Press, 1989.

1   Feldman, *The Great Disorder*, 30.
2   Feldman, 32.
3   Bresciani-Turroni, *The Economics of Inflation*, 23.
4   Bresciani-Turroni, 23.
5   Feldman, 38.
6   Feldman, 38.
7   Feldman, 45.
8   Feldman, 47.
9   Holtfrerich, *The German Inflation*, 177.
10 Feldman, 42.
11 Feldman, 52-54.
12 Taylor, *The Downfall of Money*, 16.
13 Bridgewater estimates. See also Bresciani-Turroni, 25; Ferguson, *Paper and Iron*, 118-20.
14 Holtfrerich, 117.
15 Taylor, 31.
16 Feldman, 45-46.
17 Feldman, 45.
18 Feldman, 44.
19 Bridgewater estimates. See also Feldman, 45-46.
20 Feldman, 47-49.
21 Feldman, 49.
22 Feldman, 48-49.
23 Webb, *Hyperinflation and Stabilization*, 4; Ferguson, 120.
24 Feldman, 146.
25 Feldman, 146.
26 Feldman, 148.
27 Feldman, 148.
28 Bresciani-Turroni, 54.
29 Feldman, 178.
30 Ferguson, 150.
31 Ferguson, 186.
32 Ferguson, 276.
33 Webb, 33, 37.
34 Holtfrerich, 132-3.
35 Feldman, 151.
36 Feldman, 152.
37 Holtfrerich, 132-3.
38 Feldman, 206.
39 Feldman, 207.
40 Feldman, 207.
41 Holtfrerich, 71.
42 Ferguson, 245.
43 Holtfrerich, 209.
44 Ferguson, 285.
45 Ferguson, 286.
46 Webb, 33.
47 Keynes, *Collected Writings*, 48.
48 Ferguson, 243.
49 Ferguson, 270.
50 Ferguson, 287.
51 Ferguson, 295.
52 Ferguson, 287.
53 Ferguson, 289.
54 Webb, 107.
55 See Ferguson, 311-2, for a discussion on the payments schedule.
56 Ferguson, 310.
57 Webb, 37; Ferguson, 313.
58 Ferguson, 298.
59 Ferguson, 308.
60 Ferguson, 343.
61 Keynes, 92.
62 Ferguson, 321.
63 Feldman, 445.
64 Webb, 56.
65 Ferguson, 337.
66 Feldman, 389.
67 See Bresciani-Turroni, 188-197 for more on these dynamics.
68 Quoted in Feldman, 389.
69 Bresciani-Turroni, 294.

70 Bresciani-Turroni, 294.
71 Holtfrerich, 205.
72 Graham, *Exchange, Prices, and Production*, 28.
73 Bresciani-Turroni, 297.
74 Bresciani-Turroni, 305-6.
75 Ferguson, 335-6.
76 Feldman, 390.
77 Bresciani-Turroni, 260.
78 Quoted in Feldman, 390.
79 Eichengreen, *Hall of Mirrors*, 134.
80 Quoted in Feldman, 446.
81 Balderston, "War Finance," 21; Eichengreen, 134.
82 Feldman, 445.
83 Quoted in Feldman, 433.
84 Feldman, 505.
85 Feldman, 418.
86 Feldman, 418.
87 Webb, 56.
88 Webb, 56.
89 Ferguson, 318.
90 Webb, 57.
91 Ferguson, 338.
92 Ferguson, 383.
93 Ferguson, 341.
94 Bresciani-Turroni, 81.
95 Quoted in Ferguson, 339-340.
96 Bresciani-Turroni, 80-82.
97 Quoted in Feldman, 355.
98 Webb, 14.
99 Webb, 14.
100 Holtfrerich, 75.
101 Ferguson, 360.
102 Bresciani-Turroni, 366-7.
103 Webb, 58.
104 Rupieper, *The Cuno Government*, 113.
105 Feldman, 640-1.
106 Feldman, 643.
107 Ferguson, 371.
108 Ferguson, 371.
109 Webb, 60.
110 Quoted in Ferguson, 376.
111 Webb, 3.
112 Eichengreen, 146-7; Bresciani-Turroni, 368.
113 Bresciani-Turroni, 336.
114 Feldman, 768.
115 Feldman, 704.
116 Feldman, 728.
117 Eichengreen, 149.
118 For a thorough discussion of the negotiations, see Feldman, 453-507; 658-669; 698-753.
119 Eichengreen, 148.
120 Eichengreen, 148.
121 Eichengreen, 148.
122 Ferguson, 405; Eichengreen, 149.
123 Eichengreen, 149.
124 Peukert, *The Weimar Republic*, 286.
125 Eichengreen, 150.
126 Webb, 61; Bresciani-Turroni, 353.
127 Feldman, 784-5.
128 Bresciani-Turroni, 342-3.
129 Bresciani-Turroni, 343.
130 Bresciani-Turroni, 343.
131 Webb, 61.
132 Bresciani-Turroni, 343-4.
133 Bresciani-Turroni, 344.
134 Bresciani-Turroni, 344.
135 Bresciani-Turroni, 343; Webb 63.
136 Bresciani-Turroni, 346.
137 Bresciani-Turroni, 343.
138 Webb, 63.
139 Holtfrerich, 316.
140 Webb, 62; Feldman, 752, 787-8. Notably, even the rentenmark was not really adequately secured.

141 Bresciani-Turroni, 346.
142 Bresciani-Turroni, 348-9.
143 Bresciani-Turroni, 354.
144 Bresciani-Turroni, 354.
145 Webb, 61-62.
146 Webb, 62.
147 Holtfrerich, 316-7.
148 Eichengreen, 147.
149 Eichengreen, 147.
150 Feldman, 770.
151 Bresciani-Turroni, 356.
152 Webb, 61.
153 Webb, 62.
154 Eichengreen, 146.
155 Eichengreen, 146.
156 Eichengreen, 146-7.
157 Bresciani-Turroni, 356.
158 Bresciani-Turroni, 356-7; Eichengreen, 146.
159 Bresciani-Turroni, 322.
160 Bresciani-Turroni, 322.
161 Bresciani-Turroni, 322-3.
162 Webb, 71.
163 Webb, 71; Bresciani-Turroni, 353.
164 Bresciani-Turroni, 348-351.
165 Bresciani-Turroni, 349.
166 Bresciani-Turroni, 349.
167 Bresciani-Turroni, 350-2.
168 Eichengreen, 150.
169 Eichengreen, 150.
170 Eichengreen, 150.
171 Eicehngreen, 151.

Since the gold-denominated mortgage bonds that backed the rentenmark paid 5 percent, while market interest rates for stable-value loans were much higher, these mortgages traded below par. The "real" exchange value of the rentenmark, therefore, was well below its par value. The implicit backing of the Reichsbank's gold reserves was crucial, therefore, when it came to supporting the value of the new currency. For a more detailed discussion of the rentenmark's backing. See Bresciani-Turroni, 340-1.

US Debt Crisis and Adjustment (1928–1937)

US Debt Crisis and Adjustment (1928–1937)

This section gives a detailed account of the big US debt cycle of the 1920s and 1930s, including the Great Depression, which is probably the most iconic case of a deflationary deleveraging. It takes you through the particulars of the case with reference to the template laid out earlier in the "Archetypal Big Debt Cycle." Though the Great Depression happened nearly a century ago, its dynamic was basically the same as what occurred in and around 2008. As with the other cases in this part, I both describe the timeline (which in this case is based on the library of books I've amassed on the Great Depression over the years rather than my personal experience trading through it) and provide a real-time "newsfeed" drawn from newspaper headlines and what the Federal Reserve was saying at the time that runs along the sides of the pages.

1927–1929: The Bubble

Following the world war and the recession of 1920 to 1921, the US economy experienced a period of rapid technology-led growth. The continuing electrification of rural and small-town America and the growth of the middle class opened up huge markets for new technologies. The radio was the new, hot technology and the number of radio sets owned grew from 60,000 in 1922 to 7.5 million in 1928.[1] The automobile industry also grew rapidly and by 1929 there were 23 million cars on the road—on average, about one per every five Americans (which was nearly three times higher than in 1920).[2] Technological advances also led to a productivity boom (factory worker output per hour increased 75 percent from 1922 to 1928). Technology breakthroughs filled the newspapers, driving wide-spread optimism about the economy.

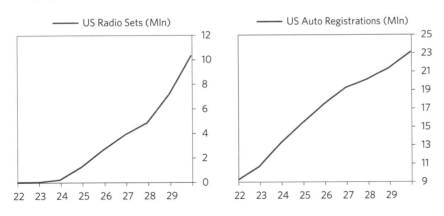

In the midst of that technology boom, the early part of the cycle (roughly from 1922 to 1927) saw strong economic growth and subdued inflation. The broader period became known as the "fat years," as both capitalists and workers experienced significant gains.[3] Corporate profits rose to postwar highs, unemployment dropped to postwar lows, and real wages rose more than 20 percent. **In the pre-bubble years of 1923 to 1926, debt growth was appropriately in line with income growth because it was being used to finance activities that produced fast income growth.** At the same time, the stock market roared higher while experiencing little volatility—investors in US

News & Federal Reserve Bulletin

January 31, 1925
Radio Corporation Gain is 100 Per Cent
"The Radio Corporation of America's earnings report for 1924, made public yesterday, shows gross income from operations of $54,848,131. This compares with $26,394,790 in 1923, and $14,830,857 in 1922."
–New York Times

January 10, 1926
Public Buying Power Took Record Output
"The motor industry again established a new high-water mark for production in turning out about 3,800,000 passenger cars last year, exceeding the previous best record of 1923 by 100,000 cars and of last year by about 500,000 cars."
–New York Times

July 25, 1926
Our Peak Year In Productivity; Industry and Trade Even Surpassed War Times, Commerce Department Year Book Says
"Industrial and commercial activity of the United States during the calendar year 1925 'reached the highest levels ever attained in our history, not even excepting the years of abnormal war activity,' says the Commerce Department Year Book, made public today."
–New York Times

August 20, 1926
Business Expansion Expected to Go On
"The last four months of the year should see expansion in the country's business activity, according to the business review of the National Bank of Commerce and the Irving Bank-Columbia Trust Company. All of the indices of trade, they say, are favorable except in a few industries."
–New York Times

January 3, 1927
Prosperity in 1927 Forecast By Bank
"The National City Bank, in commenting on the prospects for 1927, declared in a statement yesterday that the new year opens with good prospects for the continuance of prosperity."
–New York Times

January 14, 1927
Ford in 16 Years Earned $375,927,275
–New York Times

**News &
Federal Reserve Bulletin**

June 17, 1927
*$62,233,000 in Gold Now Held Abroad;
Federal Reserve Banks Show Gain of
$2,685,000 Over Amount of May 13*
—*New York Times*

August 15, 1927
*German Bank Warns of Foreign Payments;
Thinks Problem of Meeting Foreign
Indebtedness Still Far From Solution*
—*New York Times*

August 21, 1927
Durant Predicts Long Bull Market
"William C. Durant, considered one of the most
picturesque and spectacular figures identified
with the stock market, believes that 'we are
drifting into a so-called bull market
unprecedented in magnitude, which will extend
over a period of many years to come.'"
—*New York Times*

September 23, 1927
Brokers' Loans Reach New Peak
"Federal Reserve Board Report Shows Rise of
$34,499,000 for last week. Total at
$3,283,750,000."
—*New York Times*

September 24, 1927
*Over-the-Counter Trading is Slower; Major
Activity Continues in Investment Trusts*
"With trading at somewhat slower tempo and
prices showing traces of easing, the over-the-
counter market yesterday continued in much the
same position it had maintained throughout the
week. Major activity again appeared in the
investment trust issues, but in the broader aspects
of the market the general complexion was
established by the trading in bank and insurance
stocks."
—*New York Times*

October 11, 1927
*Loans To Germany Safe, Says Hahn; Banker
Denies There Will Be Difficulties in
Repayment—Points to History*
—*New York Times*

November 11, 1927
*Bank Deposits Here Biggest in World;
Five-Eighths of All Are Held in the United
States, Federal Reserve Official Says*
—*New York Times*

December 5, 1927
"Bull Market" Here a Surprise to London
—*New York Times*

December 12, 1927
Sees United States Wiping Out Poverty
"Secretary Hoover's report of economic gains
since 1921 means not that prosperity has come to
the bulk of the American people but that
widespread poverty, which has persisted among
all peoples through all the ages, may soon be
abolished in the United States, according to
Professor Irving Fisher, Yale economist, in a
copyrighted article made public for tomorrow."
—*New York Times*

stocks made over 150 percent between the start of 1922 and the end of 1927. The hottest tech stocks at the time—Radio Corporation of America (known to traders as "Radio") and General Motors—led the gains.[4]

Then a bubble began to emerge. As is classic, the bubble had its roots in the dizzying productivity and technological gains of the period and people making leveraged bets that they would continue. One writer explained the growing belief that the economy had entered a "New Era": "The New Era… meant permanent prosperity, an end to the old cycle of boom and bust, steady growth in the wealth and savings of the American people, [and] continuously rising stock prices."[5]

The US was an extremely attractive destination for investment from abroad. The US and most of the rest of the world were on a gold standard at the time, which meant governments promised to exchange their money for gold at a fixed exchange rate in order to provide assurance to lenders that they wouldn't just print a lot of money and devalue lenders' claims. Gold flowed from other countries to the US, because that was effectively how investors bought dollars. This played an important role in determining how events transpired during the lead-up to the crash in 1929, but we won't get into that now.

When other countries (France, Germany, and the UK) became worried that they were losing gold too quickly, they asked the US Federal Reserve to lower dollar interest rates to make dollars less attractive. More focused on growth and inflation than on the debt growth that was being used to buy financial assets, in the spring of 1927, the Federal Reserve Board cut its discount rate from 4 percent to 3.5 percent. This, of course, had the knock-on effect of encouraging US credit creation. This is a typical way that central banks inadvertently finance bubbles.

The economy accelerated in response to the easing, and news of the strong economy filled headlines and radio broadcasts nationwide. Over the second half of 1928, industrial production rose 9.9 percent and automobile production hit an all-time high. The boom made people euphoric. At the start of 1929, *The Wall Street Journal* described the pervasive strength of the US economy: "One cannot recall when a new year was ushered in with business conditions sounder than they are today…Everything points to full production of industry and record-breaking traffic for railroads."[6]

The easing by the Federal Reserve also produced **a bull market in stocks that showed every sign of a classic bubble**. I'll repeat my defining characteristics of a bubble:

1. **Prices are high relative to traditional measures**

2. **Prices are discounting future rapid price appreciation from these high levels**

3. **There is broad bullish sentiment**

4. **Purchases are being financed by high leverage**

5. **Buyers have made exceptionally extended forward purchases (e.g., built inventory, contracted forward purchases, etc.) to speculate or protect themselves against future price gains**

6. New buyers (i.e., those who weren't previously in the market) have entered the market

7. Stimulative monetary policy helps inflate the bubble, and tight policy contributes to its popping

After prices nearly doubled over 1927 and 1928, **stocks sold at extremely high multiples financed by borrowing (i.e., margin)**. Many stocks were valued as much as 30 times earnings.[7] The popular book *New Levels in the Stock Market*, published in 1929 by Ohio State professor Charles Amos Dice, captured **the pervasive sentiments of the bull market**. He argued that the broader base of investors in the market made higher valuations more or less permanent, proclaiming, "Among the yardsticks for predicting the behavior of stocks which have been rendered obsolete…[is] the truism that what goes up must come down."[8]

New buyers flooded the market, and many of them were unsophisticated investors with no prior experience with stocks, one of the classic signs of a bubble. Brokerage firms rapidly expanded to cater to aspiring speculators across the country; the number of branch offices outside of Wall Street increased by more than 50 percent between 1928 and 1929.[9] "Wherever one went," a broker declared in 1929, "one met people who told of their stock-market winnings. At dinner tables, at bridge, on golf links, on trolley cars, in country post offices, in barber shops, in factories and shops of all kinds."[10]

During this period, stock purchases were financed by high and rapidly increasing leverage, and more and more of this leverage occurred outside the regulated and protected banking system. Classically, new and fast-growing lending markets where a lot of levering up occurs are symptomatic of bubbles. Often, banks are able to make these new assets seem safe to investors via guarantees, or through the way the assets are combined and packaged—and without a crisis to stress-test them, it can be hard to tell how safe they actually are. These "innovations" typically lead to the next crisis if not monitored, understood, and managed by regulators. The bankers and the speculators made a lot of fast money in a symbiotic relationship (i.e., the bankers would lend to the speculators at fat spreads and the speculators would buy stocks on leverage, pushing them up and making money). In 1929, call loans and investment trusts were the fastest-growing channels for increasing leverage outside the banking system.[11]

The call loan market, a relatively new innovation, developed into a huge channel through which investors could access margin debt. The terms of call loans adjusted each day to reflect market interest rates and margin require-ments, and lenders could "call" the money at any time, given the one-day term. **Call loans created asset/liability mismatches among lenders and borrowers, since borrowers were using short-term debt to fund the purchases of risky long-term assets, and lenders were lending to riskier borrowers who were willing to pay higher interest rates. One of the classic ingredients of a debt crisis is the squeezing of lenders and borrowers who have debt/liability mismatches that they took on during the bubble.**

**News &
Federal Reserve Bulletin**

February 25, 1928
Investment Trusts Cause Albany Clash
"The Republican legislative leadership and the State Banking Department were at odds today over the investment trust bills proposed by Attorney General Albert Ottinger…Senator John Knight, majority leader, made it clear, however, that the passage of the Attorney General's legislation was on the Republican program…'The investment trusts are doing an enormous business, which is constantly growing. They need some sort of supervision.'"
–*New York Times*

February 29, 1928
New Investment Trust Formed
–*New York Times*

March 13, 1928
Violent Advance in Many Stocks, Day's Trading Breaks Records
"All doubt as to how last week's events on the Stock Exchange would affect the speculative mind was removed with yesterday's market. It reached 3,875,000 yesterday, thereby surpassing all previous achievements."
–*New York Times*

March 25, 1928
Speculative Fever Grips The Market: Stories of Large and Quick Profits Whet Public Appetite as Never Before
–*New York Times*

May 4, 1928
Companies Report an Improved Trend
"Earnings and sales of corporations for the first quarter of the current year, reported yesterday, showed distinct improvement over the same quarter a year ago."
–*New York Times*

July 25, 1928
Investment Trust Lists Rising Assets
–*New York Times*

July 26, 1928
Praises Condition Of Nation's Banks
"The capital, deposits and total resources of the banks of this country are larger than ever before, according to figures in the annual report of R.N. Sims, Secretary Treasurer of the National Association of Supervisors of State Banks."
–*New York Times*

September 2, 1928
Automobile Makers Setting New Records
"New high production records for this season of the year were established during August by several automobile manufacturers, while the industry as a whole continued to reflect the remarkable activity that has characterized it throughout the current year."
–*New York Times*

September 14, 1928
New Investment Trust: American Alliance Already Has Funds of $4,750,000 Paid In
–*New York Times*

News & Federal Reserve Bulletin

January 4, 1929
Moody Forecasts Market: Says 1929 Promises To Be Largely A Duplication of 1928
"The prosperity which has characterized this country with only moderate setbacks since 1923 is likely to continue without great variation well into the future, according to John Moody, president of Moody's Investors Service."
–New York Times

January 7, 1929
Chase Bank Assets At A High Record
–New York Times

February 2, 1929
The Reserve Bank's Admonition
"It was not considered likely yesterday that even the serious remarks of the Federal Reserve Bank regarding the hazards of corporation loans in the call-money market will have any marked effect on the total of money in that market owned by corporations and on the immediate call. Nevertheless, the central banking authority's observations on this new and unusual practice attracted a great deal of attention yesterday and drew fresh notice to what a year or so ago would have appeared to be an illogical operation."
–New York Times

February 15, 1929
Reserve Bank Keeps Rate at 5 Per Cent After Long Debate
"In a meeting that lasted for almost five hours and that added a new strain to the already frayed nerves of Wall Street, the directors of the Federal Reserve Bank of New York decided last evening to leave the bank's rediscount rate unchanged at 5 per cent."
–New York Times

February 27, 1929
Forms New Trust for Many Accounts: Farmers' Loan Develops Basic Principle of Revocable Voluntary Investment. Aims at Diversification Operation Consists of Composite Fund, With Company Acting as Trustee and Manager
–New York Times

March 14, 1929
Stocks Rally Moderately on Cheerful Industrial Reports and Easier Call Money
–New York Times

March 15, 1929
Call of Stock Expected
–New York Times

March 1929
Advances in Bill Rates and Discount Rates
"Buying rates on acceptances at the Federal Reserve Bank of New York were advanced on February 15 from 4 3/4 – 4 7/8 to 5 per cent for maturities up to 45 days and from 5 to 5 1/8 to 5 3/4 per cent for longer maturities. An advance in the discount rate from 4 1/2 to 5 percent on all classes of paper of all maturities was made at the Federal Reserve Bank of Dallas, effective March 2, 1929."
–Federal Reserve Bulletin

March 26, 1929
Stock Prices Break Heavily as Money Soars to 14 percent
"Tightening on the strings of the country's supply of credit, a development foreshadowed last week, but not considered seriously by speculators in the stock market, brought about yesterday one of the sharpest declines in securities that has ever taken place on the Exchange. Only twice in the history of the Exchange have there been broader breaks."
–New York Times

A new group of investors entered the call loan market to lend to the crowd of speculators. Because interest rates on call loans were higher than other short-term rates and lenders could "call" back their money on demand, call loans became popular as a safe place for companies to invest their extra cash.[12] Foreign capital also poured in from places like London and Hong Kong. As a historian later described it, "A great river of gold began to converge on Wall Street, all of it to help Americans hold common stock on margin."[13] The share of funds in the call loan market that were coming from lenders outside the Federal Reserve System (i.e., non-banks and foreigners) rose from 24 percent at the start of 1928 to 58 percent in October 1929.[14] This added risk to the market, since the Federal Reserve couldn't lend to these non-banks if they needed liquidity in a squeeze.

The charts below show the explosion in margin debt through the bubble and the accompanying rise in prices.

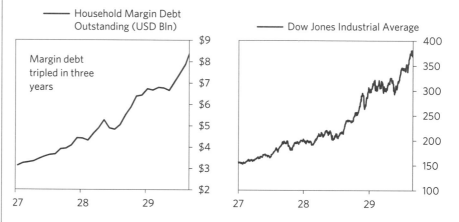

Investment trusts were another financial innovation that saw rapid growth during the bubble and helped draw new speculators into the market. First originated and popularized in Great Britain, investment trusts were companies that issued shares and invested the proceeds in the shares of other companies.[15] The well-known economist Irving Fisher praised the "wide and well-managed diversification" that trusts provided investors who lacked sufficient capital to buy shares in multiple companies.[16] As the stock market boomed, the number of trusts exploded. By 1929, new trusts were launching at a rate of nearly five per week, and these offerings were taking in one-third of the new capital raised.[17]

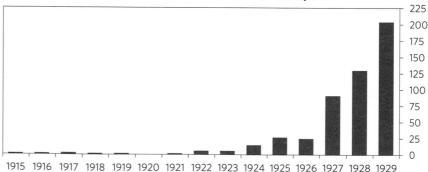

Number of US Investment Trusts Founded by Year

Promoters of trusts claimed that their diversification made the financial system safer. However, the use of leverage by many trusts to amplify returns in the bubble created risk for investors. And many speculators, unaware of the nature of the securities and believing that the recent past would continue, amplified this risk by taking out margin loans to lever up already-levered trust shares.[18]

As stock prices soared, speculators continued to lever up and make huge profits, attracting more buyers into the market to do the same. **The more prices increased, the more aggressively speculators bet that they would increase still more.**

At the same time, supplies of stocks were increasing as the higher prices encouraged their production.[19] During this phase of the bubble, the more prices went up, the more credit standards were lowered (even though it would have been logical for the opposite to happen), as both lenders and borrowers found lending and buying stocks with borrowed money to be very profitable.

The leveraging was mostly taking place in the "shadow banking" system; banks at the time by and large did not look over-leveraged. In June 1929 banks looked much healthier than they had prior to the 1920–1921 recession: not only were they posting record earnings, their capital ratios were higher (17.2 percent versus 14.9 percent) and their liabilities were stickier, as time deposits made up a greater share of their liabilities (35.7 percent versus 23.3 percent).[20] A series of large bank mergers during 1929 were viewed as a further source of strength by analysts.[21] **Classically, bank earnings and balance sheets look healthy during the good times because the assets are highly valued and the deposits that back them are there. It's when there's a run on deposits and the assets fall in value that banks have problems.**

While the Federal Reserve governors debated the need to restrain the rapid lending that was fueling stock speculation, they were hesitant to raise short-term interest rates because the economy wasn't overheating, inflation remained subdued, and higher interest rates would hurt all borrowers, not just speculators.[22] **Typically the worst debt bubbles are not accompanied by high and rising inflation, but by asset price inflation financed by debt growth. That is because central banks make the mistake of accommodating debt growth because they are focused on inflation and/or growth—not on debt growth, the asset inflations they are producing, and whether or not debts will produce the incomes required to service them.**

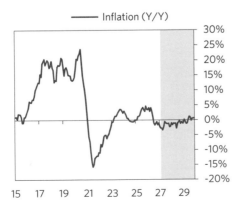

— Inflation (Y/Y)

**News &
Federal Reserve Bulletin**

March 27, 1929
Stocks Crash Then Rally in 8,246,740 Share Day
"A brisk recovery in the last hour of trading, ranging from 5 to 20 points, brought many stocks to a point where losses on the day were inconsequential, but that rally was too late for thousands of stock holders and speculators who had thrown their holdings overboard earlier in the day."
–New York Times

March 28, 1929
Stocks Rally Vigorously As Bankers Aid Market
"Calmness after the violent storms of Monday and Tuesday reigned in the markets yesterday. Stockholders regained their courage when it became evident that pivotal issues were being adequately supported and that New York bankers stood ready to supply all the money needed at the going rates."
–New York Times

April 21, 1929
U.S. Steel to Pay Bonds on Sept. 1; Call of $134,000,000 for Redemption at 115 One of the Largest Recorded
–New York Times

April 22, 1929
Investment Trust Earnings in 1928
"American investment trusts earned an average net income of 11.2 percent on invested capital in 1928, while unrealized profits brought the total to 25 percent."
–New York Times

April 23, 1929
Draft Plan to List Investment Trusts
"Pressed from many sides by its member firms which have interested themselves in investment trusts to give formal listing privileges to these securities, the New York Stock Exchange authorities are reported to have agreed in principle on the class of such securities which will be admitted to trading. The problem is one of the most important which governors of the Exchange have faced since the war because it involves securities with a market value of upward of $2,000,000,000."
–New York Times

April 25, 1929
Murphy & Co. Form Investment Trust; Graymur Corporation Will Start Business With Capital of More Than $5,000,000
–New York Times

June 21, 1929
Aldred Gains $1,464,000; Investment Trust's Stocks in Four Utilities and an Industrial Rise
–New York Times

June 24, 1929
New Investment Trust; Hudson-Harlem Valley Corp. to Acquire Bank and Trust Stocks
–New York Times

News & Federal Reserve Bulletin

July 3, 1929
Bank Borrowings Rose Here in June; Federal Reserve Reports Increase to $425,000,000, Highest in Recent Years
—New York Times

July 13, 1929
Stocks Sweep Up On Wave Of Buying
—New York Times

July 27, 1929
Investment Trust Gains in Earnings
—New York Times

August 10, 1929
Stock Prices Break As Rise In Bank Rate Starts Selling Rush
"The decision to advance the rediscount rate at the New York Federal Reserve Bank to 6 per cent from 5, for the double purpose of easing commercial credit conditions this Autumn and choking off the supply of purely speculative credit for securities stirred in its wake yesterday a storm of apprehensive selling in the country's stock markets. Foreign markets, too, were weak and unsettled."
—New York Times

August 17, 1929
Employment Fell a Little in July; But the Increase Over 1928 Was 6% and Earnings 7% Greater
"Employment decreased 0.2 per cent in July, 1929, as compared with June, and payroll totals decreased 3.8 per cent, according to a report issued by the Bureau of Labor Statistics of the United States Department of Labor."
—New York Times

August 20, 1929
Rapid Advance in Many Stocks, Led by U.S. Steel—Money Unchanged
"With no change in money rates from last week's final figures, yesterday's stock market engaged in another advance of the character that has become familiar...the very rapid bidding up of prices for half a dozen industrial stocks of various descriptions, under the lead of United States Steel."
—New York Times

August 9, 1929
Bank Rate Is Raised To 6% Here As Loans Reach $6,020,000,000
"As brokers' loans mounted to a high record for the fourth successive week, passing the $6,000,000,000 mark for the first time, directors of the Federal Reserve Bank of New York yesterday advanced the rediscount rate from 5 per cent, the level which has been held since July 13, 1928, to 6 per cent...The financial community was taken completely by surprise by the advance in the rate."
—New York Times

Rather than raising its discount rate, the Fed enacted macroprudential (i.e., regulatory) measures aimed at constraining the supply of credit via banks. Some of these regulatory measures included lowering the acceptance rate for loans and increasing supervision of credit facilities.[23] The Fed publicly released a letter it had written to regional banks, deriding the "excessive amount of the country's credit absorbed in speculative security loans" and threatening that banks attempting to borrow money from the Fed in order to fund such loans might be refused.[24] But these policies were largely ineffective.

Late 1929: The Top and the Crash
Tightening Pops the Bubble

In 1928, the Fed started to tighten monetary policy. From February to July, rates had risen by 1.5 percent to five percent. The Fed was hoping to slow the growth of speculative credit, without crippling the economy. A year later, in August 1929, it raised rates again, to six percent. **As short-term interest rates rose, the yield curve flattened and inverted, liquidity declined, and the return on holding short duration assets such as cash increased as their yields rose. As loans became more costly and holding cash became more attractive than holding longer duration and/or riskier financial assets (such as bonds, equities, and real estate), money moved out of financial assets, causing them to fall in value. Declining asset prices created a negative wealth effect, which fed on itself in the financial markets and fed back into the economy through declining spending and incomes. The bubble reversed into a bust.**

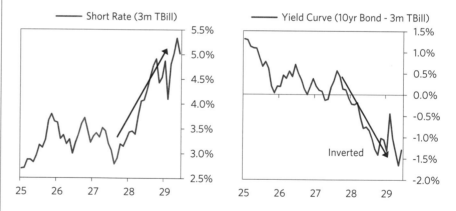

It was the tightening that popped the bubble. It happened as follows:

The first signs of trouble appeared in March 1929. News that the Federal Reserve Board in Washington was meeting daily, but not releasing details of the meetings, sparked rumors on Wall Street that a clampdown on speculative debt was coming.[25] After two weeks of modest declines and reports of an unusual Saturday meeting of the Reserve Board, the stock market broke sharply lower on March 25 and then again on March 26. The Dow fell over four percent and the rate on call loans reached 20 percent as panic gripped the market. Trading volumes reached record levels.[26] A wave of margin calls on small leveraged investors resulted in forced selling that exacerbated the decline. After the Federal Reserve Board chose not to act, National City Bank president Charles Mitchell (who was also a director of the New York Fed) announced that his bank stood ready to lend $25 million to the market.[27] This calmed the market, rates fell, and stocks rebounded. Stocks resumed their gains, but this foreshadowed the vulnerability of stocks to tightening in the credit market.

While growth had moderated somewhat, the economy remained strong through the middle of 1929. The June *Federal Reserve Bulletin* showed that industrial production and factory employment remained at all-time highs through April, and that measures of construction had rebounded sharply after falling through the first quarter.[28]

After another short-lived sell-off in May, the rally accelerated and the bubble reached the blow-off phase. Stocks rose about 11 percent in June, five percent in July, and ten percent in August. This rally was supported by accelerating leverage, as household margin debt rose by more than $1.2 billion over the same three months.

Money continued to tighten. On August 8, the Federal Reserve Bank of New York raised its discount rate to 6 percent,[29] as it became clear that macroprudential measures had failed to slow speculative lending. At the same time, concerns about the high stock prices and interest rates caused brokers to tighten their terms in the call loan market and raise margin requirements. After dropping them as low as 10 percent the previous year, margin requirements at most brokers rose to 45 to 50 percent.[30]

The stock market peaked on September 3 when the Dow closed at 381—a level that it wouldn't reach again for over 25 years.

It's important to remember that no specific event or shock caused the stock market bubble to burst. As is classic with bubbles, rising prices required buying on leverage to keep accelerating at an unsustainable rate, both because speculators and lenders were near or at their max positions and because tightening changes the economics of leveraging up.

Stocks started to decline in September and early October as a series of bad news stories eroded investor confidence. On September 5, statistician Roger Babson delivered a speech to the National Business Conference that warned about a collapse in prices due to "tight money." A 2.6 percent sell-off followed that became known as the "Babson break." On September 20, the collapse of Clarence Hatry's London financial empire on fraud charges jolted markets and forced some British investors to raise funds by selling their American holdings.[31] On September 26, the Bank of England raised its discount rate from 5.5 percent to an eight-year high of 6.5 percent and a few European nations followed suit.[32]

Together, by mid-October, these events contributed to a 10 percent sell-off in the markets from their highs. The view among investors and columnists in the major papers was largely that the worst was over and the recent volatility had been good for the market. On October 15, economist Irving Fisher proclaimed that "Stocks have reached what looks like a permanently high plateau."[33]

News & Federal Reserve Bulletin

September 6, 1929
Babson Predicts 'Crash' in Stocks; Fisher View Is Opposite
"Wise investors will pay up their loans and avoid margin speculation at this time because a 'crash' of the stock market is inevitable, Roger Babson, statistician, said today before the sixteenth National Business Conference at Babson Park, Wellesley…'Stock prices are not too high and Wall Street will not experience anything in the nature of a crash' in the opinion of Professor Irving Fisher of Yale University, one of the nation's leading economists and students of the market."
–New York Times

September 6, 1929
Stock Prices Break on Dark Prophecy
"Out of a clear sky a storm of selling broke on the stock exchange yesterday afternoon and in one hour wiped out millions of dollars in the open market value of securities of all sorts. It was one of the most hectic hours in the history of the Exchange, and wiped out thousands of small speculators who up to noon had been riding along comfortably on their paper profits. In the turbulent last hour of trading, the final quotation of which was not tapped out on Exchange tickers until almost 4 o'clock, about 2,000,000 shares of stock were handled and they hit the exchange in a torrent of liquidation."
–New York Times

October 4, 1929
Year's Worst Break Hits Stock Market
"Starting as a mild reaction, that grew in intensity with each succeeding hour, a drastic break in stock prices shook the New York Stock Exchange yesterday afternoon. Liquidation that swept through the market in the final hours cut millions of dollars from the open market value of securities. It was the widest decline of the year, accomplished in little more than two hours time. The break had been foreshadowed by the continued tightening of the financial structure as brokers' loans increased, week by week, and by the nervousness and apparent hesitation which has characterized market fluctuations during the last fortnight."
–New York Times

October 8, 1929
Recovery in Stocks Continues
"The recovery on the Stock Exchange which began on Saturday was resumed yesterday, after a brief period of hesitation. Before the day was over, numerous advances running to 10 points had been effected, and the majority of stocks closed around the day's best prices."
–New York Times

October 13, 1929
Steady Upward Trend in Earnings by Banks; Deposits also Show Advance in Third Quarter—Stocks Maintain Firm Tone
–New York Times

News & Federal Reserve Bulletin

October 13, 1929
Mortgage Returns Show Good Values; Give Higher Investment Results Than Stocks and Bonds, Reveals Survey. Insurance Reports Used Holdings of 104 Leading Companies Compared in Statistical Study
–*New York Times*

October 20, 1929
Stocks Sweep Downward Under Heavy Liquidation—Trading Almost at Record Pace
"The sweeping break in prices under which the stock market staggered yesterday was undoubtedly occasioned both by heavy professional sales for the decline and by a recurrent avalanche of forced liquidation."
–*New York Times*

October 22, 1929
Stocks Slump Again, but Rally at Close on Strong Support
–*New York Times*

October 23, 1929
Mitchell Decries Decline in Stocks; On Return from Europe, He Says Many Issues Are Selling Below True Values
–*New York Times*

October 23, 1929
Stocks Gain Sharply but Slip Near Close
–*New York Times*

October 24, 1929
Prices of Stocks Crash in Heavy Liquidation, Total Drop in Billions
"Frightened by the decline in stock prices during the last month and a half, thousands of stockholders dumped their shares on the market yesterday afternoon in such an avalanche of selling as to bring about one of the widest declines in history. Even the best of seasoned dividend-paying shares were sold regardless of the prices they would bring and the result was a tremendous smash in which stocks lost from a few points to as much as ninety-six."
–*New York Times*

October 24, 1929
Wheat Prices Drop in a Rush to Sell; Tumble in Stocks Is Reflected in Grains and Values Go Swiftly Down
"Reflecting today's drastic declines in stocks, values in the wheat market toward the close dropped 4 to 4 1/4 cents to a new low for the season."
–*New York Times*

October 25, 1929
Financiers Ease Tensions
"Wall Street gave credit yesterday to its banking leaders for arresting the decline on the New York Stock Exchange at a time when the stock market was overwhelmed by selling orders. The conference at which steps were taken that reversed the market's trend was hurriedly called at the offices of JP Morgan & Co."
–*New York Times*

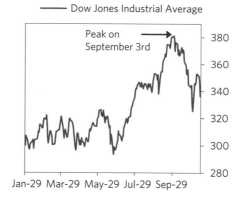

The Stock Market Crashes

Then the bottom of the market fell out. Since so much happened each day during this period, and to give you a granular understanding, I will transition into a nearly day-by-day account, conveying it via both my own description and in the newsfeed.

Stocks fell sharply on Saturday, October 19, which saw the second-highest trading volume ever in a Saturday session and the decline became self-reinforcing on the downside. A wave of margin calls went out after the close, which required those who owned stocks on leverage to either put up more cash (which was hard to come by) or sell stocks, so they had to sell stocks.[34] Sunday's *New York Times* headline read, "Stocks driven down as wave of selling engulfs the market."[35] Still, traders widely expected that the market would recover when it opened again on Monday. Over the weekend, Thomas Lamont of J.P. Morgan, looking at the economy, wrote to President Herbert Hoover that the "future appears brilliant."[36]

The week of October 21 began with heavier selling. One analyst described Monday's waves of sell orders as "overwhelming and aggressive."[37] Trading volume again broke records. Another wave of margin calls went out and distressed selling among levered players was prevalent.[38] But markets rallied into the end of Monday's session, so losses were smaller on Monday than they'd been on Saturday.

Tuesday's session saw small gains and Wednesday's opened quietly. But any hopes that the worst had passed were shattered before the market closed on Wednesday. An avalanche of sell orders in the last hour of trading pushed stocks down sharply, which triggered a fresh round of margin calls and more forced selling.[39] The Dow suffered what was then its largest one-day point loss in history, falling 20.7 points (6.3 percent) to close at 305.3.

Because the sell-off was so sharp and came so late in the day, an unprecedented number of margin calls went out that night, requiring investors to post significantly more collateral to avoid having their positions closed out when the market opened on Thursday.[40] Many equity holders would be required to sell.

Everyone who worked on the exchange was alerted to be prepared for the big margin calls and sell orders that would come Thursday morning. Policemen were posted throughout the financial district in the event of trouble. New York Stock Exchange Superintendent William R. Crawford later described "electricity in the air so thick you could cut it" before the open.[41] Then the collapse and panic came.

After a quieter opening, the avalanche of selling materialized and panic took hold of the market.[42] Sell orders poured in from across the country, pushing down prices and generating new margin calls, which in turn pushed down prices even more. The pace of selling was so frantic that operators struggled to keep up. One exchange telephone clerk captured the scene well: "I can't get any information. The whole place is falling apart."[43] Rumors of failures swirled and as news spread, huge crowds formed in the financial district.[44] By noon of what would become known as Black Thursday, the major indices were down more than 10 percent.

Around midday, a small group of the biggest bankers met at the offices of J.P. Morgan and hatched a plan to stabilize the market. "The Bankers' Pool," as they were known, committed to buy $125 million in shares. Early in the afternoon, traders acting on behalf of the bankers began to place large buy orders above the most recent price.[45] As news of the plan spread, other investors began to buy aggressively in response and prices rose. After hitting a low of 272 (down 33), the Dow Jones Industrial Index bounced back to close at 299, down only six points for the day.[46] But as it turned out, this would just be the first of many failed attempts to bolster the market. Below is the *New York Times* front page from the next day:

WORST STOCK CRASH STEMMED BY BANKS; 12,894,650-SHARE DAY SWAMPS MARKET; LEADERS CONFER, FIND CONDITIONS SOUND

FINANCIERS EASE TENSION

Five Wall Street Bankers Hold Two Meetings at Morgan Office.

CALL BREAK 'TECHNICAL'

Lamont Lays It to 'Air Holes' —Says Low Prices Do Not Depict Situation Fairly.

Wall Street Optimistic After Stormy Day; Clerical Work May Force Holiday Tomorrow

Confidence in the soundness of the stock market structure, notwithstanding the upheaval of the last few days, was voiced last night by bankers and other financial leaders. Sentiment as expressed by the heads of some of the largest banking institutions and by industrial executives as well was distinctly cheerful and the feeling was general that the worst had been seen. Wall Street ended the day in an optimistic frame of mind.

The opinion of brokers was unanimous that the selling had got out of hand not because of any inherent weakness in the market but because the public had become alarmed over the steady liquidation of the last few weeks. Over their private wires these brokers counseled their customers against further thoughtless selling at sacrifice prices.

Charles E. Mitchell, chairman of the National City Bank, declared that fundamentals remained unimpaired after the declines of the last few days. "I am still of the opinion," he added, "that this reaction has badly overrun itself."

LOSSES RECOVERED IN PART

Upward Trend Starts With 200,000-Share Order for Steel.

TICKERS LAG FOUR HOURS

Thousands of Accounts Wiped Out, With Traders in Dark as to Events on Exchange.

From the New York Times, 25 Oct © 1929 The New York Times. All rights reserved. Used by permission and protection by the Copyright Laws of the United States. The printing, copying redistribution, or retransmission of this Content without express written permission is prohibited.

After the market closed on Thursday, a group of about 35 brokers began organizing a second effort to stabilize the market. Believing that the worst had passed, they took out a full-page ad in the *New York Times* for Friday, confidently telling the public that it was time to buy.[47] That same day, President Hoover declared, "The fundamental business of the country, that is, production and distribution of commodities, is on a sound and prosperous basis."[48] Stocks were steady through the rest of the week, and the Sunday papers again showed optimism that the cheapness of stocks would support a rebound in the coming week.[49]

But the collapse and panic resumed on Monday the 28th as a flood of sell orders came in from all types of investors. Notably, significant selling came

News & Federal Reserve Bulletin

October 25, 1929
Wall Street Optimistic after Stormy Day
"Sentiment as expressed by the heads of some of the largest banking institutions and by industrial executives as well was distinctly cheerful and the feeling was general that the worst had been seen. The opinion of brokers was that selling had got out of hand not because of any inherent weakness in the market but because the public had become alarmed..."
–New York Times

October 25, 1929
Investment Trusts Buy Stocks Heavily, Pour in Their Reserves as Market Drops
–New York Times

October 26, 1929
Stocks Gain as Market Is Steadied; Bankers Pledge Continued Support; Hoover Says Business Basis Is Sound
–New York Times

October 27, 1929
Banking Buoys up Stricken Stocks
"When the financial history of the past exciting week is finally written an unusual chapter will be that devoted to the formation of a coalition of the city's leading bankers to support the stricken stock market."
–New York Times

October 27, 1929
Stocks Go Lower in Moderately Active Week-End Trading
–New York Times

October 27, 1929
Bond Dealers Report Investors Returning From Stocks to Securities With Fixed Yield
"In contrast to the depression which struck the stock markets of the country last week, trading in bonds on the New York Stock Exchange and also over the counter reached the highest levels of activity attained so far this year and to the accompaniment of rising prices."
–New York Times

October 28, 1929
Low Yield on Stocks Drove Prices Down; Berlin Sees Crash Here as Result of Abnormal Valuations for Investment Shares
–New York Times

October 29, 1929
Stocks Drop Sags Hides; Futures Close 15 to 40 Points Off on 1,720,000-Pound Total
–New York Times

October 30, 1929
Reserve Board Finds Action Unnecessary: Six-Hour Session Brings No Change in the New York Rediscount Rate, Officials Are Optimistic
–New York Times

**News &
Federal Reserve Bulletin**

October 1929
Changes in Reserve Bank Portfolio
"The additional demand for reserve bank credit was met through the purchase by the reserve banks of acceptances in the open market. Following upon the reductions in July and August in the buying rates on bills, there was a rapid growth in offerings of acceptances to the reserve banks, and bill holdings of these banks increased by more than $200,000,000 from the first of August to the last of September."
—Federal Reserve Bulletin

October 30, 1929
Further Fall of Extreme Violence in Stocks, in Largest Recorded Day's Business
"Until shortly before the end of yesterday's stock market there was no abatement whatever in the fury of liquidation. The day's actual transactions of 16,400,000 shares ran far beyond last Thursday's 12,800,000 and, in a long list of well-known shares, declines ran from 25 to 40 points."
—New York Times

October 30, 1929
General View Is That It Has Run Its Course and That Basic Condition Is Sound. No 'Catastrophe' Is Seen; Transitory Forces Held to Be Behind Decline With Prosperity Not Affected
—New York Times

October 30, 1929
Insurance Heads Urged to Buy Stocks; Conway Suggests Price Level Offers Good Purchases for Investment
—New York Times

October 31, 1929
Sharp Recovery in Stocks, a Few Further Declines—Money 6 Per Cent, Sterling Strong
"The essential fact established by yesterday's stock market was that panicky liquidation had been checked and that orders which had been placed by bona fide buyers were having their natural effect. All such hysterical declines as those of the present week are certain to end eventually with an upward rebound of prices."
—New York Times

October 31, 1929
Gains by Bank Stocks Are 5 to 500 Points; Trading Is Heavy
"Bank stocks recovered in price yesterday in a volume of trading said to have surpassed the record of Tuesday. The brisk buying sent prices up from 5 to 500 points. National City Bank led again in volume and at the closing bid was up 85 points on the day...Investment trusts moved irregularly."
—New York Times

from brokers whose loans from corporations were suddenly called amid the panic.[50] Trading volume set another record as 9 million shares changed hands over the course of the day (3 million in the last hour of trading)[51] and the Dow finished down 13.5 percent—its largest one-day loss in history—on what became known as Black Monday. The Bankers' Pool met again after the market closed, stirring optimism, but announced no additional buying measures.[52]

STOCK PRICES SLUMP $14,000,000,000 IN NATION-WIDE STAMPEDE TO UNLOAD; BANKERS TO SUPPORT MARKET TODAY

Sixteen Leading Issues Down $2,893,520,108; Tel. & Tel. and Steel Among Heaviest Losers

A shrinkage of $2,893,520,108 in the open market value of the shares of sixteen representative companies resulted from yesterday's sweeping decline on the New York Stock Exchange.

American Telephone and Telegraph was the heaviest loser, $448,905,162 having been lopped off of its total value. United States Steel common, traditional bellwether of the stock market, made its greatest nose-dive in recent years by falling from a high of 203¼ to

PREMIER ISSUES HARD HIT

Unexpected Torrent of Liquidation Again Rocks Markets.

From the New York Times, 29 October © 1929 The New York Times. All rights reserved. Used by permission and protection by the Copyright Laws of the United States. The printing, copying redistribution, or retransmission of this Content without express written permission is prohibited.

Another massive wave of margin calls went out Monday night and $150 million of call loans had been pulled from the market before Tuesday's open.[53] **The Federal Reserve attempted to counter the collapse in credit by providing liquidity.** After a 3 a.m. meeting with his directors, New York Fed president George Harrison announced before the market opened that the Fed would inject $100 million in liquidity to ease the credit crunch in the money market by purchasing government securities. Harrison needed approval from the Fed Board in Washington, but he didn't want to wait; instead he made the purchases outside the regular Open Market Investment Committee account.[54] **Classically the checks and balances designed to ensure stability during normal times are poorly suited for crisis scenarios where immediate, aggressive action is required. In the late 1920s, there were few well-established paths for dealing with the debt implosion and its domino effects.**

While the Fed's liquidity eased credit conditions and likely prevented a number of failures, it wasn't enough to stop the stock market's collapse on what became known as Black Tuesday. Starting at the open, large blocks of shares flooded the market and pushed prices down.[55] A rumor that the Bankers' Pool had shifted to selling fed the panic.[56] The members of the New York Stock Exchange met at noon to discuss closing the exchange, before deciding against it.[57] The investment trusts were hit especially hard as the leverage that buoyed returns through the bubble started to work in reverse. Goldman Sachs Trading Corporation fell 42 percent and Blue Ridge was at one point down as much as 70 percent before recovering somewhat.[58] The Dow closed down 11.7 percent, the second worst one-day loss in history. The market had fallen by 23 percent over two days and problems with leveraged speculators and their lenders were already starting to emerge.

STOCKS COLLAPSE IN 16,410,030-SHARE DAY, BUT RALLY AT CLOSE CHEERS BROKERS; BANKERS OPTIMISTIC, TO CONTINUE AID

LEADERS SEE FEAR WANING

Point to 'Lifting Spells' in Trading as Sign of Buying Activity.

GROUP MEETS TWICE IN DAY

But Resources Are Unable to Stem Selling Tide—Lamont Reassures Investors.

HOPE SEEN IN MARGIN CUTS

240 Issues Lose $15,894,818,894 in Month; Slump in Full Exchange List Vastly Larger

The drastic effects of Wall Street's October bear market is shown by valuation tables prepared last night by THE NEW YORK TIMES, which place the decline in the market value of 240 representative issues on the New York Stock Exchange at $15,894,818,894 during the period from Oct. 1 to yesterday's closing. Since there are 1,279 issues listed on the New York Stock Exchange, the total depreciation for the month is estimated at between two and three times the loss for the 240 issues covered by THE TIMES table.

Among the losses of the various groups comprising the 240 stocks in THE TIMES valuation table were the following:

Group.	Number of Stocks.	Decline in Value.
Railroads	25	$1,128,686,488
Public utilities	29	5,135,734,327
Motors	15	1,689,840,902
Oils	22	1,382,617,778
Coppers	13	824,403,820
Chemicals	9	1,621,697,897

The official figures of the New York Stock Exchange showed that the total market value of its listed securities on Oct. 1 was $87,073,630,423. The decline in the 240 representative issues there...

CLOSING RALLY VIGOROUS

Leading Issues Regain From 4 to 14 Points in 15 Minutes.

INVESTMENT TRUSTS BUY

Large Blocks Thrown on Market at Opening Start Third Break of Week.

BIG TRADERS HARDEST HIT

From the New York Times, 30 October © 1929 The New York Times. All rights reserved. Used by permission and protection by the Copyright Laws of the United States. The printing, copying redistribution, or retransmission of this Content without express written permission is prohibited.

Stocks snapped back on Wednesday, rising 12.3 percent in **one of the sharp bear market rallies that classically occur repeatedly during the depression phases of big debt crises.** Following the rally, the NYSE announced that trading would begin at noon the next day and that the exchange would be closed on the following Friday and Saturday in order to catch up on paperwork.[59]

Both the Fed and the Bank of England cut rates on Thursday. The Fed dropped its bank rate from 6 percent to 5 percent in coordination with the Bank of England's move to decrease its discount rate from 6.5 percent to 6 percent.[60] Traders also cheered the news that call loans outstanding had fallen by more than $1 billion from the prior week. Believing that the worst of the forced selling had passed, markets rallied again.

But speculators looking to capitalize on the prior week's rally raced to sell when the market opened on Monday and stocks plunged again. By Wednesday, the Dow was down 15 percent on the week. Stocks continued to fall the following week as well.

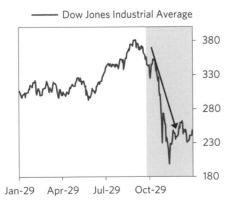

Railroad bonds and other high-grade bonds performed well during the crash, as investors sought safer investments after pulling back from stocks and call loans. At the same time, the yields between high-grade and lower-grade

News & Federal Reserve Bulletin

November 1929
National Summary of Business Conditions
"Industrial activity increased less in September than is usual at this season. Production during the month continued above the level of a year ago, and for the third quarter of the year it was at a rate approximately 10 per cent above 1928. There was a further decline in building contracts awarded. Bank loans increased between the middle of September and the middle of October, reflecting chiefly growth in loans on securities."
—Federal Reserve Bulletin

November 1929
Change in Discount Rate and Bill Rate
"The discount rate on all classes and maturities of paper at the Federal Reserve Bank of New York was reduced from 6 to 5 per cent, effective November 1. Buying rates on bills with maturities under 90 days at the New York bank were reduced from 5 1/8 to 5 effective on October 25, and effective November 1, were further reduced to 4 3/4 per cent. The buying rate on bills of 4 months 7 maturity was reduced from 5 1/8 to 4 3/4 per cent and on bills of 5-6 months' maturity from 5 1/2 to 5 percent, effective November 1."
—Federal Reserve Bulletin

November 1, 1929
Bank of England Cuts Rate; Unexpected Reduction to 6 Per Cent Cheered on Exchange—Prices Rise
"The governors of the Bank of England took the bold and unexpected step this morning of lowering the bank rate to 6 per cent after it had stood at 6 1/2 percent through five difficult weeks."
—New York Times

November 5, 1929
Stocks Sag 2 to 17 Points in Day of Orderly Selling; Sessions Cut to 3 Hours; Prices Decline Steadily
"Deprived of support by last-minute cancellations of buying orders and staggered by an unexpected rush of selling, the stock market pointed sharply downward at the opening yesterday and remained reactionary throughout five hours of orderly trading."
—New York Times

November 22, 1929
Listed Bonds Gain in Broader Trading; Government Issues in Demand, with 5 at New High Records for Year to Date
"The listed bond market showed further gains yesterday in considerably broader trading, with United States Government bonds again in brisk demand."
—New York Times

November 29, 1929
Hoover's Program as Seen by Europe; Feeling General That It Will Allay, but Not Avert, Trade Reaction
—New York Times

December 1, 1929
Hoover Stabilization Plans Require Careful Execution; Basic Principles Sound, but Discrimination Should Be Used in New Construction and Proposed Business Expansion
—New York Times

News & Federal Reserve Bulletin

December 1, 1929
What Mr. Hoover Has Done
"Too much praise cannot be given the President for the prompt and resolute and skillful way in which he set about reassuring the country after the financial collapse. Making a new use of methods which he had frequently employed on a smaller scale when he was Secretary of Commerce, he summoned to Washington leaders in business and banking and industry and agriculture and organized labor, with the aim of inducing them to do everything possible to repair the disaster."
–New York Times

December 1, 1929
To Aid Hoover Program; Fox Theatres, Inc., to Spend $15,000,000 on Construction Work
–New York Times

December 4, 1929
Wall Street Well Pleased With Hoover Message; Stocks Rise Briskly as It Comes Over the Ticker
"Wall Street appeared well pleased yesterday with President Hoover's message to Congress. The Street paid particular attention to the sections dealing with revision of the banking laws, the consolidation of railroads and supervision of public utilities...Stocks, which had been moderately firm all morning, started forward briskly during the reading of the message and continued their up-swing until the close."
–New York Times

December 5, 1929
Says Hoover Move Averted Wage Cuts; Hunt Tells Taylor Society Here President Blocked Reduction in 1921 as Well as Recently
"President Hoover's attempt to organize the economic forces of the country to check any threatened decline in business at the outset was characterized as a significant experiment toward industrial equilibrium by Dr. Wesley C. Mitchell in an address last night at a meeting of the Taylor Society held at the Hotel Pennsylvania."
–New York Times

December 10, 1929
Standard Oil Aided 129; Few Employees Buying Company's Stock Asked Help in Slump
–New York Times

December 13, 1929
Bank of England Cuts Rate to 5%; Reduction From 5, Third Drop in Eleven Weeks, Astonishes London's Financial District
–New York Times

December 31, 1929
Bonds Irregular on Stock Exchange; Domestic Issues Easier, but Foreign Loans Display Stronger Tone
"Bond prices showed considerable irregularity yesterday on the Stock Exchange, with domestic issues a trifle easier, on the average, and with foreign loans pointed upward. Liberty bonds and treasury issues were a shade lower in dull trading."
–New York Times

corporate bonds (rated BAA and below) reached their widest level in 1929, so the riskier corporate bonds were flat to down. That sort of market action—equities and bonds with credit risk falling and Treasury and other low credit risk assets rising—is typical in this phase of the cycle.

Naturally the financial and psychological impacts of the stock market plunge began to hurt the economy. As is typical, politicians and business leaders continued to talk up the strength of the economy, but stats showed weakness. Industrial production had peaked in July. More timely measures of freight car loading and steel utilization released the week of November 4 showed ongoing declines in economic activity. Sharp drops in commodity markets added to these worries. By mid-November, the Dow was down almost 50 percent from its September peak.

Policy Responses to the Crash

Although the Hoover Administration's handling of the market crash and economic downturn is now often criticized, its early moves were broadly praised and helped drive a meaningful stock rally. On November 13, President Hoover proposed a temporary one percent reduction in the tax rate for each income bracket and an increase to public construction spending of $175 million.[61] Two days later, Hoover announced his plan to invite a "small preliminary conference of representatives of industry, agriculture and labor" to develop a plan for fighting the downturn.[62] When they convened the following week, Hoover solicited pledges from business leaders to not cut spending on capital investment or wages, and from labor union leaders to not strike or demand higher wages.[63] On December 5, Hoover convened a conference of 400 of the most reputable businessmen at the time, which in turn created a leadership committee of 72 of the top business tycoons of the 1920s headed by the Chairman of the US Chamber of Commerce.[64] This mix of policies was successful for a time, as was Hoover's support for the Federal Reserve System's efforts to ease credit.

As mentioned, the New York Fed aggressively provided liquidity during the crash. Within a month, it cut its discount rate from 6 percent to 5 percent and then cut it again, to 4 ½ percent.

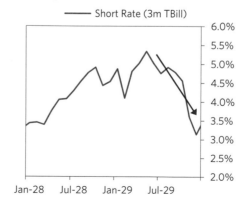

These policy moves combined with other steps by the private sector to support the stock market, most notably John D. Rockefeller's bid for one million shares of Standard Oil Co. at $50 on November 13 (effectively flooring the price at $50).[65] On November 13, the market bottomed and began what was to be a 20 percent rally going into December. A sense of optimism took hold.

1930–1932: Depression

By New Year's Day of 1930 it was widely believed that the stock market's 50 percent correction was over, which helped drive a strong rebound in the first four months of the year.[66] Stocks seemed cheap because there wasn't much evidence yet that company earnings would fall much, and investors were biased by their memories of the most recent downturns (e.g., in 1907 and 1920). In both cases, the worst was over after a correction of about 50 percent, and most assumed that events would play out similarly this time.

Helping to fuel the optimism, policy makers continued to take steps to stimulate the economy. The Fed cut rates to 3.5 percent in March, bringing the total rate cuts to 2.5 percent in just five months (sparking debate within the Fed over whether it was too much stimulation and risked weakening the dollar).[67] On March 25, Congress passed two appropriation bills for state road building and construction projects, bringing the total fiscal stimulus to about 1 percent of GDP.[68]

The consensus among economists, including those at the American Economic Association and the Federal Reserve, was that the stimulative policy moves would be enough to support an economic rebound. On January 1, the *New York Times* captured how sentiment had shifted since the crash, noting, "Lack of widespread commercial failures, the absence of serious unemployment, and robust recovery in the stock market have been factors calculated to dispel the gloominess."[69] As a further sign of optimism, banks were actually expanding their investments through 1930; member banks' holdings of foreign, municipal, government, and railroad bonds all rose.[70]

By April 10, the Dow had rallied back above 290. But despite stimulation and general optimism, economic weakness persisted. First quarter earnings were disappointing, and stocks began to slide starting in late April. **In the early stages of deleveragings, it's very common for investors and policy makers to underestimate how much the real economy will weaken, leading to small rallies that quickly reverse, and initial policy responses that aren't enough.**

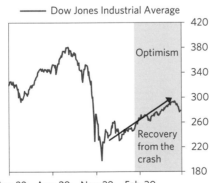

Over the second half of 1930, the economy clearly began to weaken. From May through December, department store sales fell 8 percent and industrial production fell 17.6 percent. Over the course of the year, the rate of unemployment rose by over 10 percent (to 14 percent) and capacity utilization fell by 12 percent (to 67 percent). Housing and mortgage debt collapsed. Still, at that point, the decline in the economy was more akin to a shallow recession. For example, levels of consumer spending remained above the lows of previous

News & Federal Reserve Bulletin

January 1, 1930
General Price Rise Ends 1929 Stock Trading with Wall St. Moderately Bullish for 1930
"In a burst of holiday enthusiasm, which even a tremendous volume of cash sales failed to dampen, the market on the New York Stock Exchange closed the momentous speculative year 1929 with generally higher prices throughout the list. Prices advanced from a point or so to more than 12, with the best of the principal stocks establishing the greatest appreciation."
–New York Times

January 19, 1930
Building Permits Continue Decline; But Straus Survey Indicates Cheap Money Will Aid Early Recovery
–New York Times

February 5, 1930
A Peak for the Year
"Not only did the volume yesterday establish a new high record on the Stock Exchange for 1930, but the composite averages of the New York Stock Exchange moved into the highest ground they have reached since the break of last autumn. Transactions aggregated 4,362,420 shares. It was the first time this year that business exceeded 4,000,000 shares. The last day to surpass yesterday's volume was Dec. 20, when the turnover was 5,545,650 shares."
–New York Times

March 14, 1930
Rediscount Rate Reduced to 3 1/2%; Federal Reserve Bank Here Makes Fourth Cut Since Stock Market Slump
–New York Times

March 17, 1930
Lower Money at Berlin; Day Loans Down to 3 1/2 and 5%, Discounts Cheapest Since 1927
–New York Times

April 1930
National Summary of Business Conditions
"Industrial production increased in February, while the number of workers employed in factories was about the same as in January. Wholesale commodity prices continued to decline. Credit extended by member banks was further reduced in February, but increased in the first two weeks of March. Money rates continued to decline."
–Federal Reserve Bulletin

April 2, 1930
Big Gain by Stocks Made Last Month; Values of 240 Issues Rose $2,961,240,563 on the Stock Exchange
"With heavier trading than in either January or February, prices of stocks in March showed the greatest appreciation since the market decline last fall."
–New York Times

News &
Federal Reserve Bulletin

April 1930
Changes in Discount Rate and Bill Paper
"The discount rate on all classes and maturities of paper was reduced from 4 to 3 1/2 per cent at the Federal Reserve Bank of New York, effective March 14; and from 4 1/2 to 4 per cent at the Federal Reserve Bank of Cleveland, effective March 15; at the Federal Reserve Bank of Philadelphia, effective March 20; and at the Federal Reserve Bank of San Francisco, effective March 21."

—Federal Reserve Bulletin

April 11, 1930
Farm Wage April 1 Lowest Since 1923; Situation Reflects Big Supply of Labor Due to Depression in Industrial Employment
"Farm wages on April 1 were the lowest for that date since the Bureau of Agricultural Economics began to collect their figures on a quarterly basis in 1923, the Department of Agriculture announced today."

—New York Times

April 15, 1930
Pledge Business Aid by Spending Money; Detroit Club Women Resolve on Effort to Dispel Depression Fear and Bring Out Hoarded Cash

—New York Times

April 26, 1930
Elections after Depression
"Between now and next November the uppermost political topic will be the extent to which trade reaction, coming along with a division in the Administration party and with a heavy fall in agricultural prices, will affect the Congressional campaign and the election of Governors."

—New York Times

May 1930
The Credit Situation
"The credit situation has continued to be relatively easy in recent weeks. Demand for credit from commercial sources has declined further, while demand from the securities markets has increased. During the last two months increased activity in the securities markets, a large volume of bond issues, and—until the middle of April—a rising level of stock prices have been accompanied by an increase of more than $785,000,000 in brokers' loans at New York City."

—Federal Reserve Bulletin

May 1, 1930
Studebaker Cuts Dividend Rate to $4; Directors Cite Reduction in Earnings, Due to Decreased Demand for Autos

—New York Times

recessions and many industries were not yet suffering from severe declines. The charts below show how both department store sales and industrial production had slipped but had not yet collapsed to the lows of the prior recession (the gray bars highlight 1930).

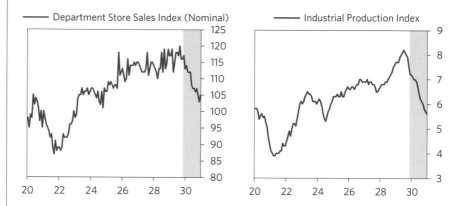

As the economy weakened, the sell-off across markets resumed. Stocks ended the period on a low note: By October of 1930, the stock market had fallen below the lows reached in November 1929. Commodities also fell sharply. Market analysts and investors alike were realizing that their hopes for a quick recovery would not materialize.[71] But Hoover remained optimistic.

Although the Federal Reserve decreased interest rates and the Treasury bond market was strong, spreads continued to widen. This increased the interest rates facing most consumers and businesses. For example, rates rose on long-term mortgage loans, and the yields on municipal bonds, which had performed well following the crash, began to rise as credit anxieties developed. Some industries were hit particularly hard by the worsening credit conditions. Railroads had large amounts of debts they needed to roll, and were facing both tighter credit conditions and decreased earnings.[72] Because railroads were considered a vital industry, the government wanted to support them, likely with a bailout. (The railroad industry's circumstances in this period parallel the struggles the auto industry faced in the 2008 financial crisis.)

Rising Protectionism

As is common in severe economic downturns, protectionist and anti-immigrant sentiment began to rise. Politicians blamed some of the weakness on anti-competitive policies by other countries, and posited that higher tariffs would help reverse the slump in manufacturing and agriculture, while restricting immigration would help the economy deal with unemployment.[73]

Protectionist sentiment resulted most notably in the passage of the Smoot-Hawley Tariff Act, which imposed tariffs on nearly 20,000 US imports. Investors and economists alike feared that the proposed 20 percent increase in tariffs would trigger a global trade war and cripple an already weak global economy.[74] As the act neared passage in early May, a group of 1,028 economists issued an open letter to Hoover imploring him to veto the bill if it passed in Congress.[75] Foreign governments also expressed opposition and hinted at retaliation.[76] However, tariffs—particularly on agricultural imports—were one of Hoover's campaign promises, so he was reluctant to renege even as the pushback against the Smoot-Hawley tariffs became more intense.[77]

Stocks sold off sharply as it became clear the tariff bill would pass. After falling 5 percent the previous week, the Dow dropped another 7.9 percent on June 16, the day before the tariff bill passed. The following chart shows the average tariff rate charged on US imports going back to the 1800s. While tariffs have sometimes increased during periods of economic downturn, Smoot-Hawley pushed tariffs to near-record levels.[78]

Average Tariff Rate on Dutiable Imports

Source: Irwin, "Clashing Over Commerce: A History of US Trade Policy"

Soon the US faced a wave of retaliatory protectionist policies. The most impactful initial response came from the US's largest trading partner, Canada, which at the time took in 20 percent of American exports. Canadian policy makers increased tariffs on 16 US goods while simultaneously lowering tariffs on imports from the British Empire.[79] As similar policies piled up in the years that followed, they accelerated the collapse in global trade caused by the economic contraction.

Restricting immigration (both legal and illegal), another common protectionist response to economic weakness, was also pursued by the Hoover administration in 1930. On September 9, Hoover put a ban on immigration, allowing travel only for tourists, students, and working professionals, describing the policy as necessary to deal with unemployment. He later reflected in his memoir his view that, "directly or indirectly all immigrants were a public charge at the moment—either they themselves went on relief as soon as they landed, or if they did get jobs, they forced others onto relief."[80]

Bank Failures Begin

Banks had largely held up well following the stock market crash, but as those they lent to were hurt by the crash and the economy weakened, they began to feel it. In 1930, bank net earnings declined about 40 percent compared to the prior year, but they remained on sound footing.[81] Several of the largest banks even increased their dividends. They looked strong at the time compared to the markets and the economy, and many analysts believed that they would be a source of support through the downturn.[82] The majority of early failures were confined to banks in the Midwest and country banks that had a lot of money in real estate loans, and were exposed to losses from a drought.[83] While the failures started small, they spread as credit problems spread.

By December, 1930 bank failures had become a meaningful risk to the broader economy. Worries about the banks led to runs on them. **Runs on**

News & Federal Reserve Bulletin

May 5, 1930
1,028 Economists Ask Hoover to Veto Pending Tariff Bill
"Vigorous opposition to passage of the Hawley-Smoot tariff bill is voiced by 1,028 economists, members of the American Economic Association, in a statement presenting to President Hoover, Senator Smoot, and Representative Hawley by Dr. Claire Wilcox, associate professor of economics at Swarthmore College, and made public here today. They urge the President to veto the measure if Congress passes it."
–New York Times

June 1930
National Summary of Business Conditions
"The volume of industrial production declined in May by about the same amount as it increased in April. Factory employment decreased more than is usual at this season, and the downward movement of prices continued. Money rates eased further, to the lowest level in more than five years."
–Federal Reserve Bulletin

June 10, 1930
Urge Tariff Cuts to Aid World Amity
–New York Times

June 14, 1930
Senate Passes Tariff Bill by 44 to 42...Europe Takes First Move in Reprisal
–New York Times

June 15, 1930
Stock Prices Sag on Passage of Tariff
–New York Times

June 16, 1930
Hoover Says He Will Sign Tariff Bill
–New York Times

July 29, 1930
Plan to Avoid Strikes Approved at Meeting; Court to Arbitrate Disputes of Building Trade Unions Tentatively Sanctioned
"A 'definite agreement for arbitration for all jurisdictional disputes' was unanimously decided upon at an all day conference between national representatives of employers and unions in the building trades at the Strand Hotel here today, it was announced as the session ended."
–New York Times

September 10, 1930
Labor Immigration Halted Temporarily At Hoover's Order
"Acting on the request of President Hoover to restrict immigration as much as possible as a relief measure for unemployment, the State Department has ordered a more strict application of that section of the law withholding visas from immigrants who may become 'public charges' after they have entered this country."
–New York Times

October 1930
Continued Monetary Ease
"Conditions in the money market remained easy through September. Although the usual seasonal trend at this time of the year is upward, there was little change in the demand for reserve-bank credit, and increase in holdings of acceptances by the reserve banks was reflected in a further decline of discounts for member banks."
–Federal Reserve Bulletin

News &
Federal Reserve Bulletin

December 11, 1930
False Rumor Leads to Trouble at Bank
"A small merchant in the Bronx went to the branch of the Bank of United States at Southern Boulevard and Freeman Street yesterday and asked bank officials to dispose of his stock in the institution. He was told that the stock was a good investment and was advised against the sale. He departed and apparently spread a false rumor that the bank had refused to sell his stock."
—*New York Times*

December 11, 1930
Stocks Decline, Trading Largest in 4 Weeks—Corn and Cotton Go Lower
—*New York Times*

December 12, 1930
Bank of U.S. Closes Doors
"While officials of the institution issued a statement expressing hope of an early reopening, leading banks of the city took steps to provide temporary relief for the depositors, offering to loan them 50 per cent of the amount of their deposits. The institution, despite its name, had no connection with the federal government. Deposits at the time of closing were approximately $160,000,000."
—*New York Times*

December 17, 1930
Severe Decline on Stock Exchange—Silver Breaks Sharply, Cotton Improves
"Yesterday's stock market was decidedly weak, under the largest trading since the break in the early days of last month culminated on Nov. 10. In yesterday's market, declines of 4 to 6 points were numerous, with losses in a few stocks running even larger. The day's declines affected shares of all descriptions, some of the high-grade stocks being for a time the points of special weakness. There was some irregularly distributed recovery before the closing."
—*New York Times*

December 23, 1930
Shut Bankers Trust of Philadelphia
"Directors of the Bankers Trust Company of Philadelphia, after an all-night conference, voluntarily turned over the bank's affairs to the State Department of Banking and neither the main office nor any of the nineteen branches of the institution opened for business today."
—*New York Times*

December 24, 1930
Topics in Wall Street: The Bank Closing
"Wall Street took the news of the suspension of the Chelsea Bank and Trust Company yesterday philosophically. The event, it was felt, while obviously unfortunate for the customers of the closed institution, had little significance for the financial world. The Chelsea Bank operated entirely outside the financial district and its closing has no bearing on the position of other banking institutions. It is, moreover, a small bank as New York banks go, not a member of the Clearing House or the Federal Reserve system."
—*New York Times*

non-guaranteed financial institutions are classic in such depressions/deleveragings, and they can lead to their failure in a matter of days.

Bank Failures Set High Records in 1930, Totaling 934, With $908,157,788 Liabilities

There were 3,446 more commercial failures in the United States, exclusive of banks, in 1930 than in 1929, and the liabilities of the companies in default in 1930 exceeded those of the preceding year by $185,000,000. The number of failures was 15 per cent higher and the total indebtedness was 38.3 per cent greater.

along with liabilities and assets, for the last sixteen years:

Year.	No.	Assets.	Liabilities.
1930	26,355	$442,799,681	$668,283,842
1929	22,909	226,028,151	483,250,196
1928	23,842	255,477,569	489,559,624
1927	23,146	256,739,633	520,304,268
1926	21,773	202,345,485	409,232,278
1925	21,214	248,066,570	443,744,272
1924	20,615	337,945,199	543,225,149
1923	18,718	388,382,154	539,386,806
1922	23,676	407,357,995	623,896,251
1921	19,652	409,038,316	627,401,883
1920	8,881	198,504,114	295,121,805

From the New York Times, 11 January © 1931 The New York Times. All rights reserved. Used by permission and protection by the Copyright Laws of the United States. The printing, copying redistribution, or retransmission of this Content without express written permission is prohibited.

Before I get into the banking failures, it's important to discuss the gold standard, since it played an important role in determining how the 1930s debt crisis transpired. As I described in prior sections of the book, when debts are denominated in one's own currency, deleveragings can generally be managed well. **Being on a gold standard is akin to having debts denominated in a foreign currency** because creditors could demand payment in gold (as was often written into contracts), and policy makers couldn't freely print money, as too much printing would lead people to redeem their money for gold. **So policy makers were working with a limited toolkit until they broke the link to gold**.

The most important bank failure of this period was that of the Bank of the United States, which had some 400,000 depositors, more than any bank in the country at the time.[84] The run on it began on December 10 because of a false rumor. Wall Street financiers—including the heads of J.P. Morgan and Chase—met at the New York Fed to determine whether they should provide the $30 million that was required to save the bank. Many within the group thought that the bank was insolvent, not simply illiquid, so they should let it fail.[85] New York Superintendent of Banks Joseph Broderick argued that its closing "would result in the closing of at least ten other banks in the city and … it might even affect the savings banks" (e.g., it was systemically important). He also noted that he believed the bank to be solvent.[86] Broderick's colleagues ultimately did not agree with him. When the bank closed its doors the next day, it was the biggest single bank failure in history.[87] The *New York Times* would later refer to its failure as "The First Domino In the Depression."[88] It was certainly a turning point for public confidence in the nation's banking system.

Banks are structurally vulnerable to runs because of the liquidity mismatch between their liabilities (i.e., short-term deposits) and assets (i.e., illiquid loans and securities), so even a sound bank can fail if it can't sell its assets fast enough to meet its liabilities. **Because of the gold standard, the Federal Reserve was restricted in how much it could print money, limiting how much it could lend to a bank facing liquidity problems (i.e., act as a "lender of last resort"). There were also legal constraints. For instance, the Fed at the time was only allowed to give direct access to its credit to member** banks, but only 35 percent of commercial banks were members.[89] So banks would often have to borrow from the private sector and sell their assets in a "fire sale" to avoid failure.

The end of 1930 also saw the political winds beginning to shift. With the downturn playing prominently in voters' minds, the Democrats swept Congress in the November mid-term elections. This foreshadowed FDR's win in the presidential election two years later.[90]

First Quarter, 1931: Optimism Gives Way to Gloom as Economy Continues to Deteriorate

At the start of 1931, economists, politicians, and other experts in both the US and Europe still retained hope that there would be an imminent return to normalcy because the problems still seemed manageable. The bank failures of the previous quarter were thought to be inconsequential, and not damaging to the overall financial system.

By March, all business indexes were pointing to a rise in employment, wages, and industrial production. Bank runs led to a less than 10 percent drop in deposits.[91] The news reflected growing economic confidence: on March 23, the *New York Times* declared that the depression had bottomed, and the U.S. economy was on its way back up.[92] New investment trusts were being formed to profit from the expected "long recovery."[93]

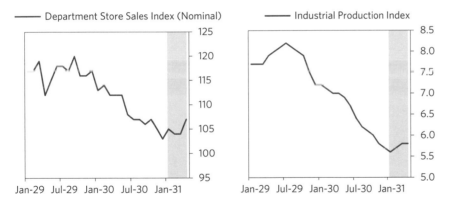

Optimism was also bolstered by the recovery of the stock market. Through the end of February, the Dow rose more than 20 percent off its December lows. The following chart illustrates the index's rise.

News & Federal Reserve Bulletin

December 1930
Recent Banking Developments
"The general level of money rates at the opening of December was as low as at any time since records became available. This ease in the money market has accompanied a further decrease in the demand for credit from the security market, which is shown by a rapid decline in brokers' loans to the lowest level in five years."
—Federal Reserve Bulletin

January 1931
A Year of Declining Business Activity
"In November and December there was a further decline in output and in employment in most manufacturing industries. Wholesale prices for many important commodities also continued to decline during the last two months of the year. Business activity, which began to recede in midsummer of 1929 after the rapid expansion of the preceding year and a half, continued to decline at a rapid rate during the last half of 1930, following a brief recovery in the spring. Almost all branches of industry shared in the decline. Employment declined, and total income of both wage earners and farmers decreased. At the same time wholesale prices throughout the world declined considerably, and retail prices also reflected this decline, although in smaller degree."
—Federal Reserve Bulletin

January 25, 1931
Wall Street Now Flooded with Optimistic Prophecies—Policies of Federal Reserve Bankers Compared
"For the first time in some months Wall Street was treated last week to a shower of optimism. Bankers and industrialists whose opinions weigh heavily with the financial community and who previously had declined to venture into the realm of prophecy struck out openly at the pessimists and with telling effect. Even the taciturn chairman of the First National Bank, George F. Baker, broke his rule of silence to the extent of telling the country that he detected signs of 'improvement in business conditions along sound lines.'"
—New York Times

February 11, 1931
Stocks Go Higher, Public Buying Again
"Another runaway market developed yesterday on the New York Stock Exchange, with the public and Wall Street professionals joining hands for the first time in a year in an enthusiastic buying demonstration which lifted the main body of stocks 2 to 6 points and sensitive specialties 7 to 14 points."
—New York Times

February 25, 1931
Stocks Rise Briskly; 330 at New Highs
—New York Times

March 1931
National Summary of Business Conditions
"Industrial activity increased in January by slightly less than the usual seasonal amount, and factory employment and pay rolls declined. Money rates in the open market declined further from the middle of January to the middle of February."
—Federal Reserve Bulletin

News & Federal Reserve Bulletin

March 1, 1931
Maximum Wage Bill is Passed by House
"The Bacon-Davis maximum wage bill, providing that the highest wage scale prevalent in any community where public works are undertaken under Federal contract, be paid to all laborers and mechanics, was passed in the House this afternoon without a roll-call. The bill goes now to President Hoover, as it already has been passed by the Senate."
–New York Times

March 2, 1931
Muller Optimistic on Business in 1931; Curb Exchange Head, in Report for 1930, Finds Hope in Theory of Cyclical Changes
–New York Times

March 13, 1931
Special Relief Measures
"To provide direct relief for their unemployed workers and to devise schemes for regularizing unemployment is the double object of several companies working generously and sensibly in the present emergency."
–New York Times

March 19, 1931
$700,000,000 Deficit in Budget Feared; Experts Admit Indications Are For Unexpected Cut in Income Taxes
–New York Times

March 23, 1931
Germany's Budget Deficit; Including Deficits Carried Over, Shortage Is 251,000,000 Marks
–New York Times

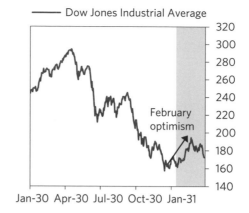

But the rally wasn't sustained. Growing concerns over Europe and indications of weak first quarter earnings caused stock prices to slip through March and end the quarter at 172.4, down 11.3 percent from their February highs.

The Growing Debate over Economic Policy

In a depression, the main ways that politics might play a role are by standing in the way of the implementation of sensible economic policies or by leading to extreme policies. These are important risks that can make a depression worse.

After more than a year of economic contraction, the political debate over economic policy was intensifying. By this time, more than six million people were unemployed in the United States and there was no agreement among policy makers and business leaders on how to deal with it.[94] Understanding this debate is key to understanding why policy makers took certain steps that ultimately worsened the crisis. It also helps illustrate many of the classic mistakes policy makers make when handling big debt crises.

The fiscal policy debate centered on whether or not the Federal government should significantly ramp up spending to support the economy. Senate Democrats, joined by some Republicans, pushed the President to increase "direct relief" for those facing particularly difficult circumstances. That would of course mean larger deficits and more debt, and it would mean changing the rules of the game to shift wealth from one set of players to others, rather than letting the game play out in a way that would provide good lessons to help prevent such problems in the future (i.e., the moral hazard perspective). There was also a strong belief that, if this money was just given away and not turned into productivity, it would be wasted. So while the Hoover administration had supported earlier fiscal stimulus, it opposed significant direct relief from the Federal government that would "bring an inevitable train of corruption and waste such as our nation had never witnessed." Hoover's administration instead advocated for what he called "indirect relief"—a mix of policies that included lobbying the private sector to invest and keep employment steady, reliance on aid from state and local governments, immigration restrictions, and macroprudential policies to encourage lending.[95]

While concerns over budget deficits limited stimulus spending, by 1931, the federal government budget deficit grew to 3 percent of GDP. The deficit was due to falling tax revenue, which had collapsed to nearly half of 1929 levels, and an increase in social spending of about $1 billion that had been approved the previous year. Treasury Secretary Mellon believed that balancing the budget was a necessary first step to restore business confidence.[96] Hoover agreed for reasons he later summarized in his memoir: "National stability required that we balance the budget."[97]

Worries over the deficit and a push for austerity are classic responses to the depression phase of a big debt crisis. Austerity seems like the obvious response, but the problem is that one person's spending is another person's income, so when spending is cut, incomes are also cut, with the result that it takes an awful lot of painful spending cuts to make significant reductions in debt/income ratios.

For all the suffering that the Depression had caused, a sense of crisis-driven urgency hadn't yet developed. The economy was still contracting over the first half of 1931, but at a slower rate than the year before. Hoover was certain that indirect relief was meeting the needs of the people and he did not see the need to use additional fiscal supports.[98] As we'll discuss later, this ultimately tipped the debate, and **the Hoover administration to make the classic rookie mistake of leaning too heavily on austerity and other deflationary levers** relative to more stimulative policies until the pain of doing these things became intolerable.

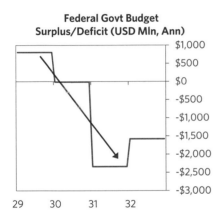

**Federal Govt Budget
Surplus/Deficit (USD Mln, Ann)**

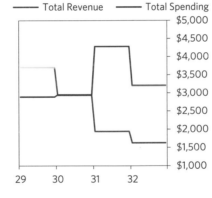

Federal Govt Budget (USD Mln, Ann)

— Total Revenue   — Total Spending

Second Quarter, 1931: The Global Dollar Shortage Causes a Global Debt Crisis and a Strong Dollar

Because dollar-denominated credit was collapsing and a lot of dollar-denominated debt that required dollar credit to service it existed around the world, a global dollar shortage emerged during the first half of 1931. **Classically, there is a squeeze in a reserve currency that is widely lent by foreign financial institutions when there is a collapse of credit creation in that currency.** Although other currencies faced a shortage amid the credit crunch, the dollar was particularly impacted because of its role as a global funding currency. At the same time, falling US imports reduced foreigners' dollar income, intensifying the squeeze. Note that virtually the same dollar squeeze dynamics occurred in the 2008 crisis for the same reasons.

As the financial markets and many other markets are global, one can't understand all that happened by looking only at the US. What happened in the US had a big impact on what happened in Germany, which led to big political changes that were felt around the world in the 1930s and early 1940s. In 1931

**News &
Federal Reserve Bulletin**

March 23, 1931
2,000,000,000 Deficit Predicted in France; February Public Revenue Down 104,000,000 Francs; Budget of 'Supplementary Expenditure' Up
—New York Times

March 25, 1931
Relief for Jobless Sets City Record; $3,175,000 Spent in February by Eleven Agencies Alone—30,000 Families Aided
—New York Times

March 27, 1931
Borah Urges Rise in Federal Taxes; Says Deficit Makes Increase Necessary and Advocates "Ability-to-Pay" Basis
"A breach in the Republican ranks over the question of Federal tax increases developed today when Senators Borah and Norris advocated action by Congress in December, despite the inclination of the regular party leaders to delay consideration until after the election next year."
—New York Times

March 29, 1931
Why the Treasury Faces a Large Deficit; Revenues Have Declined and Expenditures Increased Because of the Depression Changes in Estimate
"When the Federal Government closes its accounts on June 30, at the end of the current fiscal year, the treasury's bookkeeper will write down on the debit side of the ledger a deficit of $700,000,000 or more, if the latest unofficial estimates prove correct."
—New York Times

March 29, 1931
Red Cross to Hear Hoover on Relief; He Is Expected, at the Annual Meeting, to Amplify Views on Federal Help
"President Hoover will address the Red Cross on the drought-relief situation, and the organization will plan further measures to help the large numbers in the stricken areas who are still in want, at its two-day annual convention which is to begin in Washington on April 13."
—New York Times

March 31, 1931
Further Irregular Decline in Stocks, Trading Larger—Grain Markets Move Uncertainly
"The course of yesterday's stock market was plainly enough directed by professional pressure, applied on the theory that the company dividend reductions would have shaken financial confidence and induced actual selling. The extent to which such an influence has operated remains to be seen."
—New York Times

News &
Federal Reserve Bulletin

April 12, 1931
Expansion of Dollar Acceptances Described As Without Parallel in Financial History
"The course of yesterday's stock market was plainly enough directed by professional pressure, applied on the theory that the company dividend reductions would have shaken financial confidence and induced actual selling. The extent to which such an influence has operated remains to be seen."

—New York Times

May 1931
Money Market Conditions
"Notwithstanding the low and declining level of money rates in this country, there continued to be a large inflow of gold from abroad. Gold imports, which amounted to $100,000,000 during the first three months of the year, were proceeding at an even more rapid rate after the beginning of April. Particularly noteworthy was the receipt of $19,000,000 of gold from France in the course of one week."

—Federal Reserve Bulletin

May 1, 1931
Urge Trade Budgets to Avert Depression; National Commerce Chamber Speakers Outline System to Control Expansion

—New York Times

May 3, 1931
March Foreign Trade Grouped by Products; Percentage Decreased From 1929 in Exports Largest in Food and Manufactures

—New York Times

May 4, 1931
Favored-Nation Bid Evaded by Austria; New Trade Pact With Hungary, in Effect June 1, Employs a System of Rebates
"The proposed Austro-Hungarian trade treaty, the negotiations for which have been proceeding for months, now remains only to be paragraphed and will go into force on June 1...The origin of the Austro-Hungarian treaty was a demand by Austrian farmers for greatly increased protection, which could not be refused for political reasons, but which Hungary threatened to counter by raising the duties on Austrian industrial products."

—New York Times

May 5, 1931
Hoover Urges Arms Cut to Revive Trade in Opening World Chamber of Commerce; Foreign Delegates Attack High Tariffs; 35 Nations Represented; President Asks That Land Forces Be Reduced as Navies Are

—New York Times

Germany was the epicenter of the emerging dollar squeeze. It had previously faced great difficulty paying back the reparation debt it owed and had been forced to borrow as a result. The country had become a popular destination for the "carry trade," in which investors would lend their dollars to Germany to earn a higher yield than they would get in dollars and Germans would borrow in dollars to get the lower interest rate. Once again, this type of behavior is classic in the "good times," when there is little perceived risk and large cross-country credit creation, and sets up the conditions that make the "bad times" worse when the reversal happens. At the time, Germany was highly dependent on this flow of money that could easily be pulled, and by 1931, American banks and companies held about a billion dollars in short-term German bills (equal to about six percent of German GDP).[99] That made both the German borrowers and the American banks and companies very vulnerable.

Also, as is typical in such times, economies and wealth disparities fuel the rise of populist and extremist leaders globally, with the ideological fight between the authoritarian left and the authoritarian right. Both the German Communist party and Hitler's Nazi party made big electoral gains as the German economy struggled—with the Nazis going from under 3 percent support in the 1928 Reichstag elections to over 18 percent in September 1930. Meanwhile, the largest party (center left Social Democratic Party) slipped to less than a quarter of Reichstag seats.[100] Together, the far right and far left parties easily had enough parliamentary support to force Germany into an unstable multi-party coalition government. Germany was essentially becoming ungovernable.

The global trade war made economic conditions and the dollar squeeze worse. The collapse in global trade depressed foreigners' dollar income, which in turn made it harder for foreigners to service their dollar debts. As shown below, US imports in dollars had fallen by about 50 percent from 1929 to 1931.

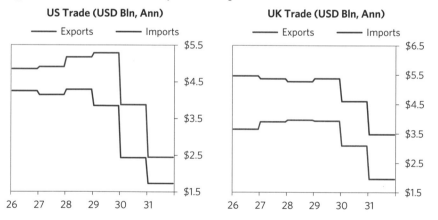

In a warning that would be echoed by global politicians and business leaders in the coming months, the president of Chase National Bank acknowledged in the August 1931 issue of *Time* magazine that companies' inability to obtain enough dollars to cover their debts was heavily affecting business. As such, he stressed the necessity for the US government to reduce debts owed to them from abroad.

The shortage of dollars made borrowing more expensive, creating a liquidity squeeze in central Europe. To alleviate the liquidity squeeze and allow the continued financing of fiscal deficits, these governments naturally turned to some money printing (since the alternative of allowing the credit crunch to spiral was worse). This increased inflation, raising fears of a return to the hyperinflation of the early 1920s in Germany. In essence, Germany was facing a balance of payments crisis. On May 7, the US Ambassador to Germany, Frederic M. Sackett, told President Hoover of Germany's economic strain, listing its pockets of weakness: capital flight, currency difficulties, unemployment, global tightening of credit, pressures for debt payments, and refusals to renew foreign held German bank accounts.[101]

Austria was also facing major losses. On May 8, Credit Anstalt, the oldest and largest of Austria's banks, announced a $20 million loss resulting partially from its role in the rescue of another failing bank in 1929 that had nearly wiped out its equity.[102] A run ensued and this spread to a run on the Austrian currency. **When risks emerge that systemically important institutions will fail, policy makers must take steps to keep these entities running to limit the impact of their failure on other solvent institutions or the economy at large. Keeping these institutions intact is also important for keeping credit pipes in place for lending to creditworthy borrowers, particularly for financial systems with a concentrated set of lenders.** But since Austria was on the gold standard, policy makers couldn't print money to provide liquidity and other frantic attempts to secure loans to stabilize the bank failed.

Geopolitical strains made the crisis worse. France feared Austria and Germany's increasingly close ties. In an effort to weaken those countries, the French government encouraged the Bank of France and other French banks to withdraw the short-term credit they had provided to Austria.[103]

Viewing the interconnectedness of global financial institutions and the weakness of Europe as potential threats to its domestic recovery, the United States began to study methods of relieving the pressure on the German economy. On May 11, President Hoover asked Treasury Secretary Mellon and Secretary of State Henry Stimson to look into relaxing Germany's significant payments for war debts and reparations. A proposal was not put forth until early the next month.[104]

In the interim, bank runs spread throughout Europe. Hungary reported bank runs starting in May, leading to the imposition of a bank holiday.[105] The German government nationalized Dresdner Bank, the nation's second largest bank, by buying its preferred shares.[106] Major financial institutions failed across Romania, Latvia, and Poland.[107]

Germany was facing capital flight. The country's gold and foreign exchange reserves fell by a third in June, to the lowest level in five years. To stem the outflow of capital, the bank tightened monetary policy, increasing its discount rate to 15 percent and its collateralized loan rate to 20 percent.[108]

**News &
Federal Reserve Bulletin**

May 12, 1931
Austria Acts to Save Biggest Private Bank
"Prompt action by the Austrian Government and banks in advancing $23,000,000 to the Kreditanstalt für Handel und Gewerbe is believed to have saved from failure the country's largest private bank. Had news of the bank's condition become known prematurely, according to its directors, a run probably would have resulted which would have forced it to close its doors within twenty-four hours."
–New York Times

May 22, 1931
Gold Imports $3,604,000; Reserve Bank Here Reported for Week also $10,000 Sent to Germany
–New York Times

May 31, 1931
The Eyes of Europe Are Again on Germany; Looking Forward to a Readjustment of Frontiers and a Revision of Debts, the Reich Is Preparing to Play an Important Role in the Era Now Opening, Wherein She Aims at Industrial Leadership
–New York Times

June 2, 1931
Sharp Fall in Stocks, Railway Shares Especially Weak—Stock Exchange Trading Larger
"The decline on the Stock Exchange continued yesterday; in a good many stocks, at an accelerated pace. While the scope of losses for the day varied widely, some of the individual declines were unusually large."
–New York Times

June 4, 1931
Stocks Up as Banks Ease Margin Policy
"Shaking off the reactionary influences that depressed prices steadily for several weeks, the stock market pointed sharply upward yesterday in the widest advance since Nov. 15, 1929, the second day of the recovery from the disastrous break of that period. Yesterday's advance, which extended to every part of the New York Stock Exchange, was accelerated by announcement that banks were adopting a more liberal policy in loans on stock collateral."
–New York Times

News &
Federal Reserve Bulletin

June 4, 1931
$25,000,000 Cut Seen by Canada's Tariff; Klein Says Increased Rates Imperil Our Export Trade to That Extent
—New York Times

June 5, 1931
Trade Group Asks Ban on Red Goods; State Chamber Also Wants Exports of Machinery to Russia Stopped
—New York Times

June 7, 1931
Drop in Foreign Trade Greater Than in 1921; Lewis Shows Exports 32% and Imports 35% Less Than in Same Period of 1929
—New York Times

June 9, 1931
Sees Politics Waning in Europe's Situation; J.G. McDonald Finds Ground for Hope Economic Interests Are Gaining Control
—New York Times

June 15, 1931
Paris Is Disturbed over German Crisis; Fears Are Created Less by Economic Difficulties Than by Political Possibilities
—New York Times

June 21, 1931
Paris Is Surprised By Plan of Hoover; Suspension of All War Payments for a Year Is Thought Perhaps Too Generous
"President Hoover's proposal for a year's suspension of war-debt and reparations payments has caused very great surprise and interest in Paris. It has proved more far-reaching than was expected even after yesterday's announcement. Until the exact terms are known and their effect on the existing arrangements are studied the French are reserving comment."
—New York Times

June 23, 1931
World Prices Soar on Debt Optimism
"Led by New York, tremendous buying enthusiasm swept over the security and commodity markets of the world yesterday in response to week-end developments reflecting the favorable reception of President Hoover's proposal for a one-year moratorium on war debts and reparations."
—New York Times

Investors took heavy losses as more and more bank failures hurt the stock market. In May, German stocks fell 14.2 percent, British stocks were down 9.8 percent and French stocks sold off 6.9 percent. In the US, the Dow sold off 15 percent in May following a 12.3 percent decline in April. The world was imploding.

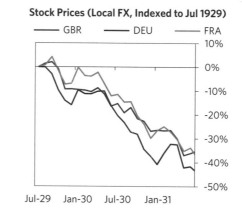

Political turmoil in Europe led funds to flow into the US, which increased demand for US Treasuries and pushed down interest rates. In an attempt to lessen the demand for dollars, the Federal Reserve reduced its discount rate to 1.5 percent.

On June 5, President Hoover suggested to his cabinet that all governments grant a moratorium of a year on all intergovernmental payments. President Paul von Hindenburg of the Weimar Republic made an appeal, stating that Germany was in danger of collapse, which helped push Hoover to swiftly adopt the plan.[109] On June 20, Hoover officially announced his proposal for a moratorium on Germany's debts for one year. Under his proposal, the US would forgo $245 million in debt service payments due over the next year from Britain, France, and other European powers. However, in order to receive these concessions, the allies had to suspend $385 million in reparations due from Germany.[110]

In what became known as the "moratorium rally," the Dow rallied 12 percent in the two days following Hoover's announcement and ended the month 23 percent above the low that it had reached on June 2. German stocks rose 25 percent on the first day of trading following the announcement. Commodity prices soared in the following weeks.

On July 6, the moratorium negotiations finally concluded. Fifteen countries agreed to it, though the share of German reparations that were suspended in the final agreement was lower than Hoover's initial proposal. France refused to participate, but did agree to re-lend their reparations back in to Germany.[111] The Dow slumped 4.5 percent on the day.

The chart below puts things in perspective; the arrow under the grey shaded area shows the moratorium rally. Notice how insignificant that 35 percent rally looks within the bigger moves. I can assure you that those sorts of moves don't seem small when you're going through them. Throughout the Great Depression, announcements of big policy moves like this one repeatedly produced waves of optimism and big rallies, amid a decline that totaled almost 90 percent. Investors were repeatedly disappointed when the policy moves weren't enough and the economy continued to deteriorate. As noted earlier, bear market rallies like this are classic in a depression, since workers, investors, and policy makers have a strong tendency to exaggerate the importance of relatively small things that appear big close-up.

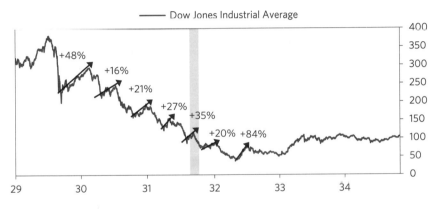

——— Dow Jones Industrial Average

Third Quarter, 1931: The Debt Moratorium Fails and the Run on Sterling Begins

It quickly became clear that the debt moratorium wasn't going to be enough to save Germany. In early July, rumors circulated that one of Germany's largest banks, Danat Bank, was on the verge of failure.[112] The Reichsbank, Germany's central bank, viewed it as systemically important and wanted to bail it out to avert the complete collapse of the German credit system, but it lacked the foreign reserves needed to do that.[113]

On July 8, just one day after the moratorium had been finalized, Reichsbank president Hans Luther began to reach out to policy makers from Britain to request further negotiations of Germany's current debts and the possibility of a new loan. Luther needed a new $1 billion loan without political concessions. Policy makers from the other countries balked at this—no one wanted to lend even more to Germany.[114] Hoover instead proposed a 'standstill' agreement, which would require all banks holding German and Central European short-term obligations to keep the credit extended, exposing them to big liquidity and potential solvency problems as they needed the cash to meet their obligations.[115]

News & Federal Reserve Bulletin

July 14, 1931
Central Banks Agree to Help Reich; Act After All-Day Meeting at Basle; German Bank Runs Bring 2-Day Closing
"Under authority granted by President von Hindenburg, the Bruening Government late tonight decreed that on Tuesday and Wednesday all banks and other credit institutions in Germany shall remain closed and that during this time the 'execution and acceptance of payments and transfers of any nature whatever at home and abroad are prohibited.'"
–New York Times

July 1931
Loss of Gold by Germany
"In recent weeks additions to this country's gold stock, which have been continuous since last autumn, greatly increased in volume. In addition to the inflow of gold from Argentina and Canada, a large amount of gold, which had previously been held under earmark for foreign account, was released in the United States. This release of gold was connected with a largescale withdrawal of short-time funds from the German market. During the period from May 31 to June 23 the Reichsbank lost $230,000,000 in gold and $20,000,000 in foreign exchange, with the consequence that its reserves were reduced close to the minimum required by law."
–Federal Reserve Bulletin

July 14, 1931
German Bonds Fall Sharply Here; Hoover Keeps in Touch with Moves to Aid Reich
"One of the worst breaks in the list of German dollar bonds since war time occurred here yesterday on the Mock Exchange when the active issues closed the day 2 3/8 to 15 points net lower."
–New York Times

July 24, 1931
News of Markets in London and Paris; English Prices Depressed on Rise in Bank Rate and Decision on Germany
"The stock markets were depressed today both by the increase in the bank rate to 3 per cent and the decision of the Finance Ministers concerning the German situation, which was not regarded as favorable."
–New York Times

July 30, 1931
Bankers to Leave Funds in Germany; British and Americans Agree With Reichsbank to Extend Short-Term Loans. Nation is More Confident
"Negotiations at the Reichsbank with British and American bankers for the prevention of further withdrawals of short-term credits from Germany were successfully concluded tonight when the bankers' representatives agreed they would leave their credits in Germany."
–New York Times

August 6, 1931
Says An Election Now Would Defeat Hoover; Farley Tells Westchester Democrats President Would Not Win Two Western States
–New York Times

News & Federal Reserve Bulletin

August 7, 1931
Hoover Seeks Means of Averting a 'Dole' for the Unemployed; Calls Julius H. Barnes and Silas H. Strawn to White House for Conference
"Realizing that another Winter is approaching with no apparent change for the better in employment conditions, President Hoover and his economic advisers are determined to work out some plan for relief with which to ward off the possible enactment of a 'dole' by the next Congress."
–New York Times

August 24, 1931
Hoover's Relief Plan Assailed as Callous; Progressive Labor Action Chairman Says President and Advisers Help Fire Revolt Spirit
"President Hoover's unemployment relief plan is condemned as 'inadequate and in many respects vicious,' in a statement issued yesterday by A.J. Muste, chairman of the Conference for Progressive Labor Action, at 104 Fifth Avenue."
–New York Times

August 26, 1931
Hoover and Mellon Consult on Britain; Treasury Head Said to Have Reported That Confidence Will Restore Situation
"Secretary of the Treasury Mellon, who returned from a European trip last night, today went over the European situation, including the British crisis, with President Hoover."
–New York Times

August 28, 1931
Hoover Reported to Favor Credits; Subject of Conferences at the White House Undivulged by the Participants
"President Hoover, it was reported late tonight, discussed the proposed bankers' loan of $400,000,000 to the English Government in his conference with New York bankers and Secretary Mellon at the White House conference last night."
–New York Times

September 5, 1931
$2,000,000,000 in Gold Finds 'Refuge' Here in Flight of Capital; Lack of Confidence Abroad Helps to Build Our Total to Record $5,000,000,000
–New York Times

September 11, 1931
Foreign Fears Bring Gold; "Security" Aims Reflected—Big Circulation Laid to Hoarding
–New York Times

September 11, 1931
French Bank Reduces All Of Its Loans; Home and Foreign Discounts Cut Down—Only Slight Increase of Gold
–New York Times

September 18, 1931
Slight Gain in Gold at Bank of France; Foreign Sight Balances Up 985,000,000 Francs, Foreign Bills Discounted 225,000,000
–New York Times

Naturally, banks were opposed to the standstill agreement and Treasury Secretary Mellon implored Hoover to reconsider. Hoover would not budge. He described his reasoning in his memoir: "This was a banker-made crisis... the bankers must shoulder the burden of the solution, not our taxpayers."[116] **Hoover's instinct to have the banks bear the cost is a classic but misguided policy response to a debt crisis. Punishing the banks in a way that weakens them makes sense for a few moral and economic reasons, as mentioned in the discussion of the archetypal template, and it can be a political necessity as the public hates the bankers at such times—but it can have disastrous consequences for the financial system and markets.**

Without a forceful policy response in support of the banks, the collapse continued and Germany's depression became much worse, inciting riots across the country.[117] Hitler was gearing up to run for Chancellor; he adopted the strongly populist stance of threatening to not repay the country's reparation debts at all. When the foreign ministers met in London on July 20, plans for a new loan slowly fizzled. Ultimately they put in place a three-month extension of an earlier loan along with a standstill agreement. The result was a classic run on the currency as described in the archetypal template.

The Run on Sterling

Germany's problems proved to be a key source of contagion. UK banks had lots of loans to Germany, so they couldn't get their money out; when foreign investors saw that the UK's banks were in trouble, they began to pull their money. On July 24, France began withdrawing gold from England. This was interpreted as a lack of confidence in the pound, which prompted more countries to pull their deposits from Britain, and the run on sterling began.[118]

To defend the currency, the Bank of England sold its reserves (a third of them in August alone) and raised interest rates, both classic moves. Foreigners were watching the weekly declines in gold reserves, so the pressure on the pound only increased.

The Bank of England also sought loans from abroad to support the currency, but these loans effectively funded the flight out of sterling. On August 1, 1931, the Bank requested that the US government organize a loan from private US banks totaling $250 million, which Hoover urged to be done right away.[119] The flight from sterling continued and the Bank of England received another loan, this time of $200 million from American banks and $200 million from French banks, which was made on August 28.[120] Hoover approved of them, but acknowledged after the fact that, "Both loans, however, mostly served to create more fear."[121]

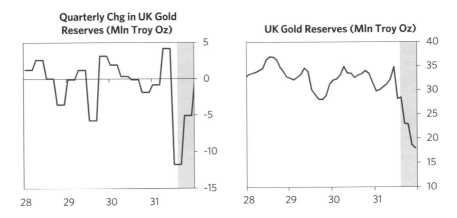

Quarterly Chg in UK Gold Reserves (Mln Troy Oz)

UK Gold Reserves (Mln Troy Oz)

On Saturday, September 19, having exhausted all of its foreign loans and with just over £100 million in gold reserves remaining, the Bank of England stopped supporting the pound and let it fall sharply, and of course the following day, officially suspended gold payments, a de facto default.[122] Initially, the public did not understand what going off the gold standard would mean for their transactions. Newspapers lamented it as the end of an era.[123]

Sterling fell 30 percent over the next three months. On the first trading day since gold payments had been halted, sterling dropped to $3.70, nearly 25 percent lower than its pre-default level of $4.86. British policy makers didn't intervene in the market to slow the fall or maintain stability. Sterling exchange rates fluctuated greatly before dropping to a low of $3.23 in December. Over the same period, the UK's equity market recovered and rose 11 percent in local currency terms.

Other countries followed the UK in abandoning gold convertibility so they could finally "print money" and devalue their currencies. Most of these devaluations were roughly 30 percent (e.g., the Nordic countries, Portugal, much of eastern Europe, New Zealand, Australia, India), in line with sterling's devaluation. The chart, below right, shows the depreciations for a few countries.

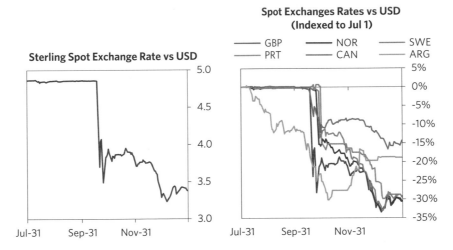

Sterling Spot Exchange Rate vs USD

Spot Exchanges Rates vs USD (Indexed to Jul 1)

Investors feared that government bonds would be defaulted on with devalued money. This led to a run out of bonds, which raised interest rates and drove bond prices down. In the United States, the Fed raised interest rates by 2 percent in order to attract foreign capital and hold the gold peg. Each government's bonds hit new lows in 1931. All except Switzerland's and France's declined at least 20 percent from their 1931 highs. Global stocks also sold off and some markets stopped trading altogether. On September 21, only the Paris Stock Exchange was open in Europe.[124]

News & Federal Reserve Bulletin

September 20, 1931
Sterling Exchange Plunges to $4.84 1/2; Cable Transfers Drop 1 5-16c, Sending Pound Lowest Here Since July 22
"Disturbed financial markets in London precipitated a wide-open break in sterling exchange here yesterday, driving the pound down to $4.84 1/2 for cable transfers, well below the gold-shipping point and the lowest price since July 22."
–New York Times

September 21, 1931
British Recovery Foreseen by Bankers Here; Gold Suspension Move Termed the First Step
"The suspension of the gold standard in England, viewed as a preliminary step to revalorization of the pound at a lower level, may prove the first step in the final solution of Great Britain's pressing economic problems, according to bankers here."
–New York Times

September 22, 1931
Would Emulate Britain; League Adviser Holds Germany May Also Drop Gold Standard
–New York Times

September 25, 1931
Sales of Gold Upset Money Market Here; Stock Prices Break; Foreigners Buy $64,000,000, Bringing 'Loss' of Metal to $180,600,000; Bankers' Bills Unloaded; Yield Rate of Acceptances Goes Up but Federal Reserve Clings to 1 Per Cent Discount
–New York Times

September 25, 1931
Sterling at $3.85 on London Market; Prices of Commodities and British Industrials Rise at Rapid Rate
"As a result chiefly of the speculative selling of sterling abroad the pound further declined today, although the prices of commodities and British industrial shares soared upward at great speed."
–New York Times

September 26, 1931
Pound Still Upsets Markets of World; Stock Exchanges in Number of Cities Remain Closed—Sterling Generally Declines
–New York Times

September 27, 1931
Stocks Move Uncertainly, Most Changes Small—Bonds Are Steadier, Sterling Recovers
–New York Times

September 29, 1931
$51,953,600 in Gold Lost to US in a Day; $31,500,000 Is Earmarked for Foreign Account—Exports of $20,453,500 Top Since 1928
"The action of Sweden and Norway in following Great Britain's lapse from the gold standard brought further confusion to the foreign exchange market yesterday and provoked foreign central banks to make additional requisitions against the gold stocks of this country for the purpose of strengthening their reserves."
–New York Times

October 1931
Changes in Discount Rate and Bill Rate
"The discount rate on all classes and maturities of paper was increased from 1 1/2 to 2 1/2 per cent at the Federal Reserve Bank of New York, effective October 9; at the Federal Reserve Bank of Boston from 2 to 2 1/2 per cent, effective October 10; and at the Federal Reserve Bank of Cleveland from 2 1/2 to 3 per cent, effective October 10. At the Federal Reserve Bank of New York buying rates on bills of all maturities were increased."
–Federal Reserve Bulletin

UK stocks and bonds sold off during the currency defense phase and continued to weaken immediately following the devaluation, but then rebounded. Because the UK's debt was denominated in its own currency, there wasn't a risk that the government couldn't pay it back. Consistent with these pressures on the bond market, the UK's 5.5 percent bonds due in 1937 had dropped to $92 after the devaluation from $104 (as interest rates rose from 4.7 percent to 5.7 percent in December), but they moved back up to $100 by the end of the year.[125]

The devaluation helped stimulate the export sector of the economy and allowed the Bank of England to ease significantly, cutting rates by one percent by the end of the year. Equilibrium was reached so that, by the end of October, banks in London were receiving money again. **In other words, the devaluation and money printing kicked off a beautiful deleveraging** (I'll go through this more later, when I discuss the US leaving the gold standard). Consistent with these pressures, UK stocks and bonds both rallied after selling off sharply through the currency defense phase and immediately following the devaluation. It is important to understand that these moves are very classic. Why they work as they do is explained in the archetypal template.

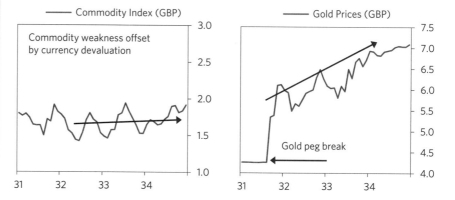

Fourth Quarter, 1931: The International Crisis Spreads to the US and the Depression Worsens

As other currencies devalued and the dollar rose, it created more deflationary/depressing pressures in the US. Sterling's devaluation in September 1931 especially stunned global investors and sent shock waves through US markets. Naturally investors and savers around the world began to question whether the US was safe from either default or devaluation, so they started to sell out of their dollar debt positions. That raised interest rates and tightened liquidity, bringing on the most painful period of the depression, lasting until FDR took the US off the gold standard eighteen months later to devalue the dollar and print money.

Stocks had sold off during the run on sterling. The Dow finished September down 30.7 percent, its largest monthly loss since the crisis began. On October 5, the market fell 10.7 percent in a single day. Amid the chaos, the NYSE once again banned short selling in a classic attempt to slow the sell-off.[126] While previously "safe" treasury bonds had rallied as stocks crashed in 1929 and 1930, they were now selling off along with stocks, reflecting the US balance of payments crisis. The yield on long-term US treasuries rose to 4 percent, nearly 1 percent above their midyear lows. Due to the US's stock of debts and their rising debt service, there were concerns about the US Treasury's ability to roll bonds that would come due in the following two years.[127] The fear of devaluation led to particularly acute runs on US banks, so banks needed to sell bonds to raise cash, which contributed to rising yields.[128]

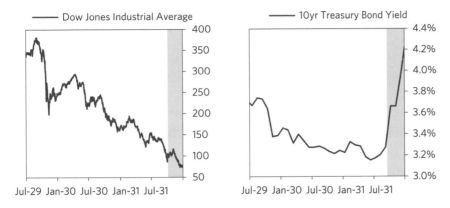

In September 1931, the dollar ceased to be a safe haven for the first time since the global debt crisis began. Gold reserves began to flow out of the US following sterling's devaluation as central banks in France, Belgium, Switzerland, and the Netherlands all began to convert their dollars to gold. The US lost about 10 percent of its gold reserves within the three weeks following the sterling devaluation.

On October 9, in an effort to attract investors, the New York Federal Reserve Bank increased the discount rate from 1.5 percent to 2.5 percent. This was no different than tightening, which is not a path to good things in a depression. **Classically, in a balance of payments crisis, interest rate increases large enough to adequately compensate holders of debt in weak currency for the currency risk are way too large to be tolerated by the domestic economy, so they don't work.** This was no exception, so a week later, the New York Fed again raised its interest rate to 3.5 percent.[129] Rumors flew that the head of the New York Fed, George Harrison, had asked the French not to withdraw any more gold from the United States.[130]

Given the domestic difficulties, investors in the US had taken to hoarding gold and cash. This led to a series of bank runs in late 1931 that caused many banks to close and resulted in a big contraction in deposits for those remaining open. As banks' deposits fell, they began to call their loans in order to build up their cash reserves. Homes and farms were forced into foreclosure, and several companies went bankrupt as investors did not roll loans they had previously extended.[131]

**News &
Federal Reserve Bulletin**

November 1931
Review of the Month
"During the 6-week period following the suspension of gold payments by Great Britain there was a decrease in the country's stock of monetary gold amounting to $730,000,000 and an increase in currency outstanding of $390,000,000. Both of these factors increased the demand for reserve bank credit, and the total volume of this credit, notwithstanding a considerable decrease in member bank reserve balances, increased by $930,000,000 during the period, and was at the end of October at the highest level in 10 years. The outflow of gold, which began at the time of the suspension of gold payments by Great Britain on September 21, was the largest movement of the metal during a similar period in any country at any time."
–*Federal Reserve Bulletin*

November 1, 1931
Hoover Gives $2,500 to Fund to Assist the Idle of District (NYT)
"President Hoover gave $2,500 today toward District of Columbia unemployment relief. E.C. Graham, chairman of the city's employment committee, was notified of the donation by a telephone call from Lawrence Richey."
–*New York Times*

November 3, 1931
Propose to Hoover Home Credits Plan; Building and Loan League Men Suggest Federal Land Bank Aid to Their Societies
–*New York Times*

November 4, 1931
Realty Credit Aid Studied by Hoover; President Confers with Glass on Bank System to Rediscount Urban Mortgages
–*New York Times*

November 5, 1931
Bennett Approves Hoover Credit Plan; Opinion to Broderick Says It Is Legal for State Banks to Participate in Pool
"Banks under the supervision of the State Banking Department may use funds legally to participate in the plan of the National Credit Corporation, which was founded at the suggestion of President Hoover to stabilize the financial situation, according to an opinion rendered yesterday by Attorney General John J. Bennett, Jr."
–*New York Times*

November 7, 1931
$350,000,000 Slash in Budget Figures Revealed by Hoover
–*New York Times*

November 8, 1931
Hoover Plans Aid for Home Builders; Conference of Bankers, Builders and Architects to Be Held in Washington Dec. 2
"The design of the average small home in the United States is defective and construction of better homes for less money is possible, in the opinion of prominent architects who are preparing a report to be submitted to President Hoover's conference on 'home building and home ownership,' which will meet in Washington, D.C., on Dec. 2."
–*New York Times*

November 8, 1931
Weekly Business Index Declines to New Low; Comparisons Made with Past Depressions
"The movement of the weekly index of business activity in the final week of October was dominated by the decline in the adjusted index of automobile production from 24.4 to the exceptionally low figure of 15.5."
–*New York Times*

News &
Federal Reserve Bulletin

November 29, 1931
An Evenly Divided Congress Faces Many Major Problems; Issues Raised by the Depression and by Foreign Events Are Added to the Usual Questions Calling for Solution
—New York Times

December 19, 1931
Ask New Lien Laws to Aid Home Owner; Realty Interests Urge a Cut in Costs of Foreclosure and in Charges of Referees
—New York Times

December 20, 1931
Urges Three Steps to Start Recovery; Col. Thompson Suggests State Spending, Foreclosure Halt and Cut in Prices
—New York Times

December 31, 1931
Credit Pool Set Up to Aid Sound Banks; Plan Suggested by President Hoover Promptly Put into Operation
"An important development of the past year in the field of commercial banking was the organization, at the suggestion of President Hoover, of the National Credit Corporation, designed to provide discounting facilities for sound bank assets not eligible under the present regulations for purchase by the Federal Reserve banks. The plan, which was devised in an effort to halt the wave of bank failures and, by restoring public confidence in the banks, to check hoarding of money, was advanced by Mr. Hoover on Oct. 7."
—New York Times

December 31, 1931
Say Reserve Banks Can Bring Recovery; Economists Recommend They Halt Liquidation by Ending Credit Contraction. Bill Buying Suggested
—New York Times

December 1931
National Summary of Business Conditions
"Production and employment in manufacturing industries declined further in October, while output of minerals increased more than is usual at this season. There was a considerable decrease in the demand for reserve bank credit after the middle of October, reflecting a reduction in member bank reserve balances and, in November, an inflow of gold, largely from Japan. Conditions in the money market became somewhat easier."
—Federal Reserve Bulletin

January 3, 1932
Congress Faces Hosts of Problems; Paramount Need Is Action on the Proposed Reconstruction Finance Board
"Foremost among problems facing Congress when it reconvenes is the bill to create a $500,000,000 reconstruction finance corporation, as advocated by President Hoover, which in many functions would duplicate the War Finance Corporation which operated in the days after the World War."
—New York Times

January 13, 1932
President to Speed $2,000,000,000 Board; He Says Reconstruction Corporation Will Start Work Soon After the Act Passes
"The Reconstruction Finance Corporation, with a contemplated lending capacity of $2,000,000,000, will be in operation a few days after Congress finally passes the bill for its creation, President Hoover told Senate leaders with whom he conferred today."
—New York Times

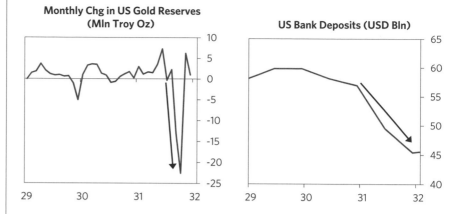

Monthly Chg in US Gold Reserves (Mln Troy Oz)

US Bank Deposits (USD Bln)

As money and credit contracted, the economy started to fall off a cliff. Over the second half of 1931, industrial production contracted by 14.3 percent and department store sales fell 12.9 percent. By the end of 1931, unemployment had reached nearly 20 percent, and domestic prices were falling 10 percent per year.

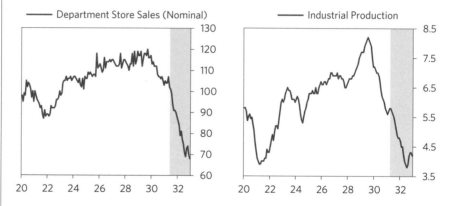

Department Store Sales (Nominal)

Industrial Production

The Hoover administration took several steps to stem bank failures and stimulate the flow of credit in late 1931. The most notable among these was the creation of the National Credit Association, which provided a pool of private money that could be lent against sound collateral to provide liquidity to banks at risk of failing (i.e., a private central bank). The funds came from the banks and totaled $500 million, with the ability to borrow another billion.[132]

At the same time, Hoover was looking for solutions for the collapsing real estate market. To stop foreclosures on mortgages of "the homes and farms of responsible people," he sought to create a system of Home Loan Discount Banks, which he did in 1932. In the meantime, he worked with both the insurance and real estate agencies to suspend foreclosures on farm loans by the Federal Land Banks, while providing the institution with $1 billion so that it could expand its lending.[133]

The policies were well received and broadly inspired confidence among investors. The stock market rallied in response, up 35 percent from its October bottom to November 9, with a jump of more than 10 percent on the day the National Credit Association was announced. The rally made some believe the worst was over, as most significant rallies do. Yet there was no significant change in the total money and credit available, so the fundamental imbalance between total debt coming due and the amount of money available to service it wasn't resolved. As was the case with so many policy announcements throughout the depression, the rally faded as it became clear that the proposals would be too small to handle the problem. Stocks reached a new low near the end of December.

First Half of 1932: Growing Government Intervention Unable to Halt Economic Collapse

The depression deepened in 1932, as the economy continued to plunge with deflation and credit problems worsening. An astounding number of businesses were struggling or failing—in aggregate, businesses experienced $2.7 billion in losses and bankruptcies hit record levels, with almost 32,000 failures and $928 million in liabilities.[134] News of bank failures filled the newspapers. As those losses rippled through the system, imposing losses on lenders and causing other businesses to close shop, the economy contracted still more.

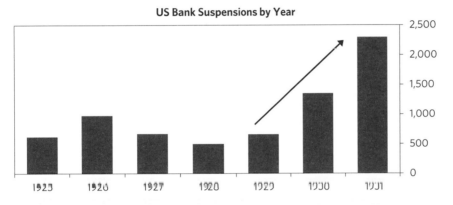

US Bank Suspensions by Year

It is classic in a big debt crisis: Policy makers play around with deflationary levers to bring down debt for a couple of years but eventually wake up to the fact that the depressing effects of debt reduction and austerity are both too painful and inadequate to produce the effects that are needed. So more aggressive policies are undertaken. As it became clear that the Hoover administration hadn't done enough to reverse the credit contraction, it announced another set of policies during the first part of 1932 in an attempt to provide liquidity to the banking system and get credit going again.

On January 23, Hoover launched the Reconstruction Finance Corporation. The RFC was funded with $500 million in capital and had the ability to borrow from the Treasury or private sources up to $3 billion; its goal was to provide liquidity to solvent banks to shore them up against failure.[135] The RFC benefited from a more extensive mandate than the Federal Reserve—it was able to lend against a wider range of collateral and to a broader range of entities. It could also lend to state-chartered banks, banks in rural areas that were not a part of the Federal Reserve System (i.e., some of the banks most affected by the crisis), and railroads, which were an important industry at the time (like the auto industry in 2008).[136] **Lending against a widening range of collateral and to an increasingly wide range of borrowers is a classic lever that policy makers pull to ensure that sufficient liquidity gets to the financial system, sometimes provided by central banks and sometimes by central governments.**

News & Federal Reserve Bulletin

January 16, 1932
Reconstruction Bill Passed by the House; $2,000,000,000 Finance Measure Is Adopted
—*New York Times*

January 17, 1932
Increased Optimism Pervades Business; Passage of Reconstruction Bill and Move Against Deflation Cheer Leaders
"The passage of the Reconstruction Finance Corporation bill by both houses of Congress and the conciliatory attitude with which the delegates to the railroad labor conference in Chicago finally met, together with the fact that the Federal Reserve System appears to have embarked on a policy to halt deflation, all served to create a better feeling in the financial community last week."
—*New York Times*

January 17, 1932
Three Banks Are Closed; Two of These Are in Chicago and One Is in Erie, Pa.
—*New York Times*

January 20, 1932
Joliet (Ill.) Bank Closes; Directors Say, However, That It Is Solvent and Predict Reopening
—*New York Times*

January 20, 1932
Rensselaer (N.Y.) Bank Closes
—*New York Times*

January 21, 1932
Two Chicago Banks Close
—*New York Times*

January 22, 1932
Hoover Asks House to Vote $500,000,000 for Finance Board
—*New York Times*

February 1932
Reconstruction Finance Corporation
"The principal development affecting the banking situation in January was the enactment of legislation creating the Reconstruction Finance Corporation with a capital of $500,000,000. The Reconstruction Finance Corporation Act, designed principally 'to provide emergency financing facilities for financial institutions' and 'to aid in financing agriculture, industry, and commerce' was approved by the President on January 22, 1932. In announcing his approval the President said of the new corporation: 'It brings into being a powerful organization with adequate resources, able to strengthen weaknesses that may develop in our credit, banking, and railway structure in order to permit business and industry to carry on normal activities free from the fear of unexpected shocks and retarding influences.'"
—*Federal Reserve Bulletin*

February 1932
National Summary of Business Conditions
"Industrial activity declined from November to December by slightly more than the usual seasonal amount, while the volume of factory employment showed about the usual decrease. Wholesale prices declined further."
—*Federal Reserve Bulletin*

News &
Federal Reserve Bulletin

February 11, 1932
Europe Withdraws $17,045,500 of Gold
"European withdrawals of gold amounting to $17,045,500 were reported yesterday by the Federal Reserve Bank of New York. Imports of $1,070,200 from Canada and $575,000 from India were also announced, and an increase of $100,000 in gold earmarked for foreign accounts was shown."
—New York Times

February 11, 1932
Changes in Reserve Act
"Development of a powerful financial machine based on revolutionary changes in the Federal Reserve System and designed to stimulate credit through a possible increase of $2,500,000,000 in the currency was decided upon at a non-partisan conference of Democratic and Republican leaders called at the White House today by President Hoover."
—New York Times

February 11, 1932
Federal Aid Stirs Sharp Senate Clash
"Senators Fess of Ohio and Borah of Idaho, both Republicans, clashed today in a lively debate over the La Follette-Costigan bill for direct Federal aid for the unemployed. Crowded galleries applauded the speakers. Vote on the measure was delayed until tomorrow, when Republican leaders count on Democratic aid for its defeat."
—New York Times

February 11, 1932
Stocks Fall, Then Recover Most of Their Losses
—New York Times

February 27, 1932
Credit Bill Voted: Hoover Signs Today
"Approved by Congress today without a dissenting vote, the Glass-Steagall credit-expansion bill reached the White House at 6:08 o'clock tonight and will be signed by President Hoover tomorrow."
—New York Times

February 27, 1932
Bank Conditions Improve in 14 Days
"A noticeable improvement has taken place in the banking situation in two weeks, according to reports received by the Federal Reserve Board and by J.W. Pole, Controller of the Currency. For eight days there have been no national bank failures, a new record for many months, while there has been an appreciable decline in failures of other member and State banks for ten days."
—New York Times

February 27, 1932
Credit Bill Voted; Hoover Signs Today; Not a Dissenting Voice Is Heard In Congress Against Passage of Bank Aid Measure
—New York Times

March 2, 1932
Senate Body Acts for Broad Inquiry on Short Selling; Banking Committee Will Go Beyond Hoover Idea in Stock Exchange Investigation
"An investigation of the New York Stock Exchange was recommended today by the Senate Banking and Currency Committee. A subcommittee, headed by Senator Walcott, Republican, of Connecticut, immediately began drafting a resolution requesting authority for such an investigation from the Senate."
—New York Times

By the end of August 1932, the RFC had lent $1.3 billion to 5,520 financial institutions, helping to reduce the number of bank failures.[137] But the RFC was only able to lend against "good" collateral. And so it was unable to provide sufficient support to some of the institutions that needed it the most.[138]

Around this time, the Fed started to experiment with money printing. Going into the crisis, the Federal Reserve was only able to lend against gold or certain forms of commercial paper. With both in short supply, policy makers were once again faced with the trade-off between further tightening and undermining the dollar's peg to gold. **The 1932 Banking Act, signed by Hoover on February 27, attempted to alleviate the liquidity squeeze while maintaining the gold standard by increasing the Federal Reserve's ability to print money, but only to buy government bonds (which 75 years later would be called "quantitative easing").**[139] This move was contentious, since it was clearly a weakening of the principles behind the gold standard, but the sense of urgency was such that the bill passed without debate.[140] As Hoover framed it, the decision was "in a sense a national defense measure."[141,] **Later that year, Congress gave the Federal Reserve additional powers to print money and provide liquidity in an emergency.**[142] **This provision—Section 13(3) of the Federal Reserve Act— would end up being critical to the Fed's response to the 2008 debt crisis.**

The Federal Reserve System bought nearly $50 million in government securities each week in April and nearly $100 million each week in May. By June, the system had purchased over $1.5 billion in government securities. The following chart illustrates the Federal Reserve's purchases and holdings of government debt in 1931 and 1932.

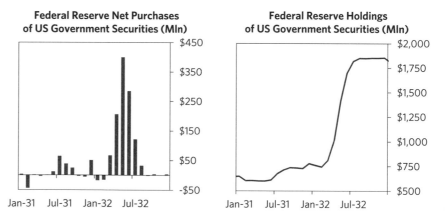

Federal Reserve Net Purchases of US Government Securities (Mln)

Federal Reserve Holdings of US Government Securities (Mln)

Once the Federal Reserve began purchases, yields on short-term Treasury securities fell rapidly with three month T-Bill yields falling more than two percent over the first half of the year. Fed purchases also relieved pressure in the market for longer-term treasury bonds, where the supply-demand imbalance for dollars had reached a breaking point amid large deficits and foreign reluctance to hold US assets. After rising above 4.3 percent in January, yields on ten-year treasuries fell below 3.5 percent over the next six months.

These moves ignited optimism and yet another rally, and the Dow Jones increased by 19.5 percent, reaching January's high. It closed above 80 in February.

Policy makers also took a number of smaller steps to support the banking system during the first half of 1932. **Another classic move was the abandonment of mark-to-market accounting for banks.** In January, the Comptroller of the Currency instructed bank examiners to use par value as the intrinsic value of bonds held by national banks with a BAA rating or better.[143] Under the prior accounting methodology, banks faced either major paper losses on the bonds they held or cash losses if they sold them. Those losses reduced their capital, forcing them to raise money or sell assets, further constraining liquidity and pushing down asset prices. The change in accounting rules relieved some of the most immediate pressure on banks.

The Hoover administration also tried to get credit going with macroprudential measures, most notably applying direct pressure on banks in an attempt to get them to lend. Hoover and Treasury Secretary Ogden Mills had blamed the banks for their inability to stimulate credit, and accused them of restricting loans and hoarding gold and cash. Hoover organized committees in the twelve Federal Reserve districts which tried to pressure large regional banks into lending, but this effort met with little success.[144]

Though some were helpful, none of these moves were enough to halt the economic collapse. Pressure on US gold reserves continued because foreigners worried that with the monetary expansion and the expanding deficit, the US would not be able to sustain the dollar's conversion to gold at existing rates.[145] As they rushed to make the conversion, gold left the country every month from March to June. In June net gold exports hit $206 million, a level last experienced following the depreciation of sterling.[146] That produced a tightening of credit.

In March, stocks sold off and the market suffered a decline that extended through 11 weeks. The Dow Jones dropped 50 percent, from 88 on March 8 to 44 on May 31. The Dow Jones closed in May on a low for the month, and volume further declined that month to about 750,000 shares per day.[147] Early in the crisis, government efforts to increase lending and spending had led to sustained rallies in asset markets. At this stage, however, investors had become disillusioned. They worried that Hoover's programs were not making enough of a difference to make up for their vast cost, and markets continued to trend downward.

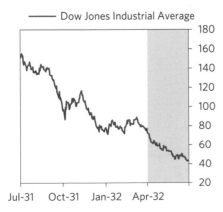

— Dow Jones Industrial Average

News & Federal Reserve Bulletin

March 10, 1932
Hoarding by Banks Put Before Hoover
"A charge that some banks were hoarding money and that their restrictive credit policies crippled industrial activities was laid before President Hoover today by the Institute of Scrap Iron and Steel through its director general, Benjamin Schwartz."
–New York Times

March 18, 1932
More Gold Taken in by Bank of France
–New York Times

March 20, 1932
Government Economy to Cut Deficit Urged; Expert Says Business Practices Should Be Adopted to Cover Federal Requirements
"Comparing the financial plight of the government at the present time to that of any large industrial organization, W. Clement Moore, economist and tax expert, asserted yesterday that the government should adopt business methods and common sense in attempting to balance the budget."
–New York Times

April 5, 1932
Gold Holdings Here Down $118,400 in Day
–New York Times

April 8, 1932
President Accepts House Bid for Help in Economy Quest
"President Hoover today accepted the invitation of the House Economy Committee to cooperate with it in reducing Federal expenditures. He requested the entire committee to meet with him at the White House at 11 o'clock Saturday morning."
–New York Times

April 9, 1932
Stocks Extend Their Decline Again, Breaking Through the Previous Lows—Bonds Also Depressed
"A stock market that has been growing steadily weaker for more than a week was subjected yesterday to further selling pressure in circumstances that served to intensify the mood of discouragement in Wall Street. Measured by points, the decline on the Stock Exchange was of only moderate scope—running from 1 to 3 points among the more prominent issues—but gauged on the basis of percentages the fall was quite sharp."
–New York Times

June 6, 1932
Congress Prepares for 2-Week Battle
"A week, or possibly a fortnight, of bitter controversy faced Congress tonight with the paramount legislative questions of taxes, economy, relief and possibly the bonus to be settled."
–New York Times

June 26, 1932
Hoover 'Wrong,' Say Relief Bill Backers
"Aroused by the President's criticism of his unemployment relief bill because of the $500,000,000 appropriated in it for public works, Senator Wagner today delivered a final plea for the measure as it was taken up by a conference of members of the House and Senate."
–New York Times

**News &
Federal Reserve Bulletin**

July 3, 1932
*Convention Throng Hails Roosevelt;
Tremendous Ovation for the Nominee Rings
Out*
–New York Times

July 24, 1932
Roosevelt to Wage Fight in Every State
"Predicting that Governor Franklin D. Roosevelt
would be elected by a greater electoral college
majority than any Democratic candidate for
President except Woodrow Wilson in 1912, James
A. Farley, chairman of the Democratic National
Committee, declared yesterday that he regarded
no State, no matter how strongly Republican in
past elections, lost to the Democratic national
ticket this year."
–New York Times

August 1932
Emergency Relief Bill
"New legislation relating to the reserve banks and
member banks has been the principal
development in the banking situation in recent
weeks. On July 21 the President signed the
emergency relief and construction act of 1932, the
text of which is published elsewhere in this issue.
This act authorizes the Reconstruction Finance
Corporation, under certain conditions, to make
available to States and Territories for the relief of
distress a total of not to exceed $300,000,000, the
amount advanced by the corporation to bear
interest at the rate of 3 per cent. It further
provides for loans by the corporation to States and
other political bodies or agencies, and to private
corporations, for self-liquidating projects of a
public or semipublic nature, such as bridges,
tunnels, docks, and housing facilities in slum
areas."
–Federal Reserve Bulletin

September 2, 1932
*Big Gain by Stocks Recorded in Month; 240
Issues on Exchange Rise $4,041,656,665,
Sharpest Advance in Three Years*
–New York Times

September 10, 1932
*Nation's Bank Clearings Up 3.6% in a Month
Due to Increase of 8.4% in Exchanges Here*
–New York Times

September 29, 1932
*Stocks of Money Larger in August; Treasury
Department Reports Increase of
$136,311,347—Gold Up $113,912,811*
–New York Times

October 10, 1932
*Hoover "Failures" Listed by Ritchie; Farm and
Tariff Relief, Prohibition and Balanced Budget
Unsolved, Governor Charges*
"Declaring that President Hoover had 'failed to
solve the four major problems' of his
administration, Governor Ritchie of Maryland
opened tonight with a speech to 2,000
Connecticut Democrats his New England
campaign tour for the Roosevelt-Garner ticket."
–New York Times

October 26, 1932
*Copeland Assails Banking "Oligarchy";
Senator Says Hoover Permits Financiers to
Impede Our Economic Recovery*
"United States Senator Royal S. Copeland of New
York, addressing a Democratic rally here tonight,
declared it was no credit to big banking interests
to boast they were '85 per cent liquid'—the boast
being as cruel as the statement of a hospital
showing 85 per cent of its beds empty, when
1,000 patients clamored for admission.'"
–New York Times

Social unrest and conflict continued to rise globally. In Germany, Hitler won the most seats in the Reichstag election. Japan slipped toward militarism, invading Manchuria in 1931 and Shanghai in 1932. In the US, strikes and protests were also increasing.[148] Unemployment was approaching 25 percent, and those still employed faced wage cuts. Outside of cities, farmers faced ruin as prices fell and a drought destroyed their crops. In one dramatic expression of discontent, thousands of veterans and their families had marched on Washington in June (and stayed there) in an attempt to pressure the government to immediately pay them their veterans' bonuses.[149] On July 28, US Army troops led by General Douglas MacArthur cleared the camp with tanks and tear gas. It was at this time that conflicts both within countries and between countries intensified, sowing the seeds of populism, authoritarianism, nationalism, and militarism that at first led to economic warfare and then military warfare in Europe in September 1939 and with Japan in December 1941.

Second Half of 1932: Further Contractions and the Election of FDR

By the summer, the big stimulation and relief to banks appeared to be helping. The downward spiral began to moderate, asset prices stabilized, and production actually increased in certain areas of the economy, like autos. From May through June, commodities, stocks, and bonds all bottomed. Markets for both stocks and bonds improved during the second half of the year. In August and September, the Dow Jones Industrial Average rallied to a peak of 80, almost double its July low. You can see trajectory of the Dow in the chart below.

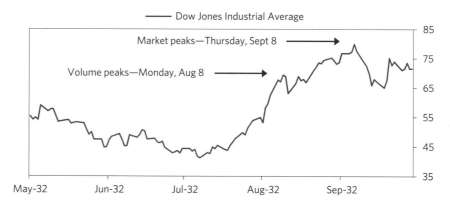

Time magazine's August 8, 1932, edition claimed that the rally occurred because the gold outflow had finally ceased, rumors had spread about the country receiving foreign capital, and a railroad merger had been approved.

As optimism about the economy and asset markets began to increase, policy makers began to pull back on their earlier stimulative measures. Also, the RFC was weakened significantly by a scandal when it bailed out Central Republic Bank and Trust, which was headed by the previous chair of the RFC. The public was outraged—the RFC now seemed like a tool of fat-cat bankers.[150] In response, Congress ordered the RFC to publish the names of all the institutions to which they had lent.[151] This effectively meant that getting a loan from the RFC also required advertising that you were in trouble, which of course worsened pressure from depositor withdrawals. Borrowing from the RFC slowed, and withdrawals began to pick up pace.[152]

Outrage over the government's role in "bailing out" financial institutions is one outgrowth of the "Main Street versus Wall Street," or "workers versus investors" conflicts that classically occur during depressions. As economic pain increases, populist calls to "punish the bankers that caused this mess" make it incredibly difficult for policy makers to take the actions that are needed to save the financial system and the economy. After all, if the bankers quit in this chaos, the system would certainly shut down.

Politics also played a part in ending the Fed's purchases of government bonds. The Banking Act passed in February had been framed as a temporary measure due to concerns that it might weaken the dollar. Members of the Federal Reserve from Chicago, Philadelphia, and Boston pushed for ending open market operations, arguing that since banks were accumulating increasing reserves but not significantly expanding credit, the program was not necessary (and the lower long-term interest rates from the program were hurting bank profitability). In July they stopped participating, and the New York Fed, unable to continue on its own, was forced to acquiesce.[153]

The administration was worried about the budget deficit ballooning, as receipts fell and expenditures rose.[154] **With almost universal support, Hoover pushed to balance the budget through a mix of tax increases and cuts to federal expenditures.**[155] On June 6, the Revenue Act of 1932 was signed into law. The act increased income taxes, corporation taxes, and various excise taxes. But despite these efforts, the budget deficit grew significantly relative to GDP because the austerity was contractionary and the economy shrank faster than the budget deficit did.[156] **As mentioned earlier, Hoover's attempt to balance the budget through austerity was a rookie move that is classic in depressions.**

As is also classic in deleveraging scenarios, the debate about what to do became antagonistically political, with strong populist overtones. Roosevelt came on the scene with what, at the time, seemed like leftist populist policies. From the outset his presidential campaign struck a strongly anti-speculator tone. It opened with a speech that railed against securities firms' abuses and called for federal control of the stock and commodities exchanges.[157] There were indications that he favored a devaluation of the dollar, which increased the pressure on the currency. To allay those fears, Roosevelt said he would not take the country off the gold standard, but investors were not convinced.[158] **By the way, politicians and policy makers frequently make disingenuous promises that are expedient and inconsistent with economic and market fundamentals, and such promises should never be believed.**

Bank failures were ticking upward, open market operations had ended, the RFC had been neutered, government spending had been reined in, and the threat of devaluation loomed large. Gold outflows resumed and prices, which had recently begun to stabilize, started to fall. The economy's downward trajectory steepened.

The renewed pressure on the banking sector moved into higher gear in November. Right before the election, Nevada declared the first statewide bank holiday, a classic response to widespread bank runs. Although Nevada was able

News & Federal Reserve Bulletin

November 2, 1932
Nevada Declares a 12-Day Bank Holiday; Low Live-Stock Prices Bring Crisis in State
"A business and bank holiday extending until Nov. 12 was declared throughout the State of Nevada today by Lt. Gov. Morley Griswold, acting in the absence of Governor Fred B. Balzar, who is in Washington."
–New York Times

November 2, 1932
46,965,230 Voters Register in Nation; Figure Is 10,166,561 Above the Record Poll Cast in the Election of 1928
–New York Times

November 6, 1932
Election of Hoover Sure, Sanders Says; A "Veritable Stampede" to the President Is Reported by Republican Chairman
"Everett Sanders, chairman of the Republican National Committee and director of the Hoover campaign, in a pre-election statement made public yesterday simultaneously in this city and in Chicago, declared that President Hoover would emerge a winner from Tuesday's election with a 'bedrock margin' of 281 electoral votes and at least twenty-one States in his column."
–New York Times

November 7, 1932
Election Is Key to New Financing; Mills Is Expected to Push Consolidation of Public Debt if Hoover Loses
–New York Times

November 9, 1932
President Is Calm in Admitting Defeat; Stanford Students Serenade Him as He Is Telegraphing to Roosevelt
"President Hoover conceded his defeat in a telegram of congratulations to Governor Roosevelt tonight just as students of Stanford University had gathered before the Hoover home to serenade him and Mrs. Hoover as they did four years ago when the election went Republican."
–New York Times

November 9, 1932
Roosevelt Pledges Effort to Restore Prosperity; Formal Statement Awaits Final Returns
–New York Times

November 11, 1932
Banker Denies Peril to Gold Standard; B.M. Anderson Jr. Says This Country Never Was Near Discarding It
"At no time in the last thirty-six years has there been justifiable ground for doubt as to the ability of this country to maintain the gold standard, Benjamin M. Anderson Jr., economist of the Chase National Bank, declared yesterday in an address before the forum on investment banking of the Graduate School of Business Administration of New York University."
–New York Times

**News &
Federal Reserve Bulletin**

November 23, 1932
**_Three Big Issues Debated at Geneva;
Manchuria, Disarmament and Depression
Absorb Delegates, with Davis Taking Part_**
"The Manchurian question, the world economic
conference and world disarmament became
intermingled in confusing fashion at meetings of
statesmen here today, with Norman H. Davis,
representative of the Washington State
Department, involved in the discussion of all
three."
—_New York Times_

December 1, 1932
**_Three Records Set in Nov. 8 Elections; Poll
Was Highest for Nation, While Roosevelt Got
Most for Winner, Hoover for a Loser_**
"Nearly complete returns from the Nov. 8
elections show that the American electorate made
three new records in casting a total of at least
39,000,000 votes and giving Governor Roosevelt
22,314,023 and President Hoover 15,574,474."
—_New York Times_

December 12, 1932
**_Holds Our Tariffs Key to Depression; German
Professor Says Issue Depends on Whether We
Lower Barriers_**
"The world will never get out of the depression
unless and until the United States lowers her
tariff barriers, according to Professor Felix
Bernstein, director of the Institute of Statistics of
Goettingen University and an adviser to the
German Government on social insurance,
taxation and other financial matters."
—_New York Times_

December 15, 1932
Nevada Ends Bank Holiday
—_New York Times_

to avert the failure of its main state bank, the holiday sparked a national panic.[159] Fearing that their bank might be next, depositors accelerated their withdrawals. Crisis dynamics were beginning to return.

The collapse of the economy throughout 1932 was breathtaking. The charts below show some of the economic stats, highlighting the period from sterling's devaluation until the end of 1932. Consumer spending and production fell by more than 20 percent and unemployment rose by more than 16 percent. Severe deflation had taken hold and prices were falling by almost one percent every month.

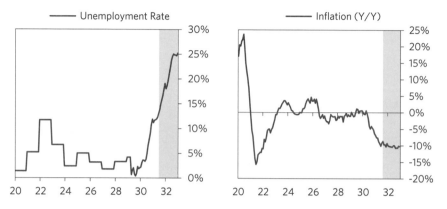

Policy makers' reliance on the deflationary levers of debt reduction had pushed the US into a severe depression/"ugly deleveraging." Since nominal interest rates were well above nominal growth rates, debt grew faster than income and debt burdens rose despite defaults.

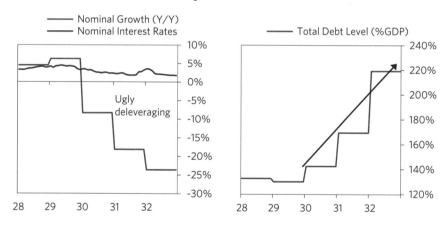

But while investors were worried about the effects of a Roosevelt presidency, the populist nature of his campaign (along with the terrible economic conditions) propelled him to victory. Roosevelt was elected in November 1932, winning 22.8 million votes against Hoover's 15.8 million, the most popular votes ever won by a presidential candidate up to that time.

Driven by weak economic conditions, an uneven recovery (in which the elite was perceived to be prospering while the common man was still struggling), and ineffectual policy makers, populism was a global phenomenon in the interwar period (the 1920s to the 1930s), leading to regime changes not only in the United States, but also in Germany, Italy, and Spain. In the United States, inequality (in both income and wealth shares) peaked in the early 1930s, but remained high for the rest of the decade. By the time of Roosevelt's election, the top 10 percent earned 45 percent of the income and owned 85 percent of the wealth while unemployment was over 20 percent. These conditions caused FDR to base his campaign on a "New Deal," which promised big changes for workers, debtors, and the unemployed.[160]

Europe had a similar set of economic conditions. Germany had experienced both a hyperinflation and the start of the Great Depression in the prior fifteen years. Inequality was also high—the top 10 percent earned about 40 percent of the income, while unemployment was over 25 percent. This set the stage for the Nazi party's ascent.[161]

1933: Preinauguration

Gold continued to flow out of the country in anticipation of Roosevelt's reflationary policies, and Roosevelt now refused to reaffirm his commitment to the gold standard. Those around him attempted to persuade him to reassure the markets. Senator Carter Glass, who was Roosevelt's likely nominee for Secretary of the Treasury, declared that he would not accept the post if Roosevelt could not guarantee the country would stay on the gold standard.[162] Hoover wrote a personal letter to Roosevelt, requesting that he clarify his policies.[163] European investors in the dollar were worried: From Paris, the *New York Times* reported that "the confusion of mind in Europe's markets concerning the future tendency of the dollar must be ascribed to lack of information regarding the definite intentions of the new American government. Declaration by Mr. Roosevelt declaring firm resolution to maintain a sound currency would have an extremely reassuring effect." But Roosevelt stayed silent.[164]

In February, the crisis deepened. Facing bankruptcy, the Guardian Detroit Union Group, the largest financial institution in Michigan, sought a loan from the RFC. The group had little good collateral, so the RFC could not, under its mandate, offer it a large loan. Perhaps more importantly, the main shareholder of the Guardian Group was auto millionaire Henry Ford. Not wanting the appearance of doing more favors for fat-cats, the RFC suggested that it could make a loan if Ford also provided some support. But Ford, recognizing that the Guardian Trust was as systemically important as the Central Republic, refused. His attempt to call the RFC's bluff failed. The Union Guardian Trust and Guardian National Bank of Commerce, two of the Guardian Group's banks, were allowed to go bankrupt and Michigan was forced to declare a statewide bank holiday.[165]

When policy makers fail to rescue systemically important institutions, the ripple effects can quickly spread to the whole system. Since Michigan was part of America's industrial heartland, the impact on other states was especially large.[166] Households and companies rushed to withdraw their savings from banks across the country. Ohio, Arkansas, and Indiana suffered bank runs. Maryland declared a bank holiday on February 25, and by March 4, there were withdrawal restrictions in over 30 states.[167]

The flow of gold out of the country turned into a wave. In the last two weeks of February, the New York Fed lost $250 million, almost a quarter of its gold reserves.[168]

News & Federal Reserve Bulletin

January 1933
Current Banking Developments
"Demand upon the reserve banks for currency in connection with holiday trade this year was about $120,000,000, compared with $225,000,000 to $275,000,000 in other recent years. This decreased demand for currency reflected both a diminished dollar volume of retail trade, due chiefly to the prevailing lower level of prices, and a continued return of currency from hoarding. The demand for currency did not result this year, as it usually does, in an increase in the outstanding volume of reserve bank credit, since additions of about $150,000,000 of gold to the country's monetary stock were more than sufficient to provide to member banks the funds necessary for meeting currency withdrawals."
–Federal Reserve Bulletin

February 1, 1933
Britain Buys Back $13,588,900 Gold; Federal Reserve Sells Final Portion of Sum Earmarked in War Payment
"The Federal Reserve Bank of New York sold yesterday to the Bank of England $13,588,900 of gold, consisting of the remaining portion of the $95,550,000 of bullion earmarked in London for the account of the local Reserve Bank on Dec. 15 in connection with Great Britain's payment of her war-debt instalment. [sic]"
–New York Times

February 1, 1933
Retail Failures Higher; Other Groups Show Drop in Week, Bradstreet's Reports
"An increase in retail failures from 404 to 417 featured business defaults for the week ended Jan. 26, according to Bradstreet's. Each of the other classifications showed a decline. The total number of failures for the week was 605, against 618 in the preceding week."
New York Times

February 4, 1933
Gold Supply Declines; $872,600 from Holland Offset by $3,670,000 in Earmarkings
–New York Times

February 8, 1933
Gold Supply Lower by $1,601,500 in Day
–New York Times

February 15, 1933
Retail Failures Up; Other Groups Are Lower for Week, Bradstreet's Reports
"Despite declines in all other classifications, the number of retail failures showed an increase during the week ended Feb. 9, according to Bradstreet's. The store defaults totaled 376, against 353 in the preceding week. The total number of failures was 509, which compares with 567 in the previous week."
–New York Times

News &
Federal Reserve Bulletin

February 15, 1933
Cash Rushed to Relieve Michigan
"With the exception of a few banks in the Upper Peninsula, all banks in Michigan were closed today following Governor William A. Comstock's early morning proclamation declaring an eight-day moratorium for the State's 550 financial institutions."
–*New York Times*

February 24, 1933
Decline Is Resumed on the Stock Exchange, with Acute Unsettlement Taking Place in Bonds
"While the Michigan banking situation showed some signs of improvement yesterday as business was resumed in that State under drastic restrictions, the security markets chose to reflect Wall Street's somber mood and there was a sharp downward revision of quoted values."
–*New York Times*

February 27, 1933
Aspects of an Unsettled Week—The Currency Talk and the New Executive
"The unsettlement of last week's stock market, the recurrent weakness in the bond market, and the indication that hoarding of currency had increased resulted partly from the not very skillfully handled Michigan episode, but they equally reflected the mental influence of the mischievous talk of experimenting with the currency."
–*New York Times*

March 1933
State Bank Holidays
"During the month of February and the first few days of March, banking difficulties in different parts of the country caused the governors and legislatures of many States temporarily to close the banks in those States or to impose or authorize restrictions upon their operations. On the morning of February 14 the Governor of Michigan declared a bank holiday to February 21, 'for the preservation of the public peace, health, and safety, and for the equal safeguarding without preference of the rights of all depositors.' This holiday in Michigan was extended, in effect, on February 21, and on February 25 a bank holiday was declared in Maryland, followed within a few days by similar action in a large number of other States. On February 25, a joint resolution was adopted by the Congress of the United States authorizing the Comptroller of the Currency to exercise with respect to national banks such powers as State officials may have with respect to State banks."
–*Federal Reserve Bulletin*

March 1933
National Summary of Business Conditions
"Volume of industrial production increased in January by less than the usual seasonal amount, and factory employment and pay rolls continued to decline. Prices of commodities at wholesale, which declined further in January, showed relatively little change in the first three weeks of February."
–*Federal Reserve Bulletin*

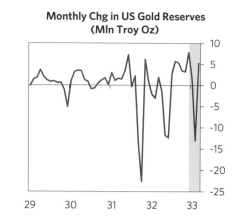

Monthly Chg in US Gold Reserves
(Mln Troy Oz)

In the face of this pressure on gold reserves, Hoover attempted to invoke the War Powers Act and introduce capital controls, a classic but ineffective response to balance of payments pressures, but the Democrats would not allow it.[169]

The economy suffered enormously. In March, business had slowed to a shocking extent. That year, the Gross National Product hit its lowest point in the entire period of the depression at $55.6 billion, which was 31.5 percent below its 1929 level in constant dollar terms.[170]

1933–1937: The Beautiful Deleveraging

1933–1934: Roosevelt Leaves the Gold Standard; the Economy Moves to a Beautiful Deleveraging

On Sunday, March 5, the day after he took office, Roosevelt declared a national four-day bank holiday, suspended gold exports (effectively delinking the dollar from gold), and set a team to work on rescuing the banking system. **It was a scramble to get as much done as possible in as short a time as possible.**

From the New York Times,6 March © 1933 The New York Times. All rights reserved. Used by permission and protection by the Copyright Laws of the United States. The printing, copying redistribution, or retransmission of this Content without express written permission is prohibited.

Before the banks were set to reopen on March 9, Congress passed the Emergency Banking Act of 1933. The act extended the bank holiday and gave the Fed and the Treasury unprecedented powers to provide liquidity and capital to the banking system. Most important, the act granted the Fed the ability to issue dollars that were backed by bank assets instead of gold, which broke the link between the dollar and gold and **allowed the Fed to print money and provide the liquidity that banks desperately needed.** So that the Fed could print money without facing a run on its gold reserves, Roosevelt banned gold exports under the 1917 Trading with the Enemy Act.[171]

Auditors began to work through the books of each US bank, starting with the largest banks and those known to be the safest. When auditors found a bank that was undercapitalized, they could either (a) recapitalize the bank by having the RFC issue preferred shares, (b) merge it with a healthier bank, or (c) close it. **Systemically important banks were always supported, while smaller banks were often allowed to fail.** Once auditors decided that a bank was sound, it would reopen with the ability to borrow from the Fed using any of its assets as collateral.[172] As part of the Banking Act of 1933, the Treasury agreed to cover any losses the Fed incurred, effectively **guaranteeing the liabilities of every bank that they chose to keep open.**[173]

On Sunday, March 12, the night before the first wave of banks was set to reopen, Roosevelt gave a nationwide radio address explaining the plan for the banks and seeking to restore trust in the banking system:

> *The new law allows the twelve Federal Reserve Banks to issue additional currency on good assets and thus the banks which reopen will be able to meet every legitimate call…It is sound currency because it is backed by actual, good assets…I can assure you that it is safer to keep your money in a reopened bank than under the mattress.*[174]

As banks in twelve cities prepared to open on Monday, policy makers and investors waited nervously to see how the public would respond. Instead of bank runs, the public proceeded to deposit more than $1 billion into the banks, which is a classic example of how debt and liquidity problems prompted by runs can be rectified by providing liquidity rather than holding it back. Banks continued to reopen in the days that followed, and within a month member banks representing 90 percent of the deposits in the system had reopened.[175] When markets finally opened on Wednesday, the Dow rose 15.3 percent and commodities also soared.

To get all that money, the link to gold had to be broken. But with all that printing, the dollar's value plunged against both other currencies and gold. This was virtually identical to what happened in August 1971, when I was clerking on the floor of the New York Stock Exchange and thought that the crisis would send the stock market and economy down. What happened was the same as what happened in 1933, and for the same reasons, but I hadn't studied what happened in 1933, so I was painfully wrong. That was the first time that I was surprised by events that hadn't happened in my lifetime but had happened many times in history. Being stung by these experiences drove me to try to understand all big market and economic movements in all time frames and all economies and to have timeless and universal principles for dealing with them. That saved my butt a number of times (e.g., in 2008). The events I am describing to you that happened in the 1930s have happened many times before for the exact same reasons.

News & Federal Reserve Bulletin

March 3, 1933
President to Ask Bank Legislation; Will Send Emergency Message Today
"Leaders of the Hoover administration and the new Roosevelt regime conferred last night and into the early morning hours today on the country's troubled banking situation, but with no tangible result."
–*New York Times*

March 5, 1933
"Business as Usual" Pledged in Crisis; Bank Holiday Not to Halt Trade, Wholesalers and Producers Are Agreed
"Faced by a nation-wide shutdown of banking facilities tomorrow and possibly for a good part of this week, manufacturers and wholesalers in the local markets indicated yesterday that they would attempt to continue business as usual, checking credits according to previous performances of customers."
–*New York Times*

March 5, 1933
Exchanges Close for Bank Holiday; All Trading Is Suspended for Third Time in History—Entire Nation Affected
"As a result of the declaration of the two-day bank holiday in this State, the New York Stock Exchange and all other security and commodity exchanges in New York City closed yesterday for the duration of the bank holiday. It was the third time in the history of the Stock Exchange that trading was suspended because of widespread unsettlement."
–*New York Times*

March 6, 1933
Banks Here Act At Once; City Scrip to Be Ready Today or Tomorrow to Replace Currency
–*New York Times*

March 7, 1933
Roosevelt Sums Up Task To Governors, Emergency Banking, with Deposits Safeguarded, Must Be Devised, He Says
"President Roosevelt met Governors and their representatives at the White House today and discussed with them measures of relief and ways of meeting the banking situation. The President did not make any definite suggestions on national policies to be carried out in the States, or indicate what his recommendations would be to Congress when it meets on Thursday."
–*New York Times*

March 7, 1933
Business Backs Scrip
–*New York Times*

March 10, 1933
Bank Bill Is Enacted; Emergency Program Put Through in Record Time of 71-2 Hours
"A record for Executive and legislative action was written today in the effort of the nation to end its banking difficulties, but progress was partly checked tonight by the inability of an administrative arm of the government to keep pace."
–*New York Times*

March 12, 1933
Exchanges Weigh Plan to Reopen; Brokers, Expecting a Brisk Demand for Stock, Hope for Full Day's Notice
"The New York Stock Exchange ended yesterday its first week of enforced inactivity since 1914 without any indication as to when trading would be resumed. None of the other security or commodity markets here have yet set a date for reopening, but the New York Cocoa Exchange announced that the board of managers had voted to extend the holiday up to and including next Tuesday."
–*New York Times*

News &
Federal Reserve Bulletin

March 12, 1933
Hopeful Feeling Marks Business; Industry Ready for Revival of Production When the Banks Reopen
—*New York Times*

March 15, 1933
Business Will Be Reopened as Usual on the Stock Exchange This Morning—Banks Continue to Resume
"Banks continued yesterday to reopen as financial confidence was restored. The resumption was on such a broad scale that business was almost on a normal basis. The security and commodity markets will start operating this morning, with the exception of the Chicago Board of Trade and the New York Cotton Exchange."
—*New York Times*

March 16, 1933
798 Banks in State Reopened in Full; End of National Holiday Finds 80% Licensed, with Most of Others Merely Delayed. All Savings Banks Open
"The banking holiday came to an end in State and nation yesterday, and business once more could be transacted with checking privileges on a nation-wide basis."
—*New York Times*

March 16, 1933
Banks Over Nation Approach Normal; Reopenings Continue in All the States as Authorities Speed Restoration
—*New York Times*

April 1933
National Summary of Business Conditions
"The course of business in the latter part of February and the first half of March was largely influenced by the development of a crisis in banking, culminating in the proclamation on March 6 of a national banking holiday by the President of the United States. Production and distribution of commodities declined by a substantial amount during this period, but showed some increase after banking operations were resumed in the middle of March."
—*Federal Reserve Bulletin*

April 22, 1933
House Nearing End of Roosevelt Bills; Leaders Say Action on Administration Measures Will Be Completed This Week
"The Democrats in the House expect to catch up with President Roosevelt's program before the end of next week. When the House adjourns Friday or Saturday all the Roosevelt measures new before it will have been disposed of, if the plans of the leaders materialize, and all the indications are that they will."
—*New York Times*

April 25, 1933
Roosevelt Ends Stalemate Over Bank Bill; Asks $10,000 Limit on Deposit Guarantee
"Banking reform legislation took on new life today when President Roosevelt unexpectedly paused in the midst of his international negotiations to discuss the Glass bill with the Senate Banking subcommittee for an hour."
—*New York Times*

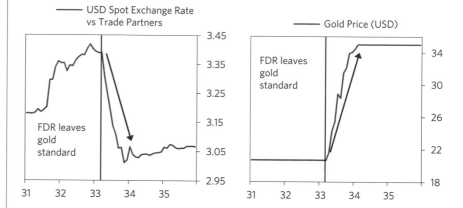

Within two weeks of leaving the gold peg, the Federal Reserve was able to decrease its liquidity injections; short-term rates decreased by one percent to two percent, bankers' acceptance rates dropped back to two percent, and call loan rates decreased to three percent.[176] The money supply increased by 1.5 percent over the next three months, and the Dow was up by almost 100 percent over the next four months. These moves ended the depression on a dime. (Most people mistakenly think that the depression lasted through the 1930s until World War II so I want to be clear on what actually happened. It is correct that it took until 1936 for GDP to match its 1929 peak. But when you look at the numbers in the charts below, you can see that leaving the gold peg was the turning point; it was exactly then that all markets and economic statistics bottomed. Still, these average numbers can be misleading because the recovery benefited the rich more than the poor, and the post-1933 period remained more difficult for a lot of people than the averages suggest, which is likely why people often think of the depression as lasting through the entire decade.)

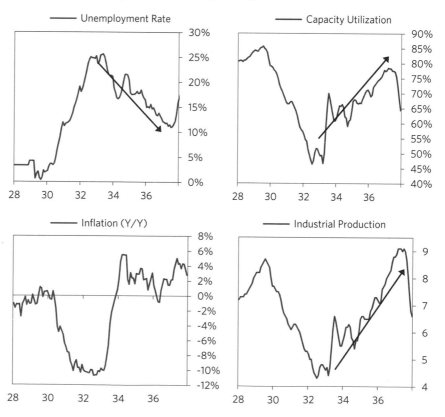

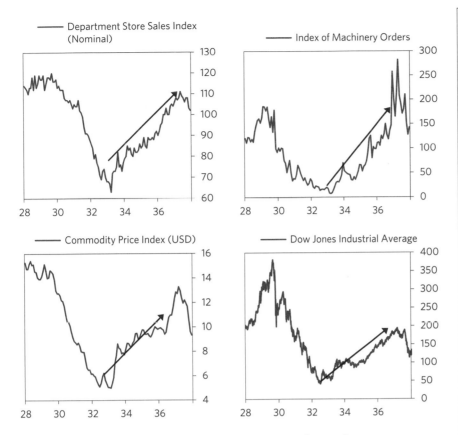

— Department Store Sales Index (Nominal)

— Index of Machinery Orders

— Commodity Price Index (USD)

— Dow Jones Industrial Average

While leaving the gold standard, printing money, and providing guarantees were by far the most impactful policy moves that Roosevelt made, they were just the first of an avalanche of policies that were unrolled during his first six months in office. The shock and awe of all those big announcements of spending, coming week after week, built confidence among investors and the public, which was critical to putting the economy on a good footing. I'll describe some of those policies below, not because the particulars are all that important, but because together they paint the picture of a bold, multifaceted, and comprehensive policy push.

While they were still working to shore up the banks, policy makers **shifted their attentions to significantly increasing financial industry regulation and oversight. Changing laws in ways that would have made the last crisis less bad are typical at the end of big debt crises.** When you read through them, focus on how they map to the template for handling debt problems.

- *April 5 and 18*: Roosevelt took additional steps to delink the dollar from gold. First he outlawed ownership of monetary gold by the public through an executive order. Two weeks later, he outlawed private gold exports and indicated support for legislation that would allow him to set the price of gold.[177] (**devaluing and printing money**)

- *May 27*: Congress enacted the Securities Act of 1933, which would regulate the sale of securities.[178] (**increased regulation**)

- *June 5*: Congress banned the relatively common "Gold Clauses" in contracts, a provision that allowed the payee to opt to be paid in gold. Since gold had increased in value after the dollar was delinked from it, this amounted to a big restructuring of debts.[179] (**restructuring debts**)

News & Federal Reserve Bulletin

April 30, 1933
Roosevelt to Seek Power to Cut Debts; He Will Ask Congress for Such Authority and Explain World's Economic Needs
"President Roosevelt, in one of the three remaining messages he will send to Congress soon, will ask for specific authority during the recess of Congress to deal individually with debtor nations with the idea of reducing war debts."
–New York Times

April 30, 1933
Roosevelt Speeds Colossal Program of Public Works; White House Conference Gets Draft of Bill—May Total $2,000,000,000 in Year
"Plans for a public works program, which will be integrated with a plan for national industrial recovery, were 'speeded up' at a White House conference today. It is expected that the...program will be completed in about a week."
–New York Times

May 1, 1933
1 1/4 Billion Sought for Construction; Public and Private Projects Financed by R.F.C. Urged Upon Roosevelt by Council
"A program of public and private construction for estimated outlays of about $1,250,000,000, much of which would be financed by advances from the Reconstruction Finance Corporation, has been placed before President Roosevelt by the American Construction Council, an organization of which Mr. Roosevelt was president from 1922 to 1929."
–New York Times

May 5, 1933
2-Month Record Set by Roosevelt; He Starts Third with Some of Major Problems Solved and Others Yielding. 14,000 Banks Reopened
"President Roosevelt began the third month of his administration today, celebrating 'the occasion' by sending to Congress his plan for an emergency reorganization of the railroads, followed by a conference at the White House with banking and currency experts to perfect his plan for a more permanent solution of the banking problem."
–New York Times

May 14, 1933
Recovery Measure Before Roosevelt in Night Council; He Will Study Proposal, Including Re-Employment Tax
–New York Times

May 28, 1933
Roosevelt Signs the Securities Bill; President Hails the New Law as Step to "Old-Fashioned Standards"
–New York Times

June 1933
National Summary of Business Conditions
"Industrial activity increased considerably during April and the first 3 weeks of May and wholesale prices of many leading commodities advanced, particularly in the latter part of April and the early part of May. Following the imposition of an embargo on gold on April 20 the exchange value of the dollar declined and on May 20 was 87 percent of its gold parity."
–Federal Reserve Bulletin

June 5, 1933
Cities Urged to Push Public Works Plans; Head of Recovery Committee Advises Speed in Asking for Federal Aid
–New York Times

**News &
Federal Reserve Bulletin**

June 23, 1933
Public Works Policies Outlined
"In its third long afternoon conference, the Cabinet board, headed by Secretary Ickes, discussed ways of pushing out over the country the $3,000,000 construction fund."
—New York Times

July 3, 1933
Recovery Program Rounds Into Shape; Swift Accord on First Code Was Reached in Spirit Rate in Trade Annals. Two Policies Emerge: 40-Hour Week, $12 Pay Not Model, and Mass-Hiring of Men Will Not Be Forced
—New York Times

July 9, 1933
Lake States See Signs of Revival; Wisconsin Finds Marked Decline in Unemployment Dependency
"In that region that skirts the western shore of Lake Michigan, and bends around its southern end, there are signs of returning prosperity. That is to say, although the almost forgotten features of the goddess who carries an overflowing cornucopia beneath her arm are not as yet clearly discernible, a form resembling her once familiar figure can be seen approaching."
—New York Times

July 27, 1933
Stocks Make Partial Recovery in Cautious Dealings—Agricultural Commodities Advance Widely
"Encouraged by the Industrial progress shown in the reports of important companies, the share market moved confidently upward yesterday but in trading that fell far short of the daily average of the last few weeks."
—New York Times

January 21, 1934
Rise in Production Cheers Steel Men; Rapid Recovery from Year-End Dip Leads Trade to Greater Optimism on Near Future
"Production of steel ingots last week was reported at 34.2 per cent of capacity by the American Iron and Steel Institute, representing a rise of 3.5 points, or 11 per cent, over the previous week. It equaled the rate reported for the week ended on Dec. 23, and there had been no higher rate since late in October."
—New York Times

April 16, 1934
Price Rise to Spur Steel Operations; Production Rate for This Quarter Forecast as the Largest Since 1930
"While the official forecast of production of steel ingots for last week was 47.4 per cent of capacity, estimates made at the end of the week were that production had been close to 50 per cent. The forecast was the highest since the series was begun last October, except that for the week ended on March 10, which was 47.7 per cent."
—New York Times

November 27, 1934
Financial Markets; Stocks Reach New High Levels for Present Recovery—Domestic Bonds Also Show Improvement
"Stocks and bonds continued yesterday to reflect returning confidence in the general business position. The share market went into new high ground for the current movement, with well distributed gains of 1 to 2 points or more, while domestic corporation bonds showed further improvement under the leadership of specially favored industrial and railway issues."
—New York Times

- *June 13*: The Home Owner's Loan Act established the Home Owner's Loan Corporation (HOLC) to assist in the refinancing of residential mortgages. Between 1933 and 1935, one million people received long term loans through the agency.[180] (**restructuring debts**)

- *June 16*: The Banking Act of 1933 (i.e., Glass-Stegall II) provided deposit insurance of up to $2,500 through the newly formed Federal Deposit Insurance Corporation (FDIC). It also empowered the Fed to regulate interest rates on demand and savings deposits (Regulation Q); set forth stringent regulations for banks; and required the separation of investment and commercial banking functions.[181] (**establish deposit insurance, increased regulation**)

Roosevelt also announced new federal agencies and programs that added up to an unprecedented fiscal stimulus. Federal spending had fallen by more than $1 billion in 1932 as Hoover tightened fiscal policy in an attempt to balance the budget. Even though he initially campaigned to balance the budget, FDR's policies would end up increasing annual spending by $2.7 billion (5 percent of GDP) by 1934. These are some of the early stimulus bills:

- *April 5*: Established the Civilian Conservation Corps (CCC), which would employ 2.5 million people in public works projects over its nine years of existence.[182]

- *May 12*: Established the Federal Emergency Relief Act to provide financial support to households with an initial funding of $500 million.[183]

- *May 18*: The Tennessee Valley Authority (TVA) undertook massive infrastructure investment, providing power, flood control, and irrigation in one of the regions most affected by the Great Depression.[184]

- *June 16*: The National Industrial Recovery Act (NIRA) created the Public Works Administration (PWA), which had $3.3 billion at its disposal to spend on large-scale public works. [185]

As a result of all of this stimulation, deflation turned into acceptable rather than horrible inflation.

As explained in the "Archetypal Long-Term Debt Cycle" section, balance is key in achieving a "beautiful deleveraging": Deleveragings become beautiful when there is enough stimulation to offset the deflationary forces and to bring the nominal growth rate above the nominal interest rate.

The economy roared to life over the next three months as terribly depressed levels of activity quickly became less terrible. Heavy machinery orders climbed by 100 percent, and industrial production increased by almost 50 percent. Between March and July nondurable manufacturing production increased 35 percent while durable manufacturing increased 83 percent. Unemployment fell and over the next three months, wholesale prices jumped by 45 percent.[186] **These were all rebounding from very depressed levels and fed on themselves to make a beautiful deleveraging.**

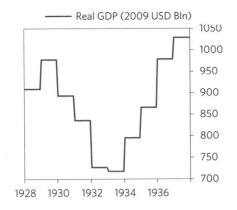

Real GDP (2009 USD Bln)

Note how the level of GDP growth was above the level of interest rates.

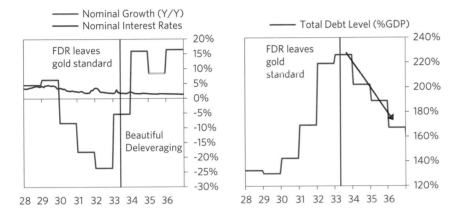

1935: The Goldilocks Period

The economy and the markets continued to recover through 1934 and into 1935, when the Federal Reserve began contemplating tightening once again. By 1935 the economy had recovered, deflation had disappeared, and stock prices had soared as a result of the Fed's earlier policies. At the time, home prices were rising faster than 10 percent per year, and the recovery in equity prices was even faster. The boost to wealth was big, though wealth and economic output remained below pre-depression, bubble levels.

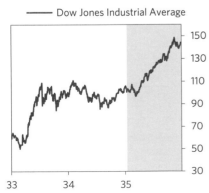

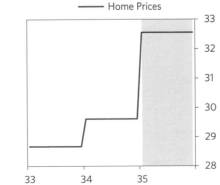

News & Federal Reserve Bulletin

December 24, 1934
Roper Cites Spurt in Business Lines; Commerce Report to Roosevelt Lists Ten Fields in Which Recovery Has Advanced
"The past fiscal year saw definite improvement in the business and financial state of the nation, Secretary Roper informed the President today in his annual report as head of the Department of Commerce."
–New York Times

January 11, 1935
Banks' Funds Rise to New High Level
"Under the seasonal influence of a return flow of currency from circulation, coupled with the further disbursement of Treasury funds and a continued rise in monetary gold stocks, excess reserves of member banks of the Federal Reserve System rose to about $1,990,000,000 in the week ended on Wednesday, according to the weekly report of the Federal Reserve System, published yesterday."
–New York Times

April 7, 1935
Deposits in Banks Now $50,000,000,000
"Based on figures compiled by the Federal Deposit Insurance Corporation today, the deposits of all banks in the United States at the end of December were estimated at close to $50,000,000,000, an approximate gain of over $3,000,000,000 in six months."
–New York Times

May 23, 1935
Cash Circulation $135,000,000 Higher
"Largely because retail trade and payrolls expanded more than seasonally, currency in circulation from Jan. 23 to April 24 showed a net increase of $110,000,000, or somewhat greater than is usual at this time of year, the Federal Reserve Board reported today in its May bulletin."
–New York Times

July 2, 1935
Gold Stocks in U.S. Expand $2,000,000,000
"The gold stock of the United States has increased more than $2,000,000,000, or about 30 per cent, since the revaluation of gold in terms of dollars at the end of January, 1934, the Federal Reserve Bank of New York points out in the current issue of its monthly review."
–New York Times

August 24, 1935
Roosevelt Signs New Banking Law
"The Omnibus Banking Bill, marking a new program of credit control by the government and involving a revision by the Federal Reserve Board, became law today when President Roosevelt signed it in the presence of Congressional leaders and a group representing the Treasury and the Reserve Board."
–New York Times

October 2, 1935
Increased Deposits Reported by Banks
"Banks here began yesterday to issue reports of their condition at the end of September. These showed gains in deposits and resources, in some cases to the highest marks in the history of the institutions. Generally, there apparently have been only slight changes in the amount of United States Government securities held, according to the reports."
–New York Times

News &
Federal Reserve Bulletin

October 2, 1935
Assets of Trusts Increase Sharply
"Reports issued yesterday by the National Investors group of investment trusts for the nine months ended on Sept. 30 showed a sharp increase in the net assets of each, resulting from the rise in the market value of their portfolios. The statements were issued by the Second National Investors Corporation, the Third National Investors Corporation and the Fourth National Investors Corporation."
—*New York Times*

November 1, 1935
Excess Funds Set Record for Banks
"Excess reserves of member banks of the Federal Reserve System surpassed $3,000,000,000 this week for the first time on record. The weekly report of the system as of last Wednesday, issued yesterday, showed member-bank reserve balances at a new high level of $5,653,000,000, up $78,000,000 in the last week, and said that of this amount $3,010,000,000 was in excess of legal requirements. This compared with an excess of $2,930,000,000 the week before."
—*New York Times*

November 30, 1935
Reserve-Bank Cut in Holdings Urged
"A recommendation that the Federal Reserve Banks allow some of their holdings of short-term government securities to run off at maturity, thus reducing excess bank reserves and the threat of credit inflation, has been laid before the Open Market Committee of the Reserve System by the Federal Reserve Advisory Council, it was learned here today."
—*New York Times*

December 1935
National Summary of Business Conditions
"Volume of industrial production and factory employment, which usually shows little change at this season, increased in October, reflecting chiefly the resumption of activity at textile mills. Wholesale commodity prices, after declining in September and October, advanced in the first half of November."
—*Federal Reserve Bulletin*

December 19, 1935
Policy Announced on Bank Reserves
"The Board of Governors of the Federal Reserve System and the Federal Open Market Committee, composed of the governors of the Federal Reserve Banks, in a Joint statement tonight opposed immediate action to reduce excess reserve of member banks, adding, however, that the situation would be watched carefully and appropriate action taken if credit expansion developed which threatened public interest."
—*New York Times*

December 22, 1935
Caution Discerned in Reserves Policy
"The joint statement issued in Washington last Wednesday by the Board of Governors of the Federal Reserve and the system's open-market committee, indicating that no immediate action to reduce excess bank reserves was contemplated, was regarded in Wall Street as the most important pronouncement of Federal Reserve policy in years."
—*New York Times*

In the spring of 1935, the Fed became increasingly concerned about the rise in excess reserves.[187] It feared that the surge in excess reserves could create an expansion in credit and inflation in the future. In March, a background memo was prepared to address the question of what the Fed should do. It recommended no action for the time being. The paper explored the question of whether excess reserves will encourage banks to lend more to the private sector by pushing down the yield on government securities, but it didn't yet see evidence of that happening, so the Fed held pat. A second issue the paper looked at was how to sell the debt that it accumulated (i.e., how to do a reverse Q.E.).[188] The paper rejected doing this for the time being, expressing the view that it would prematurely give too much weight to inflation concerns that hadn't yet shown signs of materializing, and instead advocated encouraging the expansion.

The cyclical expansion and advances in the stock market and housing price gains continued, which caused the Fed to become more inclined to tighten. In October, another memo expressed heightened concerns over the excess reserves, pondering the appropriate time to reduce them and whether to do that through 1) asset sales or 2) increasing the reserve requirement. In November, the pros and cons of these paths were explored. The argument for reducing excess reserves was to get ahead of the potential for future inflation; the argument against it was that there was no evidence yet for restraint.

In its press release of November 22, the Fed discussed the stock market boom and expressed concerns about inflation. Fears of fueling a bubble were rampant because a number of policy makers, including FDR, remembered that the bubble of the late 1920s caused the stock market bust, which had contributed to the depression. As a result, they were very worried that the steep rise in the stock market in 1935 (nearly a quadrupling!) could fuel a recurrence. The November press release from the Treasury disagreed, noting that inflation was still far off.[189]

The Fed paid a lot of attention to how the stock purchases were being financed because they had heightened concerns about "speculative credit" after the excess in margin-borrowing during the late 1920s. Raising margin requirements was considered. However, the November Fed memo noted that the purchases were being financed by money, not credit, so no action was taken.[190] Still, the stock market advance was considered an emerging bubble, and fears about too easy of a monetary policy remained, so the arguments about whether or not to apply restraints continued. One board member (George Harrison of the New York Fed) suggested raising reserve requirements to curtail the rise in stock prices. Treasury Secretary Henry Morgenthau (still on the Fed Board at the time) rejected this notion. However, he recognized the concern that a rise in reserves could lead to inflation. In December, Emanuel Goldenweiser, the Fed's head of research, warned of a potential negative psychological reaction to raising reserve requirements. He recommended that the Fed issue a press release saying that any action on reserve requirements would be "precautionary" in nature, and thought that "there is no need to worry about inflation at this time with the very large volume of unused plant capacity and unemployment." At the end of 1935, following its last meeting, the Fed issued a press release stating that the volume of reserves and gold inflows "continues to be excessive" and warned that "appropriate action may be taken as soon as it appears in the public interest."[191]

1936–1938: The Tightening Causes Recession

The debate continued at the start of 1936. FDR wanted to signal a concern around inflation ahead of the election, so he urged that reserve requirements be tightened that spring. Fed Chairman Eccles was worried that banks would accumulate a lot of bonds and loans at low rates and then get burned by inflation.[192]

In May the Fed did not move. While the Banking Act of 1935 meant Treasury Secretary Morgenthau had to resign from the board, he still had influence and was a strong proponent against acting. By that July, Fed Chairman Eccles met alone with FDR, explaining his intention to raise reserves and assuring the president he would not act if he felt interest rates would rise and that the Fed would buy bonds if they sold off. The Fed tightened reserves later that month. Eccles and the Fed moved without informing Morgenthau, who was furious. After a tiny sell off in bonds, Morgenthau ordered Harrison of the New York Fed to purchase bonds using the Treasury's accounts. The Fed Board in Washington joined in, buying bonds and selling bills as Eccles had promised the president.[193] Between August 1936 and May 1937, the Fed doubled reserve requirements from about 8 percent to 16 percent, as shown below. The first tightening, in August 1936, did not hurt stock prices or the economy.

It is typically the case that the first tightening does not hurt stocks and the economy.

Because the tightening did not have an effect, reserves were tightened more in two additional phases, the first in March 1937 and the second in May 1937. The largest increase was the first (about half the total), as shown below.

Deposit Reserve Requirements by Bank

	Prior to Aug '36	Aug '36 – Feb '37	Mar '37 – Apr '37	May '37 – Apr '38
Demand Deposits				
Central Reserve City	13.0%	19.5%	22.8%	26.0%
Reserve City	10%	15%	18%	20%
Country	7.0%	10.5%	12.3%	14.0%
Time Deposits				
All Member Banks	3.0%	4.5%	5.3%	6.0%

As a result of the reserve tightening, excess reserves fell from $3 billion to less than $1 billion.[194]

The tightening of monetary policy was intensified by currency devaluations by France and Switzerland, continuing a battle of official devaluations to gain price and trade advantages. In September 1936, the Tripartite Agreement was reached by the United States, Britain, and France, which essentially stated that each nation would refrain from competitive exchange devaluations.[195] By then, it had become obvious that all countries could just as easily devalue their currencies in response to other devaluations, creating a huge amount of economic turbulence that left everyone in the same place. At the end of the day, all currencies had devalued a lot against gold, but not so much against each other.

News & Federal Reserve Bulletin

January 26, 1936
Raising of Margins Viewed as Gesture
"The action of the board of governors of the Federal Reserve System on Friday in raising margin requirements, effective on Feb. 1, was designed primarily to check the spread of inflationary psychology, in the opinion of bankers and brokers as expressed yesterday."
—*New York Times*

February 1, 1936
New Reserve Body Takes Reins Today
"Cloaked with the most powerful centralized control over banking in the history of this country, the newly organized Federal Reserve Board will assume office officially tomorrow. The Banking Act of 1935 provided that it take office on Feb. 1."
—*New York Times*

February 5, 1936
No Harm Seen by President
"President Roosevelt at his press conference today noted the reversal of the flow of gold to this country. He declined extended comment on this movement, but remarked that the export shipments were doing this country no harm."
—*New York Times*

February 15, 1936
Dollar Declines on Inflation Move
"Quotations on the foreign exchange market experienced another abrupt reversal yesterday as a fresh wave of inflation talk cropped out in Washington and Wall Street. Renewing his drive for inflation, Representative Patman of Texas filed a petition to put before the House his plan to pay the veterans' bonus in currency."
—*New York Times*

February 22, 1936
Board Emphasizes Margins as Brake. Reserve Bank Body Intimates It Has No Fear of Speculative Stock Orgy
"The power to raise margin requirements provides an effective instrument for controlling excessive credit demands by stock market speculators, the Federal Reserve Board said today in its monthly bulletin, intimating broadly that there was no need to fear a runaway speculative market so long as this instrument was available."
—*New York Times*

News & Federal Reserve Bulletin

May 4, 1936
Flight of Capital Discerned in Paris
"A money market exists only for day-to-day loans, which cost 4 per cent, with the longer-term loans being given only by the Bank of France. The bank's return for April 24 shows a new increase in bills discounted of almost 400,000,000 francs, while the total of loans on securities and government bonds declined only 100,000,000 francs."

–New York Times

May 19, 1936
Flight of Capital Depresses the Franc
"Under the pressure of continued flight of capital the franc and other gold-bloc currencies fell further yesterday. The French currency declined to 6.58 7-16 cents, or within 1-16 point of the effective gold-shipping price, and closed at 6.58 1/2 cents, off 11-16 point. Guilders dropped 2 points to 67.59 cents and Swiss francs were off 2 points to 32.35 cents."

–New York Times

August 9, 1936
Financial Markets; Stocks Close Active and Strong; Railway Average at New High—Bonds Steady—France Loses More Gold
"To the accompaniment of the heaviest Saturday trading since July 11, the stock market extended the strong advance of Friday and closed at the best levels of the week."

–New York Times

September 27, 1936
Franc Cut to Match Dollar and Sterling
"French Yield at Last to Economic and "Budgetary Pressure and Other Nations Expected to Follow Washington and London to Aid."

–New York Times

September 28, 1936
Swiss to Devalue About 30% Today
"The Swiss Government, it is understood late tonight, plans to ask Parliament tomorrow to make the degree of devaluation of the Swiss franc about 30 per cent."

–New York Times

November 29, 1936
Volume of "Hot Money" Measured by Treasury; Nervous Capital That Flees from One Country to Another Is the Product of the World's Disorders
"The magnitude of international movements of capital during the recent period of monetary disorder was revealed for the first time last Friday when the United States Treasury made public a record of the flow of foreign money into this country since the beginning of 1935."

–New York Times

December 26, 1936
London Unruffled by Our Gold Move; U.S. Treasury's Sterilizing Action Is Considered a Sound Policy
"The decision of the United States Treasury to sterilize gold imports caused no surprise here in financial circles. It is regarded as merely another step toward giving active expression to the already announced official determination to check unwanted credit inflation or an unrestrained stock market boom."

–New York Times

By 1936, war was brewing in Europe, driving capital flight to the US, which continued to fuel advances in stocks and the economy. That year, the president and other policy makers were becoming increasingly concerned by gold inflows (which allowed faster money and credit growth).[196] The concerns were threefold:

1. *The rapid rise in the stock market.* At this time, stocks were up almost four times from their bottom in 1933 and were rising fast: by about 40 percent in 1935 and 25 percent in 1936. Policy makers worried that the gold inflows were coming from foreigners bringing in capital to buy US stocks.

2. *The inflationary impact of gold inflows increasing the monetary base.* Inflation had risen from roughly 0 percent to around 2 percent in October 1936.

3. *The US was becoming vulnerable to an outflow of gold (i.e., capital withdrawal).* The specific concern was that the European nations would finance the coming war in part by selling their US assets and pulling gold out, while preventing US holders of their assets from repatriating capital.

To neutralize the effects of these inflows, in December, FDR ordered "sterilization" to begin. Normally, when people sold their gold to the US government in exchange for dollars, the number of dollars increased (i.e., money is printed), which, given the strong economic recovery, wasn't seen as desirable. Instead, starting December 23, the gold inflows/newly mined gold were sterilized—literally, the Treasury purchased gold inflows by drawing down its cash account at the Federal Reserve instead of printing money. From the end of 1936 to July 1937, the Treasury sterilized about 1.3 billion of gold inflows (approximately 1.5 percent of GDP).[197] We can see the increase in sterilization and slowing of gold and other asset purchases in 1936/37 with money growth slowing and dropping below gold reserve growth. The Fed also tightened reserve requirements in order to take money out of circulation, as we have seen.

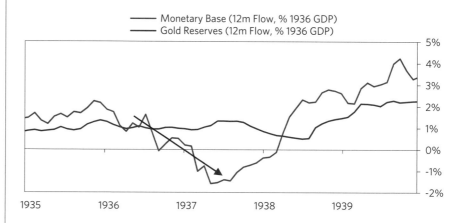

1937

The economy remained strong going into early 1937. The stock market was still rising, industrial production remained healthy, and inflation picked up to around 5 percent. The second tightening came in March 1937 and the third in May. While neither the Fed nor the Treasury anticipated that the increase in required reserves combined with the sterilization program would push rates higher, the tighter money and reduced liquidity led to a sell-off in bonds and a rise in the short rate.[198] Treasury Secretary Morgenthau was furious and argued that the Fed should offset the "panic" through open market operations to make net purchases of bonds. He ordered the Treasury into the market to purchase bonds itself. Fed Chairman Eccles pushed back on Morgenthau, urging him to balance the budget and raise tax rates to begin to retire debt.[199]

Additionally there was a fiscal tightening. Federal government outlays fell 10 percent in 1937 and another 10 percent in 1938. The Revenue Act of 1937 was passed to help to close loopholes in the Revenue Act of 1935 (which was sold as the "wealth tax").[200] That act had increased the federal income tax for the highest incomes up to 75 percent.

The federal budget deficit went from around -4 percent of GDP to neutral. The reversal in the budget in 1937 was a consequence of a large increase in taxes, mostly from a rise in the Social Security tax, along with sizable but smaller cuts in spending.[201]

There was significant pressure on the government to pass redistributive policies, as the recovery thus far was perceived to be uneven (i.e., benefiting the elites over the common man). Workers saw the gains in corporate profits, but didn't see a subsequent increase in their own compensation. Inequality bred discontent, as evidenced by the sharp increase in the number and intensity of strikes from 1936 to 1937 (the number of strikes rose by 118 percent and the number of workers involved by 136 percent).[202]

In financial markets, the combination of monetary and fiscal tightening created a significant sell-off in risky assets. Stocks fell the most, but home prices stopped their gains and dipped negative. Credit growth slowed as well, both in aggregate and across all sectors. Nonfinancial business credit creation fell to almost -2 percent, and household credit creation was slightly less negative at about -1 percent. Spending and economic activity fell as a result. With that downturn, unemployment rose to 15 percent, though it was more like a short uptick, especially in comparison to the punishingly high rise at the start of the decade. Stocks bottomed a year later, in April 1938, declining a total of nearly 60 percent!

News & Federal Reserve Bulletin

January 29, 1937
Gains in Industry Reach New Peaks; Figures for December Highest for the Recovery Period, Conference Board Finds
"On a seasonally adjusted basis, industrial activity in December advanced to a new high level for the recovery period, according to the monthly review issued yesterday by the National Industrial Conference Board."
—New York Times

February 1937
Increase in Reserve Requirements
"On January 30 the Board announced a further increase in the reserve requirements of member banks. In connection with its action the Board issued the following statement, which was released for publication on January 31: 'The Board of Governors of the Federal Reserve System today increased reserve requirements for member banks by 33 1/2 percent, as follows: On demand deposits, at banks in central reserve cities, from 19 1/2 to 26 percent; at banks in reserve cities, from 15 to 20 percent; and at "country" banks, from 10 1/2 to 14 percent; on time deposits, at all banks, from 4 1/2 to 6 percent.'"
—Federal Reserve Bulletin

April 1937
National Summary of Business Conditions
"Volume of production, employment, and trade increased more than seasonally in February and wholesale prices of industrial commodities continued to advance."
—Federal Reserve Bulletin

April 2, 1937
Morgenthau Seeks "Orderly" Market; Federal Reserve and Treasury Have Ample Funds to Aid That Purpose, He Says
"The Federal Reserve Board and the United States Treasury, working together, have ample funds to keep the government bond market orderly, Secretary Morgenthau said today. He added that money flowed in and out of the Treasury all the time and there was sufficient for that purpose."
—New York Times

May 30, 1937
Roosevelt Hopes to Get $100,000,000 from Tax Evaders; Message to Congress "Probably Tuesday" Will Ask Steps to Plug Law's Loopholes
—New York Times

June 2, 1937
Roosevelt Asks Congress to Curb Big Tax Evaders; Eight Tricks Cited
"President Roosevelt summoned Congress today to a finish fight on tax avoidances 'by a minority of very rich individuals,' not only to save millions in public revenues but to meet a challenge to 'the decency of American morals.'"
—New York Times

November 20, 1937
Leading Stocks Down 1 to 7 Points; Treasury Bonds Strong-Dollar Easier—Wheat Declines
"The stock market experienced yesterday its sharpest decline in exactly one month. Following a fractionally lower opening, stocks moved steadily lower, and the activity increased as prices receded, with the tape sometimes running a few minutes behind the market in reporting transactions."
—New York Times

December 17, 1937
Federal Deficit Reduced; Now Below $695,245,000 Estimate of President on Oct. 19
—New York Times

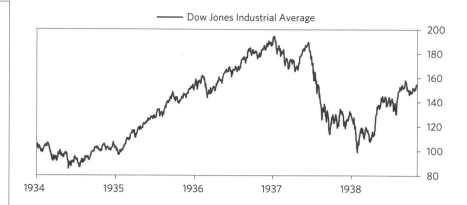

Late 1937–1938: Policy Makers Reverse Their Course

As markets and the economy turned down in 1937, the Fed accelerated a twist into longer-dated assets and started to do a small amount of net asset purchases. By the end of the year, the Treasury began to reverse its sterilization program in partnership with the Fed.[203] Money growth picked up again starting in 1938 and continued to rise with the reverse sterilization and renewed money printing. At the same time, gold inflows slowed and the economy and asset prices deteriorated. Before long, money growth had outpaced growth in gold reserves.

The Fed's twist is shown below. While the Fed didn't do much in the way of net asset purchases, it accelerated its buying of long-term bonds in 1937 while selling bills and notes (a process it had actually started in 1936). It also increased net assets by a small amount (slightly above 3 percent by 1938).

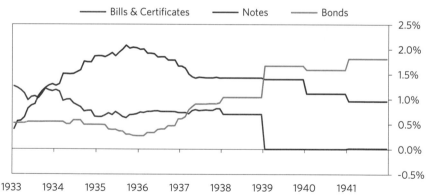

In the spring of 1938, the Fed added to the stimulus by lowering its reserve requirements back to 1936 levels, releasing about $750 million.[204] The federal government also increased deficit spending that year and again in 1939 heading into the war. While the government was almost running a balanced budget at the start of 1938, the deficit rose to almost 3 percent of GDP by the start of 1939. Deficit spending above 2 percent of GDP continued throughout the year.

In 1938, the stock market began to recover, though stocks didn't fully regain their 1937 highs until the end of the war nearly a decade later. Credit flows and the economy also recovered in 1939, following the stimulus and entry into the war.

News &
Federal Reserve Bulletin

June 1937
Recent Banking Developments
"Total deposits at weekly reporting member banks continued to decrease in April and May, reflecting declines in bankers' balances and in United States Government deposits. Other deposits, which had declined somewhat in March, increased slightly in the following weeks. Sales of securities by banks have been the most important factor in accounting for the decrease in deposits in recent months. Member bank holdings of United States Government obligations continued to decline at New York City banks during April and May, but the decline was less rapid than in earlier months, and holdings of other reporting banks showed little change. Commercial loans by banks increased further, although after the first week of April the rapid growth of previous weeks slackened."

—Federal Reserve Bulletin

October 1937
System Action to Meet Seasonal Needs
"In the monetary field the principal development of the month was the adoption by the Federal Open Market Committee of a program of supplying member banks with additional reserve funds with which to meet seasonal currency and credit demands. On September 13 the Committee issued the following statement: 'The Federal Open Market Committee met in Washington on September 11 and 12 and reviewed the business and credit situation. In view of the expected seasonal demands on the banks for currency and credit during the coming weeks the Committee authorized its Executive Committee to purchase in the open market from time to time sufficient amounts of short term U. S. Government obligations to provide funds to meet seasonal withdrawals of currency from the banks and other seasonal requirements. Reduction of the additional holdings in the open market portfolio is contemplated when the seasonal influences are reversed or other circumstances make their retention unnecessary.'"

—Federal Reserve Bulletin

January 5, 1938
Billion Deficit for 1938 Forecast; President's Resume of Financial Operations and Outlook Goes In Today
"On the eve of the sending of the annual budget to Congress, well-informed officials predicted it would indicate a $1,000,000,000 deficit. The latest official estimate of the prospective deficit for the current year was $895,245,000. Officials indicated, however, the message tomorrow would revise this figure upward."

—New York Times

April 16, 1938
Requirements Cut for Bank Reserves; Federal Board Puts Into Effect Today Virtually Same Schedule as Before May 1, 1937
"The Federal Reserve Board announced today that 'as a part of the government's program for encouragement of business recovery' it had reduced the reserve requirements on all classes of deposits of all member banks, effective at the opening of business tomorrow."

—New York Times

October 16, 1938
Stocks Up Irregularly in Increased Trading; Bonds Firm—Dollar Higher—Wheat, Cotton Steady
"The demand for low-priced stocks, especially public utility issues, continued yesterday to feature the stock market. The market as a whole closed irregularly higher. The day's business on the Stock Exchange reached 1,995,000 shares, the heaviest volume since Oct. 19."

—New York Times

The Path to War

While the purpose of this chapter has been to examine the debt and economic circumstances in the United States during the 1930s, the linkages between economic conditions and political conditions, both within the United States and between the United States and other countries—most importantly Germany and Japan—cannot be ignored because economics and geopolitics were very intertwined at the time. Most importantly, Germany and Japan had internal conflicts between the haves (the Right) and the have-nots (the Left), which led to more populist, autocratic, nationalistic, and militaristic leaders who were given special autocratic powers by their democracies to bring order to their badly-managed economies. They also faced external economic and military conflicts arising as these countries became rival economic and military powers to existing world powers.

The case is also a good example of Thucydides's Trap[205]—where rivalries between countries lead to wars in order to establish which country is more powerful, which are then followed by periods of peace in which the dominant power/powers get to set the rules because no country can fight them until a rival power emerges, at which time they do it all over again.

To help to convey the picture in the 1930s, I will quickly run though the geopolitical highlights of what happened from 1930 until the official start of the war in Europe in 1939 and the bombing of Pearl Harbor in 1941. While 1939 and 1941 are known as the official start of the wars in Europe and the Pacific, the wars really started about 10 years before that, as economic conflicts that were at first limited progressively grew into World War II. As Germany and Japan became more expansionist economic and military powers, they increasingly competed with the UK, US, and France for both resources and influence over territories. That eventually led to the war, which culminated in it being clear which country (the United States) had the power to dictate the new world order. This has led to a period of peace under that world order and will continue until the same process happens again.

More precisely:

- In 1930, the Smoot-Hawley Tariff began a trade war.

- In 1931, Japan's resources were inadequate, and its rural poverty became severe, so it invaded Manchuria, China to obtain natural resources. The US wanted to keep China free from Japanese control and was competing for natural resources—especially oil, rubber, and tin—from Southeast Asia, while at the same time Japan and the US had significant trade with each other.

- In 1931, the depression in Japan was so severe that it drove Japan off the gold standard, leading to both the floating of the yen (which depreciated greatly) and big fiscal and monetary expansions that led to Japan being the first country to experience a recovery and strong growth (which lasted until 1937).

- In 1932, there was a lot of internal conflict in Japan, which led to a failed coup and a massive upsurge in right-wing nationalism and militarism. During the period from 1931 to 1937, the military took over control of the government and increased its top-down command of the economy.

- In 1933, Hitler came to power in Germany as a populist promising to exercise control over the bad economy, to bring order to the political chaos of the democracy of the time, and to fight the communists. Within just two months of being named chancellor, he was able to take total authoritarian control; using the excuse of national security, he got the Reichstag to pass the Enabling Act, which gave him virtually unlimited powers (in part by locking up political opponents and also by convincing some moderates that it was necessary). He promptly refused to make reparations payments, stepped out of the League of Nations, and took control of the media. To create a strong economy and attempt to bring prosperity to the people, he created a top-down command economy. For instance, Hitler was involved with setting up Volkswagen to build a more affordable car, and directed the building of the national German Autobahn (highway system). He believed that Germany's potential was limited by its geographic boundaries, that it didn't have adequate raw materials to feed the industrial military complex, and that German people should be ethnically united.

- At the same time, Japan became increasingly strong with its top-down command economy, building a military industrial complex, with the military intended to protect its bases in East Asia and Northern China and to expand its controls over other territories.

- Germany also got stronger by building its military industrial complex and looking to expand and claim adjacent lands.

- In 1934, there was severe famine in parts of Japan, causing even more political turbulence and reinforcing the right-wing militaristic and nationalistic movement. Because the free market wasn't working for the people, that led to the strengthening of the command economy.

- In 1936, Germany took back the Rhineland militarily, and in 1938, it annexed Austria.

- In 1936, Japan signed a pact with Germany.

- In 1936–7, the Fed tightened, which caused the fragile economy to weaken, and other major economies weakened with it.

- In 1937, Japan's occupation of China spread, and the second Sino-Japanese War began. The Japanese took over Shanghai and Nanking, killing an estimated 200,000 Chinese civilians and disarmed combatants in the capture of Nanking alone. The United States provided China's Chiang Kai-shek government with fighter planes and pilots to fight the Japanese, thus putting a toe in the war.

- In 1939, Germany invaded Poland, and World War II in Europe officially began.

- In 1940, Germany captured Denmark, Norway, the Netherlands, Belgium, Luxembourg, and France.

- During this time, most companies in Germany and Japan remained publically owned, but their production was controlled by their respective governments in support of the war.

- In 1940, Henry Stimson became the US Secretary of War. He increasingly used aggressive economic sanctions against Japan, culminating in the Export Control Act of July 2, 1940. In October, he ramped up the embargo, restricting "all iron and steel to destinations other than Britain and nations of the Western Hemisphere."

- Beginning in September 1940, to obtain more resources and take advantage of the European preoccupation with the war on their continent, Japan invaded several colonies in Southeast Asia, starting with French Indochina. In 1941, Japan extended its reach by seizing oil reserves in the Dutch East Indies to add the "Southern Resource Zone" to its "Greater East Asia Co-Prosperity Sphere." The "Southern Resource Zone" was a collection of mostly European colonies in Southeast Asia, whose conquest would afford Japan access to key natural resources (most importantly oil, rubber, and rice). The latter, the "Greater East Asia Co-Prosperity Sphere," was a bloc of Asian countries controlled by Japan, not (as they previously were) the Western powers.

- Japan then occupied a naval base near the Philippine capital, Manila. This threatened an attack on the Philippines, which was, at the time, an American protectorate.

- In 1941, to aid the Allies without fully entering the war, the United States began its Lend-Lease policy. Under this policy, the United States sent oil, food, and weaponry to the Allied Nations for free. This aid totaled over $650 billion in today's dollars. The Lend-Lease policy, although not an outright declaration of war, ended the United States' neutrality.

- In the summer of 1941, US President Roosevelt ordered the freezing of all Japanese assets in the United States and embargoed all oil and gas exports to Japan. Japan calculated that it would be out of oil in two years.

- In December 1941, Japan attacked Pearl Harbor, and British and Dutch colonies in Asia. While it didn't have a plan to win the war, it wanted to destroy the Pacific Fleet that threatened Japan. Japan supposedly also believed that the US was weakened by both fighting a war in two fronts (Europe and the US) and by its political system; Japan thought that totalitarianism and the command military industrial complex approaches of their country and Germany were superior to the individualistic/capitalist approach of the United States.

These events led to the "war economy" conditions explained at the end of Part 1.

Works Cited:

Administration of the German Bundestag, "Elections in the Weimar Republic." Historical Exhibition Presented by the German Bundestag (March 2006). https://www.bundestag.de/blob/189774/7c6dd629f4afff7bf4f962a45c110b5f/elections_weimar_republic-data.pdf.

Ahamed, Liaquat. *Lords of Finance: The Bankers Who Broke the World*. New York: Penguin, 2009.

Allison, Graham. *Destined for War: Can America and China Escape Thucydides's Trap?* New York: Houghton Mifflin Harcourt, 2017.

Bernanke, Ben S. *Essays on the Great Depression*. Princeton, NJ: Princeton University Press, 2004.

Blakey, Roy G. and Gladys C. Blakey. "The Revenue Act of 1937." *The American Economic Review* Vol. 27, No. 4 (December 1937): 698-704. https://www.jstor.org/stable/1801981?seq=1#page_scan_tab_contents.

Board of Governors of the Federal Reserve System (U.S.). Federal Reserve Bulletin: February 1929. Washington, DC, 1929. https://fraser.stlouisfed.org/files/docs/publications/FRB/1920s/frb_021929.pdf.

Board of Governors of the Federal Reserve System (U.S.). Federal Reserve Bulletin: April 1929. Washington, DC, 1929. https://fraser.stlouisfed.org/files/docs/publications/FRB/1920s/frb_041929.pdf.

Board of Governors of the Federal Reserve System (U.S.). Federal Reserve Bulletin: June 1929. Washington, DC, 1929. https://fraser.stlouisfed.org/files/docs/publications/FRB/1920s/frb_061929.pdf

Board of Governors of the Federal Reserve System (U.S.). *Banking and Monetary Statistics: 1914–1941*. Washington, DC, 1943. https://fraser.stlouisfed.org/files/docs/publications/bms/1914–1941/BMS14-41_complete.pdf.

Brooks, John. *Once in Golconda: A True Drama of Wall Street 1920–1938*. New York: Harper & Row, 1969.

Bullock, Hugh. *The Story of Investment Companies*. New York: Columbia University Press, 1959.

Cannadine, David. *Mellon: An American Life*. New York: Vintage Books, 2008.

Dell, Fabien. "Top Incomes in Germany and Switzerland Over the Twentieth Century." *Journal of the European Economic Association*, Vol. 3, No. 2/3, Papers and Proceedings of the Nineteenth Annual Congress of the European Economic Association (April – May, 2005), 412-421. http://www.jstor.org/stable/40004984.

Eichengreen, Barry. *Golden Fetters: The Gold Standard and the Great Depression*, 1919–1939. New York: Oxford University Press, 1992.

Eichengreen, Barry. *Hall of Mirrors: The Great Depression, the Great Recession, and the Uses—and Misuses—of History*. New York: Oxford University Press, 2016.

Eichengreen, Barry. "The Political Economy of the Smoot-Hawley Tariff," *NBER Working Paper Series* No. 2001 (August, 1986). http://www.nber.org/papers/w2001.pdf.

Federal Deposit Insurance Corporation. "Historical Timeline: The 1920's." Accessed August 21, 2018. https://www.fdic.gov/about/history/timeline/1920s.html.

Federal Deposit Insurance Corporation. "Historical Timeline: The 1930's." Accessed August 21, 2018. https://www.fdic.gov/about/history/timeline/1930s.html.

Friedman, Milton and Anna Jacobson Schwartz. *A Monetary History of the United States*, 1867–1960. Princeton, NJ: Princeton University Press, 1971.

Friedman, Milton and Anna Jacobson Schwartz. *The Great Contraction, 1929–1933*. Princeton, NJ: Princeton University Press, 2008.

Galbraith, John Kenneth. *The Great Crash, 1929*. New York: Houghton Mifflin Harcourt, 2009.

Gammack, Thomas H. "Price-Earnings Ratios." In *The Outlook and Independent: An Illustrated Weekly of Current Life*. Vol. 152, May 1 – August 28, 1929, edited by Francis Rufus Bellamy, 100. New York: The Outlook Company, 1929.

Gou, Michael, Gary Richardson, Alejandro Komai, and Daniel Park. "Banking Acts of 1932: February 1932." Federal Reserve History. Accessed August 22, 2018. https://www.federalreservehistory.org/essays/banking_acts_of_1932.

Gray, Christopher. "Streetscapes: The Bank of the United States in the Bronx; The First Domino in the Depression." *New York Times*, August 18, 1991. https://nyti.ms/2nOR6rv.

Hendrickson, Jill M. *Regulation and Instability in U.S. Commercial Banking: A History of Crises*. New York: Palgrave Macmillan, 2011.

Hoover, Herbert. *The Memoirs of Herbert Hoover: The Great Depression 1929–1941*. Eastford, CT: Martino Fine Books, 2016.

Irwin, Douglas A. *Clashing over Commerce: A History of US Trade Policy*. Chicago: University of Chicago Press, 2017.

Kindleberger, Charles P. *The World in Depression, 1929–1939*. Berkeley, CA: University of California Press, 2013.

Klein, Maury. *Rainbow's End: The Crash of 1929*. New York: Oxford University Press, 2001.

Kline, Patrick M. and Enrico Moretti. "Local Economic Development, Agglomeration Economics, and the Big Push: 100 Years of Evidence from the Tennessee Valley Authority," *NBER Working Paper Series* No. 19293 (August 2013). http://www.nber.org/papers/w19293.pdf.

McElvaine, Robert S. *The Great Depression: America, 1929–1941*. New York: Times Books, 1993.

Meltzer, Allan. *A History of the Federal Reserve, Volume 1: 1913–1951*. Chicago: University of Chicago Press, 2003.

New York Times. "1,028 Economists Ask Hoover To Veto Pending Tariff Bill; Professors in 179 Colleges and Other Leaders Assail Rise in Rates as Harmful to Country and Sure to Bring Reprisals. Economists of All Sections Oppose Tariff Bill." May 5, 1930. https://nyti.ms/2MLhaBT.

New York Times. "Business Leaders Find Outlook Good; Authorities on All Branches of Finance and Industry Agree Structure Is Sound." January 1, 1930. https://nyti.ms/2o2rpE8.

New York Times. "Fisher Sees Stocks Permanently High; Yale Economist Tells Purchasing Agent Increased Earnings Justify Rise." October 16, 1929. https://nyti.ms/2JnPoGO.

New York Times. "Fixed Trust Formed to Gain by Recovery; Stein Brothers & Boyce Project to Run 5 ½ Years —Shares to be Offered at About 10 3/8." February 25, 1931. https://timesmachine.nytimes.com/timesmachine/1931/02/25/100993342.pdf.

New York Times. "Huge Bid for Standard Oil; 1,000,000-Share Order at 50 Is Attributed to J.D. Rockefeller; Exchange to Hunt Bears; Calls on Member Firms for Record of Short Sales at Close on Tuesday; A. T. & T. and 20 Others Up; But Average of Fifty Stocks Declines 9.31 Points–Sales Are 7,761,450 Shares." November 14, 1929. https://nyti.ms/2N0ZqiT.

New York Times. "Leaders See Fear Waning; Point to 'Lifting Spells' [sic] in Trading as Sign of Buying Activity." October 30, 1929. https://nyti.ms/2OZ0PH5.

New York Times. "Sterling Falls Here to the Gold Point: Cable Transfers Touch $4.84 ¾—Federal Reserve Rise Adds to British Difficulties." August 9, 1929. https://nyti.ms/2MxEwuP.

New York Times, "Stock Prices Will Stay at High Level For Years to Come, Says Ohio Economist." October 13, 1929. https://nyti.ms/2OUqCAq.

New York Times. "Stocks Driven Down as Wave of Selling Engulfs the Market." October 20, 1929. https://times machine.nytimes.com/timesmachine/1929/10/20/issue.html

New York Times. "Thirty-Three Banks Vanish in Mergers," July 21, 1929. https://timesmachine.nytimes.com/timesmachine/1929/07/21/94168795.pdf.

New York Times. "Topics in Wall Street, January 1, 1930." January 2, 1930. https://timesmachine.nytimes.com/timesmachine/1930/01/02/96015717.html?pageNumber=37.

Newton, Walter and Myers, William Starr. *The Hoover Administration: A Documented Narrative*. New York: C. Scribner's Sons, 1936.

Oulahan, Richard V. "$423,000,000 Building Plan Pressed by Mellon on Eve of Hoover's Trade Parleys." *New York Times*, November 19, 1929. https://nyti.ms/2OUQVXc.

Oulahan, Richard V. "President Hails Success; He Personally Announces Nations Concerned Are in Accord." *New York Times*, July 7, 1931. https://nyti.ms/2OSDjM0.

Piketty, Thomas. "Le capital au 21e siècle." *Editions du Seuil* (September 2013), http://piketty.pse.ens.fr/files/capital21c/en/Piketty2014FiguresTables.pdf.

Roosevelt Sr., Franklin Delano. *Fireside Chat 1: On the Banking Crisis* (Washington, DC, March 12, 1933), Miller Center, https://millercenter.org/the-presidency/presidential-speeches/march-12-1933-fireside-chat-1-banking-crisis

Sastry, Parinitha. "The Political Origins of Section 13(3) of the Federal Reserve Act." *FRBNY Economic Policy Review* (2018), https://www.newyorkfed.org/medialibrary/media/research/epr/2018/epr_2018_political-origins_sastry.pdf.

Silk, Leonard. "Protectionist Mood: Mounting Pressure Smoot and Hawley." *New York Times*, September 17, 1985. https://nyti.ms/2MI3qYE.

Smiley, Gene. *Rethinking the Great Depression*. Chicago: Ivan R. Dee, 2003.

Thomas, Gordon and Morgan-Witts, Max. *The Day the Bubble Burst: A Social History of the Wall Street Crash of 1929*. New York: Doubleday & Company, 1979.

U.S. Department of the Interior. Bureau of Reclamation. The Bureau of Reclamation's Civilian Conservation Corps Legacy: 1933–1942, by Christine E. Pfaff. Denver, Colorado, February 2010. https://www.usbr.gov/cultural/CCC_Book/CCCReport.pdf.

U.S. Department of Labor. Bureau of Labor Statistics. *Analysis of Strikes in 1937*, by Division of Industrial Relations. Washington, DC, 1938. https://www.bls.gov/wsp/1937_strikes.pdf.

U.S. Department of the Treasury. *Report of the Secretary of the Treasury: Revenue Act of 1932*. Washington, DC, 1932. https://fraser.stlouisfed.org/files/docs/publications/treasar/pages/59359_1930-1934.pdf.

U.S. Department of Transportation. Federal Highway Administration. *State Motor Vehicle Registrations*. Washington, DC, 1995. https://www.fhwa.dot.gov/ohim/summary95/mv200.pdf.

Wallis, John J., Fishback, Price V., and Kantor, Shawn E. "Politics, Relief, and Reform: Roosevelt's Efforts to Control Corruption and Political Manipulation during the New Deal." *Corruption and Reform: Lessons from America's Economic History*, (March 2006): 343-372. http://www.nber.org/chapters/c10006.pdf.

Wigmore, Barrie A. *The Crash and Its Aftermath: A History of Securities Markets in the United States, 1929–1933*. Westport, CT: Greenwood Press, 1985.

1 Klein, *Rainbow's End*, 108.
2 Klein, 29; Federal Highway Administration, "State Motor Vehicle Registrations."
3 Klein, 27-8.
4 Klein, 143.
5 Brooks, *Once in Golconda*, 90.
6 Klein, 172.
7 Gammack, "Price-Earnings Ratios," 100.
8 "Stock Prices," *New York Times*.
9 Klein, 147.
10 Klein, 190.
11 Galbraith, *The Great Crash*, 20-1, 50.
12 Klein, 160-1.
13 Galbraith, 22.
14 Klein, 146, 227.
15 Bullock, *Story of Investment Companies*, 8-9.
16 Galbraith, 86.
17 Galbraith, 49-50.
18 Klein, 130.
19 Wigmore, *Crash and Its Aftermath*, 5.
20 Board of Governors of the Federal Reserve System (U.S.), *Banking and Monetary Statistics*, 262, 264.
21 "Thirty-Three Banks Vanish," *New York Times*.
22 Klein, 175-6.
23 Meltzer, *History of the Federal Reserve*, 146, 241-2.
24 Klein, 176.
25 Galbraith, 35.
26 Klein, 178-9.
27 Ahamed, *Lords of Finance*, 323.
28 Board of Governors of the Federal Reserve System (U.S.), "June 1929," 374-6.
29 "Sterling Falls," *New York Times*.
30 Galbraith, 32; FDIC, "Historical Timeline: The 1920's."
31 Klein 197-8.
32 Thomas and Morgan-Witts, *Day the Bubble Burst*, 311.
33 "Fisher Sees Stocks Permanently High," *New York Times*.
34 Galbraith, 94-95.
35 "Stocks Driven Down," *New York Times*.
36 Ahamed, 354.
37 Cannadine, *Mellon*, 391.
38 Klein, 204-5.
39 Galbraith, 98.
40 Galbraith, 98.
41 Klein, 209.
42 Ahamed, 354.
43 Klein, 209.
44 Klein, 211.
45 Ahamed, 355.
46 Wigmore, 7.
47 Wigmore, 11.
48 Galbraith, 106.
49 Galbraith, 107.
50 Wigmore, 13.
51 "Premier Issues Hard Hit," *New York Times*.
52 Wigmore, 13.
53 Wigmore, 15.
54 Klein, 227.
55 Ahamed, 358.
56 "Leaders See Fear Warning," *New York Times*.
57 Galbraith, 116-7.
58 Galbraith, 112-13.
59 Klein, 233.
60 Wigmore, 19.
61 Oulahan, "$423,000,000 Building Plan Pressed."
62 Klein, 242.
63 Smiley, *Rethinking the Great Depression*, 11-12.
64 Klein, 244-5.
65 "Huge Bid for Standard Oil," *New York Times*.

66 "Topics in Wall Street," *New York Times*; "Business Leaders Find Outlook Good," *New York Times*.
67 Wigmore, 117.
68 Klein, 263; Ahamed, 362.
69 Klein, 250.
70 Wigmore, 119.
71 Wigmore, 137.
72 Wigmore, 147.
73 Hoover, *Memoirs of Herbert Hoover*, 47-48.
74 Eichengreen, "Political Economy of Smoot-Hawley," 5, 23.
75 "1,028 Economists Ask Hoover," *New York Times*.
76 Irwin, *Clashing over Commerce*, 400-1.
77 Gray, "Streetscapes."
78 It's worth noting that some of the rise in tariff rates can be attributed to falling import prices. Some tariffs were charged per unit (e.g., 2 cents per bushel of wheat), so the effective tariff rate rose as import prices fell.
79 Irwin, 401-2.
80 Hoover, *Memoirs*, 47-48.
81 Board of Governors of the Federal Reserve System (U.S.), *Banking and Monetary Statistics*, 262-3.
82 Wigmore, 160-1.
83 Friedman and Jacobson Schwartz, *A Monetary History*, 308.
84 Gray.
85 Ahamed, 387.
86 Friedman and Jacobson Schwartz, *A Monetary History*, 309-10.
87 Smiley, 16.
88 Gray.
89 Board of Governors of the Federal Reserve System (U.S.), *Banking and Monetary Statistics*, 16.
90 Hoover, *Memoirs*, 58.
91 Board of Governors of the Federal Reserve System (U.S.), "April 1929," 257, 299; Board of Governors of the Federal Reserve System (U.S.), "February 1929," 162.
92 Hoover, *Memoirs*, 59.
93 "New Fixed Trust Formed," *New York Times*.
94 Hoover, *Memoirs*, 53.
95 Hoover, *Memoirs*, 42, 53-55.
96 McElvaine, 76.
97 Hoover, *Memoirs*, 132.
98 Hoover, *Memoirs*, 53.
99 Ahamed, 324, 402.
100 Administration of the German Bundestag, Research Section, "Elections in the Weimar Republic," 2.
101 Hoover, *Memoirs*, 64.
102 Ahamed, 404-6.
103 Ahamed, 406.
104 Hoover, *Memoirs*, 67.
105 Eichengreen, *Golden Fetters*, 270.
106 Wigmore, 297.
107 Bernanke, *Essays on the Great Depression*, 91-2.
108 Wigmore, 297.
109 Hoover, *Memoirs*, 68-69.
110 Ahamed, 410.
111 Oulahan, "President Hails Success."
112 Eichengreen, *Golden Fetters*, 275.
113 Ahamed, 415.
114 Ahamed 415-6.
115 Hoover, *Memoirs*, 75.
116 Hoover, *Memoirs*, 77-79.
117 Wigmore, 296.
118 Hoover, *Memoirs*, 81.
119 Hoover, *Memoirs*, 81.
120 Ahamed, 428.
121 Hoover, *Memoirs*, 82.
122 Wigmore, 301.

123 Ahamed, 433.
124 Wigmore, 302.
125 Wigmore, 303.
126 Jones, "Shorting Restrictions," 2.
127 Wigmore, 289.
128 Ahamed, 435.
129 Friedman and Jacobson Schwartz, *The Great Contraction*, 39.
130 Friedman and Jacobson Schwartz, *A Monetary History*, 397.
131 Hoover, *Memoirs*, 82-3, 87-8.
132 Hoover, *Memoirs*, 84.
133 Hoover, *Memoirs*, 88, 93-95, 114.
134 Wigmore, 315.
135 Hoover, *Memoirs*, 98, 111.
136 Gou, et al., "Banking Acts of 1932."
137 Wigmore, 318.
138 Eichengreen, *Hall of Mirrors*, 158.
139 Gou, et al.
140 Eichengreen, *Hall of Mirrors*, 158.
141 Hoover, "Statement on Signing."
142 Sastry, "Political Origins of Section 13(3)."
143 Wigmore, 312.
144 Wigmore, 313, 326.
145 Friedman and Jacobson Schwartz, *The Great Contraction*, 47-8.
146 Eichengreen, *Golden Fetters*, 315.
147 Wigmore, 331.
148 McElvaine, 91.
149 Smiley, 24.
150 Eichengreen, *Hall of Mirrors*, 163.
151 Friedman and Jacobson Schwartz, *The Great Contraction*, 52.
152 Wigmore, 325.
153 Smiley, 68.
154 Wigmore, 308-9.
155 Wigmore 309.
156 United States Department of the Treasury, "Revenue Act of 1932," 13, 20-21.
157 Wigmore, 313-314.
158 Friedman and Jacobson Schwartz, *The Great Contraction*, 63.
159 Smiley, 27.
160 Piketty, "Le capital au 21e siècle," 1, 70.
161 Dell, "Top Incomes in Germany and Switzerland," 415-6.
162 Smiley, 69-70.
163 Hoover, *Memoirs*, 203.
164 Hoover, *Memoirs*, 205-6.
165 Wigmore, 434, 438-9.
166 Wigmore, 444.
167 Ahamed, 443; Wigmore, 444-5.
168 Ahamed, 444.
169 Hoover, *Memoirs*, 210-2.
170 Wigmore, 428.
171 Smiley, 75.
172 Friedman and Jacobson Schwartz, *A Monetary History*, 420-2.
173 Ahamed, 454.
174 Roosevelt, *Fireside Chat 1*.
175 Smiley, 76.
176 Wigmore, 450.
177 Smiley, 76-77.
178 Smiley, 80.
179 Smiley, 77.
180 Smiley, 80.
181 Hendrickson, *Regulation and Instability*, 143-6.
182 Pfaff, "The Bureau of Reclamation," 5, 15.
183 Wallis, Fishback, and Kantor, "Politics, Relief, and Reform," 347; Smiley, 81.
184 Kline and Moretti, "Local Economic Development," 5-6.
185 McElvaine, 152.

186 Ahamed, 463.

187 Friedman and Jacobson Schwartz, *A Monetary History*, 518.

188 Meltzer, 492-3.

189 Meltzer, 497-8.

190 Meltzer, 498-9.

191 Meltzer, 498.

192 Meltzer, 502-3.

193 Meltzer, 500-3.

194 Board of Governors of the Federal Reserve System (U.S.), *Banking and Monetary Statistics*, 395-6, 400.

195 Meltzer, 539-40.

196 Meltzer, 503-5.

197 Meltzer, 506.

198 Meltzer, 509-10.

199 Meltzer, 510.

200 Blakey and Blakey, "Revenue Act of 1937," 698-9.

201 Meltzer, 521.

202 United States Department of Labor, "Analysis of Strikes," 3.

203 Meltzer, 523-4.

204 Eggertsson and Pugsley, "Mistake of 1937," 11; Meltzer, 531.

205 Allison, *Destined for War*, xvi.

US Debt Crisis and Adjustment (2007–2011)

US Debt Crisis and Adjustment (2007–2011)

This section provides a detailed account of the most recent big US debt crisis, focusing on the period from 2007 to 2011. It was written with reference to the template laid out in the "Archetypal Big Debt Cycle" section but also pays close attention to the enormous number of particulars that occurred during this period. Please note how well the particulars of this case fit with the generalizations described in the template. For example, when you read about the pooling and securitization of mortgages, the levering up of investment banks, and the rapid growth of derivatives that were traded off of regulated exchanges, see these as new ways of providing leverage outside the protection and regulation of authorities. If you don't make the connection between the particulars of this case and the generalization, then you will miss how classic this debt crisis really was.

In providing you with this narrative, I'm also hoping to convey an up-close feeling of what it was like to go through the experience day-by-day. I encourage you, at each point, to think about what you would do a) as an investor and b) as a policy maker. I will give you that experience by describing the timeline week-by-week (and sometimes day-by-day), while showing on the sides of each page a "newsfeed" (primarily *New York Times* articles). I will also include excerpts from Bridgewater *Daily Observations*, which show what we were thinking at the time. However, I will not describe how we moved our investment positions around because how we do that is proprietary. Because there is so much here, I've organized it so that it's easy to skim by reading just the bold passages.

The Emerging Bubble: 2004–2006

In the early and healthy part of the typical debt cycle, debt grows appropriately in line with income growth because the debt is being used to finance activities that produce fast income growth to service debts. The debt-to-GDP ratio is a proxy of whether or not this is happening in a balanced way, but a rough one because, at first, the amount of income a debt will produce is a matter of conjecture. During the 1990s, debt-to-GDP ratios increased only a little in the US—and it was a period of relatively strong income growth and low unemployment. The 2001 recession, which was caused by the tightening of monetary policy, the bursting of the dot-com bubble, and the shock of the 9/11 terrorist attacks, prompted the Federal Reserve to lower interest rates all the way from 6.5 percent to 1 percent. Note how close the US rate was to 0 percent at this point. The big rate cuts stimulated borrowing and spending, especially by households. This made the 2001 recession a short-lived and shallow one, but it set the stage for the subsequent bubble period, which was building most rapidly between 2004 and 2006.

During this period, US economic conditions looked excellent by most measures. Growth was relatively steady at 3 to 4 percent, the unemployment rate was below its long term average at between 4 and 5 percent, and inflation was mostly between 2 and 3.5 percent—a bit higher than desirable, but not worrisome by traditional measures. At the same time, the economy was classically entering its "late cycle" phase as capacity constraints began to appear (e.g., the GDP gap was 2 percent and growth in demand was above growth in capacity). Financial and housing markets were very strong, financed by debt.

**News &
Bridgewater Daily Observations
(BDO)**

January 22, 2004
Home Building Keeps Driving the Economy
"The Commerce Department said yesterday that construction began on a larger-than-expected number of homes in December, capping the best year for new housing in a quarter of a century and leading some industry analysts to raise their housing forecasts for 2004."
—New York Times

April 22, 2004
Greenspan Calms Investors On Growth
"One day after Mr. Greenspan rocked financial markets by declaring that the threat of deflation had disappeared, investors in stocks and Treasury securities seemed calmed by the Fed chairman's strong hint that rising productivity and low inflation would allow the central bank to keep interest rates at rock-bottom levels a bit longer…Mr. Greenspan said that the economy had 'entered a period of more vigorous expansion.'"
—New York Times

September 26, 2004
Next Up on Reality TV: Flipping Real Estate, for Fun and Profit
"It was only a matter of time before the Southern California real estate market turned from a hair-raising reality into a hair-raising reality television show…In most parts of the country, people buy places because they want to live in them. But in markets where prices rise every month, flipping looks like an easy way to get rich."
—New York Times

News & Bridgewater Daily Observations (BDO)

October 20, 2004
Mortgage Debt Not Big Burden, Greenspan Says
"Alan Greenspan on Tuesday defended one of the most tangible results of his tenure as chairman of the Federal Reserve Board: the big increase in homeowner debt.

In his most detailed discussion yet on the subject, Mr. Greenspan disputed analysts who worry that home buyers have become swept up in a speculative housing bubble that the Fed is partly responsible for creating.'"
–*New York Times*

November 6, 2004
When Good Debt Turns Bad
"No one knows if or when accumulated debt could become unsustainable. But after years of encouraging borrowing with rock-bottom interest rates, policy makers should at least admit the possibility of a debilitating crunch—and act accordingly."
–*New York Times*

April 28, 2005
Mortgage Applications Up
"Mortgage applications increased last week as people took advantage of a decline in borrowing costs to buy homes and refinance existing loans, a private survey showed yesterday."
–*New York Times*

May 10, 2005
The U.S. Housing Bubble
"The US housing market started to look frothy a few years back and now looks to us to be in a full-blown bubble. The housing market has been a major source of strength to the US economy, and the popping of this bubble would have more dire consequences than an equity market fall. Selling one's house at a loss can be very traumatic—it is the largest and most leveraged asset of the household sector. Losing equity in one's house can devastate the household sector's net worth, and losing more than one's equity can paralyze the economy (e.g., most people couldn't sell their homes, which means that they couldn't move)."

May 25, 2005
Steep Rise in Prices for Homes Adds to Worry About a Bubble
"Home prices rose more quickly over the last year than at any point since 1980, a national group of Realtors reported yesterday, raising new questions about whether some local housing markets may be turning into bubbles destined to burst...Over all, home prices have never fallen by a significant amount, and Alan Greenspan, the chairman of the Federal Reserve, said on Friday that a national drop in price remained unlikely."
–*New York Times*

The Federal Reserve, focusing on growth, inflation, and the GDP gap more than debt growth, increased interest rates gradually, from the lows of 1 percent in 2004 to just over 5 percent in 2006.

That was not enough to slow debt-financed asset appreciation. Over those three years, the S&P 500 returned 35 percent, as earnings grew by 32 percent. While these 10 percent per year gains were good, they were not anywhere near the gains seen during the dot-com bubble of the late 1990s. With the economy strong, inflation moderate, and asset prices appreciating well, the economy appeared to most people as though it was in **a "Goldilocks" period—not too hot and not too cold**. Debt/GDP grew at an average rate of 12.6 percent during the period. **Typically that's when bubbles emerge because central banks focus on inflation and growth (which isn't a problem) and they don't adequately worry about debt-financed purchases of investment assets.**

Because debt bubbles typically emerge in one or a couple of markets, they are often hidden beneath the averages and can only be seen by doing pro forma financial stress tests of the significant areas to see how they would hold up and what the knock-on effects of them not holding up would be.

The Housing Market Debt Bubble

In this case, the most important area in which the bubble was emerging was housing. From 2004 to 2006, home prices increased around 30 percent and had increased more than 80 percent since 2000, supported by increasingly liberal lending practices. That was the fastest pace of real housing price increases in a century, except for the immediate post-WWII period. The price rise was classically self-reinforcing in a way that often creates bubbles. Because most houses are bought with borrowed money, **home price gains have magnified impacts on equity values**. For example, if a household used their savings of $50,000 as a down-payment on a $250,000 house, and that house went up in value to $350,000, then the household's investment tripled. This allowed for more borrowing and attracted other buyers and other lenders to finance them, as this lending was very profitable.

Household debt rose from 85 percent of household disposable income in 2000 to about 120 percent in 2006. Credit standards were lowered, and while all income quintiles increased their debt substantially over the period, the biggest percentage increase in debt between 2001 and 2007 was among borrowers in the bottom quintile of income earners.[1] As mortgage lending practices became more liberal, even non-home buyers ran up debts by borrowing against their home equity—home equity loans and cash-out refinancing totaled $500 billion in 2005, up five times compared to 1998.[2] That pushed overall US debt to over 300 percent of GDP.

The more prices went up, the more credit standards were lowered (even though it would have been logical for the opposite to happen), but both lenders and borrowers found lending and buying houses on borrowed money to be very profitable. The credit-fueled buying drove up prices even more, creating self-reinforcing expectations and drawing in new borrowers/lenders who did not want to miss out on the action. This is classic in bubble periods.

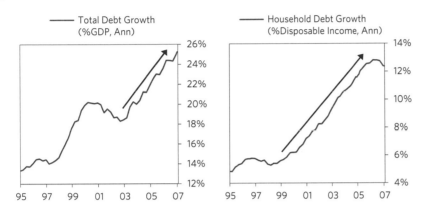

The US housing market was showing **every sign of a classic bubble**. To repeat my defining characteristics of a bubble:

1) **Prices are high relative to traditional measures.**

2) **Prices are discounting future rapid price appreciation from these high levels.**

3) **There is broad bullish sentiment.**

4) **Purchases are being financed by high leverage.**

5) **Buyers have made exceptionally extended forward purchases (e.g., built inventory, contracted forward purchases, etc.) to speculate or protect themselves against future price gains.**

6) **New buyers (i.e., those who weren't previously in the market) have entered the market.**

7) **Stimulative monetary policy helps inflate the bubble, and tight policy contributes to its popping.**

All of these were true for the US housing market. Prices rose quickly and were widely expected to continue doing so (e.g., "home flippers" would buy a home, do some renovations, and aim to take advantage of rising prices to make a short-term profit). Homebuilders were ramping up supply that wouldn't come on line for months or years, in anticipation of high prices being sustained—new single family home construction doubled between 1995 and 2005.[3] As people saw their friends and neighbors becoming richer through homeownership, more people wanted to buy homes. At the peak of the bubble, just shy of 8 percent of households were buying a home each year (around 50 percent more than today). A *TIME* magazine cover from the summer of 2005 (roughly the peak) conveyed the speculative mania, asking "Will Your House Make You Rich?"

**News &
Bridgewater Daily Observations
(BDO)**

May 31, 2005
Fed Debates Pricking the U.S. Housing 'Bubble'
"Mr. Greenspan and other officials have long argued that it is not their job to influence the price of assets whether stock prices or real estate. Rather, they contend, the central bank's job is to keep inflation low and to promote the maximum sustainable growth without fueling inflation."
–New York Times

July 9, 2005
Boom in Jobs, Not Just Houses, as Real Estate Drives Economy
"The real estate industrial complex, the economic engine that has become one of the few reliable sources of growth in recent years. Encompassing everything from land surveyors to general contractors to loan officers, the sprawling sector has added 700,000 jobs to the nation's payrolls over the last four years, according to an analysis by Economy.com, a research firm."
–New York Times

August 17, 2005
Healthy Housing Market Lifted the Economy in July
–New York Times

August 28, 2005
Greenspan Says Housing Boom Is Nearly Over
"Looking forward to the time after he steps down as chairman of the Federal Reserve, Alan Greenspan predicted here on Saturday that the nation's frenzied housing boom—and the consumer spending that it has spurred—is near an end."
–New York Times

October 4, 2005
Slowing Is Seen in Housing Prices in Hot Markets
"A real estate slowdown that began in a handful of cities this summer has spread to almost every hot housing market in the country, including New York."
–New York Times

December 17, 2005
New Strategy for Growth at Citigroup
"For the first time in at least five years, Citigroup is focusing on expanding existing businesses. It will broaden its retail presence in the United States by adding about 300 branches and banking centers, largely in areas like Philadelphia and New Jersey, where it already has customers."
–New York Times

**News &
Bridgewater Daily Observations
(BDO)**

January 8, 2006
***Warning: Beware of Warnings About Real
Estate***
"Fund investors who amassed colossal gains in
real estate over the previous few years were
warned not to expect a repeat in 2005. The
long-running rally could lose steam, some
analysts predicted, which meant that it was time
to consider selling. But those naysayers turned out
to be wrong. Many investors who stayed the
course and ignored the warnings about real estate
bubbles continued to profit: the sector ended yet
another year among the top fund categories."
–New York Times

February 1, 2006
***Exit Greenspan, Amid Questions on
Economy***
"Stepping down on Tuesday after 18 years as
steward of the nation's economy, Alan Greenspan
left his successor a wide berth to set his own
policy but some major uncertainties about the
future.

But the handoff also meant that Mr. Bernanke
would face murkier choices at a time of
substantial risks that increase the chances for
serious missteps."
–New York Times

February 10, 2006
US Trade Deficit Hit Record High In 2005
"The U.S. trade deficit jumped nearly 18 percent
in 2005, the government reported Friday, hitting
its fourth consecutive record as consumer demand
for imports increased, energy prices soared and
the dollar strengthened against other currencies...

The $725.8 billion gap, which is almost exactly
twice the deficit in 2001, was driven by a 12
percent jump in imports and a more muted 10
percent increase in exports, the Commerce
Department reported in Washington. The nation
last had a trade surplus, of $12.4 billion, in 1975."
–New York Times

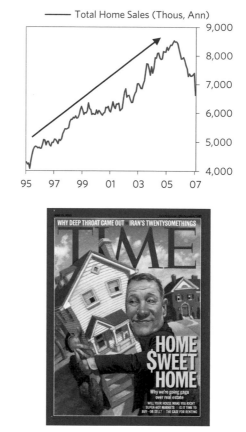

— Total Home Sales (Thous, Ann)

From TIME, 12 June © 2005 Time Inc. All rights reserved. Used by permission and protection by the Copyright Laws of the United States. The printing, copying redistribution, or retransmission of this Content without express written permission is prohibited.

In other words, there was **leveraging up to bet more aggressively on prices
continuing to increase. At the same time, supplies were increasing as the
higher prices encouraged production. Logic should dictate precisely the
opposite behavior: those betting on price changes ought to be more inclined
to deleverage or sell, and those who lend to them should be more cautious
when these things are happening. However, this sort of nonsensical
thinking is typical in bubbles.**

Just as there was a mania to buy houses, there was a mania to lend to people
to buy houses. The chart on the left on the next page shows aggregate
mortgage rates. As a result of the Fed's easy monetary policies, they fell to
lows in 2003 not seen since the 1950s, and stayed near those lows well into
the housing bubble. Leveraging up took off in 2003-2007, even after rates rose
by about 1.5 percent in 2005-2007. The chart on the right shows the loan-to-
value ratio of new housing loans—higher numbers mean mortgages had
smaller down-payments and larger loans. The fast increase to 80 percent was
an indication that banks were more eager to loan and willing to make riskier
bets. Other signs of housing loan froth were common. Banks often didn't
require borrowers to show proof of income before receiving a mortgage and
they pushed adjustable rate mortgages that enticed borrowers with low "teaser"
rates now before rates increased later on. "Subprime" mortgages (e.g., riskier
ones) became 20 percent of the market. And as we'll discuss later in much

more detail, banks were able to package this debt in ways that obscured its underlying risks (i.e., "securitization"), helping fuel the easy availability of credit and low interest rates.

News & Bridgewater Daily Observations (BDO)

April 19, 2006
Fed Signals Policy Shift on Rates
"The Federal Reserve hinted Tuesday that it might stop its campaign to raise interest rates as early as next month, a possibility that set off a surge in stocks even as crude oil prices rose above $71 a barrel...Officials suggested that, after nudging up short-term interest rates 15 times in nearly two years, the increase in May might be the last one for some time."
—*New York Times*

July 10, 2006
Paulson Sworn In As Treasury Secretary
"Former Goldman Sachs chief executive Henry M. Paulson was sworn in as the nation's 74th Treasury secretary on Monday, and he pledged to make sure the United States does not retreat from the world economy.

'We must always remember that the strength of the U.S. economy is linked to the strength of the global economy,' Paulson said in remarks during a brief ceremony."
—*Associated Press*

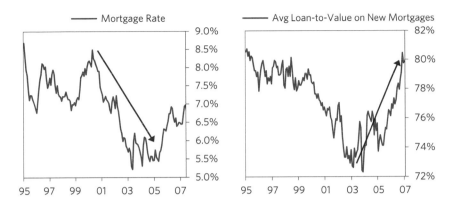

For all of the debt build-up and frenzied housing activity, the economy didn't overheat and inflation remained moderate, so the Fed, looking at the average numbers, remained unconcerned. **It is typically the case that the worst debt bubbles (e.g., the US in 1929, Japan in 1989) are not accompanied by high and rising goods and services inflation, but by asset price inflation financed by debt growth. Typically, central banks make the mistake of accommodating the debt growth because they are focused on goods and services inflation (as measured by the CPI) and/or growth. They are not focused on debt growth, which is what they are creating, and on whether the debts will produce the incomes to service them**, which is what they should be thinking about if they want to prevent bad debt crises.

As you can see in the charts below, as inflation was mostly between 2 and 3.5 percent—a bit higher than desirable but not worrisome—the Fed kept interest rates low well into the expansion. In fact, US short-term interest rates were below inflation (i.e., real short-term borrowing costs were negative) from late 2001 until early 2006. Even when the Fed did begin raising short-term rates in mid-2004, long-term nominal interest rates remained roughly flat, and real long-term interest rates declined.

News &
Bridgewater Daily Observations (BDO)

August 23, 2006
How Big A Problem Will the Housing Slowdown Be?
"The economy in aggregate is continuing to hum along with the exception of housing. Is housing the dead canary in the coal mine, or will the economy churn along despite the housing slowdown? We're wrestling with this…"

August 24, 2006
New Signs of Cooling in Housing
"The housing market is deteriorating by the month. In the latest and strongest indication that the home buying and selling frenzy is over, the National Association of Realtors reported yesterday that sales of previously owned homes fell to the lowest level in July in more than two years, prices flattened and sellers waited longer and longer to find buyers for their homes."
—*New York Times*

September 14, 2006
Foreclosures Are Up on Some Mortgages
"Foreclosures on prime adjustable-rate mortgages rose to a four-year high in the second quarter, a sign that more homeowners with good credit ratings are having trouble paying their bills…The rate of subprime ARM's — representing lending to people with poor credit histories — that were entering foreclosure rose to 2.01 percent, the highest since the fourth quarter of 2003, the report showed."
—*Bloomberg*

As shown below, the same was broadly true across the developed world.

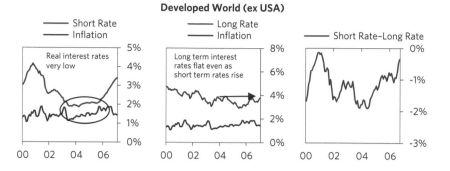

For all these reasons, a global financial bubble was emerging.

In the middle of 2006, Hank Paulson was confirmed as George W. Bush's Treasury Secretary. He came to that job from the position of chairman and CEO of Goldman Sachs, which gave him an exposure to the markets that made him generally concerned about the excesses in the financial markets, so he convened and held regular meetings with the President's Working Group on Financial Markets, which was comprised of the top members of the Bush economic team and key regulators.[4] The primary benefit of these meetings was that they built close working relationships among the members, most importantly between Paulson, Fed Chairman Ben Bernanke, and New York Fed President Tim Geithner, and their agencies.

In all financial crises, the personalities, capabilities, and ability to work well together play crucial roles in influencing the outcomes. In this case, the most important relationships were between Paulson (an extroverted former CEO who was used to making bold decisions), Bernanke (an introverted economist who was well-schooled in the Great Depression), and Geithner (a practical operator experienced in the workings of government economic policy making). Their complementary qualities, in combination with their often hourly coordination and their shared willingness to be bold and quickly evolve policies based on new learnings, were critical to their navigating through this crisis.

While all three men had concerns about the "dry tinder and gathering storm," and tried to lean against the excesses that they perceived, the problems weren't clear enough to them to prompt them to move quickly or forcefully enough to prevent what was to come. They noted the excesses in the subprime market, but none saw these excesses spilling over to the overall housing market, which had not seen a nationwide decline since World War II. Paulson, however, was very concerned about the risks posed by Fannie Mae and Freddie Mac (known as Government Supported Entities, or GSEs), which Larry Summers also highlighted when he was Treasury secretary in the Clinton administration. That prompted Paulson to get President Bush's support in the fall of 2006 to begin working on legislation with Barney Frank (then the ranking minority member of the House Financial Services Committee) to reform those entities, though that push didn't lead to progress until the crisis came to a head in the summer of 2008.[5]

The Emerging Broader-Based Bubble

The broader economy also showed signs of a bubble. Savings rates declined from low to lower and the US aggressively sucked in capital from abroad. US manufacturing employment fell and the US was rapidly losing global export market share to emerging countries, especially China. However, the increase in housing-related activity camouflaged this; for instance, construction employment in support of building houses increasingly financed by debt rose by around 50 percent compared to 1995.

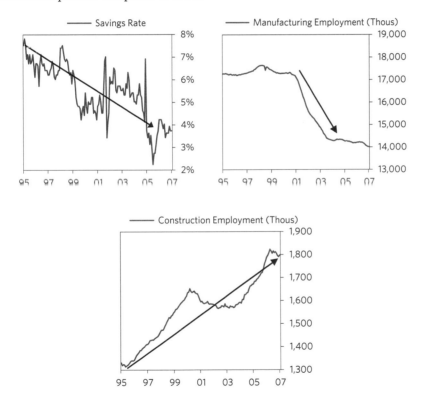

In addition, a lot of money to fund consumption was also borrowed via mortgages and other types of debt instruments. **High debt growth to fund consumption rather than investment is a red flag, since consumption doesn't produce an income, while investment might.**

News & Bridgewater Daily Observations (BDO)

October 24, 2006
This Time, It's Not the Economy
"President Bush, in hopes of winning credit for his party's stewardship of the economy, is spending two days this week campaigning on the theme that the economy is purring. 'No question that a strong economy is going to help our candidates,' Mr. Bush said in a CNBC interview yesterday, 'primarily because they have got something to run on, they can say our economy's good because I voted for tax relief.'"
–*New York Times*

October 27, 2006
New-Home Prices Fall Sharply
"Home builders, struggling to keep ahead in a weakening market, cut prices and offered a variety of other discounts in September to help sell their newly constructed houses, the latest government and industry statistics show. The Commerce Department reported yesterday that the median price of a new home plunged 9.7 percent last month, compared with September 2005, falling to $217,100, the biggest such drop since December 1970."
–*New York Times*

November 7, 2006
In Arizona, 'For Sale' Is a Sign of the Times
"Until recently, this fast-growing area was a paradise on earth for home builders. Fulton Homes' developments, for example, were so popular last year that it was able to raise prices on its new homes by $1,000 to $10,000 almost every week...Today, the number of unsold homes in the area has soared to almost 46,000 from just a few thousand in early 2005. And builders are pulling back as fast as they can."
–*New York Times*

December 6, 2006
What Statistics on Home Sales Aren't Saying
"The truth is that the official numbers on house prices—the last refuge of soothing information about the real estate market on the coasts—are deeply misleading. Depending on which set you look at, you'll see that prices have either continued to rise, albeit modestly, or have fallen slightly over the last year. But the statistics have a number of flaws, perhaps the biggest being that they are based only on homes that have actually sold."
–*New York Times*

Typical of such periods, a lot of foreign money came pouring in to participate in the bubble, as reflected in both capital inflows and our current account deficit swelling (to 6 percent of GDP). A lot of this money was coming from emerging economies such as China, which were running huge current account surpluses at the time and were choosing to save/invest in US assets. Strong capital inflows allowed US citizens to borrow so they could continue consuming more than they were earning.

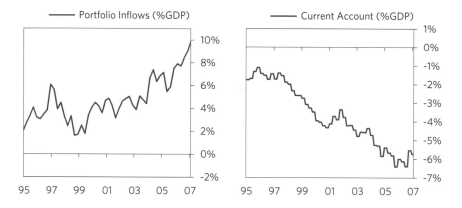

Strong demand for US assets abroad also helped keep long-term borrowing costs low even as the Fed began raising short-term interest rates in late 2004.

Many of these flows went to lending that would not produce the income to service the debts. They supported a dynamic that was unsustainable: The savings rate can't fall indefinitely, and the wave of lending can't increase forever. As the debts came due, there would be cash flow problems. When we ran our pro forma financial numbers, we could see that when all these flows tapered off, there would be cash flow problems.

During this period, lending increased and became riskier, and it increasingly occurred outside the regulated and protected banking system. Growth of new ways of lending outside of the normal banking system—often called the "shadow banking" system—is a common feature of bubble periods. Typically, financial institutions build new channels that get around the more established and better-regulated ones because it is initially advantageous to everyone involved. Fewer regulations make it cheaper to lend, borrowers get lower rates and easier terms, and investors get a small boost to returns. Often, shadow banks are able to make these new debt assets seem safe to investors via guarantees or through the way the assets are combined and packaged. Without having been through a crisis to stress-test them, it can be hard to tell if they really are as safe as they're made out to be. Often, these "innovations" lead to the crisis. That was true in this case.

In the early-to-mid-2000s, a number of new channels for increasing leverage popped up, and a number of existing less-regulated channels became larger. Many of these were short-term in nature and unregulated and thus were particularly vulnerable. During the bubble, there were five key components that helped fuel leveraging outside the traditional banking system:

1) <u>Use of repo agreements and commercial paper.</u> These developed into huge channels through which banks and corporations could borrow over short periods of time. Ben Bernanke notes that "repo liabilities of US broker dealers increased by a factor of 2.5 in the four years before the crisis."[6]

2) <u>Large institutional depositors outside the protected banking system.</u> Demand for Treasury securities, especially from foreign investors, outstripped supply, so there was a shortage of safe assets for investors. This led to demand for substitutes like asset-backed commercial paper and repo.

3) <u>Development of money market funds,</u> a short-term savings vehicle which promised higher returns than bank accounts without much additional risk.

4) <u>Globalization of dollar lending,</u> leading to the explosion of dollar borrowing and lending outside of US banks.

5) <u>Securitization of lending,</u> where banks take their traditional loans (auto loans, home loans, etc.) and sell them to other investors. This creates a "moral hazard" problem in which banks have an incentive to make risky loans since they can sell them and not bear the consequences (as long as investors remain willing to buy).

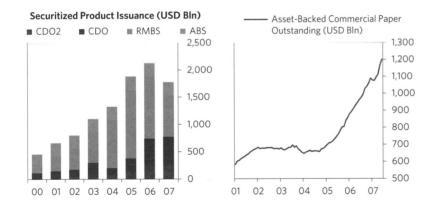

The US financial regulatory system did not keep pace with these developments. It did not provide adequate regulatory visibility into the shadow banks and markets, nor did it provide the authorities with the powers they needed to curb their excesses, though, as is typical, that wasn't apparent at first. Banks and shadow banks at the time were inadequately capitalized and over-leveraged. This meant they didn't have much cushion and would be exposed to solvency problems in a downturn. In the 1990s and early 2000s era of financial liberalization and financial engineering, regulators were more concerned about the US financial industry staying competitive with London, which discouraged them from pulling in the reins.

If the debt boom had been financed largely by the banking system, it would have been dramatically easier to manage and the run easier to contain. It still would have been a bad crisis with a bad recession, but not as bad as this crisis

**News &
Bridgewater Daily Observations
(BDO)**

January 5, 2007
Job Market Ends 2006 on Strong Note
–New York Times

January 13. 2007
Retail Sales Last Month Surprised With Big Rise
–Reuters

January 20, 2007
Consumer Sentiment Reaches 3-Year High
–Reuters

January 26, 2007
Sales of Existing Homes in '06 Had Biggest Drop in 17 Years
–Associated Press

February 2, 2007
Jobs Growth Slows but Remains Strong
–New York Times

February 5, 2007
Growing Financial Risks
"Market returns are driven by how events transpire relative to what is discounted. At this time the markets are discounting the lowest risks in decades, yet we believe that the imbedded risks in the system are quite large. We'll explain.

Right now the financial markets are awash with liquidity...It seems to us that money is now being thrown at financial instruments like it is being thrown at the art, jewelry and high-priced real-estate markets. Prices of risky assets, particularly those with positive carry, are being driven up, and yields/carries are being driven down, making expected future returns low. Simultaneously volatility has shrunk; as a result, low volatility is being assumed to continue and reaching for yields has caused increased leverage to be employed in order to try to squeeze more return out of the puny spreads/carry trades."

February 8, 2007
HSBC Reports Rise in Troubled Loans
"HSBC Holdings, a bank based in Britain, said on Wednesday that its charge for bad debts would be more than $10.5 billion for 2006, some 20 percent above analysts' average forecasts, because of problems in its mortgage portfolio."
–Reuters

February 27, 2007
Black Tuesday in China
"They're calling it Black Tuesday in China: local stock markets unexpectedly sold off, losing nearly 9% of their value, and putting pressure on equity prices around the world.

Analysts said the Shanghai and Shenzhen markets were reacting to widespread rumors of plans by the Chinese government to raise interest rates or institute a capital gains tax, measures that would serve to temper local stock markets that were up about 10% for the year before Tuesday's decline."
–Forbes

**News &
Bridgewater Daily Observations
(BDO)**

March 6, 2007
Stocks Rise in Asia, Europe and U.S.
"The five-day slide in Asian stock markets halted today, as investors took advantage of low prices and started buying again, sparking relief in the region."
–*New York Times*

March 10, 2007
Investors Get a Break, but Some Lenders Absorb Blows
"The crisis in mortgage loans to people with weak, or subprime, credit intensified as a large lender, New Century Financial, stopped accepting loan applications because several of its financial backers cut off access to credit lines... Several dozen mortgage companies have gone out of business because of high default rates on mortgages written last year when lending standards were significantly more relaxed."
–*New York Times*

turned out to be. There would have been less forced selling and a less dangerous margin spiral, as the FDIC's systemic risk exemption powers to guarantee liabilities, combined with deposit insurance and the Fed's discount window, would have had more power and reach.

So it was not just low interest rates that fueled the bubble, but rather a combination of easy money, lax regulation, and risky financial innovations. As the Fed was looking at inflation and not debt growth when setting interest rates, and as policy makers allowed the lax regulation of shadow lending channels to continue, the bubble was allowed to grow.

Borrowers and lenders had severe asset/liability mismatches, which left them especially vulnerable in a downturn. This is a classic ingredient of a severe debt crisis. Most commonly these mismatches come in the following forms:

1) **Borrowing short-term and lending long-term, leaving them to be squeezed when those who lent to them short-term don't want to lend to them anymore or only want to lend to them at interest rates much higher than what they are earning on the loans they have already made.**

2) **Lending to risky borrowers who will pay higher interest rates than they borrowed at in order to collect the credit spread—until the default rates pick up to a level greater than the credit spread.**

3) **Borrowing in one currency and lending/investing in another. When the currency they borrowed in rises, it forces borrowers to pay back the loan at a higher exchange rate or a higher interest rate than they can manage.**

All these things happened during this bubble, which made these financial intermediaries and those who trusted them with their money very vulnerable to runs and credit problems.

One classic asset/liability mismatch that developed occurred via European banks actively borrowing dollars with short-term debt and then lending them to the world. When dollar credit tightened in the summer of 2007, these banks lost access to funding from the US money markets and became transmitters of contagion around the world.

Still, the economy continued to grow above potential. The GDP gap rose to 3 percent, while inflation rose to 3.7 percent. The Fed continued to tighten to bring the nominal short rate to 5.25 percent and the real short rate to 1.5 percent in 2007.

By 2007, I was sure that we were in a bubble because it had all the classic signs previously described, plus when we did cash flow projections for companies and financial institutions, we suspected that they would not be able to secure the amount of new lending they needed to allow them to roll over their debts that were coming due, while at the same time increasing their borrowing to sustain what they were doing. Without that new lending, there would be a debt crisis. We regularly reported our thinking and estimates to policy makers, giving them the choice of believing our numbers so that they could be better prepared, or correcting our numbers so that we could see where we were wrong. They typically took the research in without comment but with questions.

The Top: 2007

The First Half of 2007

Keep in mind that up until this time, hardly anyone was concerned about hardly anything because both the markets and the economy were doing great. Stocks were reaching new highs, the job market remained strong, retail sales were strong, and so was consumer sentiment.

However the housing market and its most aggressive financers began to show some cracks. As the SEC wrote in a memo on January 4, "[t]here is a broad recognition that, with the refinancing and real estate booms over, the business model of many of the smaller subprime originators is no longer viable."[7]

Markets were flatter between February and March, and overall market volatility was pretty low and priced to stay that way. Credit spreads, a measure of the perception of the risk of lending to private companies, were relatively low compared to historical norms. In other words, the market was tranquil and priced to stay that way.

Problems emanating out of subprime mortgage lenders—those that focused on mortgages for less credit-worthy borrowers—continued to grow, with some facing considerable losses, but they did not affect the broader economy and markets. Still, bigger banks were starting to report a rise in bad mortgage debts. We summarized the situation (in our March 13 *Daily Observations*) as follows:

(BDO) March 13: Subprime Mortgage Fallout

Subprime mortgages have been grabbing the headlines, with several of the larger subprime mortgage lenders teetering on the edge of bankruptcy. The story of how the subprime mortgage sector is blowing up even with a relatively strong economy relates closely to the liquidity that is bubbling up in markets around the world. **Over the last few years, investment banks have been hard at work creating fancy new products where they can package up a bunch of assets and sell the package for more than the sum of the parts** (CDOs, CMOs, synthetic CDOs, etc.). They do this by tranching them up and getting the ratings agencies to rate the best slice AAA, the next slice AA, and so on. This financial "innovation" makes everyone happy: insurance companies get an AAA-rated bond that yields a few basis points more than their other AAA options, and so on down the line. Often hedge funds end up with the bottom piece, and that makes them happy because they get a lot of leverage/volatility. **This innovation opens up a source of credit to many risky borrowers (not**

News & Bridgewater Daily Observations (BDO)

March 22, 2007
Markets Soar After Remarks From Fed
"Wall Street rallied sharply yesterday after the Federal Reserve raised investors' hopes that it had warmed to the idea of lowering short-term interest rates.

After triple-digit gains yesterday, the Dow Jones industrial average has surged 337 points this week, its best three-day performance since November 2004.

The Fed, as expected, left short-term interest rates unchanged at 5.25 percent at the conclusion of its two day meeting. But investors, who nervously awaited the economic statement that accompanies the Fed's decision, were encouraged that the central bank had not referred to the possibility of 'additional firming' of rates as it did in January."
—Associated Press

March 22, 2007
After Sell-Off, Chinese Stocks Back at a Record
—New York Times

March 23, 2007
Existing-Home Sales Rise Most in 3 Years
—Associated Press

April 2, 2007
New Century Files for Bankruptcy
—New York Times

April 17, 2007
Shares Rally on Strong Earnings Reports
"Stocks rose yesterday as better-than-expected profits at Citigroup and a healthy increase in consumer spending renewed the optimism of investors about the economy."
—Associated Press

April 22, 2007
For the Dow, Three Record Highs in Five Days
—New York Times

April 26, 2007
Durable-Goods Picture Shows Surprising Strength
—New York Times

May 17, 2007
Mixed News About Housing Only Briefly Slows the Rally
"Wall Street shot higher yesterday after investors shrugged off a mixed reading on the housing sector and focused on a jump in industrial output, a retreat in crude oil prices and new cash pouring into the stock market."
—Associated Press

May 25, 2007
Shares Fall After a Surge in Home Sales
"Wall Street retreated yesterday after housing data showed that sales surged in April by the largest jump in 14 years, dampening hopes of an interest rate cut to stimulate the economy."
—Associated Press

**News &
Bridgewater Daily Observations
(BDO)**

June 2, 2007
Wall St. Buoyed by Economic Data
"Wall Street carved out a solid advance yesterday
after data on job creation, manufacturing and
inflation injected the market with renewed
confidence about the economy and sent major
indexes to record closes."

–Associated Press

June 5, 2007
*Shares Post Slight Gains as Slide in China Is
Shrugged Off*

–Associated Press

just households) who previously would have had trouble accessing credit markets. **The explosion in subprime mortgages is closely related to this new source of credit.** Originators paid less and less attention to underwriting standards because they were just going to hand off the mortgages to the investment banks. The investment banks were eager to package them up and sell them to investors. The investors were getting 5bps more yield for the same credit rating. Lending standards slipped to absurdly low levels, and then a small up-tick in delinquencies caused the banks to refuse to buy the loans and the originators to be stuck with the losses.

…The thing that is really hammering the subprime lenders is "early payment defaults." The agreements with the investment banks who bought the subprime loans contained provisions that the lender would have to buy back the loans if the borrower missed one of the first few payments. Without fraud, it is very rare for a borrower to miss the first payment on a mortgage. In December, New Century, the second biggest subprime lender in 2006, disclosed that borrowers had failed to make the first payment on fully 2.5% of their loans. When the banks/investors demanded New Century buy back these loans, New Century couldn't come up with the cash. Several dozen smaller subprime lenders have gone bust this way in the last few months, although New Century is the biggest.

Most people thought that these troubles in one corner of the financial markets would not cause meaningful contagion elsewhere. On March 28, Chairman Bernanke said in Congressional testimony that "the impact on the broader economy and financial markets of the problems in the subprime market seems likely to be contained."[8] I had a similar assessment at the time, though I was more concerned about the extent of leverage and tightening going on in this bubble.

The US stock market continued to rally through April and May, hitting new records. The shaded portion of the chart shows the rally in the first half of the year.

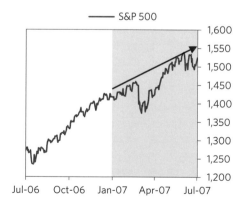

In mid-June, 10-year Treasury yields hit 5.3 percent (the highest point since 2002), and in mid-July, the 90-day T-bill rate hit 5 percent, meaning the yield curve was very flat. That was the cyclical peak because of what came next.

As interest rates rise, so do debt service payments (both on new items bought on credit, as well as on previously acquired credit that was financed with variable rate debt). This discourages additional borrowing (as credit becomes more expensive) and reduces disposable income (as more money is spent on debt service). Because people borrow less and have less money left over to spend, spending slows, and since one person's spending is another person's income, incomes drop, and so on and so forth. When people spend less, prices go down, and economic activity decreases.

Simultaneously, as short-term interest rates rise and the yield curve flattens or inverts, liquidity declines, and the return on holding short duration assets (such as cash) increases as their yields rise. As these assets become relatively more attractive to hold in relation to longer duration financial assets (such as bonds, equities, and real estate), as well as those assets with lower grade credit ratings (as the spread to these assets declines), money moves out of financial assets, causing them to fall in value. Declining asset prices in turn create negative wealth effects, which feed back into the economy through declining spending and incomes.

The tightening popped the bubble.

As interest rates rose, home prices began to decline, since debt service payments on new homes would be higher, and interest payments on many existing mortgages rose quickly because many subprime borrowers had taken out adjustable rate mortgages (ARMs). As interest rates rose, so did their debt service payments. By June, these tightening pressures flowed through to the first broad sign of financial distress: rising foreclosures and delinquencies started to translate into meaningful losses for bigger banks. In mid-June, two hedge funds run out of the investment bank Bear Stearns that invested in subprime mortgage-backed securities (MBS)—one of them leveraged about 20:1[9]—faced growing losses and a wave of investor redemptions. That required them to do a fire-sale of $3.6 billion of the securities, a large amount for the market.[10] The leveraged financial buying shifted into deleveraging selling. As the prices of securities they held fell, the hedge funds faced huge losses and forced liquidations. In the end, Bear Stearns promised a $3.2 billion loan to bail out one of the funds (later reduced to $1.6 billion), and other banks that seized collateral from the hedge funds cooperated to ensure that the market remained stable (e.g., not selling more subprime MBS). The funds would eventually be wiped out. These were relatively small funds, and the initial reverberations were limited.

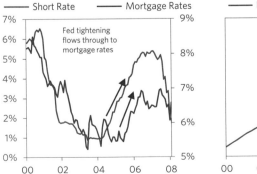

News & Bridgewater Daily Observations (BDO)

June 8, 2007
Yields on Treasuries Climb; Shares Tumble Again
"Not long ago, Wall Street trembled when it looked as if the slowing American economy might be getting worse. But now, anxiety over the potential for higher inflation, driven by a strong global economy, is preoccupying investors.

Yesterday, that fear again took its toll on stocks and bonds, giving share prices their steepest three-day decline since markets dropped around the world in February, and the interest rate on the benchmark 10-year Treasury note rose above 5 percent for the first time since last summer."
–New York Times

June 13, 2007
Bond Yields Soar, Driving Shares Down
–New York Times

June 15, 2007
Wall Street Rises on Tame Inflation Data
–Associated Press

June 15, 2007
More Trouble in Subprime Mortgages
"Delinquencies and foreclosures among homeowners with weak credit moved higher in the first quarter, particularly in California, Florida and other formerly hot real estate markets, according to an industry report released on Thursday. The report, published by the Mortgage Bankers Association, came as the Federal Reserve held a hearing on what regulators could do to address aggressive abusive lending practices."
–New York Times

June 21, 2007
Bear Stearns Shares Off Collapse at Hedge Funds
–New York Times

June 23, 2007
Bear Stearns to Bail Out Troubled Fund
–New York Times

July 3, 2007
Glancing at Implied Vols
"Recent market action has begun to show a slight pickup in implied volatility across all markets, but these increases have come from levels that were as low as they have been in more than 10 years. Looking broadly across markets, we continue to see very low expected future currency, bond, and commodity volatility, while future expected volatility in the equities is low but closer to normal relative to history."

July 13, 2007
Fitch May Downgrade Bonds Tied to Subprime Mortgages
–Bloomberg

July 14, 2007
Dow and S.&P. 500 Set Record Highs
"In a week in which the Dow swung more than 450 points and rose 283 points in Thursday's session alone, investors grappled with unease over soured subprime loans and the broader economy before casting off such concerns and bidding stocks higher amid signs the consumer might yet again pull through and give Wall Street reason to climb."
–Associated Press

News &
Bridgewater Daily Observations
(BDO)

July 16, 2007
ABX Crash
"The market for subprime mortgage debt got significantly worse Monday helping to pace treasuries, and the price action suggests a player, larger than the Bear Stearns funds that blew up in June, is going bust. The Bear Stearns collapse in June hit the low rated tranches; last Friday and Monday the rout began in the higher rated tranches. The triple A rated tranches of subprime mortgage pools were in free-fall on Monday. For instance, the triple A tranches on 2007 mortgages covered by the ABX originally slated to pay a meager 9bps of spread are now trading at 440bps of spread."

July 26, 2007
Market Falls Sharply on Housing and Oil Worries
"Wall Street hit a sharp skid today as more worrisome signs about the health of the housing market emerged and oil prices remained near record levels."

—*New York Times*

The Summer of 2007

Economic growth remained healthy and US equity markets hit new highs in mid-July. The most prominent question was whether the Fed's next move would be to tighten because of inflation concerns, or ease because of housing concerns.

Stress in the housing market was gradually building. The indices of subprime MBS (called the ABX indices) continued to see big price declines (even the AAA bonds, which were likely seen as "riskless" when purchased, fell around 5 percent), and some of the mortgage lenders started reporting increasing numbers of borrowers missing loan payments. One large mortgage lender looked to be closer to bankruptcy, and a small German bank exposed to mortgage loans faced big losses and ended up needing to be acquired by Germany's state bank. New home sales were falling very quickly. As this news emerged, the markets sold off a bit (ending July down 6 percent from the peak).

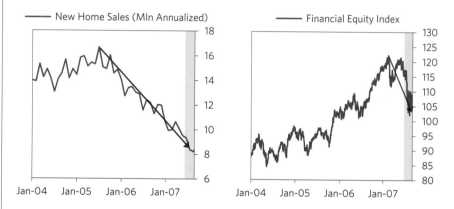

I expected this debt crisis to be self-reinforcing because of the impact that mark-to-market accounting and high leverage would have on lenders. **Debt crises and downturns are self-reinforcing behaviors because as losses occur, both lenders and borrowers are less able to lend and borrow, which worsens conditions. For example, when losses occur, one's capital declines, and because there are limits to how much one can hold in assets relative to one's capital, that means assets have to be sold, or the buying of assets has to be curtailed. That in turn makes asset prices and lending weaker, producing more losses and reinforcing the cycle further.** Because we could get very detailed financial information on banks that allowed us to know their exposures, we could estimate what the values and losses on their positions would be by knowing the pricing of analogous liquid assets. As a result, we constantly did our mark-to-market stress tests, which showed us that the financial sector and those dependent on it were incurring losses before they reported them. We could also get detailed financial information on public companies and our pro forma financial projections showed that many were facing debt squeezes.

Here is what I wrote to our clients and policy makers at the time.

(BDO) July 26: Is This the Big One?
You know our view about the crazy lending and leveraging practices going on, creating a pervasive fragility in the financial system, leading us to believe that interest rates will rise until there is a cracking of the financial system, at which

time everything will reverse (i.e. there will be a move to focusing on fear from focusing on greed, volatilities will increase, and carry and credit spreads will blow out). We had (and now have) no idea exactly when this will occur and if what's happening now is the big one. We just know that 1) we want to avoid or fade this lunacy and 2) no one knows how this financial market contagion will play out.

How it will play out is a function of who is carrying what positions and how these positions and players knock up against each other. **A few months ago we undertook an extensive study to see which market players held what positions, especially via the derivatives markets.** So we read all the studies by government overseers and financial intermediaries, we gathered and examined all the data we could obtain, and we delved into 10-K reports of financial intermediaries. **And we concluded that no one has a clue. That is because one can only vaguely examine these exposures one level deep.** In other words, while it is easy to see some parties' exposures (particularly those of regulated financial intermediaries), it is impossible to see who is carrying these and other positions in order to ascertain the net positions of the important parties. For example, the dealers who are at the epicenter of this know who their counterparties are, but they don't know their counterparties' total positions. But we do know that these exposures have grown rapidly (about four times as large as five years ago) and are huge (about $400 trillion).

At the time, growth still looked good as the debt and tightening conditions hadn't yet passed through to the economy. On July 31, we wrote: "Tuesday's slew of stats continued to convey a picture that the real economy was just fine heading into the recent market action," but we were extremely concerned that the Fed was too sanguine. In its August 7 monetary policy statement, the Fed said: "Financial markets have been volatile in recent weeks, credit conditions have become tighter for some households and businesses, and the housing correction is ongoing. Nevertheless, the economy seems likely to continue to expand at a moderate pace over coming quarters, supported by solid growth in employment and incomes and a robust global economy."

In early August 2007, the mortgage market began to seriously unravel. On August 9, BNP Paribas, France's largest bank and one of the largest in the world by assets, froze $2.2 billion worth of investments in three of its funds because its holdings in US subprime mortgages had exposed it to big losses. Banks in Europe became more nervous about lending to each other, prompting the European Central Bank (ECB) to inject 95 billion euros into the banking system to get rates back to the ECB's target, and another 61 billion the next day. The US also saw a squeeze in safe Treasury bills and higher yields on riskier commercial paper and interbank lending rates. Money market funds, the main holders of asset-backed commercial paper, saw hits to their asset values and required assistance from their sponsors, banks, and fund families in order to avoid "breaking the buck." (By "breaking the buck" I mean falling in value below the amount deposited, which is something depositors assumed would never happen but did.)

The unraveling could be seen in interbank markets. The following chart shows a classic measure of interbank stress, the TED spread, in which a higher number means banks are demanding a higher interest rate to compensate for the risks of lending to each other. It was clear that the top in the debt cycle was being made.

News & Bridgewater Daily Observations (BDO)

August 1, 2007
A Rise in Confidence Amid Mild Inflation
"Personal spending rose at its slowest rate in nine months in June while inflation moderated, but consumers' moods brightened considerably in early July, data showed yesterday."
–Reuters

August 3, 2007
Stocks Fall Sharply Amid Credit Fears
–New York Times

August 7, 2007
American Home Mortgage Seeks Chapter 11 Bankruptcy Protection
–Associated Press

August 7, 2007
Fed Leaves Rate Steady; No Sign of Future Cut
"The Federal Reserve today largely sidestepped the growing anxiety over how tightening credit standards will affect the economy, deciding to leave its benchmark interest rate unchanged at 5.25 percent. More important than the decision to hold rates steady—which was widely expected—the Fed did not significantly adjust the language in its statement explaining the decision."
–New York Times

August 9, 2007
Government May Raise Limits on Home-Loan Purchases
"Alphonso R. Jackson, the secretary of housing and urban development, said yesterday that the government might raise the limit on purchases of home loans by Fannie Mae and Freddie Mac to increase liquidity in the mortgage market. Mr. Jackson said that he and Fannie Mae's chief executive, Daniel H. Mudd, talked about Fannie Mae's request to be allowed to buy mortgages beyond a current $728.5 billion federal limit."
–Bloomberg

August 9, 2007
Paribas Freezes Funds as Subprime Woes Keep Spreading
"France's biggest listed bank, BNP Paribas, froze 1.6 billion euros ($2.2 billion) worth of funds on Thursday, citing problems in the United States subprime mortgage market. The warning, which came a week after subprime-related losses drove two Bear Stearns funds into bankruptcy protection, sent shivers through nervous financial markets. 'The complete evaporation of liquidity in certain market segments of the U.S. securitization market has made it impossible to value certain assets fairly regardless of their quality or credit rating,' BNP said. Its shares fell more than 3 percent, and stock futures in the United States moved sharply lower."
–New York Times

August 10, 2007
Stocks Tumble as French Bank Reacts to Home Loan Worries
–New York Times

News & Bridgewater Daily Observations (BDO)

August 10, 2007
Fed Injects Reserves Into System
"The Federal Reserve, trying to calm turmoil on Wall Street, announced today that it will pump as much money as needed into the financial system to help overcome the ill effects of a spreading credit crunch. The Fed, in a short statement, said it will provide 'reserves as necessary' to help the markets safely make their way. The central bank did not provide details but said it would do all it can to 'facilitate the orderly functioning of financial markets.'"
                              —Associated Press

August 11, 2007
Central Banks Intervene to Calm Volatile Markets
"Central banks around the world stepped up efforts to slow the losses. The Bank of Japan added liquidity for the first time since the market problems began. The European Central Bank injected money into the system for a second day, adding another 61 billion euros ($84 billion), after providing 95 billion euros the day before. The Federal Reserve yesterday added money by lending $19 billion against mortgage-backed securities, then another $19 billion in reverse repurchase agreements."
                              —New York Times

August 11, 2007
Europeans Are Wondering About Subprime Exposure
                              —New York Times

August 16, 2007
Countrywide's Big Credit Draw Fuels Market Fears
"Stocks fell sharply Wednesday in the United States, set off by worries that Countrywide Financial, the largest mortgage lender in the nation, could face bankruptcy if liquidity worsens after a Merrill Lynch analyst flagged that possibility. The mood grew even more grim Thursday morning, when the lender said it tapped its entire $11.5 billion credit line to boost cash on hand."
                              —New York Times

August 18, 2007
Fed Cuts Lending Rate in Surprise Move
"The Federal Reserve today approved a half-percentage point cut in its discount rate on loans to banks, saying that it now feels that 'tighter credit and increased uncertainty have the potential to restrain economic growth going forward.' Stocks immediately surged when markets opened on Wall Street, but shed much of the gains in morning trading."
                              —New York Times

August 22, 2007
Bank of America Takes Countrywide Stake
                              —Associated Press

August 22, 2007
Top U.S. Banks Draw Upon Fed Discount Window
"More banks have stepped forward and said they have availed themselves of the Federal Reserve's discount-lending rate cut amid the credit market's turmoil last week. The four biggest banks in the United States — Citigroup, J.P. Morgan Chase, Bank of America and Wachovia — said that they each borrowed $500 million through the so-called discount window by taking out loans directly from the Fed."
                              —New York Times

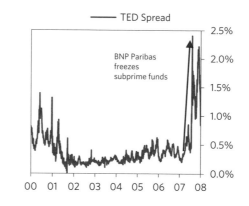

Here is what I wrote to clients and policy makers the next day:

(BDO) August 10: This Is the Big One

By that, we mean that this is the financial market unraveling that we've been expecting—the one in which there is an unwinding of widely held, irresponsibly created positions that occurred as a result of financial middlemen pressing to invest for high returns the immense amount of liquidity that has been flooding the financial system—i.e., another 1998 or 1994 (which occurred for the same reasons), just bigger. I want to reemphasize that what we know about this is less than what we don't know because how exactly the cards will fall will depend on who is holding what positions and how they all knock on with each other. Despite us doing an awful lot of work to try to get this all mapped out over the last two years, we couldn't map this out to an extent that's worth much because our knowledge of these positions is so imprecise and the array of possible permutations is so wide that forecasting where we will be in a couple of weeks is a bit like predicting how a hurricane will run its course two weeks ahead. We are also highly confident that others, including the key regulators (who have the best windows in), can't give you a forecast that's much more reliable, so they are reacting to events. However, having seen this dynamic (i.e., a self-reinforcing panic move away from high risk investments to low risk investments in which badly positioned leveraged players get squeezed) many times before (1998 is the most recent case), we are pretty confident we know some things about how it will play out. This will run through the system with the speed of a hurricane (over the next four to six months), and it will leave weaker financial credits dead or damaged and stronger financial credits in the catbird seat…

…We have a game-plan (developed over many years) that we have confidence in because we planned for times like this, but for safety's sake, we are checking that all the hatches are battened down and that the expensive radar we've developed is working well. That game-plan doesn't just pertain to our investment strategy; it includes our strategy for handling counterparty risks and transactions costs in an environment of extreme risk-aversion and illiquidity.

What I was referring to as a game plan for this is what we called a "Depression gauge." Because big debt crises and depressions had happened many times before and we had the template explained in this study, we had created this gauge as a simple algorithm based on the proximity of interest rates to 0 percent, a few measures of debt vulnerability, and indications of the beginning of debt deleveraging that would lead us to change our overall portfolio and risk controls (including our counterparty risks).

Less than a week later, news emerged that Countrywide, the US's largest mortgage issuer, had exhausted its credit line, and was at risk of declaring bankruptcy. While notable because it was a canary in the coal mine, Countrywide was not a systemically important financial institution.

Over the next several days, stocks fell sharply and yields on commercial paper spiked. The Bank of Japan, the ECB, and the Fed all responded to the market stress by providing liquidity to banks. The worst of the stock sell-off ended when the Fed surprisingly cut interest rates by 0.5 percent—doing so between its regularly scheduled meetings—an unusual move. Chairman Bernanke said he would do more if needed.[11] And Bank of America shored up Countrywide by investing $2 billion in exchange for a large stake in the company. These moves alleviated most of the funding strains in the market, and equities recovered a bit. Below is a chart of the stock market up until that time. Note that it was still near its highs.

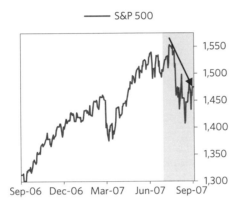

Coming out of this episode, most policy makers and investors thought that the problems in the risky part of the mortgage market would be contained, so the flow-through to the real economy wouldn't be substantial. Based on our calculations, we saw it differently and wrote: "the day of reckoning will be pushed forward, probably to when there is a big tightening by the Fed or a big turndown in the economy."

Why Banks and Investors Were So Exposed to Risky Mortgage Securities

Why were investors, banks, rating agencies and policy makers misled into thinking mortgage securities were less risky than they actually were? A key reason is the way risk is analyzed. Consider the conventional way investors think about risk. At the time, Value at Risk (VAR), which is a measure of recent volatility in markets and portfolios, was commonly used by investment firms and commercial banks to determine the likely magnitude and occurrence of losses. It typically uses recent volatility as the main input to how much risk (i.e., what size positions) one could comfortably take. As a simplifying illustration, imagine an investor that never wants to lose more than 20 percent. If the most that a subprime mortgage has ever lost in a month is 5 percent, then investors might plug that 5 percent number into a model that then says its "safe" for them to borrow until they own three times leveraged subprime.

This way of thinking about risk caused many investors to increase their exposures beyond what would normally be seen as prudent. They looked at the

News & Bridgewater Daily Observations (BDO)

August 31, 2007
Bush Offers Relief for Some on Home Loans
"President Bush, in his first response to families hit by the subprime mortgage crisis, announced several steps today to help Americans who have credit problems meet the rising cost of their housing loans.

In remarks this morning at the White House, Mr. Bush said he would work to 'modernize and improve' the Federal Housing Administration 'by lowering down payment requirements, by increasing loan limits, and providing more flexibility in pricing.'

Administration officials said...that the goal would be to change its federal mortgage insurance program in a way that would let an additional 80,000 homeowners with spotty credit records sign up, beyond the 160,000 likely to use it this year and next."
—New York Times

September 1, 2007
Soothing Words and a Big Gain
"Wall Street closed out another erratic week with a big gain yesterday after investors took comments from President Bush and the Federal Reserve chairman, Ben S. Bernanke, as reassuring signs that Wall Street would not be left to deal with problems in the mortgage and credit markets on its own."
—Associated Press

September 6, 2007
Stocks Slip as Fed Says Credit Crisis Is Contained
—New York Times

September 7, 2007
Rate of Home Foreclosures Hits Record
New York Times

September 7, 2007
The Bigger Problem
"In our opinion, what is happening here is bigger than what the world now commonly refers to as the 'credit crisis.' Normally, credit problems occur when borrowers get into a lot of debt and cash flows suffer, either because interest rates rise or the economy falls. But imagine a dynamic in which the credit keeps flowing and debts keep increasing. That is the dynamic that's happening. It is an extension of having too much credit/liquidity, not too little.

...The American household sector as a whole is now in pretty bad shape (i.e., has a bad balance sheet and poor cash flow outlook), so that pushing more money into its hands will lead to worse and worse financial problems pretty quickly, so we expect that there will be spreading of credit problems even though interest rates will decline and credit will be readily available. And we believe that this will continue until foreign investors increasingly realize that the US is not a good place to invest."

September 8, 2007
Stocks Tumble as Job Report Leads Investors to Shift to Bonds
"Shares fell sharply yesterday and investors sought safety in government debt after a Labor Department report showed an abrupt drop in employment in August and raised fears of a recession.

The Standard & Poor's 500-stock index closed down 1.7 percent...The yield on the 10-year Treasury note, which moves in the opposite direction from the note's price, fell to its lowest level, at 4.37 percent, in more than a year and a half. On Thursday evening, the yield was 4.51 percent."
—New York Times

**News &
Bridgewater Daily Observations
(BDO)**

September 14, 2007
Credit Fears Ease, and Markets Climb
–New York Times

September 14, 2007
British Lender Offered Emergency Loan
"The British government said it had authorized
the Bank of England to provide a 'liquidity
support facility' of unspecified size to Northern
Rock, a mortgage lender based in Newcastle,
England, that has expanded aggressively in recent
years...Northern Rock's need for emergency
financing represents a significant broadening of the
effects of the crisis in global financial markets,
analysts said, because until now problems at
European banks have stemmed mostly from their
direct exposure to United States subprime loans."
–New York Times

September 19, 2007
Global Markets Rise Sharply After Rate Cut
–New York Times

September 20, 2007
Fed Chief Calls for New Mortgage Rules
"Ben S. Bernanke, the chairman of the Federal
Reserve, said today that the growing turmoil from
increasingly permissive subprime lending had
demonstrated a need for tougher restrictions on
what borrowers and lenders can do."
–New York Times

September 21, 2007
*Credit Turmoil Bruised Most on Wall Street,
but Pain Was Not Shared Equally*
"Wall Street's first reports since this summer's
credit storm revealed extensive damage, but
better-than-expected earnings this week from
four brokerage firms offered some comfort. There
was clear separation among the investment banks,
as Goldman Sachs powered through the turmoil
in the credit markets to post a 79 percent increase
in profit yesterday, its third-best quarter ever. At
Bear Stearns, earnings fell 61 percent on sharp
losses related to its hedge funds and exposure to
subprime investments."
–New York Times

September 21, 2007
*Economic Indicators Drop the Most in 6
Months as Confidence Ebbs*
–Bloomberg

September 22, 2007
*Fed Governor Warns Against Shielding
Investors From Their Losses*
–Bloomberg

recent volatility in their VAR calculations, and by and large expected it to
continue moving forward. **This is human nature and it was dumb because
past volatility and past correlations aren't reliable forecasts of future risks.**
But it was very profitable. In fact, when we were cutting back on our positions,
our clients urged us to increase them because our VAR was low. We explained
why we didn't do that. Extrapolating current conditions forward and imagining
that they will be just a slightly different version of today is to us bad relative to
considering the true range of possibilities going forward. If anything, I believe
that one should bet on the opposite of what happened lately, because boring
years tend to sow the seeds of future instability, as well as making the next
downturn worse. **That's because low volatility and benign VAR estimates
encourage increased leverage.** At the time, some leverage ratios were nearing
100:1. To me, leverage is a much better indicator of future volatility than VAR.

In 2007, many banks and investors were heavily exposed to subprime
mortgages, since the instruments had not yet had a loss cycle or experienced
much volatility. VAR was also self-reinforcing on the down side, because
increased market volatility at the peak of the crisis in 2008 made their statistical riskiness look even higher, causing even more selling.

The Fall of 2007

With stocks on the rebound after the bumpy summer, policy makers started to
consider how they should approach the problems emanating from the mortgage
market over the longer term.

Beginning in the fall of 2006, Paulson and the Treasury had begun working
with Barney Frank and the House Financial Services Committee to reform
Fannie and Freddie. They focused on curbing the excesses and increasing the
authority of the regulator. A bill passed the House in the spring of 2007 but,
stalled in the Senate. Due to significant political opposition, there was no
possibility of getting Federal funding to modify mortgages for struggling
homeowners. So the Bush Treasury worked with lenders, mortgage servicers,
and counselors to motivate these private sector institutions to modify and
restructure mortgages with some modest but meaningful success. Also, the
Treasury began working with the Fed to jointly develop what they dubbed as
the "break the glass" option to go to Congress and get the authority to
purchase illiquid mortgage securities if and when this became politically
feasible. This was the forerunner of what would become the Troubled Asset
Relief Program, or TARP.

The Fed signaled its willingness to ease monetary policy to mitigate any
spillover effects the mortgage-related stress might have on the broader
economy. Although the data and news showed a steady deterioration in
fundamentals, most market participants believed that policy makers would be
able to make it through smoothly.

Bernanke began a push within the Fed (in close collaboration with Hank
Paulson and the Treasury staff) toward what they dubbed "blue-sky thinking"—unrestricted brainstorming in anticipation of the possibility that conventional policy easing might not be enough.[12] **As financial contagion spreads
beyond the banking sector, increasing numbers of players in the real
economy can no longer access credit through the usual channels.** In what
would become a crucial pillar of the Fed's response to the crisis, **Bernanke**

considered the possibility of the Fed lending directly to a broader range of counterparties than just depository institutions. This would be a big, bold move, and so unprecedented that Bernanke had to check the rulebook to see if it was allowed. The provision of the Federal Reserve Act that authorized such lending—Section 13(3)—hadn't been invoked since the Great Depression, but it was still valid. **Knowing which needed actions in a crisis are permitted (or not permitted) by law and how to have them approved is a classic challenge in democracies with rigid regulations and robust checks and balances systems.**

Worsening circumstances led to expectations for a rate cut from the Fed. Still, there were reasons to ease and reasons not to ease. Two considerations especially weighed against easing. The first concerned inflation: the dollar had been steadily weakening and oil prices steadily rising. Easing would contribute to dollar weakness, higher oil prices, and higher inflation. The other consideration was that the problems all stemmed from wrongheaded speculation, and anything that the Fed did to ameliorate the problems of those speculators would only encourage them to take excessive risks again in the future.

This notion of "moral hazard" was one that the Fed (and Treasury) would have to wrestle with many times throughout the crisis. **How the "moral hazard" question is dealt with during big debt crises is one of the biggest determinants of how these crises turn out.** Because undisciplined lending and borrowing was the cause of crisis, it is natural to want to let those who were responsible experience the consequences of their actions, and to impose lots of discipline by tightening lending and borrowing. But that's like putting someone who just suffered a heart attack because they're too fat straight on a diet and a treadmill. At such times, **above all else, the most important thing is to provide life-blood (i.e., stimulants) to keep the systemically important parts of the system alive.** It is dangerous to try to be overly precise in getting the right balance between (a) letting those who borrowed and lent badly experience the consequences of their actions and (b) providing judicious amounts of liquidity/ lending to help rectify the severity of the contraction. It is far better to err on the side of providing too much than to provide too little. Unlike in the Great Depression, when the Fed allowed banks to fail en masse, the Fed took the view that although it would be good to minimize moral hazard when possible, its top priority had to be saving the economy.

Tim Geithner, who was the president of the New York Fed at the time, shared my thinking. He believed the moral hazard framework was the wrong way to think about policy during a financial crisis because policy needs to be very aggressive in taking out catastrophic risk, and one can't move slowly or precisely.[13] That has proven true time and time again. Providing plenty of liquidity during a liquidity crisis leaves the government open to less risk and leaves the system healthier. In contrast, the moral hazard framework leads people to believe that if you let things burn, the government will assume less risk. In reality, if you let everything burn, the government will end up taking on all of the risk, as it will have to nationalize the system in a much more costly and damaging way.

In the end, policy makers responded to the crisis by guaranteeing almost everything, explicitly or implicitly, and carrying out a dramatic, explicit injection of cash. Geithner told me that the interesting thing about this

News & Bridgewater Daily Observations (BDO)

September 24, 2007
Beware Moral Hazard Fundamentalists
"The term 'moral hazard' originally comes from the area of insurance. It refers to the prospect that insurance will distort behaviour, for example when holders of fire insurance take less precautions with respect to avoiding fire or when holders of health insurance use more healthcare than they would if they were not insured. In the financial arena the spectre of moral hazard is invoked to oppose policies that reduce the losses of financial institutions that have made bad decisions. In particular, it is used to caution against creating an expectation that there will be future 'bail-outs.'"
—*Financial Times*

September 27, 2007
S.E.C. Inquiry Looks for Conflicts in Credit Rating
"The Securities and Exchange Commission has opened an investigation into whether the credit-rating agencies improperly inflated their ratings of mortgage-backed securities because of possible conflicts of interest, the head of the commission told Congress on Wednesday."
—*New York Times*

September 28, 2007
Home Sales and Prices Fall Sharply
—*New York Times*

October 2, 2007
Stocks Soar on Hopes Credit Crisis Is Over
"Blue-chip stocks pushed into record territory yesterday as investors seemed to shrug off this summer's problems with subprime mortgage lending...The advances came as two banks, Citigroup and UBS, predicted declines in third-quarter earnings or losses related to problems with mortgage-backed securities and loans...But the profit warnings eased anxiety about the long-term effects of problems that began in mortgage lending, analysts said, leaving Wall Street with a sense that the worst of the fallout from this summer's credit crisis had passed."
—*New York Times*

October 6, 2007
A Big Loss at Merrill Stirs Unease
—*New York Times*

**News &
Bridgewater Daily Observations
(BDO)**

October 9, 2007
Tranquil Session Before Earnings Data
"Wall Street finished a quiet session mostly lower
yesterday as investors cashed in some gains from
last week's rally and awaited quarterly corporate
earnings reports...Earnings are expected to
reflect the difficulty some companies,
particularly in the financial and housing
sectors, have faced because of upheaval in the
credit markets amid overly leveraged debt and
defaults in subprime mortgages."
–New York Times

October 10, 2007
*New Moves in Washington to Ease Mortgage
Crisis*
"House Democrats squared off against the Bush
administration today over measures to help
homeowners trapped in a vise of unaffordable
subprime mortgages and falling home prices.

The Democratic-controlled House passed a bill
that would require the nation's two government-
sponsored mortgage finance companies and the
Federal Housing Administration's insurance
program to channel up to $900 million a year into
a new fund for affordable rental housing."
–New York Times

approach was that instead of losing 5 to 10 percent of GDP on the cost of the financial rescue, we actually earned something like 2 percent of GDP, depending on how you measure it. That's a dramatic outlier in the history of financial crises, and Geithner credits it to the Fed and Treasury's very aggressive response and their willingness to put moral hazard concerns aside. I agree.

On September 18, 2007, the Fed cut rates by 0.5 percent, compared to the 0.25 percent expected by the market. As Bernanke put it, "the hawks and doves flocked together."[14] The Fed's bigger-than-expected move sparked a stock market rally that the *New York Times* described as "ecstatic," which brought the S&P 500 back to within 2 percent of its all-time high.

More important than the stimulation that would come from the Fed's interest rate cuts was the message this sent the markets—that the Fed was willing to take decisive action as needed to help contain the problems that had caused the market turmoil in August. At the same time, it was clear to those who ran the numbers that **easing wouldn't solve the more fundamental problems of financial intermediaries, debtors, and creditors holding more debt assets and liabilities than could be serviced**.

The banks' (and investment banks') balance sheet and liquidity problems were on both the asset side and the liability side. On the asset side, the problems stemmed from the banks' ownership of subprime mortgages through securitizations. On the liability side, the banks had become dependent on risky sources of funding. Banks had always relied on short-term funding, but historically this had consisted largely of deposits, which could be controlled with guarantees. Savers can always pull their deposits, and widespread fears about bank solvency had led them to do just that in the Great Depression. This led to the founding of the FDIC in 1933, which dealt with this problem by insuring bank deposits (up to a certain amount). That mostly eliminated the incentives the depositors had to flee, because even if a bank failed, their deposits would be protected.

But by relying on what was known as "short-term wholesale funding," modern banks had set themselves up for a similar situation to what banks had experienced between 1930 and 1933. Short-term wholesale funding took a variety of forms, but at its core, it was a lot like an uninsured deposit—meaning the depositor had a big incentive to pull it from the bank at the first sign of trouble.

Banks and investment banks had also gotten themselves into trouble by virtue of their central role in what we'll call the "securitization machine." **At its heart, the securitization machine started with the issuance of risky mortgages and ended with the sale of very safe bonds to institutional investors.** Lots of players were involved, but these financial intermediaries played a major role. Basically a mortgage lender would make the loans and sell them to a bank, which would package them up into a bundle of say 1,000 loans. The combined cash flows of these 1,000 loans were thought to be much safer than any individual loan because they benefited from diversification—if one borrower couldn't repay their mortgage, that might create a loss on one loan, but that wouldn't affect the ability of the other 999 borrowers to repay their loans. On average, most borrowers had historically been able to repay their mortgage loans, so the result of the packaging was (supposedly) to reduce the overall risk profile of the loans.

The bank would then slice up the total cash flows from the 1,000 loans and distribute them in chunks: 70 to 80 percent would become a super-safe AAA-rated bond, another 10 to 15 percent might become a slightly riskier but still pretty safe AA-rated bond, 5 to 10 percent would become a BBB-rated bond, and some small unrated residual (the "first-loss" piece) would take the losses of the first few borrowers that might default. **This was a classic case of data-mining history rather than using sound logic to assess risk. People were leveraging themselves up by betting that they were safe, because the thing they were betting against had never happened before.** When the bet went wrong, the self-reinforcing dynamic on the upside shifted to a self-reinforcing dynamic on the downside.

Banks would sell off whatever bonds they could to investors, typically retaining the first-loss piece in order to make the deal work. They carried bonds as inventory (sometimes with the intention of eventually selling them; other times to hold the exposure for return). This worked, which encouraged them to do it more until it didn't work. To varying degrees, the banks were holding large inventories of these bonds when demand dried up in the third quarter of 2007.

That happened when the write-downs due to mark-to-market accounting began. Bear Stearns saw its 3Q07 earnings drop by 61 percent due to losses related to the hedge funds that had blown up and other exposures it had to subprime mortgages. Morgan Stanley and Lehman Brothers took 7 percent and 3 percent hits to earnings, respectively (relatively small losses). Citigroup, UBS, and Merrill Lynch followed suit, reporting meaningful but manageable losses. Citigroup initially wrote down the largest loss, at $5.9 billion (keep that number in mind in comparison to the numbers later in our story).

Around this time (fall 2007) we started running our own loss estimates and "stress tests" of the financial system—gathering balance sheet data on banks to see their assets and liabilities, and applying liquid market prices as proxies to their illiquid holdings to estimate what they would have to report long before they would have to report it. This was invaluable in anticipating what was going to happen. On October 9, 2007, the S&P 500 closed at its all-time high. That high in stocks wouldn't be reached again until 2013.

It was clear to most people in the business that banks had a problem with subprime mortgages, though it wasn't yet clear to them that the whole economy had a major debt problem. To help alleviate the situation and build confidence, a number of major banks proposed joining forces and creating a fund that would aim to raise $75-100 billion for buying distressed subprime mortgage securities. Like other observers, we viewed it as a natural response to the credit crunch that would help to alleviate the risk of contagion. However, by the end of the year, efforts to establish this fund had been abandoned, as the collaborating banks decided that it was "not needed at this time."[15]

Meanwhile, despite optimism at home, the credit crunch spread from the US to Europe through two main mechanisms. The first was that some European banks (most notably the British bank Northern Rock) had come to rely on money markets for short-term wholesale funding. When that source of funding began to dry up in the summer of 2007, Northern Rock experienced a classic "run," with depositors lining up to withdraw funds for three straight days in the middle of September.[16] The UK had a similar deposit insurance scheme as

News & Bridgewater Daily Observations (BDO)

October 11, 2007
Democrats and White House Split Over Mortgage Relief Plans
"The Democratic-controlled House passed a bill that would require the nation's two government-sponsored mortgage finance companies and the Federal Housing Administration's insurance program to channel up to $900 million a year into a new fund for affordable housing."
—*New York Times*

October 15, 2007
Banks Create a Fund to Protect Credit Market
"Citigroup, Bank of America and JPMorgan Chase will create a fund, called a conduit, that will be able to buy around $75 billion to $100 billion in highly rated bonds and other debt from structured investment vehicles, or SIVs. Those vehicles own mortgage-backed bonds and other securities and have had trouble obtaining financing since early August, when the credit markets froze up."
—*New York Times*

October 17, 2007
Paulson Says Housing Woes to Worsen
—*New York Times*

October 17, 2007
Foreigners Shedding U.S. Securities
—*Bloomberg*

October 18, 2007
Core Inflation Remains Steady, Presenting a Puzzle to the Fed
—*New York Times*

October 19, 2007
Earnings Reports Trigger Steep Stock Sell-Off
—*New York Times*

October 22, 2007
China Bank to Buy $1 Billion Stake in Bear Stearns
—*New York Times*

News &
Bridgewater Daily Observations
(BDO)

October 24, 2007
Loss and Larger Write-Down at Merrill
"Merrill Lynch, the brokerage firm, reported its first quarterly loss in nearly six years today, after it increased the amount of its write-down by $2.9 billion for a total of $7.9 billion...Much of the loss and write-down was tied to problems in the subprime mortgage market and writing down the value of collateralized debt obligations."
–New York Times

October 25, 2007
Home Sales Slump at 8-Year Low
–New York Times

October 25, 2007
New Signs in Europe of U.S. Mortgage Fallout
"The ill tidings came in several European capitals on Thursday: from a reduced growth forecast in Germany to a report by the Bank of England, which said financial markets were still vulnerable to shocks from the crisis that originated in the American home-mortgage market."
–New York Times

October 27, 2007
Homeownership Declines for Fourth Consecutive Quarter
–Bloomberg

October 30, 2007
UBS Reports a Larger-than-Expected Loss
–New York Times

November 2, 2007
New York Says Appraiser Inflated Value of Homes
–New York Times

the US, but with a lower cap on insured deposits (£35,000). To stem the run, the British government guaranteed all of Northern Rock's deposits.

The second mechanism resulted from the investments that many European banks had made in subprime securitizations. The largest ones, like UBS and Deutsche Bank, owned stakes in securitizations as a corollary to their role in producing the securitizations themselves. Many smaller banks had simply wanted a piece of the action. After all, many slices of subprime securitizations had been rated AAA, meaning that rating agencies had stamped them as having extremely low risk. During previous periods of stress, such as the savings and loan crisis of the 1980s and the dot-com bubble of the early 2000s, corporate bonds rated AAA had a default rate of 0 percent, according to Standard & Poor's, one of the big three rating agencies.[17] Plus, the subprime securitizations rated AAA offered a premium (though in hindsight, one that was far too small, given the level of risk) relative to corporate bonds of the same rating.

As our risk measures of the banks, investment banks, and broker dealers that we dealt with changed, we shifted our exposures from the riskier ones to safer ones, and also moved into safer assets.

In late October, 2007, sentiment began to turn for the worse as predictions of the overall losses on subprime securitizations started to increase. US stock prices suffered a steep 2.6 percent decline on October 19, after JPMorgan posted a $2 billion write-down and Bank of America announced much weaker-than-expected earnings.

It was becoming clear that losses on subprime mortgages were going to be a bigger problem than previously thought for the banks, but it wasn't yet clear just how severely the stress in the housing market was going to hit US households, whose consumption represents the bulk of US GDP (around 70 percent). Here's what we wrote about it at the time:

(BDO) October 30: Falling Home Prices and Wealth

The weakening housing market affects the US economy in a number of ways ranging from falling construction, to falling expenditures on housing-related items, to less cash used from mortgage borrowing on non-housing-related consumption, to falling wealth. As we have described previously, the drop in financing alone (money borrowed against houses to spend on other things) made up over 3% at the peak and will likely be negative soon (and will have to be made up some other way if consumption growth is to remain where it is) while the decline in construction at a 20% annual pace is translating to about a 1% drag on real growth...Real estate assets as % GDP peaked at 167%, so the drop in wealth will equal about 50% of GDP.

The impact on households was showing up in a variety of statistics: rising delinquencies on mortgages, slowing purchases of new and existing homes, slowing retail sales growth, etc. Policy makers understood that the situation was about to get worse: the roughly two million of those borrowers with adjustable-rate mortgages we discussed earlier were scheduled to have their teaser rates expire in 2008, and thus were about to see their interest costs jump. Treasury Secretary Paulson announced various measures to help modify mortgages to extend teaser rates for stressed borrowers, but stopped short of putting taxpayer money behind the plan, limiting its potential impact.

Meanwhile, at Bridgewater, we completed our first look loss estimates and stress test by examining the balance sheet data of banks. For us, the exercise was so eye-opening that on November 21 we released what we called a "Special Report," excerpted here:

Bridgewater Special Report:
What We Think Will Be Contained & What We Think Won't Be Contained

- Some credit problems have surfaced and some haven't.

- We believe that the credit problems that have surfaced (i.e., the subprime/SIV problems) will spread (i.e., there will be a contagion) but they will be contained (i.e., won't spread beyond being manageable and won't sink the economy, though they will weaken it). That is because their size is manageable, their ownership is dispersed, and the demand to acquire these positions from buyers of distressed securities is relatively large because of the current environment of plentiful global liquidity. Management of this crisis will of course require wise decision-making and coordination of central banks, finance ministries, legislators and financial institutions in much the same way as management of past financial crises required these. We expect this wise management and coordinated decision-making, especially by central banks and finance ministries, because we have relatively high regard for the people involved and because the actions that are appropriate are relatively clear.

- We also "believe" that the credit problems that lie beneath the surface are much larger and more threatening than the ones that have surfaced. These latent credit problems are the result of a) there being an enormous amount of liquidity that is looking to be invested and b) investors increasingly and imprudently reaching for higher returns via structured, levered, illiquid, risky investments. Like subprime and other credit crunch problems before they surfaced, we and others (including government regulators) do not adequately understand these exposures, so it is difficult to say for sure where the problems lie or to know how they will behave individually and in interaction with each other in a stressful environment. What we do know is that these exposures have grown exponentially, are very large, and are based on many imprudent, sometimes seemingly nonsensical strategies. We also believe that if these problems surface, containing them will be challenging…

News & Bridgewater Daily Observations (BDO)

November 3, 2007
Citigroup Chief Is Set to Exit Amid Losses
—*New York Times*

November 3, 2007
Auto Sector's Role Dwindles, and Spending Suffers
—*New York Times*

November 3, 2007
Big Drop in Merrill Stock on Hint of New Troubles
"Merrill Lynch, still operating without a permanent chief executive, saw its shares fall sharply yesterday on the possibility that it might have to write down more of its high-risk credit exposure."
—*New York Times*

November 6, 2007
Bond Buyers Are Losing Confidence
"Investors say they are most troubled by the accelerating pace of write-downs and credit downgrades in the residential mortgage area, but they are also starting to question the value of bonds in related areas like commercial mortgages and consumer debt."
—*New York Times*

November 7, 2007
G.M. Posts Its Biggest Quarterly Loss
—*New York Times*

November 8, 2007
Morgan Stanley Takes a Hit on Mortgages
—*New York Times*

November 10, 2007
Another Steep Plunge Ends Harsh Week for Stocks
—*New York Times*

November 10, 2007
3 Big Banks See Troubles; Barclays Falls on Rumors
Three big banks [Wachovia, Bank of America, and JPMorgan Chase] warned yesterday about continuing losses in the credit markets, while Barclays of London denied speculation that it was facing a huge write-down of assets."
—*New York Times*

November 20, 2007
New Worries About Credit Drive Down Stock Markets
—*New York Times*

November 24, 2007
Housing History Sends Recession Warning
"The Federal Reserve Board forecast this week that there will be no recession in the United States in the foreseeable future…If the Fed is right, and the economy does stay out of recession, with the unemployment rate barely rising at all, then it will be the first time ever that a housing slowdown this severe has not coincided with a recession."
—*New York Times*

**News &
Bridgewater Daily Observations
(BDO)**

December 3, 2007
Mortgage Relief Impact May Be Limited
"The Bush administration's effort to help at least
some people in danger of defaulting on their
subprime mortgages could affect only a small
share of those who took out such loans during the
final two years of the housing bubble, industry
analysts said today."
–New York Times

December 5, 2007
*Wall Street Firms Subpoenaed in Subprime
Inquiry*
–New York Times

December 11, 2007
Mortgage Crisis Forces the Closing of a Fund
"Losses on investments weakened by the
deepening housing crisis have forced Bank of
America to close a multibillion-dollar high-yield
fund, the largest of its kind, after wealthy
investors withdrew billions of dollars in assets."
–New York Times

December 11, 2007
Fed Cuts Rate a Quarter Point; Stocks Dive
–New York Times

December 12, 2007
Fed Leads Drive to Strengthen Bank System
"A day after the Federal Reserve disappointed
investors with a modest cut in interest rates,
central banks in North America and Europe
announced on Wednesday the most aggressive
infusion of capital into the banking system since
the terrorist attacks of September 2001."
–New York Times

December 13, 2007
*3 Big Banks See No Relief as Write-Offs
Mount Up*
–Bloomberg

December 14, 2007
Investors Shrug Off Global Cash Injection
–New York Times

December 19, 2007
E.C.B. Makes $500 Billion Infusion
–New York Times

December 19, 2007
*In Reversal, Fed Approves Plan to Curb Risky
Lending*
"The Federal Reserve, acknowledging that home
mortgage lenders aggressively sold deceptive loans
to borrowers who had little chance of repaying
them, proposed a broad set of restrictions Tuesday
on exotic mortgages and high-cost loans for
people with weak credit."
–New York Times

December 21, 2007
*Big Bond Insurer Discovers That Layers of Risk
Do Not Create a Cushion*
"On Thursday, shares of the nation's biggest
insurer of financial risk, MBIA, fell 26 percent
after it disclosed that it was guaranteeing
billions of dollars of the kind of complex debt
that unnerved the credit market this summer.
The move came a day after Standard & Poor's
downgraded another bond insurer and assigned
a negative outlook to four companies, including
MBIA."
–New York Times

- Though we do not believe that the "below the surface problems" will come to the surface any time soon, we also want to make sure that we have no or minimal exposures to, and ample protections against, widening credit and liquidity spreads, declining equities, undoing carry trades, increasing volatility and deteriorating counterparties.

- <u>When we include all of the credit crunch related exposures that exist for all entities, we think that the mark-to-market losses as of today are in the $420 billion range globally, which represents about 1% of global GDP</u>… we estimate their unrealized losses to be much larger than their realized losses so we expect much larger write-downs to come.

So we ran the numbers and were extremely concerned by both what we knew and what we didn't know. The biggest unknowns, even after we ran the numbers on potential bank losses (which were enormous), were how these losses might ripple through the market, especially via the derivative markets. Derivatives are financial contracts whose value is determined by the value of some underlying asset, rate, index, or even event. Unlike stocks or bonds, they are not used to raise money for spending or investment. Instead, they are primarily instruments for hedging risks and for speculating on changes in prices. They are made through private contracts rather than on exchanges and are unregulated. They were also enormous and opaque to everyone, so no one could get their heads around the exposures that existed—and nobody could really know how the bank and non-bank lender losses would cascade.

More specifically, in the three decades leading up to the crisis, a huge market in over-the-counter derivative contracts (i.e., those not traded on regulated exchanges) developed. In December 2000, Congress clarified that as long as these over-the-counter contracts (OTC) were between "sophisticated parties," they did not have to be regulated as futures or securities—effectively shielding OTC derivatives from virtually all oversight.[18] Over the next seven years, the OTC market grew quickly. By June 2008, the notional value of these contracts was $672.6 trillion.

A key derivative that would play a major role in the financial crisis was the credit default swap (CDS). A CDS plays a role that is similar to insurance. When an issuer sells a CDS, they promise to insure the buyer against potential defaults from a particular exposure (such as defaults creating losses from mortgage-backed securities) in exchange for a regular stream of payments. CDS's allow purchasers of mortgage-backed securities (and other assets) to transfer default risk to the party selling the CDS. AIG, for instance, sold lots of this "insurance," but only kept very small reserves against it—meaning they didn't have the capacity to pay out if there were large losses.

As noted earlier, I shared my concerns with the Treasury and White House, but they thought that the picture I was painting was implausible because nothing like that had happened in their lifetimes. While I am hesitant to speak about policy makers in general because there are so many differences in what they are like individually and the different seats they sit in (e.g., in the Treasury, White House, Congress, SEC, etc.), I must say that they are much more reactive than proactive, which is understandable because, unlike investors, they are not in the business of having to bet against the consensus and be right, and they operate within political systems that don't act until there is a broad consensus that there is an intolerable problem. As a result, policy makers generally don't act decisively until a crisis is on top of them.

As 2007 came to an end, the S&P 500 was down 6 percent from its October peak, but in positive territory for the year as a whole. December's biggest market sell-off came on a day that the Fed lowered interest rates by 0.25 percent—even though rate cuts ordinarily help stocks—since it was less than the 0.5 percent cut that the markets were expecting. Bond yields had declined more sharply, from yields around 5 percent back in June before the credit crunch began to around 4 percent at the end of the year. The dollar index was down 8.6 percent over the year. Oil, meanwhile, was up a whopping 55 percent to $96, just a hair beneath its all-time high.

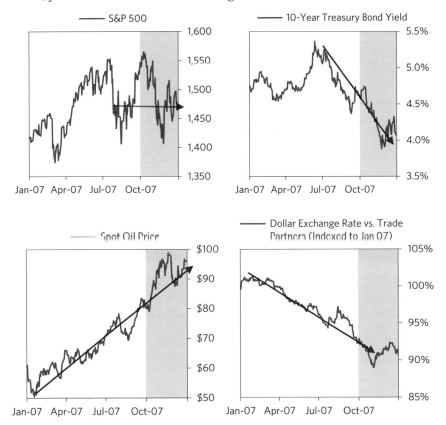

**News &
Bridgewater Daily Observations
(BDO)**

December 22, 2007
Big Fund to Prop Up Securities Is Scrapped
–*New York Times*

December 24, 2007
Merrill to Get $6.2 Billion Cash Injection
–*Reuters*

December 28, 2007
Weak Data Puts Shares in a Tailspin
–*New York Times*

December 31, 2007
Markets End Lower to End the Year
"For the first time since 2002, when the last bear market ended, Treasuries outperformed the S&P 500. Including dividends and interest payments, the S&P returned 5.5 percent while a Merrill Lynch index that tracks government-backed debt returned 8.5 percent."
–*New York Times*

News & Bridgewater Daily Observations (BDO)

January 2, 2008
Stocks Drop on Manufacturing Report
"Manufacturing activity unexpectedly shrank in December, reviving fears of an impending recession."
–*New York Times*

January 4, 2008
Weak Job Growth Numbers Prompt Stock Selloff
"The unemployment rate surged to 5 percent in December as the nation added only 18,000 jobs, the smallest monthly increase in four years."
–*New York Times*

January 15, 2008
Stocks Plunge on Economic News and Bank Woes
"Stocks fell sharply on Tuesday after Citigroup announced a $9.8 billion quarterly loss and...retail sales fell in December."
–*New York Times*

January 17, 2008
Dow Plunges More Than 300 Points on Grim Outlook
"Shares of MBIA and Ambac...tumbled Thursday after credit ratings firms said they would re-examine the company's financial health."
–*New York Times*

January 18, 2008
Bush Calls for $145 Billion Economic Aid Package
"To provide 'a shot in the arm to keep a fundamentally strong economy healthy' and avert a slide into recession."
–*New York Times*

January 21, 2008
Stocks Plunge Worldwide on Fears of a U.S. Recession
–*New York Times*

January 22, 2008
Fed Cuts Rate 0.75% and Stocks Swing
"It was the biggest short-term cut since October 1984."
–*New York Times*

January 23, 2008
Fed's Action Stems Sell-Off in World Markets
"The Federal Reserve confronted by deepening panic in global financial markets about a possible recession in the United States...stopped a vertigo-inducing plunge in stock prices."
–*New York Times*

January 31, 2008
Fed Cuts Key Rate as Stimulus Plan Advances
"The Federal Reserve cut short-term interest rates on Wednesday for the second time in eight days... the Senate pushed ahead on a $161 billion plan to prop up Main Street with tax rebates."
–*New York Times*

Depression: 2008

January–February 2008

At the beginning of the year, cracks began to appear in the economy and the markets. US manufacturing, retail sales, and employment reports were relatively poor. Then came the inevitable announcements of big write downs (i.e., losses) at Citigroup ($22.2 billion) and Merrill Lynch ($14.1 billion), as well as the downgrade of Ambac and MBIA, two bond insurers which had collectively guaranteed about $1 trillion worth of debt and had big exposure to subprime mortgage securities. These repeated losses were due to a combination of previous market declines in their holdings and accounting rules requiring them to be marked to the market and passed through their income statements and balance sheets. By January 20, the S&P 500 was down about 10 percent. Global equity markets were in even worse shape and fell even more, as shown in the chart below, left.

Witnessing all this, the Fed realized that it needed to act. Bernanke told the Federal Open Market Committee that although it wasn't the Fed's job to prevent sharp stock market declines, events seemed to "reflect a growing belief that the United States is in for a deep and protracted recession."[19] Emphasizing the need for immediate action, he said "we are facing, potentially, a broad crisis. We can no longer temporize. We have to address this...we have to try to get it under control. If we can't do that, then we are just going to lose control of the whole situation."[20]

Following an emergency meeting on January 22, the Fed cut rates by 75 basis points (i.e., 0.75 percent) to 3.5 percent, citing a "weakening of the economic outlook and increasing downside risks to growth." A week later, the Fed cut rates again, this time by 50 basis points, citing "considerable stress" in the financial sector, "a deepening of the contraction," and tight credit for "businesses and households." The combination of these cuts resulted in the largest calendar month decline in short rates since 1987. The Senate also passed a stimulus package (about $160 billion) to boost demand via tax rebates for low and middle income households.

Equity Prices (Indexed to Jan 1)

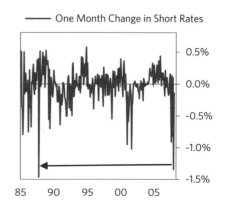

Stocks bounced, but despite the magnitude of the easing, they failed to recoup their losses, and by the end of February, stocks were back to where they had been before the Fed intervened. Credit and economic conditions continued to deteriorate along the way. Massive write-downs were announced at AIG ($11 billion), UBS ($14 billion), and Credit Suisse ($2.8 billion), indicators of service sector growth and consumer confidence hit 7- and 16-year lows, and a much publicized report from UBS estimated that losses from mortgage-backed securities could total $600 billion in the US financial system.

Reflecting on events at the time, we thought it was important to remind our clients that this was not going to be a typical recession but rather a deleveraging/depression-type dynamic, which is quite different in terms of both its potential magnitude and the linkages that drive the contraction. In our *Bridgewater Daily Observations* on January 31, we wrote:

(BDO) January 31: The Really Big Picture; Not Just a Normal Recession
The "R" word has been used a lot to describe the possible contraction in economic activity because all contractions are now called recessions. However, to use that term to describe what's happening would be misleading in that it connotes an economic contraction like those that occurred in the US many times before, as distinct from those that occurred in Japan in the 1990s and in the US in the 1930s, which are better characterized by the "D" word (e.g., deleveraging).

Contrary to popular belief, a "D" is not simply a more severe version of an "R"—it is an entirely different process…An "R" is a contraction in real GDP, brought on by a tight central bank policy (usually to fight inflation) that ends when the central bank eases. It is relatively well managed via interest rate changes…A "D" is an economic contraction that results from a financial deleveraging that leads assets (e.g., stocks and real estate) to be sold, causing asset prices to decline, causing equity levels to decline, causing more forced selling of assets, causing a contraction in credit and a contraction in economic activity, which worsens cash flows and increases asset sales in a self-reinforcing cycle. In other words, the financial deleveraging causes a financial crisis that causes an economic crisis.

March 2008–Rescuing Bear Stearns

The first ten days of March saw equities sell off about 4.5 percent (with much larger losses for financials), following high profile defaults at Carlyle Capital ($22 billion in assets under management or AUM), two funds operated by London-based Peloton Partners ($3 billion AUM), and news that Thornburg Mortgage ($36 billion in AUM) was missing margin calls. They were all heavily exposed to mortgage-backed securities and lenders were increasingly hesitant to lend them money.

These concerns quickly spread to major brokerages, especially those known to hold significant exposures to MBS, such as Bear Stearns, Lehman Brothers, and Merrill Lynch, all of which saw their borrowing costs spike. **The problems were passing to systemically important financial institutions, threatening the entire system. Even so, the danger was not widely appreciated.** Writing on March 10, we noted in our *Bridgewater Daily Observations* that conditions were quickly "slipping away" and that "Broker/dealers in our experience cannot survive with financing costs close to Bear's current levels."

**News &
Bridgewater Daily Observations
(BDO)**

February 5, 2008
Dow Off 370 Points on Weak Business Survey
"Stocks plummeted on Wall Street on Tuesday after a business survey provided another strong signal that the United States may be in the early stages of a recession. The Dow Jones industrial average closed down 370 points…The Institute for Supply Management reported that activity in the non-manufacturing sector contracted in January for the first time since March 2003."
–New York Times

February 11, 2008
White House Remains Optimistic on Economy
"The White House predicted on Monday that the economy would escape a recession and that unemployment would remain low this year, though it acknowledged that growth had already slowed sharply…The administration's official forecast calls for the economy to expand 2.7 percent this year and for unemployment to remain low at 4.9 percent. That is much more optimistic than those of many analysts on Wall Street."
–New York Times

February 16, 2008
Signs of Consumer Pullback Weigh on Shares
"The Dow industrials and the Nasdaq slipped Friday on concerns about retail spending after an index of consumer sentiment fell to a 16-year low and…A Reuters/University of Michigan index of consumer sentiment sent a shiver through the market as it dropped in February to a level associated with past recessions."
–Reuters

February 28, 2008
Write-Down Sends A.I.G. to $5 Billion Loss
–New York Times

February 29, 2008
Economic Fears Put End to 4-Day Winning Streak
"Stocks sank Thursday as investors fretted over a rise in unemployment claims and the prospect of more bank failures…In testimony to Congress, the Federal Reserve chairman, Ben S. Bernanke, said Thursday that large American banks would probably recover from the recent credit crisis, but other banks were at risk of failing. Three small banks have failed since the summer."
–Associated Press

March 6, 2008
Credit and Mortgage Woes Sink Stocks
"Renewed anxiety about the availability of bank loans — and fears that the Federal Reserve may be unable to curb the credit slump — sent stock markets down sharply on Wall Street on Thursday…The credit market troubles arrived on the day of a report that home foreclosures reached an all-time high in 2007."
–New York Times

March 6, 2008
Mortgage Defaults Reach a New High
"The number of loans past due or in foreclosure jumped to 7.9 percent, from 7.3 percent at the end of September and 6.1 percent in December 2006. Before the third quarter, the rate had never risen past 7 percent since the survey began in 1979."
–New York Times

News &
Bridgewater Daily Observations
(BDO)

March 7, 2008
Stocks Slide on Renewed Fears of Recession
"Stocks slid on Wall Street on Friday as investors digested a discouraging employment report that revived fears the nation may already be in a recession.

The Dow Jones industrials dropped at the opening bell after the Labor Department reported that the economy lost 63,000 jobs in February, an unexpected and ominous decline."
—*New York Times*

March 10, 2008
Slipping Away
"As you know we have a vague fear that the degree of levered counterparty positions that have built up over the years creates a kind of house of financial cards. With financial markets making new lows, new problems are popping up.

More and more entities are failing on margin calls, and this is flowing through to the dealers who have the exposures when entities fail on margin. Financials were crushed Monday as rumors of liquidity trouble at Bear Stearns flew. While we don't have any view on rumors, the quantity of major entities failing on margin calls (TMA, Carlyle Financial) is likely creating trouble at many dealers. The counterparty exposures across dealers have grown so exponentially that it is difficult to imagine any one of them failing in isolation.

Bear Stearns has entered a non-equilibrium situation, as its business, in all likelihood, cannot be sustained at current market prices. Either things are going to get a lot better, or a lot worse for Bear. Broker/dealers in our experience cannot survive with financing costs close to Bear's current levels."

March 11, 2008
Fed Plans to Lend $200 Billion to Banks
"Scrambling to ease the strain on the credit market, the Federal Reserve announced a $200 billion program on Tuesday that would allow financial institutions, including the nation's major investment banks, to borrow ultra-safe Treasury money by using some of their riskiest investments as collateral."
—*New York Times*

March 11, 2008
Dow Climbs 416.66 for its Biggest Gain in Over 5 Years
"Wall Street enjoyed its best trading day in more than five years on Tuesday — complete with a 400-point gain in the Dow Jones industrial average — after the Federal Reserve injected a burst of financial adrenaline into the ailing banking system."
—*New York Times*

March 11, 2008
More Liquidity (Good), But No Accounting Change (Bad)
"We think that three things are required to prevent the avalanche/deleveraging from getting unmanageable—1) providing liquidity to financially strained financial intermediaries, 2) changing accounting rules so that the losses can be written off over adequate time to prevent their ruin and/or material contractions in their balance sheets, and c) improving confidence by making it clear that these actions will keep the financial system operating effectively. The Fed is doing its part. The Treasury, Congress and accounting regulators aren't doing their parts yet."

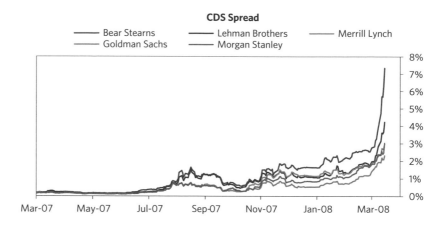

Bear Stearns was the most stressed of the major investment banks. Although Bear was the smallest of them, it still held $400 billion worth of securities that would be dumped onto the market if it failed. Moreover, Bear and its nearly 400 subsidiaries had activities that touched almost every other major financial firm. It had 5,000 trading counterparties and 750,000 open derivatives contracts. As Bernanke put it in his memoirs,[21] "size alone wasn't the problem. Bear was big, but not that big compared to the largest commercial banks." It was not "too big to fail," it was "too interconnected to fail." Bernanke's greatest fear was that a Bear bankruptcy could trigger a collapse in the $2.8 *trillion* tri-party repo market (a significant credit pipe for financial institutions), an event that would have "disastrous consequences for financial markets and, as credit froze and asset prices plunged, the entire economy."

Classically, **when a financial institution starts to show early signs of stress, it can experience "runs" that can accelerate into a failure in a matter of days, because runs can lead to losing liquidity**. That's because these institutions rely on short-term borrowing, often overnight borrowing, to hold longer-term, illiquid assets. At the first sight of trouble, it is logical for those who are providing this short-term credit to stop lending in order to avoid losses. We certainly didn't want to have exposure to a financial institution that was stressed. As more and more market participants change their behaviors in this way, it creates the liquidity crisis that leads to failure. That was what was happening to the financial institutions shown in the chart above to the degrees conveyed by the spreads. The Treasury and the Fed just had a few days to figure out their responses.

Big financial institutions have failed many times in the past. As I described in the prior sections of the book, *if the debt is in one's own currency, and if policy makers have both the knowledge of what it takes to manage it and the authority to do so, then they are capable of handling these situations* in a way that *minimizes spill-over effects and limits economic pain (though some pain is inevitable)*. This is a theme we will return to time and time again.

In 2008, the US had a team of policy makers that understood what it would take to manage a debt crisis about as well as one could expect given that debt crises of this magnitude happen about once in a lifetime. I want to reemphasize how significant it was that the economic leadership team had the qualities they had. Treasury Secretary Hank Paulson had more than thirty years of financial market experience at Goldman Sachs, including eight years as CEO, so he brought a good understanding of how financial institutions and markets worked and a forceful leadership style with experience in making tough decisions under pressure. Chairman Bernanke was one of the most prominent economists of the time, and one of the world's foremost experts on the Great Depression, which obviously provided critical perspective. Tim Geithner, president of the Federal Reserve Bank of New York (which takes a leading role in overseeing the biggest banks and implementing monetary policy), had around two decades of experience in economic policy, including prominent roles at the Treasury and at the IMF, which gave him exposure to the handling of financial crises.

Geithner, Paulson, and Bernanke told me that they were extremely lucky to be on a team that trusted one another and had complementary skill sets, and they all believed that they needed to do whatever they could to prevent the failure of systemically important institutions. In other words, they agreed on the important things that had to be done and they were great at cooperating to do all in their power to get it done. I saw up close how lucky we all were, because without such cooperation and cleverness, we would have had such a terrible disaster that it would have taken decades to recover from it.

The biggest problem Geithner, Paulson, and Bernanke faced is that they didn't have all the legal authority they needed to make some of the moves that were necessary. For example, by law, the Treasury could only use funds for purposes designated by Congress. While handling a failing traditional bank (e.g., one that took retail deposits) had a clear playbook, primarily administered by the FDIC, there was no authority for the Treasury, the Fed, or any other regulator to provide capital to a failing investment bank. At this point, to save an investment bank, there would have to be a willing private sector buyer to take on the exposure. This limitation proved incredibly consequential.

The urgent need for flexible authority is a classic challenge for policy makers in the midst of crises. The system that is designed to ensure stability during normal times is often poorly suited to crisis scenarios in which immediate, aggressive action is required.

The Treasury and the Fed ran into this challenge with Bear Stearns, so the Fed turned to the plans it sketched out in late 2007, exercising its section 13(3) powers—which hadn't been used since the Great Depression—to arrest what Bernanke would later call "self-feeding [downward] liquidity dynamics."[22] It announced a $200 billion new program, the Term Securities Lending Facility (TSLF), through which it would allow financial institutions, including major brokerage firms, to borrow cash or treasuries by using risky assets, including nongovernment mortgage-backed securities, as collateral. Markets applauded the injection of liquidity, with stocks posting their largest daily gain (about 4 percent) in over five years.

Despite the announcement of the TSLF, the run on Bear continued. In just four days (March 10-March 14) Bear Stearns saw an $18 billion cash buffer disappear as its customers quickly began withdrawing funds. Treasury Secretary Paulson feared the brokerage could collapse within 24 hours as soon he heard it was facing such a run on liquidity.[23] This was because Bear had been making loans of up to 60 days while remaining almost completely reliant on overnight funding. By Thursday, March 14, those fears were confirmed. Lenders in the repo market refused even to accept Treasury securities as collateral when making overnight loans to Bear Stearns.

News &
Bridgewater Daily Observations
(BDO)

March 14, 2008
JPM and Fed Move to Bail Out Bear Stearns
"With the support of the Federal Reserve Bank of New York, JPMorgan said...it had 'agreed to provide secured funding to Bear Stearns, as necessary, for an initial period of up to 28 days.'"
—New York Times

March 14, 2008
Stocks Tumble on Bank's Troubles
"Stocks took a sharp dive on Friday after an emergency bailout for Bear Stearns, the troubled investment bank, rocked Wall Street's confidence in the fragile credit market.

...Early in the day, the Fed issued a statement that it would 'continue to provide liquidity as necessary' to keep the wheels of the financial system turning. But investors seemed to take little solace in the pledge.

...The news from Bear Stearns came after the bank had insisted for days that its finances were in adequate shape. But its chief executive said the bank's liquidity had 'significantly deteriorated' since Thursday."
—New York Times

March 14, 2008
One can look at today's developments for Bear Stearns...
"One can look at today's developments for Bear Stearns and other US investment companies as either today's events or the latest manifestation of the deleveraging process. If you look at these developments as just today's news, it won't do you much good in preparing you for what might come next. So, before discussing today's developments for Bear Stearns and other investment companies, we will remind you of the situation that investment companies are in."

March 17, 2008
Fed Acts to Rescue Financial Markets
"The Federal Reserve on Sunday approved a $30 billion credit line to engineer the takeover of Bear Stearns and announced an open-ended lending program for the biggest investment firms on Wall Street."
—New York Times

March 18, 2008
Dow Surges 420 Points on Fed Rate Cut and Earnings
"Investors sent stocks soaring to their highest gains in five years on Tuesday as shares of financial firms surged in the hopes that the Federal Reserve has finally taken hold of the credit crisis. The Dow Jones industrial average gained 420 points."
—New York Times

**News &
Bridgewater Daily Observations
(BDO)**

March 17, 2008
We think that the Fed has done a fabulous job....
"We think the Fed is doing a great job. We wouldn't do anything different because doing anything different would produce intolerable results. Of course we have moral hazard concerns; we believe the Fed does too. But the line has to be drawn somewhere and we think that it is at that point that the equity of the financial intermediary is essentially gone and before the point that the credit problems pass to others—and that is taking it right to the edge (perhaps a bit too far).

While we believe the Fed is acting appropriately, that does not mean that we are confident that things will be all right. That's because the Fed can't do it alone (i.e., as you know, we think we need the accounting changes and they are for others to provide). Also, what probably will be required of the Fed boggles the mind.

The good thing is that the regulators now realize how serious the problems are. The question is whether they can move fast enough. As mentioned, an avalanche can be prevented, but it can't be reversed."

March 23, 2008
With the Fed to the Rescue, Stocks Surge
"It was a week of extraordinary intervention in the financial markets by the Federal Reserve, and of wild swings in prices."
–*New York Times*

March 27, 2008
A Downturn as Data Revives Pessimism
"Wall Street pulled back on Wednesday after a drop in durable goods orders for February injected more pessimism about the economy into the stock market. The Dow Jones industrial average fell nearly 110 points...Investors were disappointed to see a 1.7 percent dip last month in orders for durable goods, which are costly items like refrigerators, cars and computers. The drop followed a decline of 5.3 percent in January."
–*Associated Press*

Bernanke, Geithner, and other Fed officials agreed that another loan from the Fed wasn't going to help Bear Stearns. It needed more equity—an investor to fill the hole created by all the losses. At this point, the Treasury didn't have the authority to be that investor. **A private sector solution—a healthier institution to acquire Bear—was the best option.** To buy time, the Fed, along with JP Morgan, promised on March 13 to extend Bear Stearns "secured funding...as necessary, for an initial period of 28 days."

JPMorgan, the third largest bank holding company in the country at the time, was the most natural candidate to buy Bear, because it was Bear's clearing bank, served as an intermediary between Bear and its repo lenders, and was thus considerably more familiar with Bear's holdings than any other potential suitor. Only JPMorgan could credibly review Bear's assets and make a bid before Asian markets opened on Sunday, a process which importantly included guaranteeing Bear's trading book. However, JPMorgan was not willing to proceed if it meant having to take over Bear's $35 billion mortgage portfolio. To push a deal through, the Fed promised to provide JPM with a $30 billion non-recourse loan to buy out the brokerage (at $2 a share—its peak was $173), secured by Bear's mortgage pool, meaning that future losses on the mortgage portfolio would be borne by the Fed—and ultimately the taxpayer. They also created a new lending facility where twenty investment banks/brokerages could borrow unlimited sums while posting MBS for collateral.

On Tuesday, the Fed additionally cut rates 75 basis points (bringing the policy rate down to 2.25 percent). The rescue and aggressive injection of liquidity had the desired effect. Stocks rallied and remarkably ended the month flat. Using taxpayer money to save Bear Stearns would prove a controversial decision, but as we noted in our *Daily Observations* at the time, failure to do so would have resulted in the "financial system...passing the point of no return (i.e., the point at which the blowing out of risk and liquidity premiums would be self-reinforcing)."

Although the markets rebounded, Paulson, Bernanke, and Geithner worried because they saw that, without a buyer, they didn't have the authority to prevent the bankruptcy of an investment bank in the midst of a panic, and they immediately began to worry about Lehman.[24]

Paulson and Bernanke met with House Financial Services Committee chairman Barney Frank and told him that they were concerned about Lehman and needed emergency authority to wind down a failing investment bank in the midst of a panic. Frank told them that this would be impossible to get from Congress unless they made a compelling public case that Lehman was about to fail and that its failure would damage the US economy. Paulson and Geithner maintained frequent communication with Lehman's CEO in an unsuccessful attempt to convince him to sell the bank or raise equity from a strategic, cornerstone investor.[25]

Later in April, Paulson used the Bear failure to convene a meeting with Senators Chris Dodd and Richard Shelby (the current and former chairmen of the Senate Banking Committee) and Daniel Mudd and Richard Syron (the CEOs of Fannie Mae and Freddie Mac).[26] This led to the Senate taking up the GSE reform legislation, which had passed the House in May of 2007 but had stalled in the Senate.

The Post-Rescue Rally: April–May 2008

In response to the rescue of Bear Stearns and the big easing, stocks rallied and bond yields rose through most of April and May, as markets became increasingly confident that the Fed would do whatever was necessary if things got bad enough. Prominent policy makers struck a tone of cautious optimism, with Treasury Secretary Paulson noting that the economy was beginning to rebound and that he also "expected to see a faster pace of economic growth before the end of the year."[27] The charts below are some of the key markets at the time. You might give some thought to what bets you would've made then.

US Assets

The "expansions of balance sheets" (i.e., the increased lending and buying of assets) through borrowing was beginning to slow, and, as a result, economic conditions continued to weaken as reflected in the economic stats, which came in below expectations. Unemployment continued to climb, consumer confidence and borrowing continued to fall, housing delinquencies and foreclosures continued to rise, and manufacturing and services activity continued to contract. Simultaneously, fresh rounds of write-downs were announced at UBS ($19 billion), Deutsche Bank ($4 billion), MBIA ($2.4 billion), and AIG ($7.8 billion). Reflecting on the market action in the months following the Fed's rescue, we likened it to a "currency intervention that temporarily reverses the markets but doesn't change the underlying conditions that necessitated the action."

**News &
Bridgewater Daily Observations
(BDO)**

April 1, 2008
Stocks Surge on Hopes Financial Woes Are Easing
"Despite the discouraging numbers—$19 billion in write-downs at UBS and nearly $4 billion at Deutsche in the first quarter alone—investors appeared hopeful that the bad news could signal the last of Wall Street's subprime woes."
–New York Times

April 2, 2008
The Loan Losses Are Still to Come
"Financial institutions lost money in many instruments that did not even exist in past financial crises...While the new ways for banks to lose money have gathered the markets' focus and a lot of them are now priced in, the losses from the old way (bad loans) are just about to come to a head."

April 3, 2008
The Real Economy Is Still Weak
"While financial markets have bounced off lows in recent weeks, the real economy is still weak (close to zero growth) and still gaining momentum on the downside. Employment, production, demand, and investment are all weak and weakening."

April 4, 2008
Unemployment Rate Rises After 80,000 Jobs Cut
"Sharp downturns in manufacturing and construction sectors led the decline, the biggest in five years."
–New York Times

April 15, 2008
Rising Oil and Food Prices Stoke Inflation Fears
"A gauge of prices paid by American producers jumped 1.1 percent in March, the Labor Department said on Tuesday, sharply accelerating from a 0.3 percent increase in February."
–New York Times

April 17, 2008
Tracking the Economy's Response to Stimulation
"The Fed's efforts to stimulate the economy...have so far prevented a total collapse of the financial system but have not improved conditions in the real economy."

April 25, 2008
Stocks Mostly Up as Investors Overcome Economic Worries
"Wall Street ended its second consecutive winning week with a moderate advance Friday, overcoming concerns about consumer confidence and inflation."
–Associated Press

April 30, 2008
Fed Cuts Rates by a Quarter Point, and It Signals a Pause
"The Federal Reserve...reduced short-term interest rates Wednesday for the seventh time in seven months, and signaled a likely pause from any additional cuts for now."
–New York Times

April 30, 2008
On Wednesday the Fed eased for what is priced in to be the last time in this easing cycle

May 1, 2008
Market Bounces on Bear Rescue
"The Bear rescue was the equivalent of a currency intervention that temporarily reverses the markets but doesn't change the underlying conditions that necessitated the action."

**News &
Bridgewater Daily Observations
(BDO)**

May 2, 2008
Fed Moves to Ease Strains in Credit Markets
"The Fed said it was stepping up the amounts offered in its Term Auction Facility auctions...to $75 billion from $50 billion."
–Reuters

May 9, 2008
Bad Investments and a $7.8 Billion Loss at A.I.G
"The company's chief executive, Martin J. Sullivan, conceded...that A.I.G. had badly underestimated the extent of the problems."
–New York Times

May 21, 2008
Tough Choices for the Fed lie ahead
"...The headaches for central bankers, and most investors for that matter, come when the growth and inflation aspects of the central banks' mandates give diverging signals...The recent market action and Fed rhetoric suggests there is growing concern about the divergence of growth and inflation."

June 2, 2008
Real events are starting to feed back onto financial events
"Markets in recent weeks have been trading off of a favorable shift in perceptions that is not well-grounded in reality. Monday's announcement by S&P to cut the long-term debt ratings of Morgan Stanley, Merrill Lynch and Lehman was a renewed dose of reality."

June 3, 2008
Downgrade of 3 Banks Revives Credit Fears
"Shares of Lehman Brothers, Merrill Lynch and Morgan Stanley...sank after a major rating agency, Standard & Poor's, said it had lost some confidence in the banks' ability to meet financial obligations."
–New York Times

June 4, 2008
Dow Plunges 100 Points on Credit Strife
"The market...tumbled in early afternoon after reports that Lehman Brothers planned to raise $4 billion in capital became a rumor that the investment bank had approached the Federal Reserve to borrow money."
–Associated Press

Simultaneously oil prices continued to climb (hitting $130 in late May) and the dollar continued to fall. These moves added to the Fed's dilemma, as it would have to balance keeping its policy accommodative to ward off an economic contraction and a further deterioration in financial conditions with concerns over price stability. The minutes of the Fed's April meeting reflected this, with the committee acknowledging "the difficulty of gauging the appropriate stance of policy in current circumstances." Two members even expressed "substantial concerns about the prospects for inflation" and warned that "another reduction in the funds rate...could prove costly over the long run."

It should be noted that **using interest rate and liquidity management policies that affect the whole economy to deal with the debt problems of certain sectors is very inefficient at best.** Macroprudential policies are more appropriate (and in fact would've been appropriate much earlier, such as in 2007 when they could've been used to control the then-emerging bubbles). They were not to be put to use until much later, when pressing circumstances required their use.

Collectively, the combination of new-found optimism in the financial system and growing concerns over price stability meant that when the Fed cut rates in late April, markets priced it as the end of the easing cycle.

Summer of 2008: Stagflation

In June the S&P fell by 9 percent because surging oil prices led to a spike in inflation at the same time that there were renewed credit problems in the financial sector and poor economic stats.

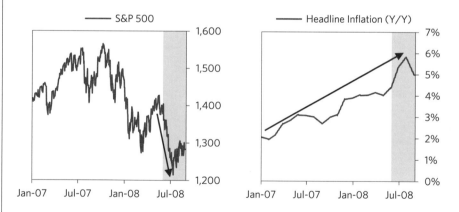

In terms of credit problems, the month began with downgrades of Lehman Brothers, Merrill Lynch, and Morgan Stanley by Standard & Poor's, with the rating agency noting that it had lost some confidence in these banks' ability to meet their financial obligations. This was followed by rumors that Lehman had approached the Fed for emergency funding and a release from Moody's that MBIA and Ambac (two of the country's largest bond insurers) were likely to lose their AAA ratings (thereby severely impairing their ability to write new insurance). By the end of the month, Moody's had cut the insurers' ratings and placed Lehman on credit review, while home foreclosures and mortgage delinquency rates, the underlying drivers of the strains, continued to accelerate.

As we looked at these institutions' balance sheets, estimated the losses they would have to report, and imagined what the reduced capital from those losses would mean for their lending and sales of assets, it was clear to us that they were headed for serious trouble that would have serious knock-on effects. Basically, they were getting margin calls, which meant that they would have to raise capital or sell assets and contract their lending, which would be bad for the markets and the economy.

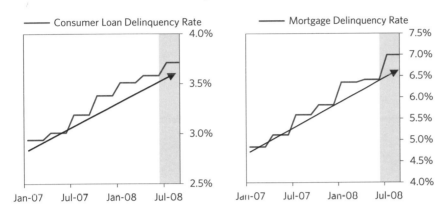

As a result of the contraction in credit, unemployment surged to 5.6 percent (the largest monthly increase in two decades), manufacturing activity declined for the fourth month in a row, and consumer confidence hit a 16-year low. Simultaneously, a CPI print showed that headline inflation rose to 4.4 percent in May, its sharpest increase in six months, and spiked fears of stagflation amidst poor growth and rising inflation expectations.

To ease or not to ease—that was the question. The cross-currents made the answer less than obvious. Throughout the month, policy makers repeatedly alluded to concerns for both economic growth and price stability. Bernanke called rising oil prices unwelcome, and Paulson emphasized that they would be "a real headwind" for the economy. With respect to the exchange rate, Bernanke emphasized that the Fed would "carefully monitor" its implications for inflation and inflation expectations, while Paulson even suggested that he "would never take intervention off the table."[28]

The pickup in inflationary pressures prompted a shift of the Fed's priorities from preventing debt and economic risks to growth and toward assuring price stability. As early as June 4, Bernanke noted that further interest-rate cuts were unlikely due to concerns over inflation, and suggested that the current policy rate was sufficient to promote moderate growth.[29] A few days later Bernanke gave a speech noting that the rising commodity prices and the dollar's depressed value posed a challenge for anchoring long-term inflation. Finally, on June 25, the Fed left rates unchanged, noting that "although downside risks to growth remain, they appear to have diminished somewhat, and the upside risks to inflation and inflation expectations have increased." Ugh. See the charts below.

**News &
Bridgewater Daily Observations
(BDO)**

June 3, 2008
U.S. Manufacturing Slips as Inflation Gauge Surges
"United States manufacturing declined in May for the fourth consecutive month while inflation surged to the highest in four years, heightening fears of stagflation."
                                        –Reuters

June 4, 2008
Fed Chairman Signals an End to Interest Rate Cuts Amid Concerns About Inflation
"The Federal Reserve chairman, Ben S. Bernanke, signaled on Tuesday that further interest rate cuts were unlikely because of concerns about inflation."
                                –Associated Press

June 5, 2008
Moody's May Downgrade Ratings of MBIA and Ambac Units
"Moody's Investors Services said on Wednesday that it was likely to cut the top ratings of the bond insurance arms of MBIA and Ambac Financial, in a move that may cripple their ability to write new insurance."
                                        –Reuters

June 7, 2008
Oil Prices and Joblessness Punish Shares
"Wall Street suffered its worst losses in more than two months on Friday after crude oil prices spiked over $138, an increase of nearly $11, and the unemployment rate rose more than expected."
                                –New York Times

June 9, 2008
Global Shift in Inflation Expectations
"Short rates have been getting hammered in recent weeks as the markets are awakening to the shift in emphasis that central bankers are putting on inflation in relation to economic growth."

June 10, 2008
Paulson Won't Rule Out Dollar Intervention
"Mr. Paulson...said record oil prices were 'a problem' for the American economy. 'There's nothing welcome about it and it's a real headwind,' he added."
                                        –Reuters

News &
Bridgewater Daily Observations
(BDO)

June 11, 2008
Concerns on Economy Are Shifting to Inflation
"There is a growing sense among investors that the Fed has shifted its focus to the fight against inflation, leaving behind—for now—concerns about the outlook for economic growth."
—*New York Times*

June 14, 2008
Moody's Is Reviewing Lehman's Credit
"Moody's Investors Service said on Friday that it had placed Lehman Brothers Holdings on review for a possible downgrade, citing the investment bank's demotion of both its president and chief financial officer."
—*Reuters*

June 15, 2008
A Mixed Bag, with Inflation a Top Worry
"On Friday, the Labor Department reported that the Consumer Price Index in May rose at a 4.2 percent annual rate, its fastest pace in six months."
—*New York Times*

June 20, 2008
Moody's Cuts Insurer Ratings
"Moody's Investors Service stripped the insurance arms of Ambac Financial Group and MBIA of their AAA ratings, citing their impaired ability to raise capital and write new business."
—*Reuters*

June 25, 2008
Consumer Confidence Declines to a 16-Year Low
"Consumer confidence dropped to its lowest point in 16 years in June while home values fell in 20 metropolitan areas across the country, according to two economic reports released Tuesday."
—*New York Times*

June 26, 2008
Shares Advance Modestly as Fed Leaves Rates Alone
"Wall Street ended an erratic day with a modest gain after the Federal Reserve left interest rates unchanged and issued a mixed assessment of the economy."
—*Associated Press*

June 28, 2008
Oil Hits New High as Dow Flirts with Bear Territory
"With a 145-point slide on Friday, the Dow Jones industrial average flirted with bear market territory, meaning that it is down 20 percent from its high on October 9, 2007...Another surge in the price of oil, which traded above $142 on Friday afternoon after gaining $5 a day earlier, discouraged investors and had helped nudge the Dow down 1.1 percent to 11,327 at 2 p.m."
—*New York Times*

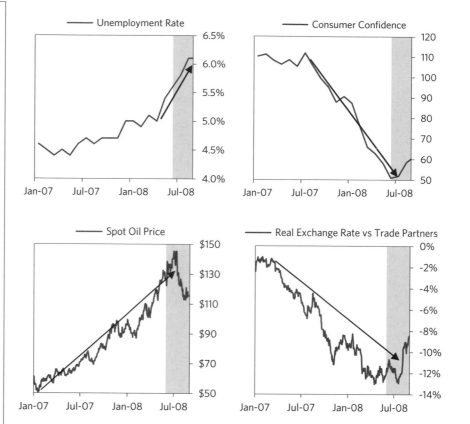

Markets continued to decline, oil prices rose, and a series of ratings downgrades, write-downs, and poor housing stats surfaced during the first two weeks of July. Financial stocks went into a free fall as it became clear that the Fed was behind developments and that the credit problems would not be fixed up via a blanket easy Fed policy even if it aggressively eased. The mortgage crisis and who it would affect next also became clearer. Shares of Freddie Mac and Fannie Mae came under extreme selling pressure, following a report by Lehman Brothers, published on July 7, stating that the two mortgage giants would need a capital infusion of as much as $75 billion to remain solvent. According to Paulson, the report "set off an investor stampede," with shares of Freddie Mac and Fannie Mae declining by about 45 percent each respectively in the week following the report's release.[30]

In mid-July, markets bounced because oil prices declined sharply (leaving more room for the Fed to ease) and policy makers made a series of interventions to shore up confidence in the financial sector—most importantly with respect to Freddie Mac and Fannie Mae. Also, the SEC placed restrictions on shorting 19 financial stocks (including the two mortgage lenders), the Fed extended its emergency lending program for investment banks and brokerages, and the Treasury and the Fed announced a plan under which Freddie Mac and Fannie Mae would be able to tap into public funding (i.e., be bailed out) if on the verge of collapse.

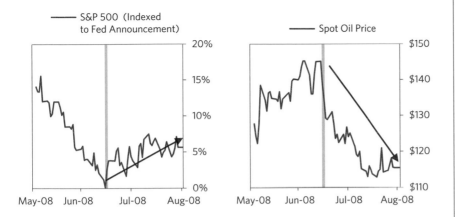

S&P 500 (Indexed to Fed Announcement)

Spot Oil Price

Taking Control of Fannie and Freddie

Of all the interventions, the guarantee to use public funds to support Fannie Mae and Freddie Mac was the most unprecedented. Fannie Mae and Freddie Mac were two government-sponsored enterprises (GSEs), created by Congress in 1938 and 1970 respectively, with the former being part of Roosevelt's New Deal following the Great Depression. They were created to stabilize the US mortgage market and promote affordable housing. They did this primarily by buying mortgages from approved private lenders, packaging many together, guaranteeing timely payment on them, and then selling them back to investors.

At first glance, everyone looked to benefit from this arrangement. Private lenders had a ready buyer for about as many mortgages as they could originate. Fannie and Freddie profited greatly from buying riskier mortgages and turning them into a safe asset (i.e., buying something cheap and selling it for more). Banks and other investors were happy to have a greater supply of safe assets to invest in, earning slightly more than they would on equivalent treasury bonds. And households benefited from cheaper borrowing rates.

Of course, all this was based on an implicit guarantee that the government would backstop Fannie and Freddie—it was only that guarantee that allowed the securities issued by GSEs to be seen as about as safe as treasuries, giving them very low borrowing rates. At times, the spread on their debt to treasuries essentially hit 0 percent.

Agency 10Yr Spread to Treasuries

Fannie Mae   Freddie Mac

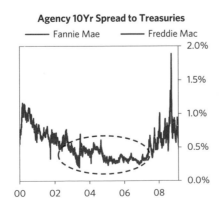

News & Bridgewater Daily Observations (BDO)

June 30, 2008
Markets are tightening while the economy is deteriorating and financials are in free-fall
"In the past three months since the Bear Stearns rescue a set of economic and market conditions have transpired that are inherently unsustainable and self-defeating. While the tax refunds and a few other unsustainable sources of money have stabilized spending and the economy, market prices that directly impact the economy have responded in a way that is uniformly restrictive. At the same time, the bounce in financial stocks that originally conveyed a more positive tone to the financial landscape has largely disappeared. Instead, deteriorating credit conditions in the real economy are feeding back onto the financial system, leaving behind a very big pile of financial institutions whose stock prices are in free-fall and whose market value of leverage is exploding. This high market value of leverage (assets divided by market cap) implies that on the margin, ever smaller declines in the value of their assets will wipe out ever larger chunks of equity value, the classic over-leveraged death spiral. Bigger losses lie ahead and the banking industry does not have enough healthy entities to absorb the dying ones. And, the sovereign wealth funds have lost their appetite for large doses of bank equity. The inadequacy of bank capital combined with the coming need to liquidate ever-larger portfolios of bank assets will further constrain credit growth in the economy. In the meantime, market prices are acting as a restrictive force against growth at the same time that the financial sector is collapsing."

July 6, 2008
Oil Climbs as Stocks Fall. Sound Familiar?
"In a pattern that has been repeated for weeks, oil prices rose and the stock market fell."
–*New York Times*

July 10, 2008
Sharp Fall for Stocks Amid Angst in Lending
"Freddie Mac...was the worst performing stock in the S & P 500. Its shares dropped 23.8 percent."
–*New York Times*

July 15, 2008
Stocks Fall Back After Early Gains on Rescue Plan
"The United States treasury secretary, Henry Paulson Jr., and the Federal Reserve chairman, Ben Bernanke, acted after the shares of Freddie Mac and Fannie Mae came under enormous selling pressure last week."
–*New York Times*

July 16, 2008
S.E.C. Unveils Measures to Limit Short-Selling
"The Securities and Exchange Commission, under pressure to respond to the tumult in the financial industry, announced emergency measures on Tuesday to curb certain kinds of short-selling that aims at Fannie Mae and Freddie Mac, as well as Wall Street banks."
–*New York Times*

News &
Bridgewater Daily Observations
(BDO)

July 19, 2008
Freddie Mac Takes Step Toward Raising Capital
"The nation's two beleaguered mortgage finance giants continued to win back investors on Friday, as Freddie Mac, the smaller of the two companies, took a crucial step toward raising capital.

After more than a week of sharp swings, the price of Freddie Mac's shares jumped once again, this time after the company registered with the Securities and Exchange Commission and reiterated its commitment to raise more capital."
–*New York Times*

July 20, 2008
As Oil Slides, Rallies for Dow and S.& P.
"On Sunday, the Treasury secretary, Henry M. Paulson Jr., proposed a broad rescue plan for Fannie Mae and Freddie Mac, the mortgage finance giants. The Federal Reserve also announced that Freddie and Fannie would have access to cheap loans from the Fed's discount window."
–*New York Times*

July 21, 2008
Trouble at Fannie Mae and Freddie Mac Stirs Concern Abroad
"For more than a decade, Fannie Mae and Freddie Mac, the housing giants that make the American mortgage market run, have attracted overseas investors with a simple pitch: the securities they issue are just as good as the United States government's, and they usually pay better...Now that the two companies are at risk, how their rescue is handled will ultimately test the world's faith in American markets."
–*New York Times*

July 22, 2008
All Markets are Trading as One...
"All markets are trading as one, with a recent turning point of July 15. The turning point was marked by a $17 drop in oil prices, limits on shorting financials when short interest was at a record, and a few positive earnings surprises from the banks. Of course this action can't last because the forces that drive these markets are widely varied and often conflicting, but such action is common when sentiment gets to extremes... Meanwhile, there has been no reversal in the underlying economic conditions as reflected in the economic stats through July. They have continued to weaken."

While they weren't officially guaranteed by law, and government officials had denied for years that there was any guarantee, the private market believed that the government would never let the GSEs fail, as it would hurt too many, including individual homeowners—though they couldn't be 100 percent sure because the Treasury wouldn't make that assurance. I remember a dinner meeting I had with the head of a Chinese organization that held a massive amount of bonds issued by the GSEs, in which she expressed her concerns. I especially admired how the Chinese creditors approached this situation analytically and with a high level of consideration. Ironically the larger the GSEs grew, the more "systemically important" they became, which in turn all but guaranteed a government rescue if needed, making them safer and further fueling their growth.

Although Fannie and Freddie were supposed to generate revenue primarily through insuring mortgage debt, by 2007 about two-thirds of their profits came from holding risky mortgage-backed securities. The problems associated with having these exposures were made worse by lax regulation. Congress only required Freddie and Fannie to keep 0.45 percent of their off-balance-sheet obligations and 2.5 percent of their portfolio assets in reserves, meaning that they were significantly undercapitalized, even when compared with commercial banks of equivalent size, which were also severely undercapitalized (meaning that it only took a modest loss to make them go broke). Paulson saw this and openly called them "disasters waiting to happen...extreme examples of a broader problem...too much leverage and lax regulation."[31]

By 2007, these two mortgage insurers were twenty times larger than Bear Stearns and either owned, or had guaranteed, $5 *trillion* dollars in residential mortgages and mortgage-backed securities—about half of what had been issued in the US. Financing such operations also made them one of the largest issuers of debt in the world, with $1.7 trillion outstanding, about 20 percent of which was held by international investors. They were also huge players in the short-term lending market, frequently borrowing up to $20 billion a week. It didn't take a sharp pencil to see that they were a disaster waiting to happen. The only question was what the government would do.

Doing something to rein them in would be politically challenging. Larry Summers recently described to me the challenges he faced when dealing with them in the 1990s:

> *"Fannie and Freddie had vast political power. When we said anything raising any concern about them, they had arranged for the Treasury to receive 40,000 pieces of mail saying it is important that Fannie and Freddie be fully enabled to do their vital work. When we testified on Fannie and Freddie, a congressman would pull out an envelope from Fannie with their prepared statements and what their questions were going to be. They would have a set of mayors call if you tried to mess with them. The most disillusioning experience I had with respect to the financial community was at the quarterly dinner for the Treasury Advisory Borrowing Committee. I asked them: 'What do you guys think about the GSEs?' They said that the GSEs were like a massively over-leveraged hedge fund—dangerous. They were pretty emphatic. I said, 'Would you put that in your report?' and they said they would. The report came back basically saying that Fannie and Freddie are vital contributors to our financial*

systems. I asked what happened. They said that they checked with their bosses and their bosses said we couldn't say that because we all had such important client relationships."

Paulson described this situation as follows:

"We had seen what happened in March when Bear Stearns's counterparties… abruptly turned away. We had survived that, but the collapse of Fannie and Freddie would be catastrophic. Seemingly everyone in the world—little banks, big banks, foreign central banks, money market funds—[either] owned their paper or were [their] counterparty. Investors would lose tens of billions; foreigners would lose confidence in the US. It might cause a run on the dollar."[32]

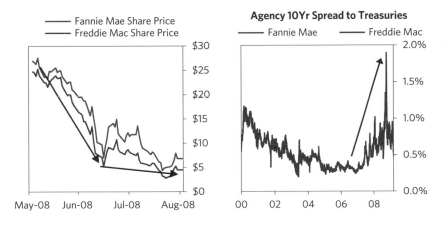

This case exemplifies the very common problem of politics creating **government guarantees (implicit or explicit) that make risky assets appear to be safer than they are. This encourages investors to lever up in them, which feeds bad debt growth.**

As losses from mortgage-backed securities mounted, shares of Freddie and Fannie plummeted because everyone knew they had a lot of bad debt. Equity holders knew they would get hit even if the creditors were protected. By July 15, Freddie and Fannie's equity prices had declined by almost 75 percent in less than a year.

Now that the crisis was at hand and undeniably obvious, it had to be dealt with. After frantic behind the scenes negotiations, the Treasury was able to get a bill passed by Congress on July 23 allowing it to use a virtually unlimited (Paulson chose the term "unspecified") amount of dollars to provide funds to the two GSEs (limited only by the overall federal debt ceiling), and expanded regulatory oversight of them. The Treasury basically acquired a blank check, backstopped by the taxpayer, to do whatever it took to keep these institutions solvent.

Nationalizing too-big-to-fail financial institutions on the brink of failure is a classic move in a deleveraging that is usually well received, as it signifies that the government is willing to provide a blanket of safety over the system. Remember that when debts are denominated in a country's own currency, the government has the power to eliminate the risks of default.

News & Bridgewater Daily Observations (BDO)

July 23, 2008
Paulson Urges Americans to Be Patient on Economy
"'Our markets won't make progress in a straight line, and we should expect additional bumps in the road,' Mr. Paulson said in remarks at the New York Public Library in Midtown Manhattan. 'We have been experiencing more bumps recently, and until the housing market stabilizes further we should expect some continued stresses in our financial markets.'"
—New York Times

July 25, 2008
Bank Failure Expectations
"The disorderly collapse of a large financial institution has yet to happen—in part because the Fed provision of liquidity has helped avoid a run (with the exception of IndyMac), and so far each time an entity has come close either a bailout or a buyout has come in order to ensure that an institution isn't forced to liquidate. Given the continued strains on financial entities, new financial institution failures are likely. Market expectations are currently pricing roughly 4% of financial institutions going bankrupt in the next 6 months, implying an asset liquidation of $600 bln…The banking sector as a whole has only about half of that amount of free equity capital available today, much of which will need to be available to absorb credit losses on old loans."

July 29, 2008
Bank Shares Retreat, Giving Up Gains
"A sell-off of stocks accelerated in late trading Monday as investors moved out of shares of investment and commercial banks, many of which have given back all of their gains from last week…A late-afternoon announcement by Treasury Secretary Henry M. Paulson Jr. that four major banks were planning to issue a new type of bond to aid the mortgage market did not stem the bank stocks' slide. The sell-off only intensified in all three major indexes just after Mr. Paulson spoke."
—New York Times

July 29, 2008
A New Tool Announced to Support Home Loans
"The Treasury Department and the nation's four biggest banks on Monday said they were ready to kick-start a market for a new tool to support home financing in the latest effort to spur a moribund housing market…The Treasury released a set of 'best practices' for institutions that issue so-called covered bonds, and Bank of America, Citigroup, JPMorgan Chase and Wells Fargo said they planned to begin issuing them.'"
—Reuters

July 31, 2008
Fed Extends Emergency Borrowing Program
"The Fed said the program, in which investment houses can tap the central bank for a quick source of cash, will be available through January 30. Originally the program, started on March 17, was supposed to last until mid-September."
—Associated Press

**News &
Bridgewater Daily Observations
(BDO)**

August 4, 2008
Developed World Entering Recession
"…Across most of the developed world growth
rates are collapsing at accelerating rates…we
expect developed central banks will be heading
toward easing while the markets are still pricing
in tightening."

August 5, 2008
*Fed Holds Key Rate Steady Amid Growth
Concerns*
                                    –New York Times

August 7, 2008
In Retail Sales, More Signs of a Slowdown
"Stocks fell sharply as sales reports revealed a
country that is ratcheting back its spending habits
and abandoning mid-tier and discount shopping
mall mainstays."
                                    –New York Times

August 7, 2008
*A.I.G. Posts a Large Loss as Housing Troubles
Persist*
"American International Group lost more than $5
billion in the second quarter as housing values slid
and disruptions continued in the credit markets."
                                    –New York Times

August 12, 2008
*After $43 Billion in Write-Downs, UBS to Split
Main Businesses*
                                    –New York Times

Though there are undeniable advantages to a political environment in which there are checks and balances and laws, during times of crisis there exists the risk that what needs to be done might not be done swiftly enough. That's because laws are never written so perfectly that they can anticipate and specify how to handle every possible circumstance. Throughout the 2008 financial crisis, there were numerous close calls in which the parties involved did the things that needed to be done, even if that required them to get around the rules to do them.

On July 30, as soon as Congress granted the Treasury the authority to oversee Fannie and Freddie, regulators from the Treasury began working to assess just how dire the situation was. With the help of the Fed and outside accounting specialists, Treasury officials pored over the GSEs' books. They soon discovered that both Fannie and Freddie had been papering over massive capital losses. Once they had properly accounted for questionably valued intangible assets and improperly valued mortgage guarantees, they saw that both companies were at least tens of billions of dollars underwater. As Paulson later put it, "We'd been prepared for bad news, but the extent of the problems was startling."[33]

From mid-August until the bailout, the situation was analyzed; terms were finalized on September 7. The Treasury then raced to build a plan that would serve its economic goals without bumping up against legal constraints. In the end, it decided to put the GSEs into conservatorship while injecting capital through guaranteed purchases of preferred stock. Conservatorship would allow both Fannie and Freddie to keep running relatively normally following the takeover, while the guaranteed stock purchases would allow the Treasury to effectively backstop their debt, even after the 18-month limit on its authority expired. And, importantly, Paulson wouldn't have to give Fannie and Freddie any heads up—all it would take was a go-ahead from their direct regulator, the Federal Housing Finance Agency (FHFA).

Bailing out the GSEs was more of a political challenge than an economic one. The executives of both companies still believed they were on sound footing. After all, just a couple of weeks before the FHFA had sent the GSEs drafts of reports concluding they were sufficiently capitalized. If news of the planned takeover leaked, the executives of Fannie and Freddie would have time to mobilize their lobbyists and congressional allies in Washington to fight it. And if there were a fight, there was no guarantee that the Treasury would win—in Paulson's words, the GSEs were famously the "toughest streetfighters in town."[34]

Convincing the FHFA examiners required the coordination and combined influence of the Treasury, the Fed, the OCC, and the FDIC. The FHFA, which had repeatedly blessed Fannie and Freddie's books on the basis of loose statutory accounting rules, was embarrassed at the thought of reversing itself so suddenly. But after weeks of pressure from the Treasury and its allies, the FHFA examiners gave in on September 4. The next day, the news was given to the boards of the two companies. Fearing that any friction or delay in the takeover might send markets plunging, Paulson set out, in his own words, "to ambush Freddie and Fannie" with no advance warning.[35]

---

* Rules create a clarity of expectations that facilitates decision making that is more structured and less arbitrary and politicized.

Paulson described the Fannie-Freddie situation to me as follows. In July 2008, when Fannie and Freddie were beginning to fail, the Treasury asked for very expansive emergency powers. As Freddie and Fannie combined were nine times larger than Lehman Brothers and the dominant sources of mortgage financing during the crisis, they could not be allowed to fail. However, Paulson's political people had told him that if they put a big dollar number in front of Congress for approval, Congress would likely get spooked. As Paulson couldn't ask for unlimited authority to inject capital into the two GSEs, he decided to ask for "unspecified" authority.

However, when the Treasury finally got the "unspecified" authority, it was temporary, i.e., it expired in October 2009. This presented a challenge, because Fannie and Freddie had long-term debt and insured long term mortgages. So it took some creative financial engineering to turn this expansive authority, which Congress had intended to be only temporary, into what was for all intents and purposes a long-term guarantee. To do this, policy makers used their ability to immediately issue long-term preferred stock. Then they used these preferred shares to backstop Fannie and Freddie and absorb any potential losses.

This particular move—with its legal finagling—and the need to convince numerous lawmakers to set aside their ideological opposition to bailouts for financial institutions, while at the same time getting Congress to raise the debt ceiling sufficiently to allow for a potentially meaningful capital injection, were unprecedented and remarkable. But as Paulson described it later, "if Congress failed to come through, markets would implode. The stakes were enormous."[36]

In early August, falling oil prices and the Treasury's unprecedented intervention helped usher in an interval of relief, with equities rallying modestly through August (about 2 percent), financials down only 1 percent, and the free fall of Freddie and Fannie stock halted. However, despite the growing perception that financial markets were stabilizing, the underlying drivers of credit problems, and their feedback mechanisms into the real economy, had not changed.

On August 18, I reminded the readers of our *Daily Observations* that the worst was yet to come.

(BDO) August 18: Entering the Second Stage of the Deleveraging

It seems to me that we have been through much of the first stage and are now entering the second stage (i.e., the avalanche stage) of the deleveraging. While the Fed did a great job of providing liquidity where it reasonably could, the accounting adjustments (e.g., allowing losses to be written down over several years) weren't made, so **we are approaching a solvency crisis that we think is about to result in an avalanche of asset sales.** So now the question is whether they will create a safety net in time to catch these assets so that they don't crash and bring down the financial system and the economy with it. Frankly, we think that this will be a race to the wire.

News & Bridgewater Daily Observations (BDO)

September 2, 2008
Oil Prices Plunge to Five-Month Low
"The drop in oil prices dragged down the entire commodities sector, and initially lifted the stock markets as investors hoped that cheaper energy could nudge up consumer spending."
  —*New York Times*

September 3, 2008
Investor Jitters Produce Mixed Markets
"One bright spot in the market Wednesday was the troubled financial sector, which drew some bargain hunters because of positive news on a few big names: the Ambac Financial Group, Freddie Mac and Lehman Brothers Holdings."
  —*Associated Press*

September 3, 2008
Investments Are Faltering in Chrysler and GMAC
  —*New York Times*

September 4, 2008
Bear Returns to Wall St. as Major Indexes Plunge
"The Dow Jones industrial average plummeted 344.65 points on Thursday on a confluence of poor news about the economy, although investors could not pin the drop on any overriding reason."
  —*New York Times*

September 4, 2008
Lehman Weighs Split to Shed Troubling Loans
  —*New York Times*

September 5, 2008
U.S. Rescue Seen at Hand for 2 Mortgage Giants
"Senior officials from the Bush administration and the Federal Reserve on Friday called in top executives of Fannie Mae and Freddie Mac, the mortgage finance giants, and told them that the government was preparing to place the two companies under federal control, officials and company executives briefed on the discussions said."
  —*New York Times*

September 5, 2008
U.S. Jobless Rate Rises Past 6%, Highest Since '03
  —*New York Times*

September 6, 2008
Mortgage Giant Overstated the Size of Its Capital Base
"The government's planned takeover of Fannie Mae and Freddie Mac, expected to be announced as early as this weekend, came together hurriedly after advisers poring over the companies' books for the Treasury Department concluded that Freddie's accounting methods had overstated its capital cushion, according to regulatory officials briefed on the matter."
  —*New York Times*

September 6, 2008
Stocks Rebound After Early Losses
  —*Associated Press*

September 7, 2008
A Sigh of Relief, but Hard Questions Remain on U.S. Economy
"Investors around the world breathed a sigh of relief on Sunday after the federal government took over and backed Fannie Mae and Freddie Mac, assuring a continued flow of credit through America's wounded mortgage system.
But the takeover of the companies reinforced concerns about troubles of the American economy and highlighted its significant reliance on foreign investors, particularly in Asia."
  —*New York Times*

The Crash: September 2008

In September the crisis entered a new stage in which there was a genuine risk that the world economy would plunge into a depression. Since so much happened, I will transition into a nearly day-by-day account of events. I will convey it via both my narrative and the newsfeed on the sides of the page.

Over the first week of September, there was a mix of good and bad news in the form of oil prices falling precipitously (which reduced concern over inflation and provided a tailwind to US consumer spending). Airlines and retailers, hopeful of a pickup in consumer spending, were particular beneficiaries. At the same time, falling oil prices reflected weakening global growth.

While financial players like Lehman Brothers, Freddie, Fannie, and Ambac were struggling, it also seemed as though solutions to their problems were in the works. For example, Lehman's stock rose on news that it had made progress in negotiations to sell part of itself to the Korea Development Bank, while good news from Freddie (a successful sale of $4 billion in debt) and Ambac (the announced launch of a new insurance subsidiary) partially softened investor concerns surrounding these companies.

These positive developments were set against a continuous trickle of negative stat releases—in particular, an unanticipated spike in jobless claims and a notable uptick in the unemployment rate (from 5.7 percent to 6.1 percent). Stocks declined by 2.5 percent. Weak economic reports also filtered in from outside the US. From Canada to Australia, the story was the same—slowing demand, slowing output, and no end in sight. All in all, stocks ended the first week of September just slightly down.

The big news came after markets closed at the end of the week, when reports broke that the federal government would take over Fannie Mae and Freddie Mac.

Lehman Goes Bankrupt: September 8–15

Stocks rose about two percent on Monday, September 8, as the market responded positively to news of the nationalization of Fannie and Freddie, a bold move that would have been unthinkable months before. The *New York Times* wrote that "financial stocks led the surge, propelled by hope that the government's decision had averted a calamity and *marked a possible turning point in the credit crisis that has troubled banks for nearly a year*" (my emphasis). Boy, was that wrong.

Writers of accounts such as this one, who have the benefit of hindsight, typically paint pictures of what happened in ways that make what happened seem obvious. However, as that rally and comment reflect, it is an entirely different matter when one is in the moment. Just days before the crisis would become much worse, the *New York Times* wrote on three separate occasions (September 3, 5, and 10) about "bargain hunters" coming in with the stock market down around 20 percent from peak and many individual stocks down much more. Lehman Brothers, for instance, was trading down some 80 percent, but it was a company with a good reputation, a nearly 160-year history, and it looked to be on the verge of finding a buyer or strategic investor. Below is its share price through early September. While the picture is clearly within the downtrend, there were rallies, and in just about all of them, one could make the argument that the bottom was being made. In investing, it's at least as important to know when not to be confident and when not to make a bet as it is to have an opinion and make one.

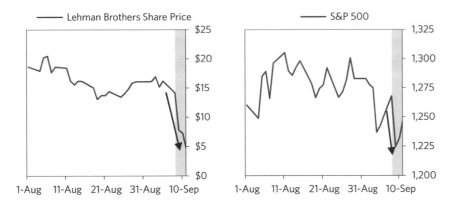

The strategic investor who would come in and save Lehman never materialized and Lehman's stock fell by almost 50 percent on Tuesday. Other major bank stocks, including Citigroup, Morgan Stanley, and Merrill, sold off 5–10 percent, while the overall market was down about 3 percent, and credit spreads widened substantially. Both investors and regulators began to wonder whether Lehman could survive until the weekend.

News & Bridgewater Daily Observations (BDO)

September 8, 2008
Stocks Soar on Takeover Plan
"Stock markets around the world rallied Monday after the federal takeover of Fannie Mae and Freddie Mac, but even the most optimistic investors worried that other problems in the economy remain unaddressed."
—*New York Times*

September 8, 2008
The Latest Step Down the Inevitable Path of Dealing With Fannie and Freddie
"At a big picture level, this is playing out in all the obvious ways... It was long ago inevitable that these GSEs were going to fail... And, it was inevitable that, when faced with this choice, the US government would stand behind its implied guarantee and defacto nationalize the GSE... Given that the big picture was so obvious, what isn't obvious to us is why the Treasury waited so long before acting."

September 9, 2008
Shares Fall on Worries About Lehman
"Stocks tumbled Tuesday after fresh concerns about the stability of Lehman Brothers Holdings touched off renewed jitters about the overall financial sector."
—*New York Times*

September 10, 2008
After a Sell-Off, Bargain Hunters Step In
"The markets ended moderately higher on Wednesday as investors bought the stocks of energy, materials and consumer-staple companies, but remained cautious about the financial sector."
—*New York Times*

September 10, 2008
Washington Mutual Stock Falls on Investor Fears
"As Wall Street scoured the financial industry Wednesday for the next weakest link after Lehman Brothers, it set its sights on a familiar target: Washington Mutual, the nation's largest savings and loan."
—*New York Times*

September 11, 2008
Market Climbs After a Bleak Beginning
"Stocks staged a strong comeback Thursday afternoon after an initial plunge at the opening bell, as a drop in oil prices helped placate fears about problems at some of the nation's biggest banks."
—*New York Times*

September 11, 2008
Investors Turn Gaze to A.I.G.
"Investors skittish about further losses in the financial industry have pounced on the American International Group, the beleaguered insurance company that has reported some of the biggest losses in the spreading credit crisis."
—*New York Times*

September 12, 2008
Markets, Distracted by Lehman's Woes, Close Mixed
—*Associated Press*

September 12, 2008
U.S. Gives Banks Urgent Warning to Solve Crisis
"As Lehman Brothers teetered Friday evening, Federal Reserve officials summoned the heads of major Wall Street firms to a meeting in Lower Manhattan and insisted they rescue the stricken investment bank and develop plans to stabilize the financial markets."
—*New York Times*

**News &
Bridgewater Daily Observations
(BDO)**

September 13, 2008
***Lehman's Fate Is in Doubt as Barclays Pulls
Out of Talks***
"Unable to find a savior, the troubled investment
bank Lehman Brothers appeared headed toward
bankruptcy on Sunday, in what would be one of
the biggest failures in Wall Street history."
–New York Times

September 14, 2008
Stunning Fall for Main Street's Brokerage Firm
"Merrill, which has lost more than $45 billion on
its mortgage investments, agreed to sell itself on
Sunday to Bank of America for $50.3 billion in
stock, according to people briefed on the
negotiations."
–New York Times

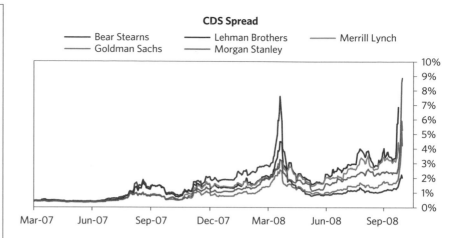

There were no clear, legally acceptable paths for saving failing investment banks, yet these investment banks were "systemically important" (i.e., they could easily take the whole system down with them). While the Fed was able to lend to Lehman to alleviate its liquidity problem, there were limitations on how much they should under these conditions. And since Lehman faced a solvency problem in addition to a liquidity problem, it wasn't even clear that more liquidity could save it.

As we described earlier, **a solvency problem can only be dealt with by providing more equity capital (or changing the accounting/regulatory rules)**. This meant that some entity needed to invest in it or acquire it. Neither the Fed nor the Treasury had the authority to provide that. Hence, there was a need to find a private sector investor/buyer, like Bear Stearns had with JPMorgan. But finding an investor for Lehman was harder than it was for Bear. Lehman was bigger, with a bigger, more complicated, and murkier mess of losing positions.

Finding a buyer was made even harder by the fact that Lehman wasn't the only investment bank needing a buyer to survive. Merrill Lynch, another iconic Wall Street investment bank, was in a similarly dire situation. As with Lehman, many believed that without an investor Merrill was no more than a week away from bankruptcy.[37]

On Thursday Lehman's shares continued their free fall, declining another 42 percent as rumors swirled that Barclays and Bank of America, though interested, were unwilling to buy without government assistance. At this point, Lehman was continually rolling $200 billion in overnight loans just to stay running, putting it at huge risk of a pullback in credit.[38]

On Friday Lehman's shares dropped 17 percent on news that neither the Fed nor the Treasury would backstop any deal. Lehman's failure would pass through the system quickly, causing a domino effect that took a toll on AIG (its stock fell 31 percent). But, remarkably, most of the market still believed that the financial sector's problems would be contained. The overall market closed on Friday up 0.4 percent, aided by falling oil prices.

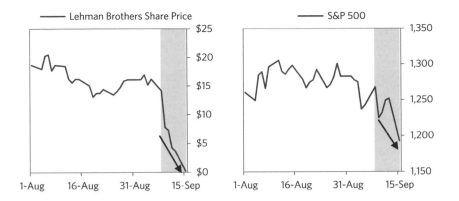

On Friday evening, reports surfaced that Fed officials had gathered the heads of Wall Street's major banks—from Goldman Sachs to the Bank of New York Mellon—to urge them to bail out Lehman. Whether there would be any takers remained to be seen. Bank of America, Barclays, and HSBC had reportedly expressed interest, but none wanted to do the deal without government support. And Treasury officials publicly insisted no support would come.

Paulson had hoped that by motivating a consortium of financial institutions to take on Lehman's bad loans, a potential acquisition of Lehman could be facilitated (as a potential buyer could leave a substantial portion of Lehman's bad assets behind when they acquired the firm). But while some progress was made with the consortium, no potential buyer emerged. Without a potential buyer, the Fed did not have any authorities which would have been effective in preventing the failure of a nonbank in the midst of a panic-driven run, according to Paulson, Bernanke, and Geithner.[39]

Bernanke and Geithner had many conversations together and with Paulson about what they could do to help prevent Lehman's failure, but, as in the case of Bear Stearns, they did not believe that a Fed loan would be effective. They believed that the legal requirement that a loan had to be "secured to their satisfaction" limited the amount they could lend, and that meant they could not lend Lehman enough to save it or guarantee its trading book. The weeks before that fateful weekend were consumed by the effort to figure out a way to prevent Lehman's failure despite those constraints. They were willing to be very creative with their authority and to take a lot of risk, but only within the bounds of what the law allowed. They erred on the side of doing more, not less, but Section 13(3) (the section of the Federal Reserve Act that allowed for emergency lending to a wider set of borrowers) did not make them alchemists. Loans were not equity, and they had to be guided by what would work in practice.

Most everyone agrees that it would have been a lot better if these policy makers had the authority to liquidate Lehman in an orderly way; this was another classic example of how political constraints together with imperfectly thought-out legal constraints can get in the way of actions that are widely agreed to be beneficial.

On Sunday afternoon the news broke that Lehman was headed for bankruptcy, and all hell broke loose. The shock was way bigger than any before because of Lehman's size and interconnectedness to other vulnerable institutions, which made it clear that the contagion would spread. Even worse, the government's failure to save it raised doubts about whether it could save the system. **Lehman's failure was particularly scary because of its large and poorly understood interconnectedness with the rest of the financial system.**

There were a couple of major channels of potential contagion. The most important (and least clear) was Lehman's substantial presence in derivatives markets. At the time of its bankruptcy, Lehman was a party to between $4 and $6 trillion worth of exposure in CDS, accounting for about 8 percent of the total market. Though many of these exposures were offsetting—Lehman did not actually owe huge sums on net—its failure sent clients scrambling to find new counterparties. At the time, no one knew how large Lehman's net exposure was, or who was on the other side of it; we were crossing the line into a big, disastrous unknown. On September 11, we wrote in the *Daily Observations*:

The uncertainty of this situation is tremendous. What happens when you go to settle a currency forward transaction with a counterparty that suddenly doesn't exist? Maybe everything goes fine, but maybe some unexpected condition bites you in the ass. What if you haven't been collecting mark-to-market gains from one of your dealers (we collect constantly from everyone), they go down, and now you are a general creditor? Who do you transfer the risk to? Maybe Merrill is right behind Lehman. What do you about that? And who might be behind it? If everyone is asking these questions the natural path is to cut back on trading and concentrate positions with a few firms. But these few firms have the incentive to ration their capacity to the highest quality financial institutions and managers. The inevitable result is substantially lower liquidity, higher transactions cost, and higher volatility. Higher volatility then feeds back into the real economy because people and businesses transact at these prices. And capital constraints in the financial sector mean that credit growth remains low, which undermines economic growth. We are getting very close to crossing this line.

While Lehman's bankruptcy was the largest in US history (and still is), with some $600 billion in reported assets, it was only about two-thirds the size of Goldman Sachs, and a quarter as large as JPMorgan. They were all connected and the losses and liquidity problems were spreading fast.

We called this stage of the crisis the "avalanche"—the point at which a smaller problem in one corner of the financial system (subprime mortgages) was building in self-reinforcing ways into much bigger problems, and fast.

Aftermath of the Lehman Collapse: September 15–18

On Monday morning, September 15, Lehman Brothers filed for bankruptcy, and the stock market fell by nearly 5 percent. No industry was spared, though the financial sector took the brunt of the pain, with shares of banks and insurers falling by about 10 percent. Credit spreads blew out and credit flow ground to a halt. Over the course of the following week, markets, policy makers, and we at Bridgewater struggled to figure out the ripple effects from Lehman, which of course we couldn't because the interrelationships and exposures were too complex and too opaque. **It was clear to us that blanket protections would have to be put into place, because the consequences of the uncertainties themselves would be devastating as everyone ran from any entity that could go under. But if policy makers couldn't or wouldn't save Lehman Brothers, how could they save the system?**

One of the Fed's immediate responses, announced the night before, was an unprecedented expansion in the "Primary Dealer Credit Facility": They were willing to lend to investment banks against almost any collateral, including extremely risky instruments—e.g., equities, subprime mortgages, and junk bonds. It should have been seen as an enormous step for a central bank to take, and in a more normal environment, it would have been. But the Lehman collapse overshadowed it.

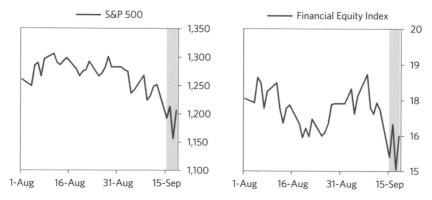

Paulson would later write in his book that **he felt constrained from even being able to explain in a forthright way why Lehman had failed without creating more problems—a common issue policy makers face when communicating during a crisis.** As he put it:

> *"I was in a painful bind that I all too frequently found myself in as a public official. Although it's my nature to be forthright, it was important to convey a sense of resolution and confidence to calm the markets and to help Americans make sense of things...I did not want to suggest that we were powerless. I could not say, for example, that we did not have the statutory authority to save Lehman—even though it was true. Say that and it would be the end of Morgan Stanley, which was in far superior financial shape to Lehman but was already under an assault that would dramatically intensify in the coming days. Lose Morgan Stanley, and Goldman Sachs would be next in line—if they fell, the financial system might vaporize and with it, the economy."*[40]

With big questions on the direction policy was heading, I wrote the following note to our clients on September 15:

(BDO) September 15: Where We Are Now

We have known about the losses that had to be taken by financial institutions for some time. They were discussed and conveyed to you in the tables that we sent to you repeatedly, over the last year. So, these problems were known. We described them as 'known and manageable' because, besides being known, we felt that they were manageable via sensible government policies—of providing liquidity (by the Fed), changing accounting rules and/or creating a safety net (by the Treasury, in cooperation with Congress)—and then clearly articulating these policies to provide the necessary confidence that would allow the debt restructuring process to progress in an orderly manner...

While we are still trying to figure out what the Treasury and Fed's approaches are, over the last few days they made some more things clear by innuendo. They made clear that they're willing to take the chance of diving into the depths of the scary unknown without a clear safety net in place. **So, now we sit and wait to see if they have some hidden trick up their sleeves or if they really are as reckless as they seem.** With interest rates heading toward 0 percent, financial intermediaries broken and the deleveraging well under way, **it appears that we are headed into a new domain in which the classic monetary tools won't work and the Japan in the 1990s and US in the 1930's dynamic will drive things.**

Meanwhile, reports came in showing how the financial meltdown was passing to the economy, leading it to plummet. A Fed report showed industrial output down sharply in August; AIG saw its credit ratings downgraded, potentially triggering additional collateral requirements; and Hewlett-Packard announced it was cutting 25,000 jobs. With America's financial system obviously in crisis, the problems quickly spread globally, prompting European and Asian central banks to announce new liquidity provision measures to shore up their own markets.

Credit markets were in turmoil. As financial players sorted through the tangle of counterparty risks and obligations created by Lehman's failure, interbank lending seized up and Libor (the rate at which banks lend to each other) settled at almost twice the prior week's levels. The contagion was spreading to everyone, even the strongest. Privately, executives from blue-chip firms like

**News &
Bridgewater Daily Observations
(BDO)**

September 15, 2008
Wall St.'s Turmoil Sends Stocks Reeling
"Fearing that the crisis in the financial industry could stun the broader economy, investors drove stocks down almost 5 percent Monday...With Lehman filing for bankruptcy and A.I.G. in distress, investors were worried that consumers and companies would have difficulty getting loans."
–*New York Times*

September 16, 2008
Fed's $85 Billion Loan Rescues Insurer
"Fearing a financial crisis worldwide, the Federal Reserve reversed course on Tuesday and agreed to an $84 billion bailout that would give the government control of the troubled insurance giant American International Group.
The decision, only two weeks after the Treasury took over the federally chartered mortgage finance companies Fannie Mae and Freddie Mac, is the most radical intervention in private business in the central bank's history."
–*New York Times*

September 16, 2008
The Fed's Balance Sheet Is the New Safety Net
"After allowing the system to go over the edge and seeing the avalanche begin, the safety net is now being quickly stitched together via the Fed having to use its balance sheet because there is nothing else in its place. While this is exactly what we would have done if you put us in their position today, it's tragic that this is the position they are in both because the Fed should not be in this position and because it is not clear that taking these actions now will save the day at this late stage."

September 17, 2008
Financial Crisis Enters New Phase
"The financial crisis entered a potentially dangerous new phase on Wednesday when many credit markets stopped working normally as investors around the world frantically moved their money into the safest investments, like Treasury bills."
–*New York Times*

GE admitted to regulators that even they were having trouble borrowing in the commercial paper market, which could put them in a cash-flow bind and force them to default. Prime money market funds started to register increasing stress, high redemptions, and losses (we'll discuss this in more detail a little later). By the end of the day, credit spreads on Morgan Stanley widened to levels greater than those for Lehman on Friday.

Throughout the day, regulators scrambled to keep up with AIG's rapid decline. AIG was one of the largest insurers, with around $1 trillion in assets at peak. Its problems centered around it having issued hundreds of billions of dollars of insurance contracts on bonds (called CDS and CDOs), which required it to pay out if a bond faced losses. Many of these insured bonds were repackaged subprime mortgages, so AIG was exposed to a staggering amount of losses. Since many other financial institutions were counting on these insurance contracts, AIG was systemically important. And it looked to be heading toward failure fast. On Sunday, it had said it would need $40 billion in funding. Now, just a day later, it was suggesting it would need $85 billion.[41]

On Tuesday, the Fed made two surprising policy moves—one far bolder than expected, the other more timid. On the one hand, the Fed, in a regularly scheduled meeting to set interest rates, decided *not* to change them, when the market expected them to be lowered—a significant disappointment that hurt the markets. Remarkably, even as the market looked to be on the verge of a depression, the Fed remained concerned about inflation, putting in their statement, "The downside risks to growth and the upside risks to inflation are both of significant concern to the Committee." In his memoir, Bernanke would later write that "in retrospect, that decision was certainly a mistake," caused in part by "substantial sentiment at the meeting in favor of holding our fire until we had a better sense of how the Lehman situation would play out."[42]

However, more importantly, the Fed also made an announcement that redefined the limits of US central banking. It courageously announced that it would provide $85 billion in emergency funding to AIG. The deal, drafted in a rush on the afternoon of Tuesday, September 16, came with tough terms attached. AIG would pay a floating interest rate starting at 11.5 percent, while giving the government an 80 percent ownership stake in the company. Because AIG did not have enough safe financial assets to secure the loan, it pledged nearly everything else it owned as collateral—including its insurance subsidiaries, financial services companies, and various real estate holdings (including a ski resort!). The Fed loan worked because the market believed AIG was solvent (because of the value of its insurance subsidiaries, which had investment-grade credit ratings). The fact that these served as collateral for the Fed's loan was also critical to the Fed's decision.[43]

But even under these terms, the loan was an unusually risky one for the Fed—after all, the companies AIG put up as collateral were not nearly as easy to value or to sell as the AAA securities the Fed accepted in normal times. And there was still a risk that AIG would go under, despite the Fed's help. Geithner would later say, "Deciding to support AIG was one of the most difficult choices I have ever been involved in in over 20 years of public service."[44]

News of AIG's bailout did not lift markets on Wednesday. Instead, stocks slid by about 4.7 percent, with shares of major financial institutions down by double digits. Rates on commercial paper continued to rise, while yields on three-month treasury bills fell to just above 0 percent (down from around 1.6 percent a week before) as investors fled to safety. Through this chaos, regulators announced a series of stabilizing measures. The SEC moved to tighten controls over short sellers (a common crisis response), and bank regulators proposed revisions to accounting rules to help dress up bank balance sheets.

Let's spend a minute on the importance of accounting, especially mark-to-market accounting. For banks, some assets are "marked-to-market," which means that every day banks take a look at what they could sell those assets for, and value them at those prices. Other assets are allowed to be valued in different ways, often by an in-house methodology that depends on the asset. When an asset that banks are required to mark-to-market is selling at fire-sale prices, any bank holding it looks like they are taking significant losses, which reduces their capital and thus requires them to raise money or sell assets, which further strains liquidity and puts further downward pressure on assets. It also scares the hell out of people dealing with them. Accounting changes that allow banks to realize losses over a longer time period (i.e., not marking assets to market) prevents some of these problems. Of course, changing accounting rules to hide losses during a financial crisis doesn't engender confidence either, so regulators have to be careful.

But accounting changes wouldn't change the more fundamental issue—that overindebted US households and financial institutions were defaulting on their debts because they were overlevered. It was clear that financial institutions needed to be recapitalized (e.g., via an equity investment), and they needed to find buyers for their more troubled assets. So Paulson turned to Congress for funding and authorization for the Treasury department to play that role.

The Government Comes Up with a Bailout Fund: September 18–31

Paulson, Bernanke, and congressional leaders (most importantly, Barney Frank) thought the best way to restore confidence was to buy troubled assets through what would become the Troubled Asset Relief Program. They could have pursued nationalizing the banks, but there was no precedent for it in the US, and when banks were nationalized in other countries, they were penalized with harsh terms. For that reason, banks were reluctant to accept capital and nationalization until just before or immediately after they failed. Paulson did not believe this was the way to go, because it would be more damaging than helpful to the task of reviving capital flows.

Buying assets seemed sensible because a big source of the banks' problems were the large amounts of complex, highly illiquid mortgage securities on their balance sheets. The theory was that if the government provided some market for them, prices would rise, capital would be freed up, and confidence would be restored, allowing the banking system to begin to recapitalize.

When Wall Street learned about the possible TARP plan on Thursday, the market rose. The rally continued on Friday, with stocks up 4 percent, as more of the details emerged. President Bush and Secretary Paulson announced that the federal government was prepared to spend $500 billion to buy up troubled mortgages, while congressional leaders promised to act quickly to pass any proposal. Then the Fed unveiled $180 billion in new swap lines for global central banks, somewhat easing fears of a dollar liquidity crunch in foreign markets. The SEC instituted a ban on the short-selling of nearly 800 financial stocks. And Goldman Sachs and Morgan Stanley came under the government's legal authority to provide a blanket of protection by voluntarily becoming bank holding companies, giving them greater access to the Fed's lending channels.

The **Treasury also unveiled a creative new move to shore up troubled money market funds, which held $3.5 trillion**. Money market funds had become very popular as an alternative to bank deposits for both retail and institutional investors. Most investors were attracted by their high interest rates and undeterred by their lack of FDIC protection; they didn't appreciate that they were delivering those higher interest rates by investing in higher-yielding and higher-risk loans. They also believed that they would not lose money in them as their principal was protected.

Prime money-market funds had been a crucial source of liquidity for all kinds of businesses, since they buy commercial paper, a type of short-term debt that businesses use to fund their operations. Because the commercial paper they hold is generally diversified and highly rated, these funds are usually considered almost riskless—like CDs or bank deposits. But a few prime funds took losses when Lehman failed, specifically the Reserve Primary Fund, which "broke the buck" on September 16. Fears that others might take losses caused many investors to pull their money. As the dollars flowed out of these funds, they had to liquidate their holdings of commercial paper. The result was that hundreds of billions of dollars that had been funding the day-to-day operations of businesses dried up in a matter of days.

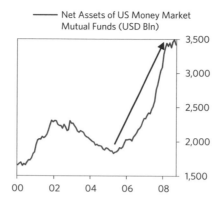

After the Reserve Fund broke the buck, Ken Wilson, who was at Treasury at the time, had gotten a call at 7 a.m. from Northern Trust, followed by others from Black Rock, State Street, and Bank of New York Mellon. All of them reported runs on their money-market funds. Meanwhile, GE had been in the news, explaining that they couldn't sell their paper. Then Coca-Cola CFO Muhtar Kent called and said they were going to be unable to make their $800 million quarterly dividend payment at the end of the week because they couldn't roll their paper. Even AAA-rated industrial- and consumer-products companies couldn't roll their paper! The situation was very quickly metastasizing from Wall Street to Main Street.

To stop the run on money-market funds, Paulson decided to guarantee them outright. The only problem was that the funds would need a substantial backstop and the Treasury couldn't immediately find the cash. To get around the problem, Treasury officials turned to a creative source—tapping the $50 billion Exchange Stabilization Fund (ESF) to back up its guarantee. This plan was announced Friday, September 19, four days after the Lehman collapse. Treasury Secretaries can get into big trouble if they spend money that hasn't been appropriated. So Paulson got his general counsel to give him an opinion that he could use that $45 billion, since if the whole economy went down it wouldn't be good for the dollar.[45] Some of Paulson's colleagues questioned whether $45 billion would be enough, given that there were $3.5 trillion worth of money-market funds. Paulson didn't know if it would be, but he didn't have a better idea.

The Treasury team was moving so fast that Sheila Bair (the head of the FDIC) called and complained that not only was she not consulted, but because of the guarantee all of the money would now go from bank deposits to money-market funds. That was a good point. So the Treasury clarified that the guarantee was only applicable to money-market funds that were in trouble as of September 19. The guarantee worked incredibly well and markets immediately turned. According to Paulson, this was because when you say something is a guarantee and not just a backstop, it is much more reassuring to investors.

The ESF was meant to be used to defend the dollar against runs, but its mandate was flexible enough that the fund could be diverted to more pressing uses. And it could be done quickly, with only presidential approval. **This was exactly the kind of quick thinking and creativity that was required to navigate the regulatory and political minefield and get what was needed done.**

The coordinated and comprehensive policy shifts were a relief to investors. Our *Daily Observations* from the day speaks for itself:

(BDO) September 18: Great Moves!

The Treasury, Fed, and Congress finally agreed to agree to build the safety net!!!!

Overnight central banks added $180 billion in liquidity!

Regulators moved against short sellers.

Morgan Stanley was frozen and is about to be dealt with, and Goldman isn't far behind, but moves are in the works to deal with them.

The week's optimism faded, however, as further details of TARP emerged (or, rather, failed to emerge) over the weekend. The formal proposal put forward by the Bush administration on Saturday, September 20, was three pages long, and was intended to be an outline rather than a fait accompli to Congress. The proposal, to be called TARP (Troubled Asset Relief Program), called for $700 billion in purchases of mortgage-related assets, but offered few details on how these purchases would be administered or what other actions might be taken—and that amount of money was a pittance in comparison to the need. As we explained to our clients when the bill was first unveiled, troubled asset purchases couldn't have much impact on their own:

(BDO) September 25: The Proposed Plan Disappoints:

Buying up $700 billion in mortgages (along with some other assets) will hardly help us at all. If these mortgages are bought at market prices it won't change the financial conditions of nearly anyone materially, the mortgages will be a small percentage of the amount that needs to be bought, and the action won't deal with most of the problems that exist. If they are bought at a premium, this will be both an unethical direct subsidy that is on the wrong side of the line, and it will mean that the amount of money spent will buy less and it still won't contain the problems.

To make matters worse, legislators were put off by the unchecked authority the bill would give the Treasury, so getting it through Congress wasn't assured. When markets opened on Monday, stocks sold off, closing down 3.8 percent and the dollar fell against most major currencies.

The evolving story of the TARP bill's difficult journey through Washington DC—set against a backdrop of poor economic releases and icy credit markets—drove the ups and downs throughout the week of September 22. Most importantly, political struggles between those who wanted to provide the support and those who didn't drove the markets Monday through Wednesday. As Bernanke and Paulson urged immediate action in testimony before Congress on Tuesday, President Bush addressed the nation in support of TARP on Wednesday. Yet little apparent progress came out of Congress. Legislative momentum was interrupted by debates over the need for a more comprehensive bill with more significant aid for homeowners and better-defined limits on the authority of the Treasury. Compensation for executives at banks became a hot-button issue. Many other issues that had some politicians anti- and others pro- led to lots of arguing and little progress.

As is classic in deleveraging scenarios, this political debate took on populist overtones. Though congressional leaders mostly supported the bill, rank-and-file members argued that it would be like a handout to the banks that caused so much trouble in the first place. Arguing over who ought to bear the costs is

News & Bridgewater Daily Observations (BDO)

September 18, 2008
Vast Bailout by U.S. Proposed in Bid to Stem Financial Crisis
"The head of the Treasury and the Federal Reserve began discussions on Thursday with Congressional leaders on what could become the biggest bailout in United States history.

While details remain to be worked out, the plan is likely to authorize the government to buy distressed mortgages at deep discounts from banks and other institutions."
                                    —*New York Times*

September 18, 2008
Great Moves!
"The Treasury, Fed, and Congress finally agreed to agree to build the safety net!!!! Overnight central banks added $180 billion in liquidity! Regulators moved against short sellers. Morgan Stanley was frozen and is about to be dealt with, and Goldman isn't far behind, but moves are in the works to deal with them."

September 21, 2008
This Newest Move by the Treasury Is Shockingly Disappointing
"The newest move to contain the credit crisis (The "Temporary Asset Relief Plan") is extraordinary in: 1) The breadth of the authority it gives the Treasury, and 2) The lack of specifics it provides. So, it doesn't engender confidence. In fact, on the heels of moves that both happened and didn't happen, it undermines our confidence."

September 22, 2008
With Bailout Picture Unclear, Markets Tumble
"Fresh concerns about the biggest government bailout in history sent stock markets down sharply on Monday, while a weakening dollar sparked a frantic rush into commodities as investors remained nervous about the health of Wall Street."
                                    —*New York Times*

September 22, 2008
What Markets Are Saying
"The market action Monday for the most part was a disaster for US policy makers. US assets were abandoned, as stocks and treasury bonds declined while the dollar collapsed and commodities surged. This action is consistent with a loss of faith in the US as a reserve currency, and, if it continues, puts the US economy and financial system even more at risk."

September 24, 2008
Economic Activity Is Slowing across Many Areas, Fed Chairman Says
"The chairman of the Federal Reserve, Ben S. Bernanke, described the nation's economy on Wednesday as one that was barely limping along and could buckle if financial institutions did not get a $700 billion crutch from the government."
                                    —*New York Times*

**News &
Bridgewater Daily Observations
(BDO)**

September 25, 2008
*As Stocks Rally, Credit Markets Appear
Frozen*
                                —*New York Times*

September 25, 2008
*Government Seizes WaMu and Sells Some
Assets*
                                —*New York Times*

September 26, 2008
*The Fed Continues the Fight on the Liquidity
Front, But it is Not Enough*
"The big picture through which we see all the
daily news is that we are in the avalanche phase of
the deleveraging, and we suspect the steps being
considered in Washington now are not nearly
adequate to reverse the situation."

September 28, 2008
*The Plan Is Pretty Good; Now We Have To See
How it Is Employed and Whether It's Too Late*
"The plan allows the government all that we had
hoped for in order to restore liquidity, solvency,
and confidence, but it is not as forceful or as
timely as we had hoped."

September 29, 2008
*Defiant House Rejects Huge Bailout; Next
Step Is Uncertain*
"Defying President Bush and the leaders of both
parties, rank-and-file lawmakers in the House on
Monday rejected a $700 billion economic rescue
plan in a revolt that rocked the Capitol, sent
markets plunging and left top lawmakers groping
for a resolution."
                                —*New York Times*

September 29, 2008
A Credibility Test
"Today's failure in the House of the bill, whose
passage was assured by those supposedly in
control, has shined the global spotlight on US
decision makers. The question of whether the US
can do what needs to get done has been further
complicated. In the end, the world's financiers
(China, OPEC) will decide whether US policy
makers have passed the test."

September 30, 2008
A Recovery in Shares on Hopes of a Bailout
                                —*New York Times*

typical during deleveragings and highly counterproductive; it can be like doctors in the emergency ward arguing over who will pay the bill. All attention needs to be directed to saving the patient—how the costs should be handled can be decided later.

Even proposing the TARP bill was risky. If it didn't pass, there was likely to be an extremely negative market reaction. And they needed it passed in very difficult circumstances: as soon as possible, weeks before a presidential election and amid a populist uproar from both the left and the right over its unprecedented size and scope. Given the vote counts in Congress, the bill would need to pass on a bipartisan basis, which by this point was extremely rare on any new important law (and has become even rarer since). If either of the presidential candidates opposed the bill, it would have been nearly impossible to get passed—McCain and Palin initially taking an anti-bailout position put the bill at risk, though they eventually supported it. (Paulson was on the phone almost daily with both presidential candidates.) The only factor working in the bill's favor was that it usually takes a crisis to get Congress to act, and the financial crisis was in its most acute stage. The difficulties in getting TARP passed are a good illustration of why regulators need broad emergency authorities versus needing to rely on Congress to act.

Financial markets pulsated in response to each undulation between "they will" and "they won't" do what was necessary in time. Credit spreads on CDS for Goldman Sachs and Morgan Stanley, which had narrowed following their transformations into bank holding companies over the weekend, widened through the week, and huge outflows from prime money-market funds and into government funds continued to put pressure on commercial paper. On Thursday night, the FDIC seized control of Washington Mutual, marking the largest bank failure in American history, before shifting its assets to JPMorgan in a $1.9 billion deal (they would seize Wachovia a few days later). As we wrote on Friday, September 26, "There is so much jam packed into each day that it is hard to pick what to comment on. The big picture through which we see all the daily news is that we are in the avalanche phase of the deleveraging."

The political stalemate in Congress seemed to break early Sunday morning, as Secretary Paulson, flanked by House Speaker Nancy Pelosi and Senate Majority Leader Harry Reid, announced that an agreement had been reached on a $700 billion bailout bill.

But when the bill came up for a vote on Monday afternoon, it failed. Stocks fell 8.8 percent in the largest single-day drop since 1987. Around the world, reverberations sent markets spiraling downward; oil prices fell by $10 because in a depression the demand for it would be much less. Central banks, meanwhile, scrambled to offer emergency loans to shell-shocked institutions. Interbank lending markets froze, while rates on short-term treasuries fell to just above zero.

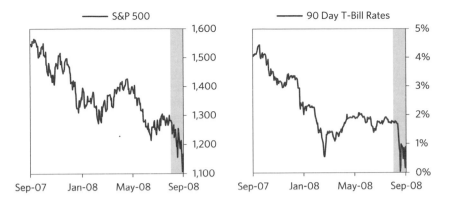

Again, among the most important aspects of successfully managing a crisis is having wise and knowledgeable decision-makers who have the authority to do whatever it takes. The Congressional vote was a sign that the Treasury would have to struggle to get the authority it needed. At the time, we wrote:

(BDO) September 29: A Credibility Test

The financing of US consumption and the global financial system operates on faith. Recent developments have obviously strained the faith in the financial system. Today's failure in the House of the bill, whose passage was assured by those supposedly in control, has shined the global spotlight on US decision makers. The question of whether the US can do what needs to get done has been further complicated. In the end, the world's financiers (China, OPEC) will decide whether US policy makers have passed the test.

Even had the bailout passed, maintaining the necessary global faith in the system would have been difficult. Today the degree of difficulty has risen and the risk of a loss of faith has increased given the chaotic process and lack of leadership illustrated in Washington. *There is still a lot to lose.*

Officials at the Treasury and Congressional leaders were working around the clock to get the bailout bill passed. The process was painful: Convincing Republicans and Democrats to work together is hard enough during a normal year, but TARP was being considered only a month before a hotly contested presidential election. Republicans hated to look as though they were abandoning their free-market principles and their commitment to fiscal responsibility just to support a bank bailout. Democrats worried about giving a major legislative win to an outgoing Republican administration just before an election. And both Obama and McCain worried that the other would try to bolster his populist credentials by taking a stand against a so-called "Wall Street bailout." If that happened, Paulson worried, the bill would have little chance of passing.[46]

But politics wasn't the only headache associated with TARP. While the Treasury had been working with Congress to get TARP passed, two of the biggest bank failures in US history occurred (WaMu and Wachovia), and several European countries had to step up and bail out their own banks. Treasury officials could see that $700 billion in purchases of toxic assets wouldn't be enough to rescue markets. But if the money was put directly into the banks as capital, they could buy many times the $700 billion because they could lever up.

Even though they said they weren't going to put capital in the banks through TARP, they pushed to get authority to do it if necessary. The question would be how to do it fast and well. Rather than try to distinguish between healthy and unhealthy banks, an analytical nightmare, which would have prompted a lot of arguing and would have taken more time than they had while stigmatizing the banks they supported (which could have worsened the runs), the Treasury instead offered to buy preferred stocks on very attractive terms. This allowed it to put capital into 700 banks very quickly.

What Paulson did was enormously unpopular because, understandably, the public wanted to punish the banks. In my opinion, the move was necessary and appropriate. It also worked out very well for the taxpayer, because the money that went into TARP's capital programs prevented a catastrophic collapse, which would have been as bad or worse than the Great Depression—not to mention that it all came back plus an almost $50 billion profit for the

**News &
Bridgewater Daily Observations
(BDO)**

October 1, 2008
After Two Days of Whiplash, a Small Decline for Stocks
"Tension mounted in the money markets on Wednesday as the Senate prepared to vote on the government's bailout plan. Many companies and banks had trouble borrowing money. Where credit was available, it was typically only on an overnight basis, rather than for weeks or months."
–*New York Times*

October 1, 2008
Manufacturing Index Shows Sharp Decline
–*New York Times*

October 2, 2008
Persistent Anxiety over Tight Credit Sends Stocks Plunging
"Stocks dropped sharply on Thursday as signs of the economy's worsening health and a continued choking of credit unnerved investors ahead of a crucial vote in Washington on a financial rescue plan."
–*New York Times*

October 3, 2008
Bailout Bill Fails to Reassure Investors
–*New York Times*

October 3, 2008
Horrible Market Action
"Price action around the TARP has been very bad, consistent with our view that the TARP won't be a game changer. Friday's price action in stocks held to the classic buy-the-rumor, sell-the-fact pattern. Except that normally you get a big rally into good news and a selloff after the news is fact, culminating in a net gain...this time...the stock market traded to new lows after the vote became fact."

October 3, 2008
159,000 Jobs Lost in September, the Worst Month in Five Years
–*New York Times*

October 5, 2008
Financial Crises Spread in Europe
–*New York Times*

October 6, 2008
Fed Considers Plan to Buy Companies' Unsecured Debt
"Under the program, the Fed said that it would buy the unsecured short-term debt that companies rely on to finance their day-to-day activities. 'This facility should encourage investors to once again engage in term lending in the commercial paper market,' the Fed said Tuesday in a statement."
–*New York Times*

October 7, 2008
U.S. Markets Plunge Despite Hint of Rate Cut
–*New York Times*

October 8, 2008
Supply and Illiquidity
"You've got increasing government supply with tight liquidity; dealers can't finance inventory, hedge funds can't borrow, foreigners are losing confidence in the dollar as a reserve currency, and the desire for cash is trumping all forms of risk, even the yield curve risk of a treasury bond."

taxpayers. This willingness to do the unpopular but right things to benefit people is both heroic and underappreciated. Too many people who have never actually been on the field throw beer cans from the stands. This can lead to disastrous results, unless the players are smart enough and courageous enough to do what is right despite the unpopularity of doing it.

With a lot of negotiating, TARP eventually got through, which was an extraordinary accomplishment because it was a very rare, consequential bipartisan action from Congress. As you can imagine, everyone was on pins and needles because of the enormity of the uncertainties. As with most such cases, it took being at the edge of the precipice to bring about the coordinated action to do the right thing. While it would be great if policy makers could take the right steps early on to prevent such crises, that's unfortunately not consistent with how political systems work. From having been through a bunch of these sorts of dramas in many countries over many years, I can attest that political systems typically make the right decisions only after heated fighting and literally just hours before disaster is about to strike.

But by the time the bill passed on October 3, there was broad agreement among investors that the bill wouldn't be enough. Stocks sold off 1.4 percent.

October 2008

For policy makers, the first days of October were **a scramble to get as much done in as short a time as possible**. With the economy deteriorating daily, nearly every regulatory department had a major policy change in the works, each with its own roadblocks, tradeoffs, and benefits.

At the FDIC, regulators worked on raising the ceiling on deposit coverage. The FDIC's analysts knew they needed to provide more coverage— Depression-style bank runs on Wachovia had made that clear—but they also worried that raising the limit too high would draw depositors from foreign banks with lower limits, choking off liquidity in Europe and Asia. So they settled on a compromise measure—raising the limit from $100,000 to $250,000 on October 3 as part of the same bill that authorized TARP— hoping it would be enough to ease pressure on struggling banks but not so much that it would start a deposit-insurance war with foreign regulators. The FDIC later followed up with the Transaction Account Guarantee Program that fully guaranteed non-interest bearing transaction accounts at participating banks.

Every day, a new wave of bad news hammered stocks. The economy was sinking fast. In the first week of October alone, PMI (a survey of purchasing managers) came in well below expectations, data on factory orders showed a 4 percent decline in August, and a payroll report showed a loss of 159,000 jobs in September—marking the worst month in five years. The following week, similarly grim economic stats came out in retail sales (down 7.7 percent year over year).

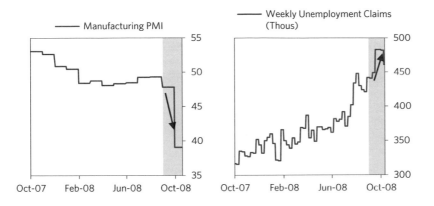

News &
Bridgewater Daily Observations
(BDO)

October 8, 2008
A.I.G. to Get Additional $37.8 Billion
—New York Times

October 9, 2008
U.S. Considers Cash Injections into Banks
"Having tried without success to unlock frozen credit markets, the Treasury Department is considering taking ownership stakes in many United States banks to try to restore confidence in the financial system, the White House said on Thursday."
—New York Times

October 9, 2008
U.S. Auto Shares Plunge on a Grim Sales Forecast
—New York Times

October 10, 2008
Whiplash Ends a Roller Coaster Week
"For three straight days, the stock market collapsed in the last hour of trading. On Friday, it merely swooned...It was one of the wildest moves in stock market history, and perhaps a fitting conclusion to the worst week in at least 75 years. The Dow and the broader Standard & Poor's 500-stock index both closed down 18 percent for the week."
—New York Times

October 10, 2008
Battered Money Funds Find Relief
"Investor confidence in money funds, long considered as safe as bank deposits, was shaken on September 16 when losses at a multibillion-dollar money fund set off weeks of withdrawals... Hardest hit were the so-called prime money funds, which have the most latitude in buying commercial paper and other short-term assets that help finance business operations. But on Thursday, both institutional and retail prime funds collected fresh assets."
—New York Times

During this period of constant bad news, stocks sold off literally every day. Between October 1 and October 10, investors in the S&P 500 took total losses of 22 percent, without a single day of gains. Crude oil continued to fall rapidly as well, ending the first half of the month at $75 per barrel. Some days saw huge routs even when there wasn't much news. On October 9, for instance, stocks sold off 7.6 percent on record volume, with virtually nothing important enough to warrant it.

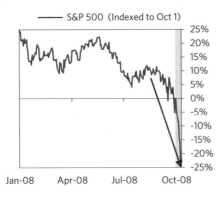

This acute pain wasn't concentrated only in the financial sector. Reports surfaced that major nonfinancial corporations were relying on credit lines to finance continuing operations as they found themselves all but shut out of corporate paper markets. Some companies announced that they were slashing dividends to keep up cash reserves, and outflows from prime money-market funds continued. In the household sector, a report showed that consumer credit had fallen in August for the first time since 1998. Similar stories were unfolding globally, as liquidity dried up in every major market, even as central banks announced unprecedented interventions.

In the face of so much pain, policy makers rolled out ever-larger initiatives to thaw frozen credit markets and ease concerns throughout the financial system. On October 7, for instance, the Fed announced an extraordinary new plan to purchase unsecured commercial paper. Since bank lending had been almost completely choked off and money-market funds had pulled hundreds of billions of dollars out of commercial paper markets, major nonfinancial companies were struggling just to continue funding normal operations. Fearing major layoffs and disruptions across the economy if these companies couldn't access funding, the Fed felt compelled to step in. To do so, it created what it called the Commercial Paper Funding Facility—technically an independent entity that would buy up

**News &
Bridgewater Daily Observations
(BDO)**

October 11, 2008
White House Overhauling Rescue Plan
"As international leaders gathered here on
Saturday to grapple with the global financial
crisis, the Bush administration embarked on an
overhaul of its own strategy for rescuing the
foundering financial system. Two weeks after
persuading Congress to let it spend $700 billion
to buy distressed securities tied to mortgages, the
Bush administration has put that idea aside in
favor of a new approach that would have the
government inject capital directly into the nation's
banks—in effect, partially nationalizing the
industry."
–*New York Times*

October 11, 2008
Bush Vows to Resolve Crisis
"President Bush sought to present a united global
front in responding to the financial crisis on
Saturday, saying the world's leading industrialized
countries had agreed on common steps to stabilize
the markets and shore up the banking system...
Mr. Bush said the countries had agreed to general
principles in responding to the crisis, including
working to prevent the collapse of important
financial institutions, and protecting the deposits
of savers."
–*New York Times*

October 12, 2008
**Margin Calls Prompt Sales, and Drive Shares
Even Lower**
–*New York Times*

October 13, 2008
Stocks Soar 11 Percent on Aid to Banks
"On Monday, for the first time this October, the
Dow Jones industrial average ended the day
higher than it began. Nine hundred and thirty-six
points higher, to be exact, making for the biggest
single-day percentage gain in 75 years. The surge
came as governments and central banks around
the world mounted an aggressive, coordinated
campaign to unlock the global flow of credit, an
effort that investors said they had been waiting
for."
–*New York Times*

October 15, 2008
GMAC Struggles with Financing
–*New York Times*

October 18, 2008
Home Building at Slowest Pace since 1991
–*New York Times*

commercial paper using loans provided by the Fed under its Section 13(3) powers. In practice, the Fed was agreeing to finance commercial paper purchases directly, with no backstop against losses by the Treasury. The move took the Fed to the edge of its statutory authority or perhaps a bit beyond (depending on who you ask), as the central bank is generally not permitted to take on much exposure with such risky credit. The Fed bravely did what it needed to do and hoped that the fees the CPFF charged borrowers could be used to cover any losses, though covering losses was appropriately not the primary objective.

Just days after the passage of TARP, Paulson began hinting that the funds might be used to capitalize the banks instead of just purchasing troubled assets, as he said he had been anticipating for weeks.[47] On October 9, at Paulson's urging, White House officials started to signal that TARP money might go to capital injections into banks.

There was so much to do, and policy-making needed to proceed at a furious pace. It was an utterly insane week.

The single largest push on the part of policy makers came over Columbus Day Weekend: October 11–13. On Saturday, October 11, President Bush met with members of the G7 in Washington to publicly commit himself to a coordinated international effort to contain what had become a global financial crisis. It was agreed that the members of the G7 would move together to inject capital into their banking institutions and increase deposit insurance guarantees. Over the next two days, officials from the Treasury raced to finalize America's part of the international commitment. The centerpieces of the new program were two bold new policy changes—a huge expansion of FDIC insurance coverage, and a massive injection of capital into the banking system.

Typically, the FDIC is only responsible for insuring the deposits of commercial banks. Under the new Temporary Liquidity Guarantee Program, however, the FDIC's authority had been stretched to guarantee the debt of any single systemically important bank and to backstop losses on all newly issued unsecured debt by banks and bank-holding companies as well as all noninterest-bearing transaction accounts. This amounted to a guarantee of nearly all bank debt. It was an extraordinary measure that many feared might have serious unintended consequences, but, as Paulson would later write, "To be frank, I hated these options, but I didn't want to preside over a meltdown."[48]

Under the new Capital Purchase Program, the Treasury planned to use its TARP money to take equity stakes in as many banking institutions as possible, up to a limit of 3 percent of risk-weighted assets or $250 billion. As explained earlier, the investments would come in the form of preferred stock with a 5 percent dividend.

Paulson needed even the healthiest banks to participate, because if only the weak ones did, participation would create a stigma that could encourage runs. And so, though the Treasury had no power to force banks to take capital, it did what it could. On Monday, October 13, Paulson invited the CEOs of nine major banks to his private conference room, and explained that he expected everyone in attendance to participate, and even prescribed the amount of capital he expected each bank to take. None left without taking government money. By the end of the meeting, Paulson had pledged $125 billion of the $700 billion Congress had given him.

But even with the cash injection, markets in the US, Europe, and Japan continued to worsen. So it became clear to Paulson, Bernanke, and Geithner that they had to act with even greater force. Bernanke and Paulson had very consequential meetings with central bankers and the finance ministers in the G7 to coordinate an international response. Paulson and President Bush also met with G20 finance ministers. Meanwhile, there were teams moving very fast at the Treasury working to develop the US response. Several people took Paulson aside and warned him that they were perhaps moving too fast, and that doing so could be dangerous. However, Paulson believed that if policy makers did not move quickly, they would have nothing that would work when all the markets opened on Tuesday after the three-day Columbus Day weekend.[49]

Paulson says that the most powerful step they took was the Temporary Liquidity Guarantee Program, in which the FDIC used its funds, which were established to protect savers, to guarantee the liabilities of financial institutions, including the unsecured liabilities of bank holding companies.[50] At one point, the FDIC's general counsel said this was illegal. However, Paulson and others spent a lot of time convincing its head, Sheila Bair, that this was the right thing to do, and she ultimately made the very courageous decision to back it—which made a huge difference.[51]

As news of the programs leaked on Monday, October 13 (and policy makers around the world announced similar projects), the markets that were open surged. Stocks rallied by 11.6 percent, the largest single-day increase in the S&P 500 since 1939.

It's worth pausing for a moment to consider how significant these announcements were in the larger story of the crisis. Up to this point, most of the government responses had come in the form of ad hoc reactions to individual disasters. The Fed had borne a disproportionately large share of the burden, and it was not at all clear that other agencies would adequately support it. But now it seemed increasingly clear that policy makers in the US and around the world were committed to taking extraordinary, coordinated action. Still, huge uncertainties lay ahead, as the underlying economy continued to deteriorate. Here's how we described this moment to our clients at the time:

(BDO) October 13: The Governments Are Doing Everything Possible; Now We Will Have to See If It's In Time

These are great moves. They are doing everything that we had hoped that they would do. While these would have worked in stage one of the crisis—e.g., if they did them instead of allowing Lehman to go bankrupt—the crisis has spread to a stage 3 condition, so we just have to wait and see. The big question is whether the massive liquidity injections and bank recapitalizations will get to those who are at the periphery of the system.

Many dominos are now falling that are beyond the reach of government. We know of lots of them that are big and scary and we are sure that we don't know of many others. So, it is hard to know for sure how these big problems will be affected by these policy changes and what the effects of these big credit/liquidity problems will be…

We are in very uncertain times. But, for the first time we can now say with confidence that the major developed countries' governments are doing all in their power to deal with this crisis.

News & Bridgewater Daily Observations (BDO)

October 19, 2008
Regions in Recession, Bush Aide Says
"President Bush's top economic adviser said Sunday that some regions of the United States were struggling with high jobless rates and seemed to be in recession."
–*New York Times*

October 20, 2008
Signs of Easing Credit and Stimulus Talk Lift Wall Street
"The tentative re-emergence of trust among lenders—a rare commodity of late—raised hopes that the immediate financial pressures on banks, businesses and municipalities could ease somewhat, cushioning the blow of a likely recession. That encouraging signs appeared at all was enough to bring a wave of relief to Wall Street, where the Dow Jones industrial average rose 413 points, or 4.7 percent."
–*New York Times*

October 20, 2008
Fed Chairman Endorses New Round of Stimulus
"The chairman of the Federal Reserve, Ben S. Bernanke, said on Monday that he supported a second round of additional spending measures to help stimulate the economy."
–*New York Times*

October 20, 2008
U.S. Is Said to Be Urging New Mergers in Banking
"In a step that could accelerate a shakeout of the nation's banks, the Treasury Department hopes to spur a new round of mergers by steering some of the money in its $250 billion rescue package to banks that are willing to buy weaker rivals, according to government officials."
–*New York Times*

October 21, 2008
Fed Adds to Its Efforts to Aid Credit Markets
"In another bold gambit to restore confidence in the financial system, the Fed announced that it would provide a backstop for the short-term debt that many money-market funds hold. The central bank will buy certificates of deposit and certain types of commercial paper from the funds, in hopes of restoring the free flow of credit and easing worries about the investments. It is the third program of its kind that the Fed has announced this month."
–*New York Times*

October 23, 2008
Rise in Jobless Claims Exceeds Forecast
–*New York Times*

October 23, 2008
Greenspan Concedes Error on Regulation
"For years, a Congressional hearing with Alan Greenspan was a marquee event. Lawmakers doted on him as an economic sage. Markets jumped up or down depending on what he said. Politicians in both parties wanted the maestro on their side. But on Thursday, almost three years after stepping down as chairman of the Federal Reserve, a humbled Mr. Greenspan admitted that he had put too much faith in the self-correcting power of free markets and had failed to anticipate the self-destructive power of wanton mortgage lending."
–*New York Times*

**News &
Bridgewater Daily Observations
(BDO)**

October 27, 2008
White House Explores Aid for Auto Deal
"The Bush administration is examining a range of options for providing emergency financial help to spur a merger between General Motors and Chrysler, according to government officials... People familiar with the discussions said the administration wanted to provide financial assistance to the deeply troubled Big Three Detroit automakers, possibly by using the Treasury Department's wide-ranging authority under the $700 billion bailout program that Congress approved this month."
–New York Times

October 27, 2008
The Fed Continues to Try to Get the Dollars Where They Are Needed
"The Fed continues to push unprecedented liquidity into the system across a variety of channels. The unprecedented push of liquidity has more than doubled the Fed's balance sheet by increasing their assets and liabilities by nearly a trillion dollars, but it has still not offset the private sector need. The world has accumulated so many dollar debts, and the ability to roll and grow these debts was so ingrained in the financial system's architecture, that the breakdown requires the unprecedented push from the Fed. Nonetheless, the risks the Fed faces in embarking on this course are numerous, and so much of the global financial system lays out of the Fed's reach."

October 29, 2008
Concerned Fed Trims Key Rate by a Half Point
–New York Times

October 29, 2008
A Rate of Zero Percent from the Fed? Some Analysts Say It Could Be Coming
–New York Times

October 30, 2008
Fed Adds $21 Billion to Loans for A.I.G.
–New York Times

Fears and uncertainties surrounding the economy kept volatility extremely high over the next week. On Wednesday, for instance, stocks fell 9 percent following grim retail sales numbers for September and a warning from Bernanke that any "broader economic recovery" would be slow to arrive.[52] The following day, the market rebounded by 4.3 percent, even in the face of a number of disappointing stat releases, and rates on commercial paper fell slightly.

But by Monday, October 20, markets had registered a meaningful easing of conditions in interbank lending and commercial paper. Rates on commercial paper touched four-week lows, while short-term treasury yields crept up. This thawing of credit conditions helped lift stocks, and represented a significant easing of the pressure on banks.

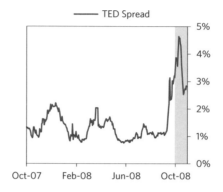

Still, most of the financial mismatches that were squeezing financial institutions and companies (i.e., borrowing short term and lending longer term, borrowing in one currency and lending in another) had yet to be resolved. There was a squeeze for dollars because foreign financial institutions that had borrowed dollars and lent them out now had to pay them back, and/or had to deal with their debtors, who had to pay them back in dollars when dollars, money, and credit were hard to come by. Though the Fed continually expanded its dollar swap lines (i.e., liquidity lending) with developed-world central banks throughout October, it was not able to provide enough dollar liquidity to alleviate this global dollar squeeze. Part of the problem lay in central banks' reluctance to lend Fed-provided dollars against locally denominated collateral because of their fears of default and logistical issues. The largest squeeze occurred in emerging markets, where major dollar debts had built up and debtors were scrambling for dollars. All in all, the dollar rallied 8 percent in October.

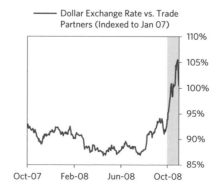

Here's how we explained the situation to our clients at the time:

(BDO) October 22: The Dollar Squeeze

A debt is a short cash position—i.e., a commitment to deliver cash that one doesn't have. Because the dollar is the world's reserve currency, and because of the dollar surplus recycling that has taken place over the past few years…lots of dollar denominated debt has been built up around the world. So, as dollar liquidity has become tight, there has been a dollar squeeze. This squeeze…is hitting dollar-indebted emerging markets (particularly those of commodity exporters) and is supporting the dollar. When this short squeeze ends, which will happen when either the debtors default or get the liquidity to prevent their default, the US dollar will decline. Until then, we expect to remain long the USD against the euro and emerging market currencies.

The actual price of anything is always equal to the amount of spending on the item being exchanged divided by the quantity of the item being sold (i.e., $P = \$/Q$), so a) knowing who is spending and who is selling what quantity (and ideally why) is the ideal way to get at the price at any time, and b) prices don't always react to changes in fundamentals as they happen in the ways characterized by those who seek to explain price movements in connection with unfolding news. During this period, volatility remained extremely high for reasons that had nothing to do with fundamentals and everything to do with who was getting in and out of positions for various reasons—like being squeezed, no longer being squeezed, rebalancing portfolios, etc. For example, on Tuesday, October 28, the S&P gained more than 10 percent and the next day it fell by 1.1 percent when the Fed cut interest rates by another 50 basis points. Closing the month, the S&P was down 17 percent—the largest single-month drop since October 1987.

November–December 2008

In the midst of this chaos, on November 4, Barack Obama was elected President amid record turnout, and would come into office with big majorities in both houses of Congress. Heading into the election, Obama had promised billions in government spending on infrastructure, unemployment insurance, and Medicaid, and was supportive of TARP—and control of Congress would allow him to move quickly.

From USA Today, 5 November © 2008 Gannett-USA Today. All rights reserved. Used by permission and protection by the Copyright Laws of the United States. The printing, copying redistribution, or retransmission of this Content without express written permission is prohibited.

News &
Bridgewater Daily Observations
(BDO)

November 1, 2008
A Template for Understanding What's Going On
"We believe that the world economy is going through a deleveraging/depression process that will be quite painful for many people…Contrary to popular thinking, a deleveraging/depression is not simply a severe version of a recession—it is an entirely different process."

November 2, 2008
U.S. Rejects G.M.'s Call for Help in a Merger
–New York Times

November 3, 2008
Automakers Report Grim October Sales
–New York Times

November 4, 2008
Obama Sweeps to Historic Victory
"According to early exit poll data, 62% of voters said the economy was their top concern. All other issues, including terrorism and the war in Iraq, were far behind…With strong majorities in Congress, President-elect Obama is likely to start fast, with a large economic-stimulus package."
–Wall Street Journal

November 7, 2008
Jobless Rate at 14-Year High after October Losses
–New York Times

November 7, 2008
Creating Liquidity but Failing to Create Credit
"Essentially, through some asset purchases and a series of swaps, the Fed has exchanged T-bills for other more illiquid, lower grade and longer duration credits, and through the process has provided many key entities with short term liquidity. But it hasn't been able to get a privately-funded credit expansion going because it is uneconomic for creditors to lend, especially when they are squeezed. Without a credit expansion, the deleveraging/depression will continue until ultimately there will be a global debt restructuring (i.e., diminishing the size of creditors' claims on debtors)."

November 10, 2008
A.I.G. Secures $150 Billion Assistance Package
–New York Times

November 10, 2008
Fannie Mae Loses $29 Billion on Write-Downs
–New York Times

News &
Bridgewater Daily Observations
(BDO)

November 11, 2008
Retail Worries Help Push Markets Lower
–New York Times

November 11, 2008
Oil Prices Drop to 20-Month Low
–New York Times

November 11, 2008
We Are Thrilled with the Fed's Management and Are Hopeful That There Will Be Excellent Management at the Treasury
"While the Fed sowed the seeds of this crisis by allowing credit growth to be fast enough to cause rapid deteriorations in Americans' balance sheets (at first under Greenspan and then under Bernanke), and the Treasury allowed the deleveraging crisis to move beyond that which was manageable, the Fed behaved superbly once the deleveraging crisis became apparent to it, thereby mitigating the implosion in credit. It has quietly, imaginatively and aggressively redefined the optimal way that central banks should behave in depressions by essentially replacing, rather than relying on, impaired financial institutions to provide credit to key entities."

November 12, 2008
Major Indexes Fall Sharply as Economic Uncertainty Spurs Fear
"The financial markets had been trading down all morning but began a sharp slide just before Treasury Secretary Henry M. Paulson Jr. appeared at a news conference to discuss the $700 billion financial bailout package. Mr. Paulson said those government assets would not be used to buy troubled securities, as originally planned, but would instead go to buying stock in banks and infusing money into other financial institutions."
–New York Times

November 13, 2008
U.S. Shifts Focus in Credit Bailout
–New York Times

While the financial contagion may have been slowed by the Treasury and the Fed's actions so far, **it became clearer in the last couple months of 2008 that the economy was falling at a far faster pace than even the most pessimistic observers feared, and that we were heading for the worst downturn since the Great Depression and into the great unknown**.

To us the economy was now in the classic early days of a deleveraging/depression, when monetary policy could not work normally. Interest rates could no longer be lowered and innumerable avenues of credit had dried up.

Most of the important economic stats released in November were worse than the already very poor expectations. Consumer spending fell at an extraordinary rate; retail sales fell by over 8 percent and auto sales were down 30 percent year over year. Businesses across industries reacted to poor results with historic layoffs. The unemployment rate moved up past 6.8 percent, the highest level since 1994, and projections for layoffs and unemployment increased dramatically. December saw the worst manufacturing reading since 1982. The economy was imploding.

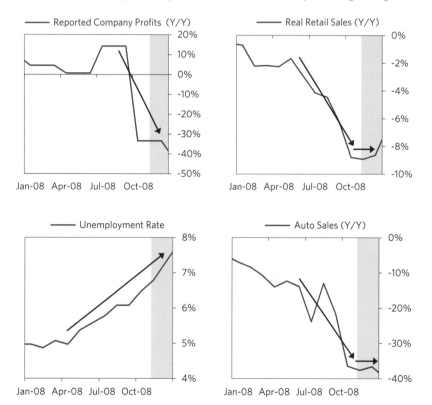

Businesses across industries looked to the federal government for aid to shore up their finances. The auto industry in particular remained in dire straits and actively sought backstops from the federal government. However, the Treasury department was reluctant to broaden the $700 billion TARP package to include industrial companies and was thus unwilling to assist major automakers. In early November, the Treasury turned down a request by General Motors for $10 billion to help finance a possible merger with Chrysler. Without funding from the federal government and with credit markets remaining nonfunctional, automakers turned to selling assets to raise cash. Both Ford and General Motors sold their stakes in other automakers during the month.

On November 10, AIG reported a $25 billion quarterly loss (while securing an additional $150 billion from the government to curtail financial contagion). Fannie Mae posted a $29 billion loss and said it might need more than the $100 billion the Treasury had already pledged to keep it afloat.

Paulson hadn't said anything publicly about how his thinking was changing, as he hadn't wanted to influence the election.[53] The market was expecting a significant asset repurchase program. However, in a mid-November postelection speech, Paulson announced his plans for modifying Treasury's use of TARP. He disclosed that Treasury no longer planned to buy illiquid assets because the market for these securities was frozen. Funds would instead be channeled to banks and nonbank financial companies (though not auto companies) as equity-like capital to better free them up to resume normal lending. Additionally, a new lending program was announced that was targeted at consumer lending markets. This new program allowed the Treasury to put up part of the funding for auto loans, credit cards, and student loans. The markets, however, reacted negatively to the adjustment. Paulson noted after the fact: "As I feared, the markets focused on the fact that there wouldn't be a program to purchase mortgage-related assets."[54] This rattled the markets and the S&P dropped 5.2 percent.

Stocks reached a new low on November 20, down over 20 percent for the month (and 52 percent from their highs). Oil collapsed (now below $50 a barrel), and home prices continued to fall. However, this new low was met with a relatively quick reversal on news that Obama would nominate Timothy Geithner to be Treasury secretary and Larry Summers (former Treasury secretary) to be director of the National Economic Council, as both were justifiably considered highly capable. Summers came into this job having been concerned about the possibility of a major debt crisis for a while (in a speech in early March before Bear's collapse, he had said, "I believe that we are facing the most serious combination of macroeconomic and financial stresses that the United States has faced in a generation—and possibly much longer than that,"[55] and he was an advocate of big policy moves in response to the crisis. He would end up as a key decision-maker in the administration's policy toward auto companies. Bernanke would of course stay at the Fed, so there was good continuity among the leaders of the economic team. These moves helped assure policy continuity between administrations.

On November 25, the Federal Reserve and the Treasury announced $800 billion in lending and asset purchases aimed at pushing down mortgage rates (to help the housing market). The central bank committed to purchases of $600 billion in debt tied to home loans. This was their first Quantitative Easing (QE) program. This was a classic and critical step in managing a deleveraging. Central bankers in the midst of crises are forced to choose between 1) "printing" more money (beyond what's needed for bank liquidity) to replace the decline in private credit, and 2) allowing a big tightening as credit collapses. **They inevitably choose to print, as they did in this case, which is when things changed dramatically.**

I hope you will read the next section, about the US debt crisis in the 1928–37 period (as well as look at the other cases) to see how true this is. What was different in 2008 was the speed with which the policy makers made this crucial step. The 1930–33 depression went on so long because policy makers were so slow to react—not because their problems were

News & Bridgewater Daily Observations (BDO)

November 13, 2008
Understanding the Changing Plans for the TARP
"Paulson's statements Wednesday and Thursday show another shift in the plans for the use of the TARP. The shift away from directly buying mortgage assets (unlevered) to injecting more capital into banks and now working on other mechanisms that further lever the funds outside the banking system via potentially guaranteeing new securitization vehicles make sense to us."

November 14, 2008
After Loss, Freddie Mac Seeks Aid
–Associated Press

November 14, 2008
A Record Decline in October's Retail Sales
–New York Times

November 17, 2008
Citigroup Plans to Sell Assets and Cut More Jobs
"In one the largest single rounds of layoffs on record, not just for the financial industry but for any industry, Citigroup said on Monday that it planned to eliminate a staggering 52,000 jobs, or 14 percent of its global work force."
–New York Times

November 17, 2008
G.M. Sells Suzuki Stake in Its Effort to Raise Cash
–Associated Press

November 17, 2008
Markets Move Lower in Late Trading
–New York Times

November 17, 2008
The Need for Bankruptcies and the Risks of Preventing Them
"Our economy's most basic problem is that many individuals' and companies' debt service payments are too large relative to the cash flows they produce to service them. As a result, they will have to go through debt restructurings that will write-down debts to levels that reduce required debt service payments to levels that are consistent with debtors' abilities to pay. Bankruptcy is the most common way of bringing about these restructurings. The more bankruptcies we have, and the sooner we have them, the quicker we can get this economic crisis behind us."

November 18, 2008
Ford, Trying to Raise Cash, Sells Stake in Mazda
–New York Times

November 18, 2008
Home Prices Decline by 9%
–New York Times

November 19, 2008
Stocks Drop Sharply and Credit Markets Seize Up
"The Standard & Poor's 500-stock index fell 6.7 percent, leaving that benchmark down about 52 percent from its peak in October 2007."
–New York Times

November 20, 2008
New Jobless Claims Reach a 16-Year High, U.S. Says
–New York Times

November 20, 2008
Oil Closes Below $50, Lowest Price since May 2005
–New York Times

News & Bridgewater Daily Observations (BDO)

November 20, 2008
Stocks Soar on News of Choice for Treasury
—New York Times

November 21, 2008
The Balance Sheet Problem
"The thaw in credit markets since the Fed decided to inject equity into banks has been insufficient in preventing the avalanche of credit market selling. The freeze that continues in credit markets is evidenced by the breakdown of basic financing relationships in markets that were taken for granted as arbitrages when financing was available. The economy will be in free fall until new credit is available at rates that make sense given economic conditions, and new credit is unlikely to be made available at such rates while there are so many dislocations to take advantage of first. Today, there is just no willingness to use up balance sheet (create credit) for even arbitrages, much less the financing of new economic activity."

November 23, 2008
Britain Poised to Announce Stimulus
—New York Times

November 25, 2008
U.S. Details $800 Billion Loan Plans
"The mortgage markets were electrified by the Fed's announcement that it would swoop in and buy up to $600 billion in debt tied to mortgages guaranteed by Fannie Mae and Freddie Mac. Interest rates on 30-year fixed-rate mortgages fell almost a full percentage point, to 5.5 percent, from 6.3 percent."
—New York Times

November 26, 2008
New Efforts for Stimulus in Europe and China
—New York Times

November 28, 2008
In Short Session, Stocks Cap 5-Session Rally
"Wall Street finished higher Friday, wrapping up its biggest five-day rally in more than 75 years, even as investors digested signs of a bleak holiday season for retailers...The stock market closed three hours early the day after Thanksgiving and locked in gains of 16.9 percent for the Dow since the rally began November 21, while the S.& P. 500 is up 19.1 percent."
—New York Times

worse, because they weren't. Still, the 2008 crisis would have been a lot less painful if the policy makers had acted even earlier.

See the chart below to get a sense of what happened in response to the news of "quantitative easing." 30-year fixed mortgage rates fell nearly 1 percent on the news (and 10-year Treasury yields declined 22 basis points).

Still, the stock market ended the month down 7.5 percent, as it wasn't clear if these moves were too little too late.

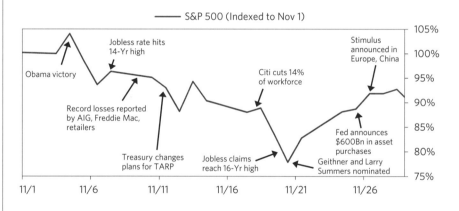

We wrote to clients on this announcement:

(BDO) November 25: Why We Expect More Shock & Awe And What It Will Mean

Though we can't speak for them, we believe that the Fed and the new Treasury folks understand the deleveraging/depression dynamic and the seriousness of the one that we're in. In fact, we believe that their understanding is now quite similar ours, so they are doing what we would do, and that they will probably do about what we would do. Along these lines, we expect shock and awe type moves from both the Fed and the Administration (i.e., the Treasury and other departments).

Today's Fed's announced moves are just the latest steps down the path of continuing to broaden the securities bought and increase the amounts spent to bring down credit spreads and add liquidity to the system. We expect more because we expect that they will do "whatever it takes" that they can get away with.

Big policy announcements were also coming from other major countries as they saw their own economies slide. For instance, the UK government announced a

$30 billion stimulus package (via a reduction in sales tax and measures to help homeowners, pensioners, and small businesses); China cut interest rates; and the EU outlined a $258 billion fiscal plan. Other central banks also increased emergency lending measures (e.g., the Bank of Japan implemented a new provision allowing commercial banks to borrow unlimited funds from the central bank, collateralized). And in December, interest rates were lowered across the developed world as the global economy slowed.

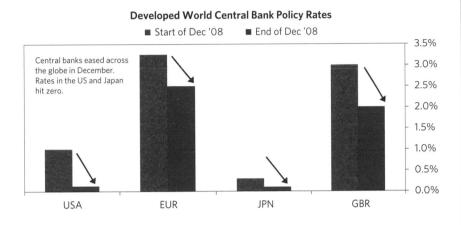

Developed World Central Bank Policy Rates
■ Start of Dec '08   ■ End of Dec '08

Central banks eased across the globe in December. Rates in the US and Japan hit zero.

As for the US Federal Reserve, it cut its overnight rate to its lowest level ever (between 0 percent and 0.25 percent), hitting the zero bound. Chairman Bernanke noted: "the decision was historic."[56] Stocks rallied and the dollar fell following the announcement, largely because it was clear that "printing money," buying debt, and providing big guarantees to do whatever was needed to reverse this debt/liquidity crisis would occur.

The increased likelihood of a deal with the auto companies funded from TARP also helped markets, not just because it helped those companies but because it was emblematic of a more forceful approach to saving the system. TARP was enacted to deal with financial institutions. Paulson repeatedly said that they didn't intend to use TARP funds for the autos, while the Bush Administration made it clear that it didn't want an auto bankruptcy and worked diligently with Congress to prevent one by trying to get the legislative authority to use a portion of the $25 billion that Congress had already appropriated to help the autos meet fuel efficiency standards for emergency loans for restructuring. There was real progress in this regard, with a bill passing in the House, but the legislation stalled in the Senate in mid-December. On December 19, just before leaving office, President Bush officially announced plans to extend $13.4 billion in emergency loans to Chrysler and General Motors. By the end of the month, the government expanded this bailout package unexpectedly, delivering additional support to the auto industry (which buoyed stocks). Because TARP money could only be given to financial institutions, the funds had to be directed through the auto companies' financing arm. Additionally, the financing affiliate of General Motors (GMAC) was approved to reorganize as a bank (to receive federal aid), which allowed GMAC to start making new loans to less credit-worthy borrowers. After that, they then helped the auto companies by recapitalizing and rescuing their finance companies just before leaving office. The market was also optimistic about the fiscal stimulus being pledged by president-elect Obama. The transition exemplified the very best of political behavior on the part of both transitioning presidents. Also, the continuity of Bernanke and Geithner on the economic leadership team helped.

News & Bridgewater Daily Observations (BDO)

December 17, 2008
OPEC Agrees to Another Cut in Production
—*New York Times*

December 17, 2008
As the Fed Flattens Rates, the Dollar Gets Bruised
—*New York Times*

December 18, 2008
How So Many Investors Lost Money in 2008 & Lessons for the Future
"From our perspective, most investors lost money because:

1. They had a lot more exposure to beta than alpha.

2. The beta exposure was much more heavily in assets that do badly during economic bad times (e.g., stocks, private equity, real estate, bonds with credit risk, etc.) than in assets that do well in bad times (e.g. Treasury bonds).

3. The risk and liquidity premiums rose a lot (which happens in bad times).

4. The alphas typically had lots of systematic biases in them to do well in good times and to do badly in bad times—e.g., the average "hedge" fund has been about 70% correlated with stocks, so it's not surprising that hedge funds are down a lot when stocks are down a lot."

December 18, 2008
Rules Aim to Protect Credit Card Users
—*Associated Press*

December 19, 2008
Stocks Jump, Then Slide Back, After Auto Bailout
—*New York Times*

December 22, 2008
Irregularity Uncovered at IndyMac
—*New York Times*

December 23, 2008
November Home Sales Fell Faster Than Expected
—*New York Times*

December 24, 2008
Fed Approves GMAC Request to Become a Bank
—*New York Times*

December 24, 2008
New Jobless Claims Hit 26-Year High
—*Reuters*

December 29, 2008
U.S. Agrees to a Stake in GMAC
—*New York Times*

December 30, 2008
Shares Climb as G.M. Gets More Money
—*Reuters*

December 30, 2008
GMAC Makes It Easier to Get a Car Loan
"GMAC said it would begin making loans immediately to borrowers with credit scores of 621 or higher, a significant easing from the 700 minimum score the company started requiring two months ago as it struggled to stay afloat. And G.M. said it would offer a new round of low-rate financing, including zero percent interest on some models."
—*New York Times*

While all these moves were big, there was of course good reason to question whether the damage already done was too great for a full recovery to occur. While stocks rallied on the hope of stimulus and progress with the automakers, December ended with volatility (uncertainty) priced to remain high.

Bridgewater closed out 2008 with significant gains for our investors, when most other investors had significant losses. What a year! What a relief!

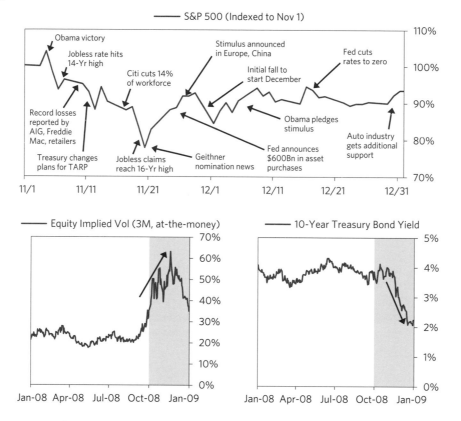

Having the template explained in Part 1 and understanding the dynamics of the Great Depression in the 1930s as well as we did (and so many other deleveragings) helped us a lot. The chart below shows interest rates and money supply (M0) since 1925 to encompass both periods. In both cases they hit virtually 0 percent and in both cases "money printing" followed. Note that these were the only times since 1900 that these things happened, and that, in both cases, immediately following this "money printing"/QE the markets and the economy bottomed.

Quantitative easing is like a giant shot of adrenalin to save a patient that is having a massive heart attack. The only question I had in late 2008 was if this overdue and great move would work or if it had come too late.

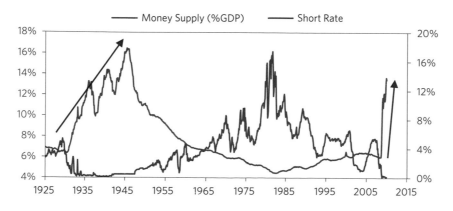

Transition from an "Ugly" to a "Beautiful" Deleveraging: 2009

It's worth briefly recapping where the US economy was at this point. Virtually every economic indicator looked to be falling extremely quickly. As an illustration, in a single day in January, reports of employment cuts across companies totaled 62,000. In addition to weak economic growth, there were still at least five major financial institutions at risk of failure: Fannie Mae, Freddie Mac, AIG, Citigroup, and Bank of America; each of these was bigger than Lehman. And a new, untested administration was about to be handed the reins. This note conveys our picture of the economy at the time:

(BDO) January 9: The US Economy Remains in Freefall…
The US economy remains in free-fall with the impact of the credit contraction now hitting where it hurts most, employment. Initially the financial sector suffered, then demand and now employment. The transition from demand to employment was sealed when business revenues fell faster than costs in the fourth quarter, compressing margins and driving earnings down (not yet reported, but almost certainly occurred). Businesses were then motivated to cut their biggest expense item, labor. The extreme pace of payroll reductions, over 500 thousand per month in November and December, reflects business's attempt to sustain their operating earnings.

This is even more important than in most economic contractions given the lack of credit. The lack of credit means that businesses must generate cash flow internally; they cannot rely on a loan to get them through a cash bind. This magnifies the pressure to lay off workers.

When President Obama took office on January 20, the markets began to focus on the administration's economic policies. Secretary Geithner's announcement of his financial stability plan on February 10 was seen as a major bellwether for administration financial policies. He outlined[57] broadly how he was going to "clean up and strengthen the nation's banks." He explained that the approach would stress test the nation's major banks to determine which institutions needed additional capital and that the administration would shore up their capital with a combination of public and private funds. Investors were uncertain about the details of Geithner's plan: Would there be nationalizations; would losses be imposed on shareholders or taxpayers? Investors were provided only with the broad strokes, leaving them to expect the worst. The S&P fell 3 percent as Geithner spoke and ended the day down 4.9 percent.

Rumors that the Obama administration was considering nationalization continued to circulate, so the Treasury, FDIC, OCC, OTS, and the Federal Reserve released a joint statement to assure[58] the public that nationalization was a last resort outcome, stating: "Because our economy functions better when financial institutions are well managed in the private sector, the strong presumption of the Capital Assistance Program is that banks should remain in private hands." The "strong presumption" wasn't enough—the S&P fell 3.5 percent on the day.

Later in the month, Geithner released further details about the plan that the Treasury and Fed had collectively worked out for the "stress test": the Federal Reserve would assess how well the country's big banks would withstand a major contraction in the economy, defined as a 3.3 percent contraction in

News & Bridgewater Daily Observations (BDO)

January 2, 2009
Manufacturing Reports Show Depth of Global Downturn
"In the United States on Friday, a crucial measure of manufacturing activity fell to the lowest level in 28 years in December. The Institute for Supply Management, a trade group of purchasing executives, said its manufacturing index was 32.4 in December, down from 36.2 in November."
—New York Times

January 4, 2009
Auto Industry Still Coming to Grips With the Damage of 2008
"Each of the six largest automakers, including foreign and domestic brands, is expected to say that its sales in the United States fell at least 30 percent in December."
—New York Times

January 5, 2009
Fed to Begin Buying Mortgage-Backed Securities
—Associated Press

January 5, 2009
Putting the Stimulus Plan In Perspective:
"Our estimates suggest the lack of both supply and demand for credit will create a hole in the economy that is around $1.2 trillion, and that at least based on what we know now, the government stimulus in 2009 will offset only about 1/3 of that."

January 6, 2009
In Fed Rate Cut, Fears of Long Recession
—New York Times

January 9, 2009
Jobless Report Sends Shares Tumbling
"Stocks slid on news that unemployment rates had hit their highest levels in 16 years as the economy slipped further into recession."
—New York Times

January 12, 2009
Bush Agrees to Obama Bailout Request
—CBS

January 15, 2009
Weak Economy and Retail Sales Hurt Shares
"Barraged by more signs of economic distress from retailers and the Federal Reserve, stocks plunged the most in weeks on Wednesday."
—New York Times

January 16, 2009
Wall Street Ends Higher After New Bank Bailout
"Some investors cheered news on Friday that the federal government had agreed to inject an additional $20 billion into Bank of America and absorb as much as $98.2 billion in losses, but for others, more financial bailouts and huge losses at Bank of America and Citigroup were dark omens of the direction of the financial markets and the broader economy."
—New York Times

January 20, 2009
Obama is Sworn In as the 44th President
—New York Times

News &
Bridgewater Daily Observations (BDO)

January 26, 2009
Senate Confirms Geithner for Treasury
—New York Times

January 28, 2009
Bank Stocks Lead Wall Street Rally
"Reports that the government was considering a deal to set up a 'bad bank' to absorb toxic assets ignited a broad rally on Wednesday, with financial companies leading the way."
—New York Times

January 30, 2009
Board Announces Policy to Help Avoid Preventable Foreclosures on Certain Residential Mortgage Assets
—Federal Reserve Press Release

February 6, 2009
Markets Rise Despite Report
"Not even the loss of 598,000 jobs could dampen Wall Street's soaring mood."
—New York Times

February 10, 2009
Secretary Geithner Introduces Financial Stability Plan
—Treasury Press Release

February 10, 2009
Stocks Slide as New Bailout Disappoints
—New York Times

February 10, 2009
There wasn't much of a surprise...
"The key takeaway for the members and staff present at the briefing seems to have been that the Treasury's plan was at its infancy and far from where members of Congress expected it to be."

February 13, 2009
Stimulus Plan Approved by Congress
—New York Times

February 17, 2009
Signing Stimulus, Obama Doesn't Rule Out More
—New York Times

February 18, 2009
$275 Billion Plan Seeks to Address Housing Crisis
"President Obama announced a plan on Wednesday to help as many as nine million American homeowners refinance their mortgages or avert foreclosure."
—New York Times

February 20, 2009
Markets Close Lower as Fears Over Banks Persist
—New York Times

February 20, 2009
The Eve of Nationalization?
"While nationalization seems to us the best option it is still extremely dangerous. The goal of nationalization is to re-capitalize these institutions in an acceptable way, while sustaining the basic underlying infrastructure of the financial system."

GDP, 8.9 percent unemployment, and a 22 percent fall in housing prices. If they lacked the capital to withstand the stress test, banks would turn to private markets first and then public funds to fill the gap. Of course Geithner couldn't yet provide the funds until the Fed finished their assessment on how exactly the shortfall would be filled. For about 18 months, we had regularly run our own estimates of bank losses by analyzing their holdings, marking them to market, and then doing scenario analysis. We were pretty confident that our estimates were good. So we were eager to see what the Fed's stress tests would look like, mostly to see if they would forthrightly show the numbers and then deal with them.

In addition to Geithner's Financial Stability Plan, the Obama administration announced a series of other fiscal policies aimed at jumpstarting the economy and getting credit flowing again. We won't go into depth on all of them here, but will give some details about the two most meaningful announcements:

- On February 17, President Obama signed into law the American Recovery and Reinvestment Act. The stimulus totaled $787 billion, with $288 billion specifically set aside for tax reductions, $144 billion for state and local governments, $105 billion for infrastructure, and the rest for federal spending programs. Notably, the tax reduction was funneled to taxpayers within days—a virtually instantaneous stimulus. The infrastructure spending, on the other hand, would take years to ramp up as projects needed to be scoped and planned for, so it mattered less in the short term.

- On February 18, the administration announced a plan worth up to $275 billion to address the housing crisis. With the goal of helping "as many as nine million American homeowners refinance their mortgages or avert foreclosure," the Homeowner Affordability and Stability Plan offered $75 billion in direct spending to keep at-risk homeowners in their homes. It also provided incentives to lenders to alter the terms of their loans to troubled borrowers to make them more affordable. And it gave Fannie Mae and Freddie Mac an additional $200 billion in financing.

Over the course of February, US policy makers also announced or expanded other policies—including the Term Asset-Backed Securities Loan Facility (TALF). TALF was a Fed policy which helped stimulate various types of consumer loans by lending up to $1 trillion on a non-recourse basis to holders of AAA asset-backed securities. It was set to begin on March 5 as an extension of a number of liquidity programs set to expire at the end of April. Despite all this stimulation, markets continued to fall, as shown in the chart below.

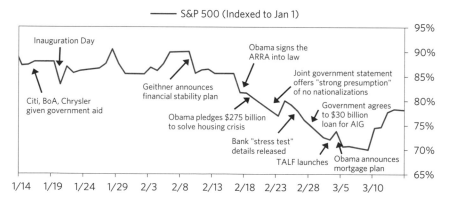

—— S&P 500 (Indexed to Jan 1)

Reports of ongoing weakness in the financial sector and economy continued to pile up. On Sunday March 1, news broke that AIG planned to report a $62 billion 4th quarter loss (the largest quarterly loss in US corporate history), and that the Treasury and Fed had agreed to provide AIG with an additional $30 billion in capital and loosen the terms of its earlier loan to the insurer. Markets plunged on Monday as fear of knock-on effects were triggered and the first economic stat releases from February showed the economy contracting at an accelerating rate. Monthly auto sales fell 5.8 percent to the weakest level since the early 1980s and the economy shed 651,000 jobs.

The next week opened with more of the same. On Monday, March 9, the World Bank came out with a very pessimistic report and Warren Buffett said that the economy had "fallen off a cliff." The stock market fell by 1 percent. Investor sentiment was extremely bearish and selling was exhausted. That was the day the bottom in the US stock market and the top in the dollar were made, though it was impossible to know that at the time.

Stocks surged 6.4 percent on Tuesday, led by a 38 percent jump in Citigroup shares, following a memo to employees from Citigroup's CEO stating that the bank was once again profitable, a well-received speech by Chairman Bernanke on reforms to financial regulation, and reports that lawmakers were close to re-instituting the uptick rule to slow short-selling of stocks.

Policy Makers Launch Coordinated Counterattack: March–April 2009

Behind the scenes, **policy makers at the Fed and the Treasury department were planning a coordinated set of "shock and awe" policies designed to shore up the financial system and provide the money needed to make up for contracting credit**. These policies were much more aggressive than earlier easings, and were released in a sequence of mega-announcements. How they were announced magnified the impact on markets.

The first of these announcements came on **March 18** when, in a move that surprised markets, the Fed announced that it was expanding its QE purchases of Agency MBS by $750 billion and agency debt by $100 billion, and that it would expand its purchases to US government bonds, making up to $300 billion in purchases over the next six months. In addition to increased QE, the Fed expanded the collateral that was eligible for TALF to a wider set of financial assets and stated its continuing expectations of "keeping rates exceptionally low for an extended period."

The market action around the $1 trillion plus announcement was huge. There was an enormous Treasury rally (the 48 basis point fall in yields was the biggest change in a couple of decades), stocks rallied, the dollar sold off, and gold rallied. The intraday charts below show how big the moves following the announcement were.

**News &
Bridgewater Daily Observations
(BDO)**

February 23, 2009
3rd Rescue Would Give U.S. 40% of Citigroup
–New York Times

February 25, 2009
Markets Lose Gains After Bank Test Details Are Disclosed
"In a reflection of the market's recent volatility, stocks fell in early trading Wednesday, giving back most of the gains from a 236-point rally in the Dow Tuesday...They rebounded in the afternoon as federal regulators announced details on the stress tests for banks worth more than $100 billion. But in the last minutes of trading, the major indexes dipped back into the red."
–New York Times

February 27, 2009
G.D.P. Revision Suggests a Long, Steep Downfall
"In the fourth quarter, the gross domestic product fell at an annualized rate of 6.2 percent, the steepest decline since the 1982 recession and sharper than the 3.8 percent reported earlier."
–New York Times

February 27, 2009
U.S. Agrees to Raise Its Stake in Citigroup
–New York Times

March 1, 2009
U.S. Is Said to Offer Another $30 Billion in Funds to A.I.G.
–New York Times

March 1, 2009
In Letter, Warren Buffett Concedes a Tough Year
–New York Times

March 2, 2009
U.S. Treasury and Federal Reserve Board Announce Participation in AIG Restructuring Plan
"The U.S. Treasury Department and the Federal Reserve Board today announced a restructuring of the government's assistance to AIG in order to stabilize this systemically important company in a manner that best protects the U.S. taxpayer. Specifically, the government's restructuring is designed to enhance the company's capital and liquidity in order to facilitate the orderly completion of the company's global divestiture program."
–Federal Reserve Press Release

March 18, 2009
Fed Plans to Inject Another $1 Trillion to Aid the Economy
"The Federal Reserve sharply stepped up its efforts to bolster the economy on Wednesday, announcing that it would pump an extra $1 trillion into the financial system by purchasing Treasury bonds and mortgage securities. Having already reduced the key interest rate it controls nearly to zero, the central bank has increasingly turned to alternatives like buying securities as a way of getting more dollars into the economy, a tactic that amounts to creating vast new sums of money out of thin air."
–New York Times

News &
Bridgewater Daily Observations
(BDO)

March 18, 2009
The Inevitable and Classic Central Bank Purchases
"Rather than being a surprise, today's Fed moves were an inevitable, necessary and very classic step in the D-process. In fact, the way we run our calculations, the Fed's purchases of Treasury securities will end up being in the vicinity of $1.5-$2.0 trillion.

At the big picture level, events are transpiring in the very classic way that happens in depressions and that is outlined in our "Template for Understanding What's Going On," *except the Fed is understandably doing these things earlier in the process than is typical.* Those who run the Fed are clearly trying to prevent the debt restructuring phase and go directly to the credit creation phase by doing all the classic debt relief things now. So are the folks in the administration. In addition to printing money, these will include initiatives to encourage credit creation (e.g., TALF, PPIF, etc.), and accounting and regulatory forbearance."

March 20, 2009
Financial Shares Lead the Market Down
"Stocks dropped on Friday as investors worried about the consequences of efforts on Capitol Hill to claw back bonuses from firms that received government bailouts...On Thursday, the House of Representatives responded to growing furor over bonuses at the American International Group by passing a bill that would impose a 90 percent tax on bonuses awarded this year by companies that received $5 billion or more in bailout money. The Senate is expected to take up its version of the bill next week."
–New York Times

March 22, 2009
U.S. Rounding Up Investors to Buy Bad Assets
"Obama administration officials worked Sunday to persuade reluctant private investors to buy as much as $1 trillion in troubled mortgages and related assets from banks, with government help."
–New York Times

March 23, 2009
U.S. Expands Plan to Buy Banks' Troubled Assets
"The Obama administration's new plan to liberate the nation's banks from a toxic stew of bad home loans and mortgage-related securities is bigger and more generous to private investors than expected, but it also puts taxpayers at great risk... Taken together, the three programs unveiled on Monday by the Treasury secretary, Timothy F. Geithner, could buy up to $2 trillion in real estate assets that have been weighing down banks, paralyzing credit markets and delaying the economic recovery."
–New York Times

March 23, 2009
Banking Plan Propels Wall St. to Best Day in Months
–New York Times

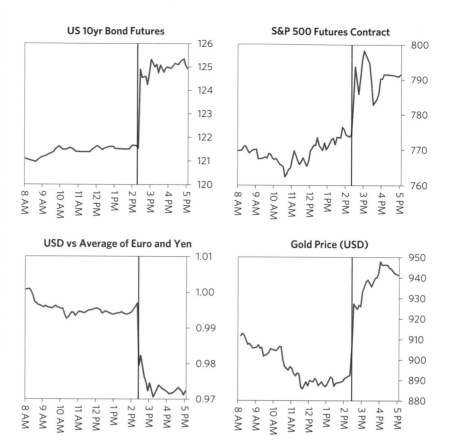

Then, on March 23, Secretary Geithner announced an expanded set of policies that aimed to buy $500 billion to $1 trillion worth of troubled assets from banks. At the heart of the program was the three-part Public-Private Investment Partnership (PPIP), which incentivized private investment firms to buy banks' bad assets using their own capital. In effect, it allowed firms to leverage their investments in troubled assets using money borrowed from the Fed, with a guarantee that they would not lose more than their initial investment if the assets fell below their initial value. In another move coordinated with the Fed, Geithner also announced a possible expansion of TALF, to finance residential and commercial MBS, and said the agencies were considering making legacy securities eligible for the program.

On the day of the announcement, the S&P rose 7.1 percent led by an 18 percent rally in financial shares.

On March 24, The Fed and the Treasury each announced plans to overhaul financial regulations and expand government power in seizing "too big to fail" banks, as well as insurers, investment banks, and other investment funds. Two days later, Secretary Geithner outlined a wider overhaul of financial regulations, which greatly increased federal regulatory oversight of insurance companies, hedge funds, and private equity funds, with expanded regulatory powers over any company deemed "too big to fail." While not a key part of the stimulative counter-attack, the move was well-received by markets.

At the end of March, Summers and Geithner oversaw a team led by Steven Rattner, a smart financier, to create the plan that would push GM and Chrysler into what Larry Summers described as a "cushioned bankruptcy." Bankruptcy would force the trade unions and creditors to negotiate ways to reduce debts, and ample US government support (including a large guarantee of GM's car warrantees) would ensure that GM could remain functioning while the company was restructured. While the automobile companies felt they couldn't function in bankruptcy, Summers thought that, with sufficient support, a bankrupt automobile company could function, and that there was no reason that the debt needed to be paid in full.

And then on April 2 came two major announcements. In the first, the G20 reported that it had reached an agreement on a greater than what we expected increase to IMF funding. Specifically, G20 countries agreed to immediately provide $250 billion in additional IMF financing, with the aim of eventually adding up to $500 billion in new lending capacity to the IMF's roughly $250 billion of existing liquid resources. The combination of dramatically expanded IMF lending capacity and more flexible lending terms was expected to dramatically reduce the immediate liquidity needs of a number of emerging-market countries. Emerging currencies soared following the announcement.

The second announcement came from the Financial Accounting Standards Board (FASB), which had passed two proposals to ease mark-to-market accounting rules. The changes, which had been expected to pass for a couple of weeks, gave banks more discretion in reporting the value of mortgage securities. While markets embraced the move, at the time we thought that these changes would have relatively little impact on banks' abilities to write off losses over time, while relieving some (but not all) of the accounting pressures on insurance companies.

The size of the coordinated government response to the credit crisis was unprecedented. At the time, we characterized the moves as "an enormous wave." The first table below, which we shared with our clients at the time, adds up all of the US government purchases and guarantees that had been announced by April 2009. **Remarkably, the US government was backstopping two-thirds of all debt, about $29 trillion dollars.**

News &
Bridgewater Daily Observations (BDO)

March 26, 2009
Geithner to Outline Major Overhaul of Finance Rules
"The Obama administration will detail on Thursday a wide-ranging plan to overhaul financial regulation by subjecting hedge funds and traders of exotic financial instruments, now among the biggest and most freewheeling players on Wall Street, to potentially strict new government supervision, officials said."
–New York Times

March 27, 2009
Bankers Pledge Cooperation With Obama
"The 13 chief executives emerged from the 90-minute meeting pledging to cooperate with the administration's efforts to shore up the banking industry and the broader economy. On a bright day with the cherry blossoms in bloom, administration officials and the bankers presented a unified message to the nation: We're all in this together."
–New York Times

March 27, 2009
Auto Sales for March Offer Hope
–New York Times

April 2, 2009
Change in Bank Rules Lifts Stocks
"Hopes that the worst days of the financial crisis are retreating lifted stock markets on Thursday after government leaders pledged huge new financial rescues and a regulatory group moved to rewrite financial regulations and accounting rules...The Financial Accounting Standards Board voted to ease mark-to-market standards, giving companies more leeway in valuing mortgage-backed securities."
–New York Times

April 2, 2009
Banks Get New Leeway in Valuing Their Assets
"A once-obscure accounting rule that infuriated banks, who blamed it for worsening the financial crisis, was changed Thursday to give banks more discretion in reporting the value of mortgage securities...During the financial crisis, the market prices of many securities, particularly those backed by subprime home mortgages, have plunged to fractions of their original prices. That has forced banks to report hundreds of billions of dollars in losses over the last year..."
–New York Times

News &
Bridgewater Daily Observations
(BDO)

April 2, 2009
The G20 Agreement on IMF Funding and Accounting Changes
"Thursday's reported developments in the form of the G20 announcement regarding IMF support and mark-to-market accounting rule changes are steps in this general direction to relieve the squeeze. The IMF announcement is a big step, while the FASB proposal will have a more limited effect on the accounting front...In our view, the most important part of the announcement relates to the commitments to immediate IMF financing already made, and to similar such commitments which are likely to be forthcoming from the US in the near future. We would expect a US commitment in the region of $100bn, which would bring the total increase in IMF resources to $350bn...we are in the process of reviewing the proposals that FASB passed yesterday. Our preliminary thoughts are that these changes will have relatively little impact on banks' abilities to write-off losses over time, while relieving some (but not all) of the accounting pressures on insurance companies."

Government Guarantees ($Mln)

Description	Asset Purchases	Hard Guarantee	Implicit Guarantee	Soft Guarantee
Agencies	40,000	577,000	6,400,891	
Fannie Mae	20,000		3,491,169	
Freddie Mac	20,000		2,740,721	
Other Agencies		577,000	169,001	
Banks	1,080,546	8,757,623	884,973	924,280
Fed Liquidity Programs	570,900			
Preferred Shares	285,646			
Remaining Capital Necessary	224,000			
TLGP		201,645		
Soft Guarantee on Senior Debt				924,280
FHLB Implicit Guarantee			884,973	
FDIC Deposit Losses		8,555,978		
Asset Purchases/ Guarantees	3,684,750	415,000		
TALF/PPIF	4,700	0		
Bank Asset Guarantees	0	415,000		
Short-Term Debt Market	3,255,650	0		
Fed Asset Purchases	424,400	0		
Other	463,285	140,193		5,700,000
AIG	121,000			
GE Capital	3,500	36,693		
Other Financial Institutions	10,000			5,700,000
Car Makers	19,785	3,500		
Foreigners	309,000	100,000		
Total	5,268,581	9,889,816	7,285,864	6,624,280
Cumulative Total	5,268,581	15,158,397	22,444,261	29,068,541

2/3rds of all debt guaranteed

While President Bush took a more hands off approach, believing his team knew best what to do and supporting them to do it, President Obama took a hands on approach, digging into the facts and numbers and being actively engaged in discussions about issues. He instituted a presidential daily economic briefing, analogous to the daily national security briefing. Every morning, the president met with his economic team, and for the first months, every one of those meetings was about the ongoing crisis. According to Larry Summers, the president read every word they sent him, and he was very much into understanding what the approach was, why they recommended it, and what alternatives were being turned down. It was a time when market and economic developments were more important than anything else.

How investors fared in the bear market varied a lot. They generally fell into three broad categories: 1) those who were clobbered and let their fears prompt them to reduce their risks (sell "risky" assets) the more they got clobbered, 2) those who were clobbered and had blind faith that in the end things would work out, so they held on or even bought more risky assets, and 3) those who had a pretty good understanding of what was happening and did a good job of selling high and buying low. There were very few in the third group.

As for us, while we had done a good job up until that point, we didn't want to take on hardly any bets at this stage. Back in the 2007 bubble, the gap between what was discounted in market pricing and what was likely appeared very large to us. Now market pricing was discounting a terrible set of conditions and the range of potential outcomes was enormous. While policy makers were making the right moves, whether they would work and what else lay beneath the surface in exposures remained unknown.

A little later in April, we wrote in reference to the degree of money printing and stimulus spending: "Like pandemics, D-processes come along very infrequently, so we don't have many to look back on and, in those that we have, this antidote was never administered in this dosage."

In these crises there is no such thing as getting everything exactly right, especially in the eyes of everyone. There was a **public uproar** over the Treasury's actions, especially about how "generous" its deal was for banks that were recapitalized, and how bankers weren't being punished. Reports that AIG had paid large, previously-committed bonuses after it received a bailout from the Treasury focused on how Secretary Geithner knew about the bonuses and allowed them to be paid out. The reports infuriated a public already upset with government bailouts of financial institutions and put the Treasury's plans for further action at risk.

Such reactions are classic. **As economic pain increases, populist calls to "punish the bankers that caused this mess" are the norm and they make it difficult for policy makers to take the actions that are necessary to save the financial system and the economy.** At such times bankers can want to stop "being bankers" by stopping investing or lending. Their doing so in the midst of the crisis would make the crisis much worse.

While the financial crisis and how it was handled contributed somewhat to the rise of populism in subsequent years, in the end saving the system is much more important than striving for precision. Larry Summers makes the comparison to battlefield medicine—it's never perfect, you're going to realize you made mistakes, and you're going to look bad, even if you do the best possible job. I can't say this enough: in my opinion, judging the policy makers in this way is unfair. The fact that they do their job anyway, and that they help as many people as they do, is what makes them heroes in my eyes.

In mid-March, at the peak of the controversy, members of Congress and the media were publicly calling for Secretary Geithner's resignation, even though he had executed his job with great skill, wisdom, and care. Had they succeeded in forcing a resignation or otherwise derailed the Treasury's bold and necessary plans to recapitalize the banking system, the bad economic consequences would have been large.

Geithner wrote the following in his book, conveying the challenge of handling public outrage:

> "The public outrage was appropriate, and I understood why the President wanted to embrace it, but I didn't see how we could ever satisfy it. We had no legal authority to confiscate the bonuses that had been paid during the boom. We had no power to set compensation for most private firms. We had more authority over firms receiving TARP funds, but we couldn't reduce bonuses to levels that the public might find acceptable without unleashing an exodus of talent from those banks, reducing their prospects of navigating their way to safety. In any case, I thought the public's rage on these issues was insatiable. I feared the tougher we talked about the bonuses, the more we would own them, fueling unrealistic expectations about our ability to eradicate extravagance in the financial industry."[59]

News & Bridgewater Daily Observations (BDO)

April 3, 2009
Big Bonuses at Fannie and Freddie Draw Fire
—New York Times

April 5, 2009
Treasury Chief Says He's Open to Ousting Heads of Frail Banks
—New York Times

April 6, 2009
Central Banks Expand Currency Swaps
"Central banks in the United States, Europe, Britain and Japan announced an agreement on Monday that could provide some $287 billion in liquidity to the Federal Reserve, in the form of currency swaps...Under the arrangement, the Fed could draw on these lines to provide more liquidity to financial institutions, this time in the form of foreign currency."
—New York Times

April 6, 2009
Muted Signs of Life in the Credit Markets
—New York Times

April 7, 2009
Fed Minutes Show Worry as Credit Seized Up
"A major economic weakening in the United States and across the world helped prod the Federal Reserve to pump more than $1 trillion into the economy last month, according to minutes of a recent Fed meeting released on Wednesday...At their latest meeting, members of the central bank's Open Market Committee worried about persistent declines in the economy and talked about the best way to loosen credit markets."
—New York Times

April 21, 2009
Markets Rally on Geithner's Reassurances on Banks
"Stock markets closed solidly higher on Tuesday, a day after Wall Street posted its biggest losses since early March and financial stocks plunged more than 10 percent. Bank stocks rebounded, bolstered by reassurances from the Treasury secretary, Timothy F. Geithner, that most banks were well capitalized...In written testimony to a Congressional oversight panel, Mr. Geithner said a 'vast majority' of banks had more capital than they needed right now."
—New York Times

April 22, 2009
Regulators to Meet With Banks on Friday on 'Stress' Tests
"Federal Regulators have quietly scheduled face-to-face meetings on Friday with leaders of the nation's biggest banks to reveal the preliminary results of the stress tests."
—New York Times

News &
Bridgewater Daily Observations
(BDO)

April 24, 2009
Wall St. Unfazed by Stress Test Details
"Investors are unlikely to know the results of the government's stress tests of major banks until May 4, but Wall Street cleared one hurdle on Friday: stocks did not lose their footing after regulators laid out how they were conducting the assessments.

Shares pushed higher even though few details were forthcoming on the ratios and metrics being used to determine whether banks need to raise more capital. Still, investors speculated that most of the 19 financial institutions were well capitalized and would not need huge new infusions of capital from private investors or the government."
–New York Times

April 24, 2009
World Finance Leaders Meet, and Cautiously Glimpse "Green Shoots" of Recovery
"Sounding slightly less terrified than they have at any time in the last six months, finance ministers from the United States and other wealthy nations said Friday that they saw 'signs of stabilization' in the global economic crisis...In a joint statement, the group went further and predicted that economic activity should begin to edge up later this year, though they cautioned that growth would be 'weak' and that the outlook could darken again."
–New York Times

April 28, 2009
A New Plan to Help Modify Second Mortgages
"The Obama administration sought to expand its $50 billion plan to reduce home foreclosures, announcing a new program on Tuesday to help troubled homeowners modify second mortgages or piggyback loans...Under the new plan, the Treasury Department will offer cash incentives and subsidies to lenders who agree to substantially reduce the monthly payments on second mortgages or forgive those loans entirely."
–New York Times

May 1, 2009
Citi Is Said to Require New Capital
–New York Times

May 1, 2009
Fed to Begin Lending Program in June
"The Federal Reserve announced Friday that it would start a much-awaited program in June to encourage commercial real estate lending...The goal is to expand the availability of these loans, help prevent defaults on commercial properties like office parks and malls and make the sale of distressed properties easier, the Fed said...The new commercial real estate component is part of a broader program introduced in March, called the Term Asset-Backed Securities Loan Facility, or TALF, that aims to jump-start lending to consumers and small businesses."
–New York Times

May 4, 2009
Existing-Home Sales Rise for a Second Month
–New York Times

The uproar ultimately faded after President Obama strongly stood behind Tim. But after what was seen as Geithner's lack of action, the House of Representatives passed a bill on March 19 that put a 90 percent tax on bonuses paid out by companies that received government bailouts worth $5 billion or more. While the scope of the tax was limited mostly to the AIG bonuses, the sense of distrust for government support among many executives in the financial sector (who saw the tax as the government changing the rules after the fact) would be a continuing source of tension.

Fortunately, the bottoms in the markets and the economy were being made, because had things gotten any worse or gone on any longer our capitalist and democratic system would've been at risk of breaking. All else being equal, prices for goods, services, and investment assets go down when a rate of buying lessens and go up when the rate of selling lessens. For that reason, **tops are typically made when the rate of buying is unsustainable (which is also when people think prices will rise) and bottoms are made when the rate of selling is at a pace that's unsustainable (typically when most people are bearish)**. In the weeks before and after the big announcements, pressures eased, signs of an economic rebound emerged, and markets rallied. A series of economic releases during the first week of April showed that while the economy continued to contract during March, the pace of contraction was slower than expected. And as the charts below show, while the major economic stats continued contracting through March at the fastest pace in decades, the contractions looked to be leveling off and maybe reversing.

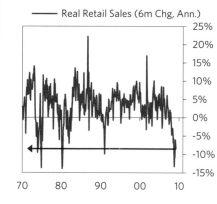

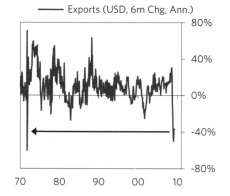

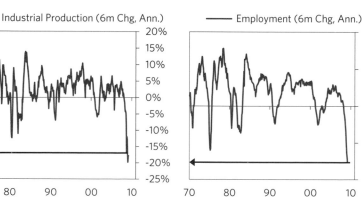

By mid-April, stock and commodity markets around the world had rebounded sharply from their March lows. The S&P was up 25 percent, oil was up over 20 percent, and bank CDS spreads fell almost 30 percent, but in level terms they remained near their extremes. This appeared to be due more to a slower rate of selling than a pickup in buying.

The obvious question at the time was whether a bottom was being made or if we were just seeing another bear market rally. After all, there had been a number of classic bear market rallies along the way—e.g., the S&P had staged a 19 percent rally over a week at the end of October and a 24 percent rally over the last six weeks of 2008 before giving up the gains of each and hitting new lows.

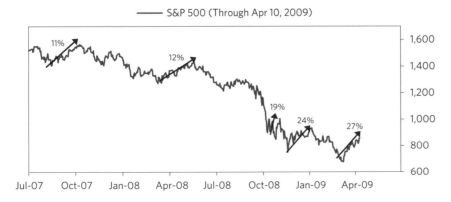

News & Bridgewater Daily Observations (BDO)

May 6, 2009
Banks Gain Ahead of Stress-Test Results
"Some of the big banks may need billions of dollars in additional capital, but Wall Street decided Wednesday to view the glass of the financial system as half full...Investors bought shares of major banks and regional banks as the government prepared to release the results of its stress tests of 19 major financial companies. Investors were speculating that the banks were in decent shape, even if they are required by the government to raise more capital to withstand deeper economic declines."
—*New York Times*

May 7, 2009
Stress Test Results Split Financial Landscape
"The stress tests released by the Obama administration Thursday painted a broad montage of the troubles in the nation's banking industry and, for the first time, drew a stark dividing line through the new landscape of American finance...Broadly speaking, the test results suggested that the banking industry was in better shape than many had feared. Of the nation's 19 largest banks, which sit atop two-thirds of all deposits, regulators gave nine a clean bill of health."
—*New York Times*

May 7, 2009
Central Banks in Europe Ease Credit Policies Again
—*New York Times*

May 8, 2009
Bank Exams Over, Wall Street Celebrates
"Stock prices climbed Friday as investors seemed to endorse the results of the government's stress tests of 19 major banks and to new figures showing that the pace of job losses was beginning to moderate."
—*New York Times*

May 8, 2009
U.S. Jobless Rate Hits 8.9%, but Pace Eases
—*New York Times*

May 8, 2009
2 Banks Cited in Stress Tests Find Ready Investors
"A day after the bank stress tests were released, two major institutions, Wells Fargo and Morgan Stanley, handily raised billions of dollars in the capital markets on Friday to satisfy new federal demands for more capital. A third, Bank of America, hastily laid out plans to sell billions of dollars in new stock."
—*New York Times*

May 18, 2009
Geithner Says He Favors New Policies, Not Pay Caps
"Treasury Secretary Timothy F. Geithner said on Monday that the government should not impose caps on executive pay at institutions that receive federal bailouts, but instead should set policies that discourage all financial companies from rewarding excessive risk-taking."
—*New York Times*

News & Bridgewater Daily Observations (BDO)

May 20, 2009
Fed Considered Increasing Its Purchase of Debt
"Seeking to keep interest rates in check and heal the credit markets, the Federal Reserve last month debated whether it should expand a program to buy mortgage and Treasury securities, according to minutes of the meeting released Wednesday."
–*New York Times*

May 20, 2009
Bank Raised Billions, Geithner Says
"The country's biggest banks have made moves to bolster their balance sheets by about $56 billion since the government disclosed the results of its financial 'stress tests' two weeks ago, Treasury Secretary Timothy F. Geithner said Wednesday."
–*New York Times*

May 21, 2009
Long-Term Job Claims Rise, but Layoff Rate Edges Down
–*New York Times*

May 21, 2009
Treasury Is Said to Plan Second Bailout for GMAC
–*New York Times*

May 21, 2009
U.S. Is Said to Be Weighing Financial Consumer Agency
–*New York Times*

May 26, 2009
Consumer Confidence Rose Sharply in May
–*New York Times*

June 1, 2009
Obama Is Upbeat for G.M.'s Future
"President Obama marked the lowest point in General Motors' 100-year history—its bankruptcy filing on Monday—by barely mentioning it, instead focusing his remarks on the second chance G.M. will have to become a viable company with more government aid."
–*New York Times*

June 4, 2009
Stocks Advance on Hopes for Economic Rebound
"Even though the economy remains weak, investors on Thursday were already looking ahead to a recovery and setting their sights on inflation...Investors seeking signs of economic stability were also encouraged by reports on Thursday showing reductions in first-time unemployment claims and continuing jobless claims for last week."
–*New York Times*

June 4, 2009
Jobless Claims Decline Slightly, the First Time in 20 Weeks
"The number of people on the unemployment insurance rolls fell slightly last week for the first time in 20 weeks, and the tally of new jobless claims also dipped, the government said Thursday...The report provides a glimmer of good news for job seekers, though both declines were small and the figures remain significantly above the levels associated with a healthy economy."
–*New York Times*

The Bank Stress Test

One of the key questions for determining whether the US was headed for a sustained recovery was the health of the banks. Despite recent drips of good news, there wasn't broad transparency on whether the banks were still encumbered by toxic assets or a big need for capital. We had been running our numbers for months and saw huge numbers that weren't being brought to light or being dealt with. But in February Tim Geithner said the Fed was going to do those stress tests. I didn't know if they would fudge the numbers to make them look better than they were or if they'd tell it like it was so they could deal with the problems appropriately.

On May 7 the Fed released its results. In response I wrote:

(BDO) May 7: We Agree!
The Stress Test numbers and ours are nearly the same!!! The regulators did an excellent job of explaining exactly what they did for this stress test and showing the numbers that produced the results. They did virtually exactly what we did since we started putting out our loss estimates nearly two years ago, and their numbers are essentially the same as ours. The differences between our numbers and theirs are more a matter of terminology than of substance. For example, the biggest difference between their estimates and ours is due to the number of years they and we are counting—i.e., their loss estimate is for the losses that will occur over the next two years and ours is for the total amount of losses that will be taken on these assets over the lives of these assets. As there will be losses in years 3, 4, etc., in addition to those in the first two years, naturally the total losses (i.e., ours) will be greater than the losses incurred over the next two years (i.e., theirs). We won't conjecture why they did it that way, though we do know from our projections that the maximum capital needs (i.e., when earnings fall short relative to losses) is probably at the end of two years. Anyway, that accounts for most of the difference in our total loss estimates, and in addition we may also have a slightly worse economic scenario than they do. Once these adjustments are made, we see essentially the same picture. What a relief!!! For the first time in the last two years we are confident that the regulators really do understand the scale of the banking problem!

Tim Geithner, who read *Bridgewater Daily Observations* daily throughout the crisis, took this one to President Obama. In his memoir, he described the moment as follows:

> "The next morning, I walked into the Oval Office for the President's daily economics briefing with a report from Bridgewater Associates, the world's largest hedge fund firm. Many experts, including Larry, regarded Bridgewater's Daily Observations as among the smartest and most credible sources of private-sector economic analysis—and among the darkest about the banks. In front of the economic team and the President's political advisers, I handed that day's Observations to the President...
>
> I wasn't dancing in the end zone, but that was a good day for the home team."[60]

We were in sync about what was and what needed to be done about it. What a relief!

The Beginning of the Beautiful Deleveraging: June–December 2009:

In the second half of 2009, the policies (i.e., providing liquidity via QE, capital via fiscal policies, and other supports via macro-prudential policies) reduced risks and increased the buying and prices of "riskier" assets, and the economy began to recover. This shift was analogous to others that produced "beautiful deleveragings" for reasons explained earlier.

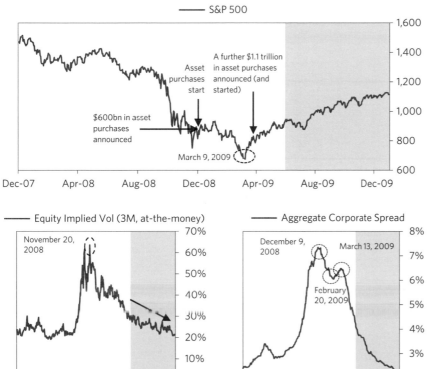

While we won't discuss all the improving news of this period in depth, we will highlight two points. First, frequent concerns over inflation stemming from the fast pace of central bank printing didn't materialize, which fortunately laid to rest the incorrect belief that printing a lot of money would cause inflation to accelerate. The Fed's "printing money" would not cause an acceleration of inflation if it was replacing contracting credit.

As we explained to our clients that summer:

- **Reflations don't necessarily cause inflation because they can simply negate deflations, depending on how far they are taken and what the money goes to.**

- It is overly simplistic to talk about "inflation" because "inflation" is an average of many things that behave differently from one another. For example, when an economy is depressed, during reflations (which is normally the case, because otherwise there's no need for reflations), there is little or no inflation in labor costs and assets that are used for

News & Bridgewater Daily Observations (BDO)

June 5, 2009
Hints of Hope Even as Jobless Rate Jumps to 9.4%
"The American economy shed 345,000 jobs in May, and the unemployment rate spiked to 9.4 percent, but the losses were far smaller than anticipated, amplifying hopes of recovery... Economists described the Labor Department's monthly jobs report, released Friday, as an unambiguous sign of improvement, yet also clear evidence of broadening national distress, as millions of households grapple with joblessness and lost working hours."
–New York Times

June 9, 2009
10 Large Banks Allowed to Exit U.S. Aid Program
"The Obama administration marked with little fanfare a major milestone in its bank rescue effort—its decision on Tuesday to let 10 big banks repay federal aid that had sustained them through the worst of the crisis—as policy makers and industry executives focused on the challenges still before them...The bank holding companies, among them American Express, Goldman Sachs, JPMorgan Chase and Morgan Stanley, plan to return a combined $68.3 billion."
–New York Times

June 10, 2009
Fed Sees Bright Spots in Weak Economy
–New York Times

June 12, 2009
U.S. Consumer Confidence Hits a 9-Month High
–New York Times

June 15, 2009
Shares in Retreat on Fear of Slow, Late Recovery
"Hopes for an economic rebound lifted Wall Street off the mat this spring. But on Monday, investors took cover in a broad sell-off as they faced the prospect that any recovery could be slow and a long way off...Two new reports helped to underscore the difficult times ahead for the American economy."
–New York Times

June 17, 2009
Financial Regulatory Reform
"While this crisis had many causes, it is clear now that the government could have done more to prevent many of these problems from growing out of control and threatening the stability of our financial system. Gaps and weaknesses in the supervision and regulation of financial firms presented challenges to our government's ability to monitor, prevent, or address risks as they built up in the system. No regulator saw its job as protecting the economy and financial system as a whole...We must act now to restore confidence in the integrity of our financial system. The lasting economic damage to ordinary families and businesses is a constant reminder of the urgent need to act to reform our financial regulatory system and put our economy on track to a sustainable recovery."
–US Treasury Press Release

June 24, 2009
SEC Proposes Rule Amendments to Strengthen Regulatory Framework for Money Market Funds
–SEC Press Release

News & Bridgewater Daily Observations (BDO)

July 2, 2009
Joblessness Hits 9.5%, Deflating Recovery Hopes
"The American economy lost 467,000 more jobs in June, and the unemployment rate edged up to 9.5 percent in a sobering indication that the longest recession since the 1930s had yet to release its hold."
–New York Times

July 8, 2009
I.M.F. Upgrades Outlook for Economy
–New York Times

July 16, 2009
New Jobless Claims Are Lowest Since January
–New York Times

July 16, 2009
Geithner Sees Evidence of a Financial Recovery
–New York Times

July 23, 2009
Dow Closes Over 9,000; First Time Since January
–New York Times

August 6, 2009
New Jobless Claims Fall, Beating Estimates
"The government said Thursday that the number of newly laid-off workers seeking unemployment insurance fell last week...The Labor Department said that initial claims for jobless benefits dropped to a seasonally adjusted 550,000 for the week ending August 1, down from an upwardly revised figure of 588,000...That was much lower than analysts' estimates of 580,000, according to a survey by Thomson Reuters."
–New York Times

August 7, 2009
Bulls Send Markets to Heights Last Seen in 2008
–New York Times

August 12, 2009
Fed Views Recession as Near an End
"Almost exactly two years after it embarked on what was the biggest financial rescue in American history, the Federal Reserve said on Wednesday that the recession is ending and that it would take a step back toward normal policy."
–New York Times

September 19, 2009
Leading Senator Pushes New Plan to Oversee Banks
–New York Times

November 16, 2009
Continuing Unemployment Is Predicted by Fed Chief
–New York Times

January 4, 2010
Manufacturing Data Helps Invigorate Wall Street
–New York Times

January 6, 2010
U.S. Service Sector Shows Modest Growth
–Associated Press

January 8, 2010
Consumer Borrowing Fell Once Again in November
–Associated Press

production (e.g., real estate, equipment, etc.), while there is inflation in assets that benefit from decreases in the value of money/currency (e.g., internationally traded commodities, gold, etc.).

Second, Congress and the Obama administration **shifted their attentions to significantly increasing financial industry regulation and oversight**. The following timeline gives a sense of how quickly these new laws and regulations were being written:

June 17: Obama delivers a speech outlining a legislative proposal for comprehensive financial services reform, which eventually led to the passing of Dodd-Frank. The proposal included heightened regulation, consolidation of existing regulatory bodies (with greater regulatory authority given to the Fed), more consumer protections, more regulation of credit rating agencies, and updated rules around winding down banks, among many other components. The bill itself wouldn't be passed until 2010.

June 24: The SEC suggested regulations for money market funds that would require them to hold some portion of their portfolios in highly liquid investments. Additionally, the proposed regulations would restrict money market funds' holdings to high-quality securities.

June 30: The Treasury Department released a bill to Congress to create a Consumer Financial Protection Agency. The agency would take control of all consumer protection programs currently run by the Fed, the Comptroller of the Currency, the Office of Thrift Supervision, FDIC, FTC, and the National Credit Union Administration.

July 23: The Federal Reserve proposed changes to Regulation Z (Truth in Lending). The changes aimed to improve the consumer disclosure laws for closed-end mortgages and home-equity credit. It would require APR and monthly payments (on adjustable-rate loans) to be communicated to the buyer.

October 22: The Fed proposed a review of 28 banking organizations' incentive compensation policies, to see whether or not they are "risk-appropriate," and to go through a similar process at smaller banks. This proposal came on the same day that the Special Master for TARP Executive Compensation released[61] the determinations for executive compensation for the "top 25 most highly paid at the seven firms receiving exceptional assistance."

December 11: The House passed the creation of the Financial Stability Council and Consumer Financial Protection Agency.

Changing laws in ways that would have made the crisis less bad are typical at the end of big debt crises. Then, over long time frames (e.g., 25 years), as the hangover wears off and a new euphoria sets in, these laws are increasingly flouted and new forms of leverage are produced by new forms of entities, leading to a new debt crisis that evolves similarly.

2010 through Mid-2011

As 2010 began, the financial markets were strong (up nearly 65 percent from their March 2009 lows) because they were flush with liquidity thanks to the Fed's QE, and they were safer due to fiscal and regulatory changes. But the economy labored because many borrowers were weaker and more cautious, and lending standards had tightened.

Now, the markets started to discount a move to normalcy. The credit markets priced in that the Fed would tighten two or three times within the year—roughly the amount of tightening you'd expect in a standard business-cycle recovery from a recession. That was odd given conditions. Unemployment rates were still a hair away from post-war highs, wage growth was stuck, homes prices were flat at well-below the prior peak (meaning many middle-class mortgage borrowers remained underwater), credit standards were tightened, and borrowers who were still okay financially remained disinclined to lever up, while those who were inclined to lever up were financially dead. It was hard to imagine there would be a normal pickup.

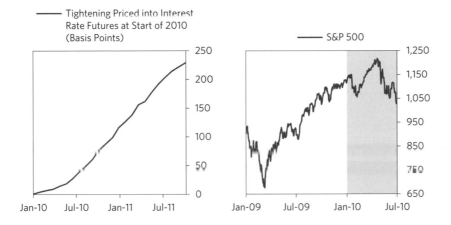

Around this time, most of the world's central banks and governments were slowing their aggressive rates of stimulus. The Fed ended the first round of quantitative easing in March after purchasing $1.25 trillion in mortgage-backed securities. The pace of fiscal stimulus from programs like the America Recovery and Reinvestment Act were set to peak later in the year. Abroad, there were pockets of tightening as countries like China increased interest rates.

Importantly, at this point it wasn't clear to investors that **merely slowing or ending quantitative easing was equivalent to tightening—and not that different from raising interest rates**. Some thought it was enough to simply pump a lot of money into the economy to stimulate it—and the Fed had certainly done that, printing over $2 trillion. But the flow of money was more important than the amount of money, as it was this flow of asset purchases that helped sustain their increases in value and the growth of lending to buyers in the economy, because credit growth remained slow. Yet the Fed's amount of stimulation was then popularly believed to be too much and irresponsible. We had a different view, doubting that developed economies would tighten as fast as what others thought and had priced in. We laid it out in the *Daily Observations* of February 17:

News & Bridgewater Daily Observations (BDO)

January 13, 2010
U.S. Regions Show Gains and Softness, Fed Reports
—New York Times

January 22, 2010
3-Day Slide Sends Markets Down About 5 Percent
"A new worry seemed to crop up daily. On Wednesday traders fretted about earnings, particularly for banks. On Thursday, President Obama's plans to restrict big banks seemed to send the market lower."
—New York Times

January 27, 2010
A Day Before Vote on Bernanke, Fed Leaves Rates Alone
—New York Times

January 27, 2010
The Fed's Withdrawal from Quantitative Easing
"Given still weak underlying economic conditions, we expect that the Fed will keep interest rates near 0% longer than currently discounted and continue to expect rolling down the yield curve to be attractive for some time."

February 1, 2010
Shares Gain on Earnings Reports and Signs of Stability in Housing
—New York Times

February 4, 2010
Investors Fear Europe's Woes May Extend Global Slump
—New York Times

February 4, 2010
Tightening + Over-indebtedness = High Risk
"As you know, we believe that monetary and fiscal policies are beginning to tighten globally and the mature industrialized countries are over-indebted, so we believe that we are about to enter a period of testing whether central banks and central governments can really 'pull back' as planned. Based on our calculations, we doubt that they can stick to the plan as outlined without causing unacceptable consequences."

February 11, 2010
Prospect of Aid for Greece Gives Wall Street a Boost
—New York Times

February 24, 2010
Bernanke Expects Extended Low Rates
—New York Times

March 3, 2010
Changes and Levels in Economic Activity and in Financial Asset Prices
"It seems that there is a great deal of confusion regarding 'how things are going' in developed countries that has arisen from observers sometimes looking at changes, sometimes looking at levels, sometimes looking at economic activity, sometimes looking at the drivers of economic activity and sometimes looking at markets. Specifically, a) those who are looking at changes in financial markets' prices are most optimistic, b) those who are looking at changes in economic activity and levels of market values are less optimistic, c) and those who are looking at the levels of economic activity and the drivers of economic activity are least optimistic."

News & Bridgewater Daily Observations (BDO)

March 5, 2010
Markets Find the Upside of the Jobs Report
–New York Times

March 31, 2010
Fed Ends Its Purchasing of Mortgage Securities
–New York Times

July 13, 2010
6-Day Winning Streak for U.S. Indexes
"Stock indexes in the United States rose for a sixth consecutive session on Tuesday, propelled by a strong start to the corporate earnings season."
–New York Times

July 14, 2010
The Template and the Slowdown
"We suspect that the most important difference between our views and others concerns the long-term debt cycle. As long-term debt cycles transpire slowly—essentially over a lifetime—most people haven't experienced many of them, unlike the business cycle which most of us have seen many of. So, while recessions are well understood, deleveragings are not well understood."

July 21, 2010
Bernanke Comment on Uncertainty Unsettles Market
–New York Times

July 21, 2010
Obama Signs Bill Overhauling Financial Rules
–New York Times

July 29, 2010
More Will Likely Be Necessary From the Fed
"While monetization policies are currently viewed as risky, we think the implications of monetary inaction during a deleveraging and deflation are riskier. Monetization should not be viewed like a light switch that works in an all-or-none sort of way; it should be viewed like a spigot that regulates the flow in degrees. It works similar to interest rate cuts or putting your foot on the accelerator of a car. When doing either, you judge the right amount primarily by watching the reactions. When things start to pick up, you start to let off. When things start to slow down, you start to press the pedal harder. The same is true for monetizations. In our view, it is time for the Fed to put its foot back down on the monetization accelerator."

August 10, 2010
Fed Move on Debt Signals Concern About Economy
"Federal Reserve officials, acknowledging that their confidence in the recovery had dimmed, moved again on Tuesday to keep interest rates low and encourage economic growth. They also signaled that more aggressive measures could follow if the job market and other indicators continued to weaken."
–New York Times

August 24, 2010
Wall Street Hit Again, This Time by Housing Data
–New York Times

September 1, 2010
Wall Street Surges After Good Reports
–New York Times

September 7, 2010
Renewed European Worry Hurts Shares
–New York Times

(BDO) February 17: The Coming Tightening

It is now the established view among the electorate, central bankers, and elected officials that central banks printing and buying of financial assets and central governments budget deficits must be reined in because these actions are financially irresponsible. We think that this universally accepted view is at best premature and at worst dangerous...When we take a sharp pencil to these plans and their implications, we conclude that it is too much restraint—unless there is either major pickup in private debt growth or a major realignment of developed and emerging country currencies, both of which appear unlikely to happen in the amounts required.

At the same time, we did our pro forma financial projections in Europe and saw a debt crisis brewing there due to a mismatch between: a) the amount of borrowing debtors needed to rollover maturing debt and sustain what they were doing, and b) the amount of lending that would be required to come from banks that had already stretched their balance sheets. In February, several of Europe's more indebted countries—Portugal, Ireland, Italy, Spain, and especially Greece—struggled to meet their debt obligations and were facing deteriorating economic conditions. While the news flow associated with this led to some day-to-day volatility in global markets, most assessed the issue to be contained to Greece (and potentially Portugal) and that it would not pose larger problems for the European monetary system or the global economy. In a note to clients in early February, we calculated that the problem would probably be much worse:

(BDO) February 4: Tightening + Over-indebtedness = High Risk

"We judge the over-indebtedness problems of the European debtor countries (PIGS) to be comparable in magnitude to some of the worst emerging-market debt problems of the past.

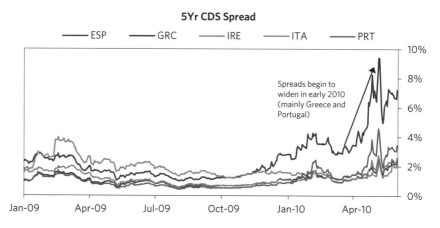

5Yr CDS Spread

Spreads begin to widen in early 2010 (mainly Greece and Portugal)

But the European debt crisis is a different story. While I won't go into it now, it is noteworthy that the same sequence of events followed, in that policy makers didn't believe they would face a debt crisis until they had it. When it came, they made the same rookie mistakes of leaning too heavily on deflationary levers like austerity and of not printing money and of not providing protections against defaults for systemically important entities until the pain became intolerable.

From May until July, the US equity market, which had rallied nearly 10 percent from the start of the year through late April, fell over 15 percent, largely on contagion worries about Europe and softness in the US economic numbers.

That weakness led to the realization that the Fed was likely to maintain its course on its 0-percent-interest-rate policy. US bond yields fell over 100 basis points over the next four months. The pace of improvement in the economy slowed in the summer of 2010. Timely reads on labor market health showed only modest improvement in unemployment claims, while the unemployment rate was still near highs. There was still a lot of slack in the economy. Weakness at this level of economic activity would have been terrible.

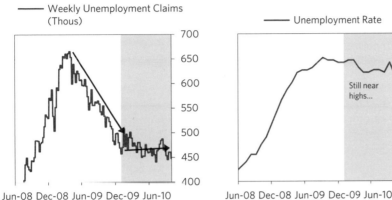

Bernanke addressed further QE in a speech in Jackson Hole, making it clear that it was a key policy option if needed, saying, "a first option for providing additional monetary accommodation, if necessary, is to expand the Federal Reserve's holdings of longer-term securities."[62] He also emphasized his belief that QE had been effective and had "made an important contribution to the economic stabilization and recovery." As the chart below shows, the 10-year break-even inflation rate had fallen by 50 basis points in the several months leading up to Bernanke's August speech, reflecting concerns of sustained very low inflation or deflation. However, after he signaled that further QE was a strong possibility, the markets rebounded strongly. The real economy response naturally lagged the essentially instantaneous market response, but it wasn't long before growth picked up as well.

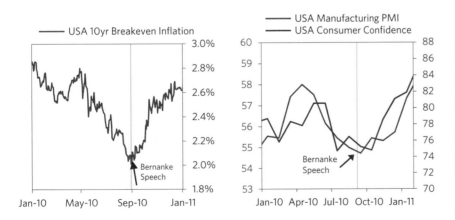

In early October 2010, New York Fed President Bill Dudley described economic conditions as "wholly unsatisfactory" and argued that "further action is likely to be warranted."[63] Dudley went on to give an assessment of the underlying drivers of US growth that was broadly similar to our own view at the time, based largely on this observation (from our October 1 BDO): "Consumers are facing slow

News & Bridgewater Daily Observations (BDO)

September 21, 2010
Fed Stands Pat and Says It Is Still Ready to Buy Debt
—*New York Times*

September 21, 2010
Another Step Toward More Quantitative Easing
"We suspect the Fed will end up having to push much harder than anyone currently expects, as it is likely that the currently planned quantitative easing will not be nearly as effective per dollar as the last stage of QE was. This is because the economic impact of the Fed printing and spending money (QE) depends on who gets the money and what they do with it."

September 24, 2010
Signs of Stability Help Extend September's Rally
—*New York Times*

October 1, 2010
In Comments, Fed Officials Signal New Economic Push
—*New York Times*

October 14, 2010
ECB Policy
"We see overall growth rates decelerating, debt problems on the periphery that at a minimum remain an intense weight on growth and a fiscal policy of austerity that is clearly a drag. It is against that backdrop that the ECB is 'normalizing' its balance sheet (both by letting its longer-term lending facilities roll off and by decreasing the pace of its asset purchases), and as a result pushing up both short-term interest rates and the euro. This de facto tightening of monetary policy seems like a mistake to us, and we suspect will cause conditions to deteriorate (likely further pressuring peripheral credits) and eventually cause the ECB to reverse course (pushing down rates and probably the euro)."

October 15, 2010
Bernanke Weighs Risks of New Action
—*New York Times*

October 25, 2010
Fed Reviewing Foreclosure Procedures
—*Associated Press*

November 3, 2010
Fed to Spend $600 Billion to Speed Up Recovery
"The Federal Reserve, getting ahead of the battles that will dominate national politics over the next two years, moved Wednesday to jolt the economy into recovery with a bold but risky plan to pump $600 billion into the banking system."
—*New York Times*

November 12, 2010
Shares and Commodities Fall on Currency Concerns
"Stocks fell Friday and commodity prices declined, reflecting concerns about global issues and the possibility of a slower economy in China...Investors were also apparently reacting to signs of financial pressures in Europe and to the possibility that China's higher-than-forecast inflation rate of 4.4 percent in October could lead to measures to slow its economy."
—*New York Times*

News &
Bridgewater Daily Observations
(BDO)

November 18, 2010
Stocks Surge Worldwide on the Prospect of a Rescue for Ireland
"Stocks in the United States rose Thursday after Ireland indicated that it would seek billions in aid from international lenders to rescue its banks. That eased concerns about the health of Europe's financial system and helped buoy investor sentiment globally."
-New York Times

November 23, 2010
Wall Street Falls, Unsettled by Debt Crisis and Korea
-New York Times

December 1, 2010
Portugal Bond Sale Highlights Stress in Euro Zone
-New York Times

December 14, 2010
Fed Goes Ahead With Bond Plan
-New York Times

December 21, 2010
Fed Extends Currency Swaps With Europe
-Associated Press

January 3, 2011
Wall Street Starts Year With a Surge
"On the first day of trading of the year, the broader market reached its highest level since 2008, led by a gain of more than 2 percent in financial shares.

Bank of America was up more than 6 percent after it announced that it made a $1.34 billion net cash payment to Fannie Mae and one to Freddie Mac of $1.28 billion to buy back troubled mortgages on December 31. In doing so, it tackled an issue overshadowing the markets."
-New York Times

February 1, 2011
Dow and S.& P. Close at Highest Levels Since 2008
-Reuters

February 8, 2011
Fed Casts A Wide Net In Defining Systemic Risk
"Federal regulators on Tuesday took an expansive view of the types of companies that could be deemed essential enough to the financial system that they should be subjected to greater oversight.

The Federal Reserve, in a 22-page proposal required by the Dodd-Frank financial legislation, outlined initial criteria for identifying 'systemically important financial institutions,' whose collapse would pose a serious threat to the economy."
-New York Times

February 16, 2011
Fed Forecasts Faster Growth as Economy Improves
-New York Times

February 25, 2011
Shares Climb as Oil Prices and Supply Concerns Ease
-Associated Press

March 3, 2011
Wall Street Gains On Upbeat Jobs Data
-New York Times

income growth, lower asset prices relative to prior to the crisis, and a much lower ability to borrow as a result of lower wealth, higher debt levels, and lower incomes. As a result, households have not responded to lower rates by saving less or borrowing." On October 6, I wrote the following:

(BDO) October 6: The Next Shoe to Drop: More QE and Devaluations

What is happening is all very classic. Though they're all different, in most ways deleveragings are basically the same and transpire via a similar sequence of events. As we have described them in the *Daily Observations* and in our "Template for Understanding What's Going On," we won't dwell on this sequence, but will remind you of a few things that we think are especially relevant now.

All deleveragings are due to declines in private sector credit growth that require increases in both central bank money creation and central government deficits in order to offset the effects of the decline in private sector credit. Though many of us are financially conservative and feel that there is something unethical about printing money to bail out debtors and creditors, it is important to recognize that austerity to deal with debt-deleveraging problems has never worked when these problems were big. When austerity has been tried, even in persistent attempts to get out of debt, it has eventually been abandoned by all governments because it didn't work, and it was too painful. That is because the decreased borrowing and spending (and consequences of these on employment and many other pain points) make this type of deleveraging as self-reinforcing on the downside as the increased debts and spending that cause bubbles is on the upside. As a result, all of the deleveragings that we have studied (which is most of those that occurred over the last couple of hundred years) eventually led to big waves of money creation, fiscal deficits and currency devaluations (against gold, commodities, and stocks).

The QE broadly worked in providing additional needed stimulus. Despite continued debt problems in Europe, the US economy and markets finished 2010 on a high note. Growth picked up after a brief lull between QE1 and QE2, the S&P 500 had 13 percent total returns for 2010, and inflation expectations had been re-anchored by the Fed's proven determination to continue stimulating as long as necessary. On March 15 of 2011, this is how we saw domestic conditions as they developed:

(BDO) March 15: Transitioning Beyond the "Sweet Spot"

As previously mentioned, it is pretty clear that the US economy is going through a post-contraction growth spurt that is being supported by monetary policy, fiscal policy and an improvement in credit growth. As this recovery is occurring with both a) considerable slack domestically (and in Europe and Japan) and b) overheating demand in emerging countries, we see limited inflation pressures, with those pressures that exist largely coming via the prices of items that are being demanded by emerging countries. **Said differently, 2010/2011 in a cyclical context appears quite like the "sweet spot" part of the cycle that typically occurs during the first two years of a recovery, when there remains adequate slack and low inflation pressures.** However, this recovery from a contraction is taking place during a deleveraging and therefore has been more dependent on the Fed's printing of money and the central government's fiscal stimulus.

By this point, it was clear that the governments different programs to support the financial system broadly worked. Compared to other countries, the US financial system experienced:

- A relatively fast speed at which the financial system was recapitalized (and that TARP capital was repaid)

- A relatively fast speed at which they unwound emergency credit programs

- Good overall financial returns on the rescue across the various programs.

We will end this case study here, because in the second quarter of 2011 real GDP returned to its pre-crisis levels. This wasn't the end of the recovery by any means. There was still plenty of slack in the economy and a self-reinforcing upward cycle. The charts below show the unemployment rate, GDP growth, the GDP gap (showing the estimated amount of slack in the economy's capacity to produce), and the S&P 500 stock market index from 2006 until the writing of this on the tenth anniversary of the 2008 Lehman debt crisis. The shaded bars show where they were in 2Q 2011. The second set of charts show existing and projected debt-to-GDP ratios from 1920 until 10 years from now. These numbers do not include non-debt obligations such as those for pensions and health care, which are considerably larger than debts. But that's another issue to be explained at another time.

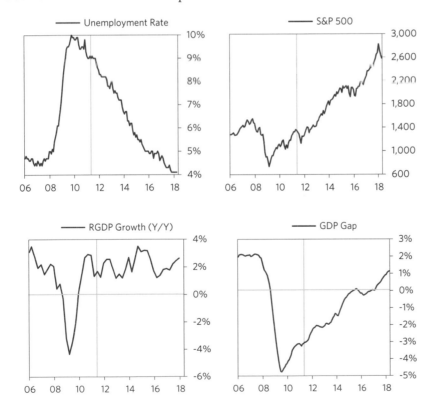

**News &
Bridgewater Daily Observations
(BDO)**

March 10, 2011
Increasing Global Divergences
"As you know, we divide the world into debtors and creditors, and we divide each of these groups into those with independent monetary policies and those with linked monetary policies. We believe that debtors with linked monetary policies (i.e., who can't print money) will experience many years of hardship and economic weakness, and that creditors who can't stop printing money because they have linked exchange rates will go through an extended period of overheating. We also believe that these pressures will intensify over the next 18 months, leading to cracks and seismic shifts in these linkages. These views influence our market positioning in credit spreads, yield curves, currencies, commodities and equities."

March 15, 2011
Stocks End Lower as Traders Focus on Japan Crisis
　　　　　　　　　　　　　-New York Times

March 20, 2011
Dow Soars Above 12,000 on AT&T Deal for T-Mobile
　　　　　　　　　　　　　-New York Times

Debt Levels (%GDP)

Government

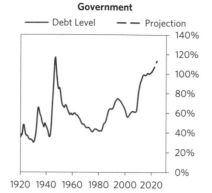

Non-Financial Business

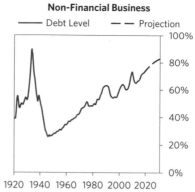

Households

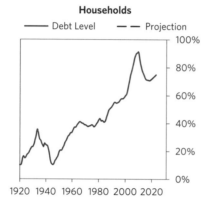

Financials

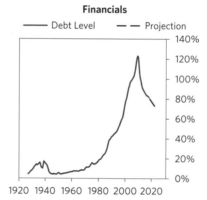

Works Cited:

Associated Press, "Fed Chairman Signals an End to Interest Rate Cuts Amid Concerns About Inflation," *New York Times*, June 4, 2008, https://nyti.ms/2BC431y.

Bernanke, Ben S. "Causes of the Recent Financial and Economic Crisis," Testimony Before the Financial Crisis Inquiry Commission (Washington D.C., September 2, 2010). https://www.federalreserve.gov/newsevents/testimony/bernanke20100902a.htm

Bernanke, Ben S. *The Courage to Act: A Memoir of a Crisis and Its Aftermath*. New York: W.W. Norton & Company, 2017.

Bernanke, Ben S. "The Economic Outlook and Monetary Policy." Speech, Federal Reserve Bank of Kansas City Economic Symposium, August 27, 2010. The Federal Reserve. https://www.federalreserve.gov/newsevents/speech/bernanke20100827a.htm

Board of Governors of the Federal Reserve System (U.S.). *Joint Statement by the Treasury, FDIC, OCC, OTS, and the Federal Reserve*. Washington, DC, 2009. https://www.federalreserve.gov/newsevents/pressreleases/bcreg20090223a.htm.

Creswell, Julie and Vikas Bajaj. "$3.2 Billion Move by Bear Stearns to Rescue Fund," *New York Times*, June 23, 2007. https://nyti.ms/2hanv9c.

da Costa, Pedro Nicolaci. "Bernanke says U.S. economy faces big threat," Reuters, October 15, 2008. https://www.reuters.com/article/us-financial-fed-bernanke/bernanke-says-u-s-economy-faces-big-threat-idUSTRE49E6Y820081015.

Dudley, William C. "The Outlook, Policy Choices and Our Mandate" Remarks at the Society of American Business Editors and Writers Fall Conference, City University of New York, Graduate School of Journalism. New York City, October 1, 2010. https://www.newyorkfed.org/newsevents/speeches/2010/dud101001.

Elliott, Larry and Jill Treanor. "The Day the Credit Crunch Began, Ten Years On: 'The World Changed,'" *The Guardian*, August 3, 2017. https://www.theguardian.com/business/2017/aug/02/day-credit-crunch-began-10-years-on-world-changed.

Ellis, David and Ben Rooney. "Banks to Abandon 'Super-SIV' Fund," CNNMoney.com, December 21, 2007. https://money.cnn.com/2007/12/21/news/companies/super_siv/index.htm?postversion=2007122116.

Federal Reserve Bank, "2016 Survey of Consumer Finances Chartbook," (October 16, 2017), 835. https://www.federalreserve.gov/econres/files/BulletinCharts.pdf.

Geithner, Timothy F. "Introducing the Financial Stability Plan." (Speech, Washington, D.C., February 10, 2009) https://www.treasury.gov/press-center/press-releases/Pages/tg18.aspx

Geithner, Timothy F. *Stress Test: Reflections on the Financial Crisis*. New York: Broadway Books, 2015.

Greenspan, Alan and James Kennedy. "Sources and Uses of Equity Extracted from Homes," Finance and Economics Discussion Series, Division of Research and Statistics and Monetary Affairs (Washington, D.C.: Federal Reserve Board, 2007–20), 16–72. https://www.federalreserve.gov/pubs/feds/2007/200720/200720pap.pdf.

Lukken, Walt. "Reauthorization: Let the Debate Begin." *Futures & Derivatives Law Report* 24, no. 6 (2004): 1-9. https://www.cftc.gov/sites/default/files/idc/groups/public/@newsroom/documents/speechandtestimony/opafdlrlukkenarticle.pdf

Memorandum from Financial Economist to Erik R. Sirri, Robert L.D. Colby, Herbert F. Brooks, Michael A Macchiaroli, Thomas K. McGowan, "Re: Risk Management Reviews of Consolidated Supervised Entities," January 4, 2007. https://fcic-static.law.stanford.edu/cdn_media/fcic-docs/2007-01- 04%20SEC%20Risk%20 Management%20Review%20of%20Consolidated%20Supervised%20Entities.pdf

Nizza, Mike. "Paulson Says Economy Is Starting to Rebound," New York Times, May 17, 2008. https://nyti. ms/2BBJJgD.

Paulson Jr., Henry M. *On the Brink: Inside the Race to Stop the Collapse of the Global Financial System.* New York: Business Plus, 2010.

Raum, Tom and Daniel Wagner. "Geithner grilled on AIG bailout," *The Post and Courier*, January 27, 2010. https://www.postandcourier.com/business/geithner-grilled-on-aig-bailout/article_e0713d80-bbf1-5e81-ba9d-377b93532f34.html.

Reuters, "2 Bear Stearns Funds Are Almost Worthless," *New York Times*, July 17, 2007. https://nyti.ms/2fHPu2b.

Reuters, "Paulson Won't Rule Out Dollar Intervention," *New York Times*, June 10, 2008. https://nyti.ms/2BAWQid.

Stolberg, Sheryl Gay and Steven R. Weisman. "Bush Talks Up Dollar as He Heads to Europe," *New York Times*, June 10, 2008. https://nyti.ms/2o1glHj.

Summers, Larry. "Opening Remarks at the SIEPR Economic Summit." (Speech, Stanford University, March 7, 2008). Accessed at: http://delong.typepad.com/larry-summers-stanford-march-7-2008.pdf

U.S. Census Bureau. "Number of Stories in New Single-Family Houses Sold." https://www.census.gov/const/C25Ann/soldstories.pdf.

U.S. Department of the Treasury. *The Special Master for TARP Executive Compensation Issues First Rulings.* Washington, DC, 2009. https://www.treasury.gov/press-center/press-releases/Pages/tg329.aspx.

Vazza, Diane, Nick W. Kraemer, Nivritti Mishra Richhariya, Mallika Jain, Abhik Debnath, and Aliasger Dohadwala. "Default, Transition, and Recovery: 2017 Annual Global Corporate Default Study and Rating Transitions," S&P Global Ratings, April 5, 2018. http://media.spglobal.com/documents/RatingsDirect_DefaultTransitionandRecovery2017 AnnualGlobalCorporateDefaultStudyAndRatingTransitions_38612717_Apr-17-2018.PDF.

1   Federal Reserve Bank, "2016 Survey of Consumer Finances Chartbook," 835.

2   Greenspan and Kennedy, "Sources and Uses of Equity," 16-17.

3   US Census Bureau, "Number of Stories."

4   Paulson, *On the Brink*, 45, 50-52.

5   Paulson, 57-58.

6   Bernanke, "Causes of the Recent Financial and Economic Crisis."

7   Memorandum, "Re: Risk Management Reviews."

8   Bernanke, "Causes of the Recent Financial and Economic Crisis."

9   Reuters, "2 Bear Stearns Funds."

10 Creswell and Bajaj, "$3.2. Billion Move to Rescue Fund."

11 Bernanke, *The Courage to Act*, 156.

12 Bernanke, *The Courage to Act*, 156.

13 Geithner, *Stress Test*, 9.

14 Bernanke, *The Courage to Act*, 160.

15 Ellis and Rooney, "Banks to Abandon 'Super-SIV' Fund."

16 Elliott and Treanor, "The Day the Credit Crunch Began."

17 Vazza, et al. "Default, Transition, Recovery"; Andrews, "Mortgage Relief Impact."

18 Lukken, "Reauthorization," 3.

19 Bernanke, *The Courage to Act*, 194.

20 Bernanke, *The Courage to Act*, 194.

21 Bernanke, *The Courage to Act*, 208, 215-6.

22 Bernanke, *The Courage to Act*, 208.

23 Paulson, *On the Brink*, 93.

24 Bernanke, *The Courage to Act*, 218.

25 Geithner, *Stress Test*, 166-7.

26 Paulson, 132-5.

27 Nizza, "Economy Is Starting to Rebound."

28 Stolberg and Weisman, "Bush Talks Up Dollar"; Reuters, "Paulson Won't Rule Out."

29 Associated Press, "Fed Chairman Signals an End."

30 Paulson, 142.

31 Paulson, 57.

32 Paulson, 4.

33 Paulson, 162.

34 Paulson, 167.

35 Paulson, 1.

36 Paulson, 147.

37 Paulson, 219.

38 Ibid, 185.

39 Paulson, 209, Geithner, *Stress Test*, 96.

40 Paulson, 225.

41 Paulson, 229.

42 Bernanke, *The Courage to Act*, 280.

43 Bernanke, *The Courage to Act*, 281.

44 Raum and Wagner, "Geithner Grilled on AIG."

45 Paulson, 252-3.

46 Paulson, 233.

47 Paulson, 342.

48 Paulson, 353.

49 Paulson, 353.

50 Paulson, 369.

51 Paulson, 357-8.

52 Da Costa, "Bernanke Says U.S. Economy."

53 Paulson, 396.

54 Paulson, 399-400.

55 Summers, "SIEPR Economic Summit," 1.

56 Bernanke, *The Courage to Act*, 378.

57 Geithner, "Introducing the Financial Stability Plan."

58 Board of Governors of the Federal Reserve, "Joint Statement."

59 Geithner, *Stress Test*, 291.

60 Geithner, *Stress Test*, 349-50.

61 US Treasury, "The Special Master for TARP."

62 Bernanke, "Economic Outlook."

63 Dudley, "The Outlook."